Multicultural News from an American Indian Perspective

January – December, 2014

Compiled with a Foreword by

# Rose Davis

BLACKROSE COMMUNICATIONS

San Diego – 2015

# MISSION STATEMENT

To advance and promote a supportive system of information sharing grounded in Native Indigenous values and traditions while developing pioneering efforts to build bridges with emerging grassroots coalitions of labor and community groups in order to create a sustainable economic environment.

# FOREWORD

The language and culture of our indigenous heritage is under siege from technological encroachment. Oral tradition which has been the traditional conveyance of our ancestral wisdom is unsustainable in the high tech age of contemporary communication. In order to preserve and protect the historical legacy of a people Indian Voices has developed a journalistic strategy to catalog, document and chronicle our human experience to reveal the inner truth of a heritage that would otherwise be hidden and forbidden. Through articles, anecdotes, traditional tales these Urban Legends contribute to the ancient and modern body of knowledge fostering independent journalism and cultural transparency while securing our heritage for the next seven generations.

Rose Davis
Publisher & Editor/Indian Voices

# CONTENTS

# ABOUT

Indian Voices Media project is the culmination of efforts on the part community members intent on assisting with the development of an entrepreneurial journalistic endeavor dedicated to bringing the voices of the marginalized and e indigenous members of our society into the national discourse, to not only influence policy makers but to enhance the pool of educational material to inform the mainstream about the important role of indigenous people whose enduring presence in the development of our history and society assures its future.

Particular emphasis is given to exploring and revealing the historically strong connection that exists between the Black/Indian cultures.

This loose affiliation of volunteers and change agents contribute to the production of a hard copy newspaper and a developing cutting edge website offering academicians and social critics a platform for expression

This ongoing project has been under guidance and supervision of Rose Davis a long time advocate of a sustainable and healthy, balanced living environment and whose work toward this end is her raison d'etre.

www.indianvoices.net

OUR 28ᵀᴴ YEAR    MULTI-CULTURAL NEWS GLOBAL NETWORK    JANUARY 2014

# David Vows to Slay Goliath

*by Rose Davis*

It was a standing room only crowd that assembled at the home of Dr. Shirley Phelps and her daughter Cheryl Althea Phelps for a condensed, power-packed, speed drill political education. Progressive San Diegans heeded the call to come together. The think tank caucus was held at a festive holiday fundraiser.

SEE **David Alvarez, page 2**

Photography by Rochelle Porter/ Peaché Photo Memories

David Alvarez candidate for Mayor of San Diego has sparked a movement that has enlivened the the city's populist coalitions. He appeals to his large and growing group of supporters at an amimated holiday fundraiser at the home of Cheryl Alethia Phelps.

## In this issue... THUNDER from the 4TH

**www.indianvoices.net**

## Health Center Names Chief Medical Officer from Menominee Nation

*Story and Photos by Alaina Dall*

Covering the back wall of Dr. Melissa E. H. Deer's office is a Pendleton medicine wheel blanket woven in earthy colors representing the four directions. Her parents gave it to her in recognition of one of her greatest accomplishments – becoming a medical doctor. As of October 1, 2013, Dr. Deer is the new Chief Medical Officer at San Diego American Indian Health Center.

Now in its 35th year, SDAIHC serves thousands of urban American Indians each year, providing medical, dental, and behavioral health services, as well as cultural and traditional programming such as weekly talking circles, cultural arts classes, and a youth center. Established in 1979 and contracted with the Indian Health Service to serve individuals of American Indian ancestry, the organization has grown to become a comprehensive community clinic open to everyone. SDAIHC is conveniently located on 1st Avenue, just west of Balboa Park, San Diego, CA.

Dr. Deer comes from a family of health

providers. Her grandmother was a nurse, and her mother and aunt are nurses as well. Her aunt has championed national Indian policies in the course of her career.

The importance of education was emphasized in her family, and she knew from her early teens that she wanted to be a physician. She describes the profession as a calling inspired by "a desire to help other people and to address the injustices that have happened to Native people that I have seen play out in my own family."

While Dr. Deer had strong role models in her family, she also saw the effects of despair. "I saw how alcoholism ruin family dynamics. It is a common narrative that our people experience."

Her grandfather was a full-blooded Menominee, a tribe located in Wisconsin. He was removed from his home at an early age and put into a boarding school. While there, he wasn't allowed to speak his native language and he felt shame as his cultural identity and traditions were methodically stripped away from him.

Her father grew up on the Menominee reservation in a one-room log cabin with-

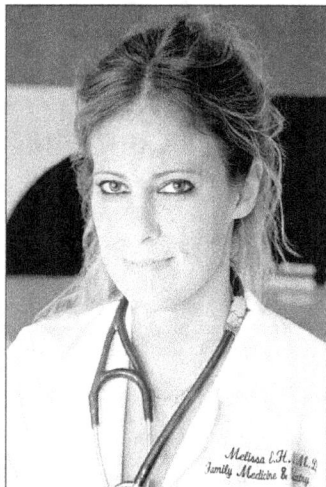

out running water or electricity. He is a Vietnam veteran, and suffered from post-traumatic stress disorder – a poorly understood affliction at the time -- upon his

SEE **Medical Officer, page 4**

## David Alvarez

Continued from page 1

Cheryl Phelps and David Alvarez welcome the guests to the fundraising gala.

The animated crowd thirsted for the primal need of communion and unity.This multi-generational/cultural assemblage had a collective agenda which transalated into getting David Alvarez elected mayor of San Diego. The relaxing sounds wafting through the air promoted open, candid communication. The Phelps'collection of museum quality African masks and artifacts seemed to call for indigenous wisdom.

After an enjoyable meet and greet the

political message was cast: time for the gavel to fall on the main agenda item. The leadership arm of the San Diego progressive community was locking arms preparing to march forward against the developer cabal.

Seasoned political veterans, elected officials, political scientists, business people wanting to be on the winning side, democratic loyalists, truth seekers and everybody else was there.

David Alvarez was born in. 1980. He serves as a San Diego City Councilmember representing City Council District 8. He is a Democrat. District 8 includes the neighborhoods of Barrio Logan, Egger Highlands, Grant Hill, Golden Hill, Logan Heights, Memorial, Nestor, Ocean View Hills, Otay Mesa West, Otay Mesa East, San Ysidro, Sherman Heights, Southcrest, Stockton, and the Tijuana River Valley.

Alvarez was born in San Diego to Jose and Maria Alvarez and has four brothers and one sister. He grew up in Barrio Logan. He attended local public schools: Perkins Elementary, Memorial Junior High, and San Diego High School. He was the first in his family to graduate from high school and college. He graduated with honors from San Diego State University. Alvarez, his wife Xochitl, and their daughter reside in Logan Heights.

Dr. Shirley Weber took center stage indicating her commitment to getting David Alvarez elected. As the first black assembly woman elected to represent San Diego. It was deja vu all over again. The Grand Dame of electoral politics and community icon has "been there done that".

### Moving forward

Forward motion is the theme. Little comment was wasted alluding to the reason why this special campaign was even necessary. Dr. Weber stated, "As it turned out, the good old

days weren't the good old days for us. We will work to make sure that the 11th floor at City Hall represents our interests and not just those of developers."

The people are awakening. For many indigenous people silence has been a safe and comfortable path to walk. This is understandable considering that it is just over a hundred years ago that there was a bounty on the head of a Kumeyaay, forcing them into the mountains or into blending with the Mexican community. In alliance with other groups there is now a chance to educate the power elite and encourage them to evolve from the reptilian brained cocoon with a new value structure not based on greed. They can be encouraged to abandon their pathologically confused concept of morality and get in touch with their humanness. Dr Weber introduced David Alverez who articulated a down to earth people oriented focus. The inter-connectedness of the group resonated. "I need your ongoing help, not just getting elected but assist-

David Alvarez, Mayoral Candidate; Hon. Leon Wiliams, Former SD County Supervisor and Cheryl Althea Phelps join the discussion.

ing with confronting those who undermine the democratic process.

The afternoon was enlightening, motivational, encouraging and powerful. There was much touching, hugging and love.

TJ Dunnivant, Kathleen Harmon and Carol Jeffries, Members of the Black American Political Association of California - San Diego Chapter lock arms to move forward.

Mary Salas, Chula Vista Councilwoman; Hon. Leon Wiliams, Former SD County Supervisor; CA Assemblymember Shirley Weber; Dr. Shirley Phelps and Cheryl Althea Phelps.

## Asian American Pacific Islander Leaders Endorse Councilmember David Alvarez

A diverse group of Asian American Pacific Islander (AAPI) leaders, including Asian Pacific American Labor Alliance (APALA) President Johanna Hester and entrepreneur, Dr. Allen Chan, joined Councilmember David Alvarez to endorse his candidacy for Mayor at Bay Terraces Community Park San Diego, CA Friday, January 10, 2014

• Johanna Hester, APALA President
• Dr. Allen Chan - Entrepreneur & Business Owner, Jasmine Seafood Restaurant
• Frank Vuong – President & Co-Founder, Little Saigon San Diego Foundation
• David Alvarez, City Councilmember

and candidate for Mayor
• Asian American Pacific Islander community supporters

The AAPI communities, north and south of Interstate 8, have had a rich history in San Diego and are one of the fastest growing minority groups across the city. This event highlights Councilmember Alvarez's plans to support sustainable and revitalized neighborhoods through parks and recreation centers, fostering a growing economy, and increased funding for services that working families need.

More information can be found at www.AlvarezforMayor.com

# INDIAN VOICES

Multicultural News from an American Indian Perspective

## PUBLISHED BY BLACKROSE COMMUNICATIONS
Member, American Indian Chamber of Commerce

Email: rdavis4973@aol.com
Website: www.indianvoices.net
Editorial Board: Rose Davis

| | | | |
|---|---|---|---|
| Editor: | Rose Davis | Writer: | Jaclyn Bissonette |
| Managing Editor: | Yvonne-Cher Skye | Entertainment Writer/ | |
| Outside Support: | Mel Vernon | Photographer LA/SD: | Rochelle Porter |
| LV Entertainment Writer: | Z. Z. Zorn | Reporter de Espectaculos: | Omar DeSantiago |
| Associate Editor: | Sis Mary Muhahmmad | Reporter de Espectaculos: | Michelle Banuet |
| Writer: | Kathleen Blavatt | Proofreader: | Mary Lou Finley |
| Writer: | Roy Cook | Graphic Artist: | Elaine Hall |
| Writer: | Marc Snelling | Staff Photographer: | Abel Jacome |
| Writer: | Scott Andrews | | |

| | |
|---|---|
| Las Vegas, NV | 111 South 35th St. |
| (619) 534-2435 | San Diego, CA 92113 |
| (619) 234-4753 | (619) 234-4753 |
| | (619) 534-2435 (cell) |
| | Fax: (619) 512-4534 |

Member of the Society of Professional Journalists
Member of New America Media

# Southern California Tribal Chairman's Association Substance Abuse Update

*Meeting Date: December 13th, 2013*

*Update from David "Wolf" Diaz*

On October 30, 2013 a very special meeting took place in honor of all who have gone before us. This meeting brought the Southern Indian Health Clinic, the Rincon Indian Health Clinic, the Riverside-San Bernardino Indian Health Clinic, the Substance Abuse Committee and guest speaker Eddie Grijalva together in one room with the intentions of saving lives and walking the healing circle. There were a total of 24 participants from the above mentioned organizations. The agenda and discussions for this meeting centered on creating a culturally appropriate adult residential treatment facility within one of the local reservations.

As we discussed various aspects of this proposed facility and asked the right questions it was decided that there should be members from each organization represented and elected to form an expanded subcommittee to achieve this

goal of creating this treatment facility. Our guest speaker Eddie Grijalva impressed upon us the importance of including the Trauma Informed Care combined with the ACE study as one of the latest cutting edge evidence-based modalities not only for the clients but the staff as well as at this facility. Chairman Pico contacted SIHC and they will keep him informed they will be getting together with the Northern Indian Health Council in the next couple of weeks to begin the process of an adult treatment facility further stating they will keep him abreast on the progress.

We will be needing copies of the new committee members from SIHC, IHC, UIHC, and SBIHC. The Substance Abuse Committee will be having a February 2014 meeting with the recently expanded committee on the new treatment facility. Our next Substance Abuse Committee meeting will be held on January 17th 2013.

Now, for a Walk of the Warrior update, I have recently returned from London, England after being invited by

Lord Stone to attend a meeting at the Palace of Westminster and the House of Lords. Lord Stone of Blackheath is a Parliament Member who has expressed interest in Walk of the Warrior and my involvement with SCTCA and the Substance Abuse Committee. Upon discussing our interest in creating a treatment facility Lord Stone offered us help in raising funds through the form of allowing us to write an article in a widely published award winning European magazine called "Resurgence & Ecologist".

Part of this magazines vision statement is that humanity is at ease with itself and is in harmony with the natural world; a vision where spiritual fulfillment and material wellbeing are in balance and science is in constant conversation with wisdom; their vision is not driven by doom and gloom; rather it is inspired and motivated by love of nature, respect for the earth, reverence for all life and a fair 'deal' to all people, believing that the power of love is greater than the force of fear and despair. Resurgence presents and promotes a positive perspective which is based on a foundation of optimism and hope. Resurgence (now Resurgence & Ecologist) magazine has been in publication for the past 45 years and in order to

secure its future The Resurgence Trust has been formed in the conviction that humankind is capable of rising to the challenges of our time by using its potential, its imagination and its creativity. The transforming power of the human spirit can bring about social, political and economic transformation to ensure the wellbeing of future generations. The Resurgence Trust, in collaboration with like-minded individuals and organizations, will work towards the realization of such a vision as we believe that urgent action is needed to stem the tide of global catastrophe, but that action must be embedded in human wisdom which can help us to live joyfully and justly within the carrying capacity of the earth.

This is an incredible opportunity because of the great love and interest in Europe for American Indian teachings and traditions. It is in my knowledge that only the Creator can open these kinds of doors and present these kinds of situations. I have been invited back by other Parliament Members who have expressed similar views and more will be revealed.

*Substance Abuse Committee: Eric LaChappa, Mark Romero, David "Wolf" Diaz & Anthony Pico SCTCA Staff: Denis Turner, Executive Director & Recording Secretary*

# First Native American Judge Appointed

*by Richard K. De Atley*

Sunshine S. Sykes is the first Native American to sit on the Riverside County Superior Court bench. Attorney Sunshine S. Sykes became Riverside County Superior Court's first Native American judge when she appointed to the bench by Governor Jerry Brown Thursday, Dececember 5. At the same time Brown also announced the appointment of Khymberli S.Y. Apaloo as San Bernardino County Superior Court judge. She had been serving as a commissioner. Apaloo, 43, is from Rancho

Cucamonga. Sykes, 39, of Riverside, has been a a deputy county counsel at the Riverside County Office of County Counsel since 2005. The graduate of Stanford University Law School, where she also earned her undergraduate Bachelor of Arts degree, is a member of the Navajo Nation. She was a contract attorney at the Juvenile Defense Panel from 2003 to 2005. Sykes was a staff attorney and Equal Justice Works fellow at the California Indian Legal Services from 2001 to 2003, according to a release from the governor's press office. Sykes fills the vacancy created by the retirement of Judge Randall White. Riverside County Superior Court Presiding Judge Mark Cope said Sykes will be sworn in to her new post before the first of the year. "I have heard so many good things about her," Cope said in a phone interivew. " I am thrilled not only to have an appointment, but this particular appointment. It sounds like she is going to be a fantastic addition to our bench, " he said of Sykes. Khymberli S. Y. ApalooBefore Apaloo was appointed a San Bernardino County commissioner in 2012, she was a partner at the Haslam and Perri law firm from 2003 to 2012 and an associate attorney at Covington and Crowe from 1998 to 2003. She earned her law degree from the New York University School of Law and a Bachelor of Arts degree from University of California, Berkeley. Apaloo fills a vacancy created by the retirement of Judge John Martin.

# Nevada Governor's Conference on Tourism

**Domestic, international buyers offer business-building opportunities at 2013 Governor's Conference**

For the first time in Las Vegas, the 2013 Governor's Conference on Tourism includes a robust business-building opportunity for Nevada tourism entities. The Nevada Marketplace will bring 41 domestic and international buyers for one-one-one meetings with conference attendees. The buyers represent travel agencies, tour operators, airlines and wholesalers from key international markets including China, South Korea and Japan.

"The informational and networking opportunities at the Governor's Conference are instrumental in keeping our travel industry competitive," said. Lt. Gov. Brian Krolicki's "Tourism is the state's primary industry, generating $58 billion in spending in 2012; we want to safeguard this industry and to help it continue its upward trajectory."

Attendees also heard from a stellar lineup of internationally renowned speakers, including noted author and consumer insights expert James A. Taylor; brand and destination marketing guru Duane Knapp; generational marketing pioneer Chuck Underwood; and global tourism safety consultant Peter Tarlow.

The conference offered general ses-

sions and several concurrent sessions. Of particular interest was Focus on Asia panel — Lt. Gov. Krolicki moderated a panel discussing how to maximize opportunities in the Asian market. Panelists are NCOT Deputy Director of Tourism Larry Friedman; Karen Chen, NCOT representative in China; Amy Lee, NCOT representative in South Korea; Kyoko Okabe, the Las Vegas Convention & Visitors Authority representative in Japan; Ruth Kim of the LVCVA; and Andrew Edelfsen of U.S Commercial Services.

"By focusing on the most relevant topics in tourism today, we hope to provide Nevada's tourism professionals with the tools they need to develop innovative marketing platforms," Claudia Vecchio, director of the Nevada Department of Tourism and Cultural Affairs, said.

Indian Voices welcomed the opportunity to network and build relationships with the attendees in order to further assist with the establishment and growth of tourism in San Diego and Southern California . Meeting Sherry Repurt, Indian Commission Executive Director of was a wonderful experience Another highlight was meeting and sharing information with Cory Brooks of the Blue Man Group who encouraged networking and staying in touch.

Please see Tourism Conference photos on page 9

## Medical Officer

Continued from page 1

return. Despite these hardships, he pursued a college education, as did three out of four of his siblings.

Dr. Deer's parents had the expectation that she would graduate from college as well, and she did with a Bachelor of Science in Sociology from the University of Wisconsin-Madison.

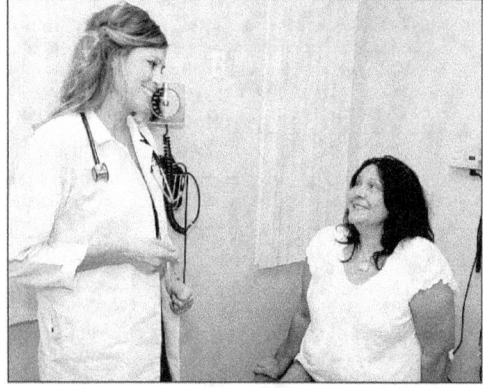

"There was always a strong commitment to give back in my family, as it is in the Native community. If you are given gifts, such as education, you give back. It was something that I didn't question. It was something that was in my blood," she said.

While attending the University of Minnesota Twin Cities Medical School in Minneapolis, she continued the tradition of giving back. She became involved in the urban Indian community by engaging in Indian advocacy activities with other Native students at the university, and encouraging minority high school and undergraduate college students to consider medical school.

After completing medical school, Dr. Deer went to the University of California San Diego's Combined Family Medicine and Psychiatry Residency Program. Again, advocacy and cultural awareness were important motivations for her at this time. She worked with other residents in her program to add a cultural training component to psychiatry grand rounds at UCSD, and she designed and implemented a cultural curriculum for psychiatry residents.

While completing her residency, much of which was providing health and psychiatry services at a homeless shelter in downtown San Diego, she created and worked part-time at a psychiatry clinic at

San Diego American Health Center in 2009, a service that continues today.

### HEALTH CENTER

Dr. Deer keeps sage available for patients needing psychiatry services that request smudging, which is a cleansing ritual used prior to any traditional Native gathering, prayer or ceremony. A small dream catcher hangs on the adjacent wall. Diego, a Border collie mix that visits the behavioral health clinic a couple times a week, lies quietly in the sunlight. Dr. Deer said he immediately puts patients at ease, some of whom are seeking mental health services for the very first time.

Said SDAIHC Chief Executive Officer Joe Bulfer, "We value the importance of integrating the primary care medical practice with behavioral health services. Because Dr. Deer is board certified in both family medicine and psychiatry, she will be able to integrate the two to a much

higher degree than we have been able to before."

Many staff members are part of the Native community, and Indian symbolism is evident throughout the clinic. Exam rooms have Native motifs stenciled on the walls. Photographs of Native people appear in the clinic, as does Indian art work.

"The traditions of our culture need to be reverberated through the clinic in order for us to be successful at reaching out to the community and providing good care," said the medical director.

A flier is posted on the bulletin board advertising a Wellbriety gathering, "promoting holistic health, sobriety and wellness utilizing Native American cultural teachings, traditions and spirituality," taking place weekly. A notice for the youth center describes service offerings such as tutoring, an American Indian life skills development class, talking circles, intertribal sports, games and field trips.

Medical Providers here treat health problems prevalent in Native communities everywhere, including obesity, diabetes, high blood pressure, high cholesterol, heart disease and tobacco dependence, and other health concerns. The health center's goal is to reduce the significant disparities of San Diego's urban American Indian population by increasing access to care and improving the quality of that care.

"Dr. Deer will enable us to excel at the objectives that we set in our strategic plan. In the end it is going to improve patient care," said Mr. Bulfer, CEO.

Part of that plan is to create a medical home for SDAIHC's patients in which all of the patient's health care needs are met under one roof, or coordinated with serv-

ices outside of the health center.

Another part of the plan is to enroll patients in Covered California, the health coverage made available by the Affordable Care Act. This insurance will cover services that the Indian Health Service program does not currently pay for, such as medical specialists, tests, prescription drugs, emergency room visits and hospital care.

But now, for Dr. Deer, it is time to get back to seeing patients. She wears a bracelet of blue, gold and orange beads made by the Menominee tribe. Her stethoscope is adorned with a small band of beads, and she changes into moccasins before walking past the medicine wheel blanket on her wall and heading to the medical clinic. She continues to give back to the Native community in her new role as medical director.

# Sycuan Culture Gathering 2014

*by Roy Cook*

Another 'New Year' with another traditional land area returned and a new page in opportunities to present Kumeyaay traditional song, gaming and tribal hospitality. The Sycuan Band has nearly tripled the size of its reservation and is utilizing it for culture gatherings and recreation. Using gaming profits, the tribe has acquired 2,000 acres over several years and annexed 1,350 acres to the reservation. Another 600 acres will be kept as

separate conservation space.

Over fifty singers of all ages, bands and Colorado River tribes were on the line bringing the songs and activities to the Dehesa valley. Pit cooked beef, beans and handmade tortillas were served to all attendees. It makes my mouth water to think of missing these delights, regretfully my strained knee kept me from being there this time.

Today there are many more occasions on the reservation to learn the songs and be a part of the rich aspects of Kumeyaay culture. In the previous generation many opportunities were linked to someone's passing or the one year memorial wake. Those responsibilities are still a cultural priority but there are now other occasions for the children to participate and indelibly be a part of the Kumeyaay future for all the people. Additional incentive for participation was a dance competition and two step quality songs were led by Paul 'Jr' Cuero. Many singers, many Kumeyaay songs and many invited guests came together for a wonderful start for a new year of possibilities.

Black Path Commentary: Critical Analysis on Culure, Community, & Struggle

## Honoring the Heritage of Dr. King: Emulating a Model of Moral Magnitude in achieving Optimal Health

*by Min. Tukufu Kalonji*

Within the unique, awesome, extensive and special narrative of Afro American history there is an expansive list of saints, saviors, prophets, practitioners, and servant leaders of the good. Both men and women who struggled to bring into being a truly just and moral society. These men and women; teachers of the good; and messengers of moral magnitude, walked righteously in worthiness in the world before history, humanity, and heaven, sought to build what the Rev. Dr. Martin Luther King constructs as the Beloved Community; by speaking truth, doing justice, by way of serving God through serving the people! The Most Honorable Rev. Dr. Martin Luther King is without a doubt, such a person; and this month of January, we honor him and celebrate his ethical life of service, struggle, and achievement as our ancestor servant leader. His death as does his life provides us very useful lessons on how we are to see ourselves today as the struggle for justice continues in and on all fronts. It is as articulated by another ancestor soldier for rightness and good in the world, Paul Robeson who, in a speech declared "The battlefront is everywhere, there is no sheltered rear."

Therefore, with the battle front everywhere with no sheltered rears then let us review and revere Kings legacy in the context of striving toward excellence in struggle to reach Optimal Health. For clarity the operational definition of optimal health here is the practice of NERDS, i.e., Nutrition, Exercise, Rest, Detoxification, and Stress Management. Moreover, for clarity we use the modifier of Proper to emphasize high quality or excellent before each of the categorical areas, thus Proper nutrition, exercise, rest, detoxification and stress management. Consequently in gaining greater insight as to how we see ourselves, this also implies a greater understanding of ourselves and finally as how we assert ourselves in the world. And in the struggle for optimal health, Rev. King's legacy and lessons is as relevant to our wellbeing and development as it is in any other area of our thought and activity.

Rev. King's legacy is a continued lesson on seeing the value of our life and all human life as sacred. Sacred here means human life is special and not to be violated under any rationale for oppression

and barbarism for humans are by virtue of the creators, the ancestors, and the universe, dignity bearing divine beings. The Americas as a country has yet to learn this lesson as we continue to see the onslaught of racism, class exploitation, sexism, materialism and military imperialism in its varied and sundry forms. For example, the ill gotten immoral wars in the world; which America either initiates, supports or both. The ongoing misappropriation of wealth and power by the ruling race and class; and of focus in this commentary, the insidious policy, programs, and practices of the Unholy Alliance of the Food Industry, the disease Management Industry, Pharmaceutical companies and their assorted cohorts in crime such as the American Medical Association, American Cancer Society, the Food and drug Administration, American Heart Association etc.

In Rev. Kings philosophical stance he deemed us, Black people as the moral vanguard whose social circumstances, pain, and intense spiritual grounding, positions us for a mission of liberation that is divinely inspired, manifested in our thought and action building a liberation movement, with anticipated ramifications of peace, freedom, and an abundance of goodness for all at the end of our days of struggle. There is no where today where Rev. Kings model of moral magnitude could be more needed than engaging the struggle to obtain optimal health as a people.

As I have articulated elsewhere; "Afro Americans, have the highest disparity rates of obesity, diabetes, hypertension, prostate cancer, stroke, heart attacks and related diseases; and San Diego is not exempt from this atrocity as evidenced by County of San Diego, (2013)'s Health Status of Black Residents in San Diego County, (in Critical Issues in the Struggle for Optimal Health, Kalonji, Dec, 2013)." The battle for optimal health will of necessity include efforts in the political, economic, and social realm of human thought and activity. Moreover, like the overall liberation movement, it is both communitarian and personal; and the focal point of this article is primarily in the interest of personal/communitarian development. There are four points of Rev. Kings, philosophy, practice and

model of moral magnitude addressed here. They are his position on Self Help, Revolution, and Activism & Achievement. On Self Help, Rev. King writes us in his seminal text Stride Toward Freedom that "Black people must come to see that there is much we can do about our plight. Whether educated or not, or stricken with poverty; these handicaps most not prevent us from seeing that we have the power to alter our fate." In other words as I have written elsewhere in,

Change begins with one person; as one person changes they affect the rest of the population. One person has the power within them to bring massive change in any circumstance through creating change within themselves. But we cannot bring well-being to others unless we have conquered that in our own life, (in A Maxim for Optimal Health; Kalonji, Dec, 2013).

Moreover, inherent in this position on Self Help is Rev. King's contention that it "is immoral to collaborate in one's own oppression." One collaborates by their accepting oppression, turning a blind eye or ignoring oppression, and become evils accomplice. So a people ignoring its poor state of health and continuing to demonstrate the behavior that got them unhealthy is collaboration in one own oppression. Thus, there is as argued earlier, no reason that we as a people cannot eradicate our health crisis. Regardless of the systemic manipulation by the Unholy Alliance, if we do as the Nguzo Saba principles of Kujichagulia (Self Determination) and Ujima (Collective Work and Responsibility) instruct us, we no doubt will overturn our weakness and turn it into a strength, subsequently empowering ourselves to be the best of who we are as African peoples living a quality lifestyle free of disease and systemic death predicted and promoted by the established orders disease management mechanisms.

On Revolution, King contends that "indeed we are engaged in revolution, a social movement that changes people and institution; and that our hope today lies in our ability to recapture the revolutionary spirit and go out into a hostile world." Linked to King's position on revolution is his contention that we have the

SEE **Black Path, page 13**

## CalVet to Co-Host CA Black Veterans Summit

Throughout American history, Black veterans and Black military personnel have played a vital role in the development, economic vitality and security of our State and our Nation. To honor that legacy, CalVet will co-host the first California Black Veterans Summit.

**California Black Veterans Summit
February 24, 2014 • 8:00AM-4:30PM
California African American Museum
600 State Dr., Los Angeles, CA 90001**

This inaugural Black Veterans Summit seeks to develop lines of communication between the Black veterans' community, Black military history organizations and CalVet. Dynamic speakers will offer key insights on issues that are germane to Black veterans and their environments. Subject matter experts and other panelists will discuss current data and trends to bridge the information gap that exists for Black veterans regarding the education, employment, housing, health and other benefits they have earned through military service and to guide them through the benefits claims process more efficiently.

For more information, call 916-653-1402 or go to http://www.calvet.ca.gov/Minority/BlackVeteranSummit.aspx to register.

## Southern Indian Health Council Hosts 2nd Annual Native American Veterans Holiday Breakfast

On December 6th, over 80 veterans attended the above event held at the Barona Indian reservation. Mr. Leon Altamirano and Eleanor Miller were the hosts. A fine breakfast was enjoyed by all those who attended. I, Virgil Osuna/Vice Commander for AIVA gave thanks to the Barona Donation Committee for their generous donation toward the purchasing of rifles for our Honor Guard. The rifles will used for military burials and events. Chairman, Clifford LaChappa presented a check at this event. On behalf of all veterans, we thank the Barona Band for their support and dedication.

To improve the quality of life of those who recognize themselves and choose to be recognized by others as "Indigenous Peoples of Color of the Americas" and in support of The American Indian Rights and Resources Organization (AIRRO).

## Christmas Day Freedom Fighters: Hidden History of the Seminole Anticolonial Struggle

*by William Katz*

On Christmas day 1837, 176 years ago, the Africans and Native Americans who formed Florida's Seminole Nation defeated a vastly superior U.S. invading army bent on cracking this early rainbow coalition and returning the Africans to slavery. The Seminole victory stands as a milestone in the march of American liberty. Though it reads like a Hollywood thriller, this amazing story has yet to capture public attention. It is absent from most school textbooks, social studies courses, Hollywood movies, and TV.

This daring Seminole story begins around the time of the American Revolution when 55 "Founding Fathers" broke free of British colonialism and wrote the Declaration of Independence. About the same time, Seminoles—suffering ethnic persecution under Creek rule in Alabama and Georgia—fled south to seek independence. Africans who has escaped bondage and became among its first explorers welcomed them to Florida.

The Africans did more than offer Seminole families a haven. They taught them methods of rice cultivation they had learned in Senegambia and Sierra Leone, Africa. Then the two peoples of color forged a

## Lucinda Fixico the Indian Princess of Seminole County

Earlier, this year, a gentleman contacted me from Seminole County, Oklahoma, with information that solved a decades old mystery for the Fixico family. My relatives and Ancestors who came to California were Black Indian Refugees from Oklahoma. When they fled Oklahoma after my grandfather Pompey Bruner Fixico was gunned down, in Wewoka, Okla. The result of which, saw the perpetrator, go free just like, George Zimmerman did in the Trayvon Martin tragedy. My family who came here from Oklahoma, brought many things, however, what was left behind was the truth. One unsolved mystery was "Whatever happened to Pompey's older sister Lucinda Fixico"? The Gentleman who contacted me, had information that solved part of the puzzle. He is White male in his 40's and was not only born and raised in Seminole County, his family owns the land where, Lucinda Fixico, my Great-aunt and Pompey's sister is buried (see photo). He has known about her tombstone for 40 years. The tombstone was so expensive for the area, that the local legend was that she must have been a Princess with magical powers.

My new hero, is named, Kevin Brinker, formerly a detective with the Wewoka, OK Police Department of Seminole County, he wants to submit the story known locally as, "Lucinda Fixico, the Indian Princess of Seminole County", to the "Oprah" Production and Publishing Empire. Let's see if this episode, of a tremendous saga will finally

capture the imagination of America and the world. I believe our history can be revealed by looking at the current descendants of the Pioneers who settled the land and the Children, of the era of Slavery and Indian Removal. The effects of Manifest Destiny are not on trial, but we must look at it's effects, in order to understand how we all, can come together in the spirit of Reconciliation. I have worked on this question for 14 years, what Mr. Brinker did marks an important milestone. If they assign a Producer and a Writer to the idea, there is more than enough content and documentation to make it a candidate for production. Another, phase of this cross country, episode is that Kevin Brinker, who is a wonderful human being, got interested in the story enough to encourage the county's oldest area newspaper, "The Seminole Producer" to do a story on it. The paper is published by Mr. Stu Phillips, his Senior Editor is Karen Anson, a famous author in her own right, Ms. Anson wrote a Frontpage masterpiece, that is worthy of serious praise. Therefore, the Bureau of Black Indian Affairs, recommended that this, 'Salt of the earth' trio be recognized by the "Semiroon Historical Society". Mr. Kevin Brinker, has been presented with the "Humanitarian of the year Award 2013", and Owner/Publisher Mr. Stu Phillips, has been given a "Lifetime Achievement Award 2013" and finally Ms. Anson has

received the award for "The Best Journalist 2013". The story was named, "Play Could Begin Renaissance for Seminole Culture" the play in question was being performed in Los Angeles at the prestgious Los Angeles Theater Center. It was entitled, "the road weeps, the well runs dry". It was written by Marcus Gardley and Directed by Shirley Finney, both of whom are descendants of Oklahoma Black Indians. Finding the location of Lucinda Fixico's resting place, has not answered all the questions, but it did prove that there are great people on the West coast and in Seminole County, that have have much in common. The fact that this story crossed-over to a location where the demographics are approximately, 70% White, 19% Indian and 6% Black, proves that a Hollywood movie could be successful. The idea of which is being circulated in Hollywood right now, I know because, I'm circulating it.

All the best, Phil "Pompey" Fixico, Seminole Maroon Descendant, California Semiroon Mico (Nation of One).

Seminole Chief Osceola (1804–1838). Image: WikiCommons.

prosperous multicultural nation and a military alliance ready to withstand the European invaders and slave catchers. The Seminoles were led by such skilled military figures and diplomats as Osceola, Wild Cat, and John Horse.

This alliance drove U.S. slaveholders to sputtering fury. They saw Seminole unity, prosperity, and guns as a lethal threat to their plantation system. Here was a beacon that enticed escapees and offered them a military base of operations. Further, these peaceful communities destroyed the slaveholder myth that Africans required white control.

And these armed black and Indian communities lived a stone's throw from the southern U.S. border. The U.S. Constitution of 1789 embraced slavery and protected slaveholder interests. From George Washington to the Civil War, slave owners sat in the White House two-thirds of the time, were two-thirds of speakers of the House of Representatives, two-thirds of presidents of the U.S. Senate, and 20 of 35 U.S. Supreme Court justices. With the support of their Northern trading partners—merchants and businessmen, and the politicians who served them—slaveholders were able to direct U.S. foreign policy.

Slaveholders and their allies kept up a drumbeat for U.S. military intervention in Florida, and in 1811 President James Madison authorized covert U.S. invasions by slave-catching posses called "Patriots." Then in 1816, General Andrew Jackson ordered General Gaines to attack the Seminole alliance and "restore the stolen Negroes to their rightful owners." A major U.S. assault began

on hundreds of people living in "Fort Negro" on the Apalachicola River. As U.S. Army Colonel Clinch sailed down the Apalachicola he wrote: "The American Negroes had principally settled along the river and a number of them had left their fields and gone over to the Seminoles on hearing of our approach. Their cornfields extended nearly fifty miles up the river and their numbers were daily increasing."

When a heated U.S. cannonball hit Fort Negro's ammunition dump, the explosion killed most of its more than 300 defenders. The survivors were marched back to slavery. Then in 1818 General Jackson invaded and claimed Florida, the United States "purchased" it ($5,000,000) from Spain in 1819, and sent a U.S. army of occupation for "pacification."

But suddenly the U.S. faced the largest slave revolt in its history, its busiest Underground Railroad station, and the strongest African/Indian alliance in North America. The multicultural

SEE **Seminole Struggle**, page 7

# The Civil War as a War Against Bondage/War of Genocide

On August 1, 1865, John Evans was removed from his post as Governor of Colorado by Secretary of State Seward for being the official who presided over and ordered the Sand Creek massacre. The Congressional Joint Committee on the Conduct of the Civil War investigating Sand Creek had called for his resignation.

Evans was a friend and associate of the Republican Party with Lincoln and they had been involved in the railways together in Illinois. Lincoln is famed for extending the Union Pacific, as Marx put it in Capital, with the "speed of seven league boots" across the whole country .

The Union Pacific had gone through Kansas where officials, threatening coercion, had negotiated with the indigenous people to leave their lands and hunting grounds. This was part of a process of belligerence, thievery, killing and settling other people on the land. It imposed grave hardship on indigenous people. They had to change their way of life, become farmers among whites, or farmers on reservations, and they were made dependent on American promises. They were continuously expelled into "Indian Territories," no longer independent nations but racial subordinates to the United States Government.

Some cooperated to an extent, to save themselves: the Pawnee, for example, against the Sioux. It was, over time, ethnic cleansing. American leaders, for instance, General William Tecumseh Sherman, spoke of exterminating native americans... "St. Louis, December 28, 1866.

General Grant: Just arrived in time to attend the funeral of my adjutant general, Sawyer. I have given general instructions to General Cooke about the Sioux. I do not yet understand how the massacre of Colonel Fetterman's party could have been so complete. We must act with vindictive earnestness against the

Sioux, even to their extermination, men, women and children. Nothing less will reach the root of this case. W. T. Sherman, Lieutenant General" With the surrender of the Confederacy, the War against bondage ended in 1865. But the War of genocide extended from before the Civil War, was heightened during it in the West (the driving of indigenous people out of Mankato and Minnesota as well as Colorado), and extended in the Great Indian Wars till the massacre at Wounded Knee in 1890. Starting with Lincoln's Presidency, one might date this Civil War from 1861-1890.

*John Evans professor at the Josef Korbel School of International Studies at the University of Denver*

## History is Important

*by refixico*

A great thinker named George Santayana, once said: "Those who do not remember the past are condemned to repeat it".

The world forgot the African Holocaust of the Trans-Atlantic Slave Trade and the Holocaust of the Native American 500 Year War. By forgetting the past of others we repeated similar events, like the Jewish Holocaust of World War II.

Hitler's actions, proved Santayana's point. Hitler didn't forget the past, he mentioned in his book, "Mein Kampf", that in his opinion, the American Indians presented the same situation to the "Aryans" of America, as the Jews did, to the "Aryans" of Germany. He applauded the techniques used by the American Presidents Jackson and Van Buren during the Indian Removal Era, that led to the, "Trail of Tears" of the 1830's and he used the same tactics on a much bigger scale.

As our technology, increases our need to be mindful of historical similarities must also increase. When Hitler applied the technological advances of his day, to the logistical strategies of 1830's America, the effect was exponentially more devastating.

Yes, history is important. It's crucial, that we continue to use education and commemorate the good and the not so good. If we face those realities, we can better promote and celebrate more positive paradigms for our future. I have been blessed to have had my Semiroon Historical Society confirmed as a Private Sector Partner, for the U.S. Dept. of Interior/National Parks Service/National Underground Railroad/Network to Freedom Program. I intend to show my respect for the Past, by working in the Present, with this worthy program to ensure a brighter Future, for everyone, regardless of race, religion, color or creed.

Yours Truly,
Phil "Pompey" Fixico, Private Sector Partner, NUGRR/NTF

## Seminole Struggle

Continued from page 6

Seminole forces carefully moved families out of harm's way from 1816 to 1858 as they resisted the U.S. through three "Seminole Wars." Today many Seminoles still claim they never surrendered.

In June 1837 Major General Sidney Thomas Jesup, the best informed U.S. officer in Florida, described the danger posed by the Seminole alliance: "The two races, the Negro and the Indian, are rapidly approximating; they are identical in interests and feelings ... Should the Indians remain in this territory the Negroes among them will form a rallying point for runaway Negroes from the adjacent states; and if they remove, the fastness of the country will be immediately occupied by Negroes."

Then on Christmas Day 1837, 380 to 480 Seminole fighters gathered on the northeast corner of Florida's Lake Okeechobee ready to halt the armies of Colonel Zachary Taylor, a Louisiana slaveholder and ambitious career soldier. He was building a reputation as an "Indian killer." Taylor's troops included 70 Delaware Indians, 180 Tennessee volunteers, and 800 U.S. infantry soldiers.

As Taylor's huge army approached, Seminole marksmen waited perched in trees or hiding in tall grass. The first Seminole volleys sent the Delaware fleeing. Tennessee riflemen plunged ahead until a withering fire brought down their commissioned officers and then their noncommissioned officers. The Tennesseans headed home.

Then Taylor ordered the U.S. Sixth Infantry, Fourth Infantry, and his own First Infantry Regiments forward. Pinpoint Seminole rifle fire brought down, he later reported, "every officer, with one exception, as well as most of the noncommissioned officers" and left "but four ... untouched." That Christmas Day Colonel Taylor counted 26 U.S. dead and 112 wounded, seven dead for each slain Seminole, and he had taken no prisoners. After the two and a half hour battle the Seminoles took to their canoes and sailed off to fight again.

Lake Okeechobee became the most decisive U.S. defeat in more than four decades of Florida warfare. But after his survivors limped back to Fort Gardner, Taylor declared victory—"the Indians were driven in every direction." The U.S. Army promoted him and he later became the 12th president of the United States.

Lake Okeechobee took place during the Second Seminole War that took 1,500 U.S. military lives, cost Congress $40,000,000 (pre-Civil War dollars!), and left thousands of American soldiers wounded or dead of disease. Seminole losses were not recorded.

The truth of Lake Okeechobee remained buried. When President Taylor died in office, in Illinois Abraham Lincoln memorialized him on July 25, 1850. "He was never beaten," Lincoln said, and added: " ... in 1837 he fought and conquered in the memorable Battle of Lake Okeechobee, one of the most desperate struggles known to the annals of Indian warfare."

A century and a half later noted Harvard historian and author Arthur Schlesinger Jr. wrote in The Almanac of American History: "Fighting in the Second Seminole War, General Zachary Taylor defeats a group of Seminoles at Okeechobee Swamp, Florida." Some textbooks such as Holt McDougal's United States History (2012) now reference the Seminole Wars. However they classify them not as anticolonial struggles, but as minor impediments in "Manifest Destiny's" triumphant march.

The United States needs to face its past. Americans of all ages have a right to know and to celebrate the freedom fighters who built this country, all of them. Our schools, children, teachers, and parents deserve to learn about a daring Christmas day that has been too long neglected and distorted.

*William Loren Katz is the author of Black Indians: A Hidden Heritage, and 40 other books on African American history. His website is www.williamlkatz.com.*
*This article was adapted from Black Indians: A Hidden Heritage.*

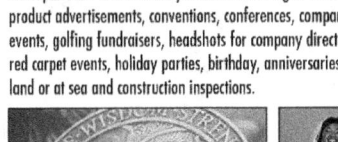

# *CELEBRATION*

Joe Rentaria was honored on Saturday, December 7th at a luncheon hosted by the American Indian Heritage Foundation at Barrio Station, 2175 Newton Ave.

The winter celebration is held in San Diego to honor American Indian leaders in the community to recognize them for their work and contribution to the world. A massive outpouring from our indigenous community came out to enjoy, celebrate and honor each other. Much enthusiasm and support from the volunteers inspired by Paula Brim made this a memorable and heart felt occasion. Flute playing, feasting and storytelling made a great holiday event

Joe Renteria, a retired Naval Photographer was presented with many awards by the Events Committee Chair, Ms. Paula Brim.

# Nevada Governor's Conference on Tourism

**December 3-5**

Bethany Drysdale and the Nevada Tourist Bureau brought together a dynamic business networking event. Held at the Red Rock Casino in Las Vegas, industry leaders from around the world came to exchange ideas and opportunities. Chinese and Japanese tourist professionals were eager to reach out to the attendees.

Although snow storms prevented the Governor from attending the conference was an enormous success.

# A Tongva Calendar Story

*Edited Excerpt by Valena Dismukes from an article by Bryn Barabas Potter*

For some Native Californians, the New Year begins on Winter Solstice. For the Tongva (Gabrielino), the New Year will begin on December 21, 2013, followed by a year of ten months. For the first time, a modern calendar based on the traditional Tongva has been printed.

Most of the world has been following the familiar twelve-month Gregorian calendar since 1582. Prior to that, other civilizations devised their form of tracking the years. In terms of timekeeping, what was happening in Southern California? The question intrigued Glenn Miller, Jr, a local astronomer of Tongva

descent who currently teaches astronomy at Pasadena City College. As he learned more about his maternal heritage, he came across the 1822 writings of Friar Boscana that mentioned the traditional indigenous year.

Ever the scientist, Miller took on a challenge---to recreate an indigenous California version of 2013. He brought the idea to a group of volunteers at the Haramokngna American Indian Cultural Center (the Center), and the idea evolved. With a committee composed of Kat High, Glenn Miller, Jr., Bryn Potter, Peggy Ronning, Valena Dismukes, the idea slowly evolved. Miller's Tongva heritage, use of Tongva words, and the location of the Tongva homeland in the San

Gabriel Mountains is what made this version "A Tongva Calendar."

A Tongva Calendar is innovative and cutting-edge, yet also basic and ancient. How does a ten-month year work? Simply put, the year begins on the Winter Solstice. Months generally start with the new crescent Moon. As lunar phases vary year to year, "vacant days" occur which don't belong to any month. In this calendar, months 5 and 10 have "vacant days," noted by a slightly different color.

This is a useable, contemporary calendar, full-color, 8.5 x 11 wall calendar with beautiful Native American artwork to enjoy day and boxes for each day in which to write notes. The Gregorian and Tongva systems are artfully combined, with an unexpected twist but still in a functional format. Astronomical events

like solstices and eclipses are noted, as are Daylight Saving Time and American holidays. Days are listed Sunday through Saturday with standard Gregorian numbering and Tongva names. Most of the months include information about the Tongva culture and language.

By looking at months in a different way, maybe minds cam be opened to an alternate way of viewing the year. Malcolm Margolin (author, and publisher of HeyDay books) summed it up in these words: "It is an art project that will allow people to reconceptualize their world."

A Tongva Calendar is available at Haramokngna for $20. All of the proceeds of this volunteer production with benefit the Center and its programs. To order, visit the Haramokngna website (Haramokngna.org).

# A San Diego Political Sea Change as David Alvarez Fights for Barrio Logan

Barrio Logan is in the eye of a political hurricane in San Diego. Recognizing that politics is local, David Alvarez , a Home Grown Home Boy is indellably connected to this community. He could not be better positioned to lead the charge for the people that he represents. Affordable housing advocates, union and community groups are allied with him against corporated funded referendums. "Juntos venceremos" they chanted.

Barrio Logan is a neighborhood in San Diego, California bordered by East Village and Logan Heights to the North, Shelltown and Southcrest to the East, San Diego Bay to the West, and National City to the South. I-5 forms the Northeastern boundary.

In 1871, Congressman John A. Logan wrote legislation to provide federal land grants and subsidies for a transcontinental railroad ending in San Diego. A street laid in was named Logan Heights after him,

and the name came to be applied to the general area. Plans for a railroad never successfully materialized, and the area was predominantly residential by the turn of the century, becoming one of San Diego's oldest communities. Its transformation began in 1910 with the influx of refugees of the Mexican Revolution, who soon became the majority ethnic group. For this reason, the southern part of the original Logan Heights neighborhood came to be called Barrio Logan.

The area was originally residential with access to the beach at San Diego Bay. During World War II this beach access was lost due to the expansion of Naval Station San Diego and other military facilities on the waterfront. The neighborhood continued to degrade during the 1950s and 1960s due to rezoning that permitted industrial uses, the construction of Interstate 5 through the heart of the community in 1963, and the construction of

the San Diego-Coronado Bridge in 1969, which covered much of the community with a concrete "roof" supported by gray concrete pillars.The city council promised to build a community park under the bridge approaches, and a site was approved in June 1969. When construction began in April 1970 at the designated site, but the community learned that the work was intended to create a state building instead of a park, there was a nonviolent community uprising. Students and others occupied the site and forced a halt to the construction. The occupation of the site lasted twelve days. Residents planted landscaping, and a local artist, Salvador Torres, proclaimed his vision of covering the freeway support pillars with murals. After intense negotiation between the city and the state (which owned the land in question), the site was reclaimed for park use, and Chicano Park was built and dedicated. It was expanded several times and in 1990 it was extended all the way to the bay, restoring beach access to the community

Barrio Logan is the home of Chicano

Bobby Godinez, President of the Shipyard Workers Union Local 1998. He says all unionized shipyard workers support the Barrio Logan Community Plan and will vote against repealing it. "The Maritime Industry gave us lies and deception."

Park, a Chicano-themed public park created in large part by the local residents. It is located at the site of a 1970s demonstration, land takeover, and cultural renaissance for the Mexican-American community. It features more than 60 colorful murals painted on the concrete support piers for the San Diego-Coronado Bridge

SEE **Barrio Logan**, page 14

# Rally to Vote NO on Fast Tracking the TPP

**Coalition calls on Rep. Susan Davis to Join Bipartisan Opposition**

**Congress' Constitutional Duty Would Be Usurped by Fast Track!**

As we mark 20 years since the signing of the North American Free Trade Agreement (NAFTA), the potential impacts on working people of the secretly negotiated TPP are cast in stark relief. Under NAFTA, the United States suffered a net loss of 700,000 jobs to Mexico, as manufacturers took advantage of Mexico's cheap labor and lack of environmental and safety standards. Labor unions and human rights groups point out that fair labor standards have either eroded or were simply nonexistent in both countries during the past two decades.

A 2012 Angus Reid Public Opinion

"Hit it" chimes Norrie Robbins (left) of Occupellas.

poll says more than half of Americans want the U.S. to withdraw or renegotiate NAFTA. Only 15 percent believe that the U.S. should continue its current participation in NAFTA. When President Obama ran in 2008, he said he voted against the Central American Free Trade Agreement, he never supported NAFTA, and that he would not support NAFTA-style free trade agreements in the future. Yet now he is aggressively pushing the the TPP, which has been described by critics as "NAFTA on steroids."

Kicking off the Rally is Richard Barrera, Secretary-Treasurer of the San Diego and Imperial Counties Labor Council which includes 135 affiliated unions. He is also a twice-elected Trustee of the San Diego Unified School District, the second-largest school district in California.

"Fast tracking trade deals like the Trans-Pacific Partnership hurt America's working families by eliminating access to a reasoned and thoughtful democratic process. We urge Congress to vote 'no' on rushing through any deal that favors corporate profits over the rights of American workers." — Richard Barrera, Secretary - Treasurer, San Diego and Imperial Counties Labor Council

The celebrated Occupellas choral group of Women Occupy San Diego performed

Fast Tracking the secret, undemocrat-

**San Diego Congressmembers Say NO to Fast Tracking the TPP**

**Where are Susan Davis & Darrell Issa**

Mt. Rushmore cries out for a leader.

ic Trans-Pacific Partnership Agreement (TPP) is expected to be introduced in Congress when it returns from holiday recess today, and it could be voted on between January 8-11. If Fast Tracking passes, there will be virtually no Congressional debate on the TPP, which has been negotiated in secret by the Obama Administration and 600 corporate lobbyists with 10 other nations. For more info on the TPP, see http://www.citizen.org/tpp//

Congressmembers Susan Davis and Darrell Issa have not joined their San Diego County delegation colleagues Duncan Hunter, Scott

Peters and Juan Vargas in opposing Fast Tracking. Women Occupy San Diego and the San Diego Overpass Light Brigade are working in a national coalition of 400+ labor, environmental, health, democracy and other advocacy groups to target our local Congressmembers with phone calls to Vote NO on Fast Tracking the TPP, and this Rally is intended to highlight the importance of this vote. We call upon Congresswoman Davis to join 178 of her colleagues from BOTH PARTIES who have publicly opposed Fast Tracking to Vote NO on "Fast Track" Trade Promotion Authority or any other mechanism that continues to exclude Congress from having a meaningful role in the formative stages of trade agreements and throughout negotiating and approval processes.

TPP protestors in front of Congresswoman Susan Davis' office.

## GAMBLING AND THE LAW®:
# Adelson's Bad Bet

*"If Churchill were alive today, he would have said about this election, 'Never have so few spent so much to affect so little.'"* – James Carville

The gaming industry won most of its battles at the ballot box, but lost the public relations war.

In Maryland, voters passed Question 7, 52% to 48%. This will not only allow the five previously authorized slot casinos to add table games, it permits a giant sixth Las Vegas style casino, right next to Washington, DC. MGM's Prince George's County casino will have as many as 3,000 slot machines.

Rhode Island voters approved adding table games to the slot halls at Twin River and Newport Grand, giving the state two full-scale casinos. Geneseo, Illinois, voters narrowly recommended the city have video gaming.

Oregon again voted against privately owned casinos. But that is mixed news, since it would have meant competition to the state's Indian casinos.

The continuing Democratic majority in the U.S. Senate means Nevada casinos keep one of the best friends they have ever had, Harry Reid (D.-NV), as majority leader. Tribal gaming also keeps its friend, Barack Obama, as president, and added individuals like Heidi Heitkamp (D.-ND)

to the upper house. For Internet gaming, die-hard supporter Barney Frank (D.-MA) may have retired, but so did opponent Jon Kyl (R.-AZ).

All of these successes pale in the face to the major p.r. hit casinos took in the media on November 6 and the days that followed. The fault lies primarily with two individuals: Donald Trump and Sheldon Adelson. But Steve Wynn and Penn National Gaming did their share to hurt gaming's reputation.

There is not much to say about Trump. I have to admit that I used to admire him. I have taught law school classes in negotiating, and I respect not only his skill but his willingness to do whatever it takes to win. When one of his Atlantic City casinos went bankrupt, he threatened the bondholders to tie up the proceedings in messy litigation for years. He knew as an equity holder he had almost no legal rights. But he also knew the lenders were big investors from Japan, who would do anything to avoid having their names dragged into a public fight. So, they let Trump keep his name on the casinos, and gave him shares in the new business.

Similarly, I often work as a consultant and expert witness. This means getting people to know my name, so they will hire me. Until recently, no one could compete with Trump when it came to self-promotion.

But his lack of restraint led to headlines like this:

"Trump calls for revolution, blasts

Electoral College"

"Donald Trump goes berserk on election night"

"Donald Trump Wins Election Night's 'Most Unhinged Conservative' Award"

NBC reporter Brian Williams said, on-air, "Donald Trump, who has driven well past the last exit to relevance and peered into something closer to irresponsible here, is tweeting tonight." Trump's response led to new headlines: "Donald Trump Twitter Tirade Continues with Criticism of Brian Williams."

Trump was most upset that Barack Obama appeared to have won the electoral college but not the popular vote. Trump had not complained in 2000, when George W. Bush was elected president with fewer votes than Al Gore. Common sense would have told Trump to wait until the votes from the West Coast had been counted: Obama beat Mitt Romney by more than 3 million votes.

Fortunately for the gaming industry, Trump is so well known, that most stories never mentioned his casinos. Not so with Sheldon Adelson.

Adelson bet very big on Romney and other conservative Republicans in nine Senate races. Many stories noted that the money he contributed in 2012 made him the largest political donor in American history. And every news report included his ownership of casinos.

All of his money was wasted, with the possible exception that the GOP kept the U.S. Senate seat in Nevada. But it was more than thrown away: Adelson actually campaigned against himself.

The owner of the Las Vegas Sands ("LVS") started the year as the biggest backer of Newt Gingrich. There is general agreement that without Adelson's millions, Gingrich would have dropped out of the primaries after his early losses. Instead, Gingrich had the cash to run attack ad after attack ad against Romney, focusing on his "vulture capitalism" at Bain Capital. This reinforced the image of Romney that the Obama campaign was pushing. And it extended the primary fights, forcing Romney to take extreme right-wing positions that were caught on tape.

Forbes lists Adelson as the 11th richest

American, and his political contributions show just how much money he has. Americans have trouble thinking about the difference between "million" and "billion." I like the British terminology better, which calls the larger number "a thousand million."

Adelson has somewhere around $25 thousand million, give or take a few thousand million. This means he has more money than was spent by Obama and Romney and the Democratic and Republican parties and all independent groups on the presidential election – four times as much. Ironically, he probably made more money under Obama than any other individual. His LVS stock was at $5 a share when Obama took office; it is now above $43.

Adelson gave people like Romney and Karl Rove about $53 million. This is an enormous amount, for an election. But not for Adelson. As a nice comparison, a couple of weeks after the election, Adelson had LVS declare a special dividend, giving him about $1.2 billion. That's $1,200 million; $53 million really is the size of a rounding error.

It is about two-tenths of one percent of his assets. If you own a home that is above water and have some money in the bank, you might be worth about $100,000. Donating 0.2% would mean just writing a check for $200.

The problem for the gaming industry is that it looks like it is filled with people with money to burn, and who have their own agendas at best, or who are divorced from reality at worst.

Howard Stutz wrote an "Inside Gaming" column in the Las Vegas Review-Journal entitled "Piles of cash, torrents of tweets and lots of crazy." In it, he discussed not only Trump and Adelson, but also Wynn's constant attacks on President Obama.

Wynn characterized Obama as a socialist, while praising Communist China. Here are the actual quotes: "The guy keeps making speeches about redistribution, and maybe we ought to do something to businesses that don't invest, they're holding too much money. We haven't heard that kind of talk except

SEE **Gambling**, page 14

---

# The Pauma Band of Mission Indians Honors Vets

*by Adam Rodriguez*

The Pauma Band of Mission Indians honored their Veterans at a ceremony on November 9, 2013 at 11:00 am at their Graveyard in Pauma Valley.

The first Veteran Memorial was made out of adobe and over the years has deteriorated. The Pauma Tribe wanted to honor their Veterans before the Veteran Day Holiday. The names of the Pauma Tribal Veterans well be on a temporary

nameplate until their bronze plate is ready after Veterans Day.

The Tribes Gaming Revenue funded the Pauma Tribal Veteran's Memorial.

Father Ray, from the Pala Mission conducted the Blessing of the Memorial.

In addition the Southern California Veterans Association Honor Guard conducted the customary military honors

A festive lunch followed the ceremony at the Pauma Tribal Hall.

# TRADING POST BUSINESS DIRECTORY

## CALIFORNIA

**ADVOCACY**
Alan Lechuza Aquallo
Advocate for Native Youth and Scholarships
alan@blackphonerecords.com

**ATTORNEYS**
Aaleman & Associates
Henry Mendibles Associate
220 Sage Road El Cajon, CA 92012
619-593-1754 • treefuzz@cox.net

Marshall Law PC
Daniel E. Marshall, Attorney at Law
619-298-5778 • marslawbmw@gmail.com

**BAKERY**
Historic San Luis Rey Bakery
490 N. El Camino Real Oceanside, CA 92058
760-433-7242

La Nueva Mexican Bakery
4676 Market St. Ste. A-3, San Diego, CA
619-262-0042

**BEEKEEPERS**
Liz • 619-504-2655

**BEVERAGES**
ExFuse / Vandana Chima
702-401-1404
vandana@teamchima.com
www.teamchima.com

**CARE GIVER**
Private Duty– References
Terms to be discussed
619-504-2455 Ask for Liz

**CLERICAL**
Your Girl Friday International
Marketing, Operations & Promotional
Services • 619-961-0531
yourgirlfriday3512@gmail.com

**CONSULTING**
Taspan Consulting Company
Shirley Murphy, President
5457 Sycuan Road, El Cajon, CA
619-994-5796 • www.taspan.org

**CONTRACTORS**
Rivero Builders / Carlos Rivero
General Contractor, Residental, Commercial
760-715-8003

**CULTURE**
Kumeyaay
www.kumeyaay.com • larry@kumeyaay.com

Worldbeat Cultural Center
619-230-1190
www.worldbeatculturalcenter.org
info@worldbeatculturalcenter.org

**DRIVER**
Driver for Hire
Clean DMV Class ABC
619-504-2455 Ask for Liz

**FINANCIAL ADVISORS**
Merrill Lynch / Elke Chenevey
Vice President & Financial Advisor
Office: 619-699-3707
Fax: 619-758-3619

Summit Funding
The Home Loan Experts
Jeff Ellenz, Branch Manager
760-568-0300 • jellenz@summitfunding.net

**FURNITURE**
Ladies Mahogany Dresser
3 Mirrors - Good condition
$2,000
619-504-2455 Ask for Liz

**HEALTH**
Rady's Children Hospital

San Diego, CA
800-869-5627 • www.rchsd.org

Regenerative Medicine Institute
www.regenerativemedicine.mx

**HEALER-SHAMAN**
Transitions / Vera A. Tucker
vtucker1212@gmail.com
619-987-0372

**HOUSEKEEPING**
Cleaning, windows, floors
4 hours $60 - 8 hours $100
619-504-2455 Ask for Liz

**INSURANCE**
State Farm / Jack Fannin
1154 E. Main St. El Cajon, CA 92021-7157
619-440-0161 Business
619-440-0495 Fax
jack.fanninjroi@statefarm.com
www.jackfannin.com

Bradley Insurance
Doris Bradley, Agent
619-309-5394 • 619-698-4783
bradleyinsurance@yahoo.com

Earthquake Insurances
www.EarthquakeAuthority.com

**MARKETING**
International Marketing Systems
Eddy Michaelly
www.imsbarter.com

Jahaanah Productions
Marketing, Media, Public Relations, Graphic
Design • 832-978-0939

**NOTARY PUBLIC**
Sis. Evon X. Nana
San Diego, CA 92113 • 619-549-5792
evonx@yahoo.com

**PHOTOGRAPHY**
Peache Photo Memories
619-697-4186 office
619-549-0968 contact
http://peache-1.smugmug.com
peachephotos@cox.net

**PUBLISHERS**
Blackrose Communications
111 South 35th St. San Diego, CA 92113
619-234-4753
www.indianvoices.net • davis4973@aol.com

**RADIO**
91.3PM Kopa
Pala Rez Radio
www.palatribe.com • 91.3@palatribe.com

**REGALIA**
Carla Tourville
Native Regalia Custom Design
Yokut Tule River Tribe
San Diego, CA • 619-743-9847

**REPARATIONS**
Mr. Peoples Reparations
200 N. Long Beach Blvd. Compton, CA
310-632-0577

**RESTAURANT**
Awash Ethiopian Restaurant
4979 El Cajon Blvd. San Diego, CA
619-677-3754

**RETAIL – CLOTHING**
Full Blood Apparel
P.O. Box 3101 Valley Venter, CA 92082
www.fullbloodskates.com • 760-445-1141

**SOCIAL SERVICES**
Tribal Tanf
Temporary Assistance for Needy Families
San Diego Office 866-913-3725
Escondido Office 866-428-0901

Manzanita Office 866-931-1480
Pala Office 866-806-8263

**VETERANS**
AIWA – American Indian Warriors
Association
William Buchanan, President
858-234-8715

## NEVADA

**ADVOCACY**
Adams Esq.
Special Needs Children
500 N. Rainbow Blvd. Ste 300
Las Vegas, NV 89107
702-289-4143 Office • 702-924-7200 Fax

**COMMUNITY**
Native American Community Services
3909 S. Maryland Pkwy #205 Las Vegas, NV
89119-7500

**PUBLISHERS**
Blackrose Communications
111 South 35th St. San Diego, CA 92113
619-234-4753
www.indianvoices.net • davis4973@aol.com

## TEXAS

**HEALTH**
The Circle: A Healing Place
Joanna Johnson, MSW, CFAS
Longview Behavioral Hospital
22 Bermuda Lane, Longbiew, Texas 75605
www.longviewhospital.com
www.oglethorpeinc.com
850-228-0777

## Black Path

Continued from page 5

moral right and responsibility to resist wrong include disobeying the established orders and unjust laws. Thus in the context of our struggle of prevention and intervention of disease disparity and death of our community, we are obligated by history and heaven to rise up in opposition to evil and wrong doing as King states " that when man-made law conflicts with moral reasoning, we not only have the right but also, the responsibility to resist it. Rev. King goes onto say that "justice will not come from court decision or legislation but rather form a "rad-

ical restructuring of our society"; and that is ever evident in the struggle for liberation via reaching optimal health in our community.

Lastly, Rev. King's stance on Activism & Achievement is affirmed through his contention that "Freedom is never given to anybody, activism is necessary to achieve libration because oppression does not yield unless strong pressure is applied against it by the oppressed." Furthermore, King argues that after one has discovered what he/she is made of and for, they should surrender all of the power of their very being to the achievement of their goals" Rev. King urged excellence in work o matter what the

work might be." Therefore I contend that without any doubt whatsoever, in order to do as Rev King rightly encourages us to do we must also adhere to the principle and practices of the Nguzo Saba principle, Nia (Purpose), which states "to make our collective vocation the building and developing of our community in order to restore our people to their traditional greatness" and part of our greatness is that our ancestors brought to the world naturopathic protocols for living long and prosperous healthy lives. Therefore we have no business playing cultural children to Europe and its descendant, buying into their profit making schemes about health and medicines

and dying at unparalleled rates in comparison to other others in the process.

In the final analysis, it is up to us Black people to continue our legacy as being this country's moral vanguard and thus let us remain steadfast and compelled to build on Rev Kings legacy and honor his heritage by assuming and infusing his positions and Practices of Self Help, Revolution, Activism & Achievement in our struggle to establish a Model of Moral Magnitude in achieving Optimal Health !

*Min. Tukufu Kalonji is Founder/Kasisi of Kawaida African Ministries. For info contact @ tkalonji@hotmail.com*

# NEVADA NEWS

For Nevada Information: 619-234-4753 • 619-534-2435

## Reid, Sandoval Announce Nevada Selected As UAV Development Center

Sandoval Announce Nevada Selected As UAV Development Center Washington, D.C. – The Federal Aviation Administration (FAA) today announced that Nevada has been selected as one of six locations to be a center for Unmanned Aerial Vehicle (UAV) development in the United States. As a UAV development site, the most likely economic forecast shows that there could be thousands of jobs for UAS direct employees with an average wage of approximately $62,000; an estimated $2.5 billion in economic impact in present dollars; and an estimated $125 million in annual state and local tax revenue.

"This is wonderful news for Nevada that creates a huge opportunity for our economy," said Senator Harry Reid. "Nevada has long been a leader in the UAS Industry, and no state makes a better candidate than ours. With this application approval, Nevada will continue to lead in new and innovative technologies of the 21st century, along with creating a large and profitable industry. I appreciate the work of all those involved and I look forward to working with Governor Sandoval to ensure a successful implementation of the award, and subsequent creation of the testing sites in Nevada."

"Being selected as one of six sites for UAV development in the country is a historic moment for Nevada," Governor Brian Sandoval said. "With the climate and air space of Nevada, we are uniquely equipped to help expand the development of UAVs.

We have also partnered with private industry and academia to establish the curriculum necessary to create the UAS civilian workforce of the future in Nevada. Our state has been preparing for this selection and we are ready to enter this new era of aviation history. I thank Senator Reid for his tireless work on this issue and the opportunity to work together on this momentous day for our state." In 2012, Senator Reid led passage of the FAA Modernization and Reform Act of 2012, establishing the Federal Aviation Administration program to begin testing for the integration of Unmanned Aerial Vehicles--commonly referred to as drones--into the National Airspace System.

Awarding Nevada the FAA test sites will have far reaching implications on the economy of Nevada. The range of jobs created includes, but is not limited to: teachers, machinists, aircraft mechanics, software developers, electrical engineers, and human resource professionals. The selection follows Nevada's application, submitted to the FAA in May of 2013. Nevada's application included the state as the direct applicant, and a 28 member team including the Nevada System of Higher Education, the Nevada National Guard, Bowhead Systems, Navigator Development and Drone America.

Team members, who represented a cross-section of public and private partners, industry and academic leaders, within the northern and southern regions of the state, identified three Test Ranges and four test sites in the State's Application. "The FAA designation of Nevada as a UAS Test Site is an incredible step forward for the State of Nevada," said Steve Hill, Director of the Governor's Office of Economic Development. "It allows us to establish a leadership role and be at the forefront of a new and important future industry.

The job creation and economic impact will be significant - growing during the testing phase and expanding as Unmanned Aerial Systems (UAS) becomes a commercial industry. We look forward to working with the FAA and other Test Sites to develop an industry that is safe and secure while creating good jobs and providing the benefits that stem from commercial applications. I want to thank everyone who directly worked to make this a reality, and I also want to thank elected officials and communities throughout Nevada for their unwavering support."

## Gambling

Continued from page 12

from pure socialists." "September will be our fifth anniversary in the People's Republic of China in Macau, and we love it there. We are so grateful to be part of that market and to be allowed to participate in that community. We find the political environment, the regulatory environment, the human resource environment that we're in to be absolutely delicious."

Stutz also wrote about Penn National Gaming's over the top attacks on Maryland's Question 7, which feared the potential competitors that would be created for its West Virginia casino. This

## Barrio Logan

Continued from page 10

and Interstate 5. It was designated an official historic site by the San Diego Historical Site Board in 1980.

Barrio Logan is part of City Council District 8 represented by Councilman David Alvarez. The Barrio Logan Community Planning Area was granted status as a redevelopment area but the state of California abolished all redevelopment areas in 2012.

Barrio Logan is home to the Naval Station San Diego, also known as 32nd Street Naval Station, as well as the NASSCO shipyard and other military-related facilities, which is were the have vs the havenots turff war begins.

At a recent press conference Alvarez stated "out-of state billionaires launched and funded a referendum process to scare voters and overturn he democratically created and approved plan. I put y tust in the voters to see the referendum process for what it is. A greedy attempt to keep the status quo at the expense of the hard working residents in an attempt to hijack our community.

included funding ads attacking legal gaming as creating compulsive gamblers and underage betting.

Elections matter. They not only determine who wins and how they will govern. They also focus the public's attention on issues that they otherwise ignore.

It is important to win. But it is more important not to lose in a way that completely destroys your credibility forever.

© 2013, I. Nelson Rose. Prof. Rose is recognized as one of the world's leading experts on gambling law, and is a consultant and expert witness for governments, industry and players. His latest books, INTERNET GAMING LAW (1st and 2nd editions), BLACKJACK AND THE LAW, GAMING LAW: CASES AND MATERIALS and GAMING LAW IN A NUTSHELL are available through his website, www.GAMBLINGANDTHELAW.com.

Reid All About It.

Special to Indian Voices from Senator Harry Reid
United States Senator for Nevada • Majority Leader • http://reid.senate.gov/

# Native American Self-Determination

As we begin to close out 2013 and look back at the accomplishments this year, we realize that Native American communities have much to be proud of.

Congress passed historic provisions in the Violence Against Women Act by restoring criminal jurisdiction to Indian tribes over non-Indians who commit domestic violence in Indian Country.

Congress awarded long overdue gold medals to Native American Code Talkers who were invaluable to help end both World Wars. Much awareness and understanding has been brought to bear about the denigrating effects of the name

"Washington Redskins." I sincerely hope that the team's owner will change this name that is so offensive to Native Americans and their history.

The first Native American woman, Diane Humetewa, has been nominated to the federal bench in Arizona—something that I look forward to moving along in the Senate.

In Nevada, final distribution of the Western Shoshone judgment was made to tribal members. I worked on this matter for many years to make sure that the Department of the Interior kept its obligation to make these final payments. But we

still have so much work to do.

The Native American Housing Assistance and Self-Determination Act expired in September. These programs are crucial to building homes, infrastructure and communities in Indian Country. I remain committed to working with the Committee on Indian Affairs to bring this bill to the floor and to the President's desk.

Construction of the largest commercial solar power plant on Indian Lands is scheduled to begin in full in early 2014.

The Moapa Band of Paiutes' project will create dozens of jobs, and contribute to the tribe's economy while creating energy

independence. And we must continue to work on reauthorizing energy and other tax extenders which are so important for continued investment in developing energy independence in Indian Country.

Under sequestration we must work harder to protect tribal programs like the Indian Health Service from harsh funding cuts.

As the Majority Leader of the Senate, and Nevada's Senior Senator, I look forward to working with the tribes in Nevada and the rest of Indian Country to ensure that Congress upholds its trust and treaty obligations to American Indian and Alaska Native people.

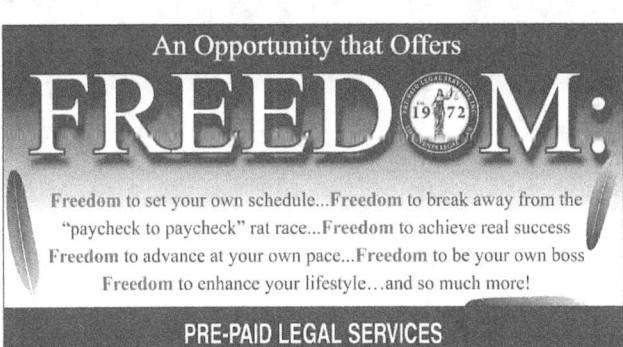

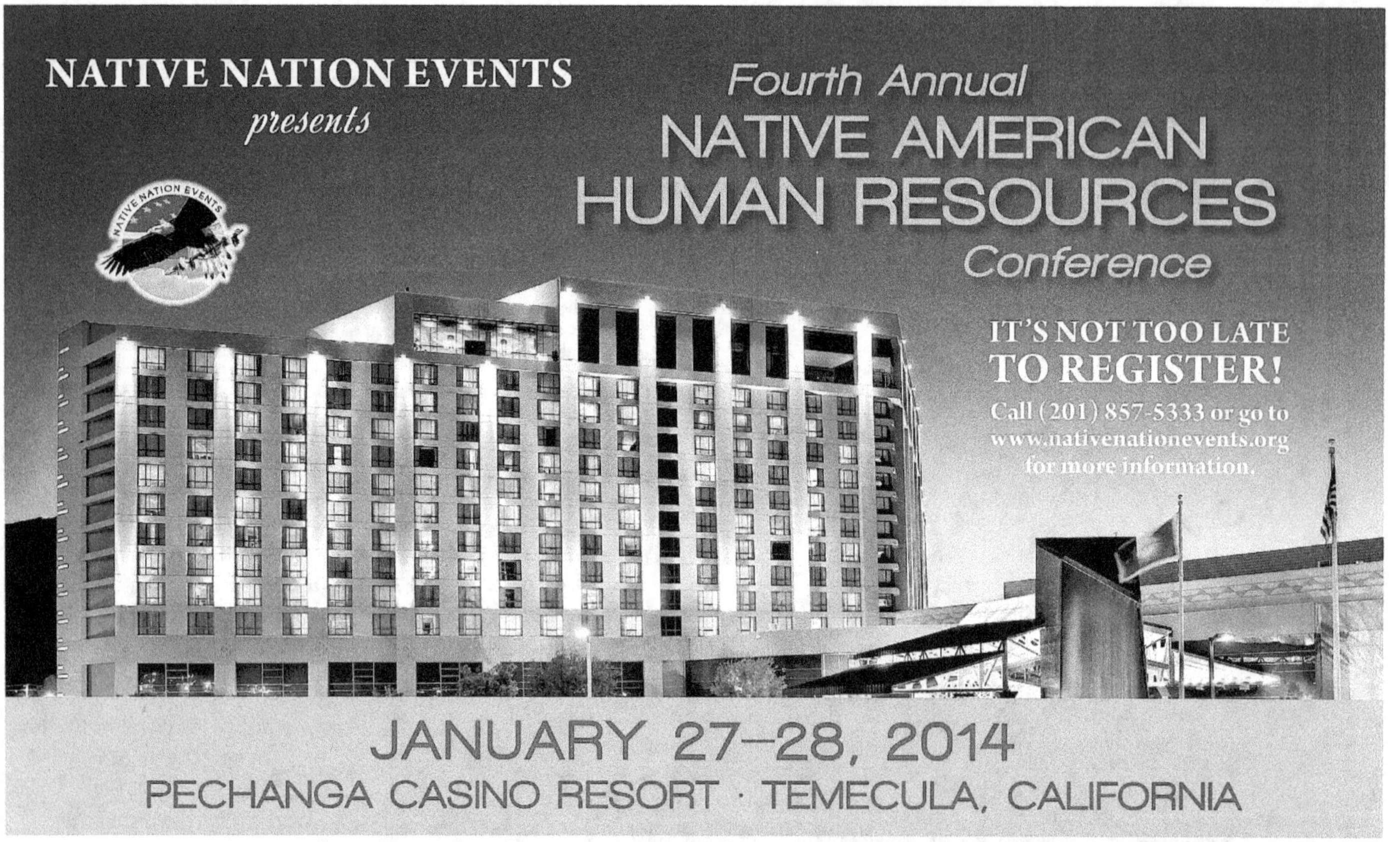
NATIVE NATION EVENTS
presents
Fourth Annual
NATIVE AMERICAN
HUMAN RESOURCES
Conference
IT'S NOT TOO LATE
TO REGISTER!
Call (201) 857-5333 or go to
www.nativenationevents.org
for more information.
JANUARY 27–28, 2014
PECHANGA CASINO RESORT · TEMECULA, CALIFORNIA

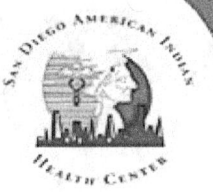

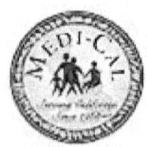

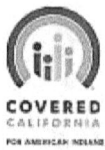

**OUR 28ᵗʰ YEAR**　　　　**MULTI-CULTURAL NEWS GLOBAL NETWORK**　　　　**MARCH 2014**

# Healing a Nation

*"...everything on the earth has a purpose, every disease an herb to cure it, and every person a mission. This is the Indian theory of existence."*

Robert Hayward prepares a ceremonial Sweat Lodge which is part of the Sober Ranch experience.

## Introducing Sober Ranch

*by Robert Hayward*

My roots go deep onto the soil on this continent. My grandmother was Ho-Chunk, from Wisconsin, taken as a child with all of her 9 siblings and sent to a boarding school, then adopted into a Dutch family, never fully recovering from the damage done. Like millions of Indian people across this country, that hurt and pain was passed on to me, in what we are now recognizing as Generational Trauma, and Cultural Trauma.

It comes in many forms, the most common result is alcoholism, addiction, depression, and suicide. In my case, it was extreme addiction and alcoholism,

for over 26 years.

I began drinking and using at age 14, which is now a late start for most Indian children. I spent much of my teen years on a Southern California Reservation perfecting my drinking and drug abuse. I wrote a book about these experiences and how returning to my culture and traditions brought sanity and sobriety back into my life. (The Thirteenth Step; Amazon)

After sobering up, I learned all I could about this insidious disease, and received degrees in Drug and Alcohol Counseling, and became a CAADAC Certified Counselor, and a trained Interventionist. Last year The Creator presented me with an opportunity to put my experience, strength and hope into practice. I took over ownership of Sober Ranch, a 67 acre remote mens Drug and Alcohol Treatment Center on top of

SEE **Sober Ranch**, page 3

# Palomar's Friendly Hermit

*by Laura M. James*

If you go to Palomar Mountain by the old West Grade road, just as you enter the trees, pause and go back from the road a short distance. You will find a small clearing, a pile of rocks, a few dead apricot trees, and a dry dilapidated watering trough. The rocks once formed the walls of a small house, the trees were part of a lovely orchard, and the watering trough once overflowed with cold mountain spring water.

In former years here lived at the roadside an old Negro man who was friend to both man and beast. All who traveled this steep grade, which, for years was the only road connecting the mountain with the valley below, looked forward to reaching this spot. They knew that they would be met by this small, smiling man who would first hand them a gourd of

ice-cold water, then see that their horse was watered, or their boiling radiator cooled, as the case might be.

"Nate" was a friendly person, yet very little is known of his early life. All of his life story was never told, even to his best friends, and, try as hard as they would, no one could ever get him to tell the name of his master, for Nate was once a slave. When he passed on in 1920 his true story was buried with him.

There are many versions as to how he came to California. Some say he was the body servant to an Army officer who brought him around the Horn to the gold diggings in the northern part of the state. In order to get to make the trip he had promised to work in the mines for the officer. This he did for one day, then declared his independence, and went to work on his own, and for years did freighting for the miners. Another story is that he came from Kentucky to Sedalia, Missouri, where he waited for several months while a wagon train was being made up to come overland to Merced and on to the mines. However, the following is what Nate told two of his friends, one a lady from the South who lived for years on the mountain,

and the other an Indian friend who used to spend a lot of time up at the cabin.

Nate told them he was from the state of Mississippi. When a boy of about sixteen he and a number of other slaves were put up for auction. As he was small of stature (caused, he claimed, because

SEE **Nate Harrison**, page 4

# Facing the Truth of Today

*by Gretchen Burns Bergman*

My unique, adorable and cherished son lives in a sweet hallowed spot in my memory. He isn't gone, but he is lost. I know that he is somewhere inside of the stranger that I see today, but it is easier to close my eyes to find him.

I remember my sunny, funny, freckle-faced boy who met the world with imp-ish delight and exuberant glee. He was athletic and agile, throwing physical caution to the wind, leaping down flights of stairs, skateboarding, surfing, and doing flips off the high-dive. He could swim before he could walk.

His quirky talents entertained us all. With focused patience and attention he could catch flies and fish with his own bare hands, and he learned to tie cherry stems into knots with his tongue. He was a creative musician who taught himself to play a mean blues harmonica. Although he played naughty pranks, he had a solid sense of fair play. In his youth my beautiful blue eyed boy was a loving, affectionate and exuberant little elf.

How can I accept the truth of today: a life interrupted and stuck for decades. I'm sure that his loss of self further frustrates and angers him, allowing him to continue to lose himself further into depression and drugs.

What do we do with our older children who have had so many opportunities at treatment, but can't find or sustain recovery? What can we do when the pain of loss has beaten us down and the answers keep slipping away? What can we say when the world has thrown up their hands in frustration, declaring them to be unlikable, untreatable misfits?

Parents who can't accept living with the gnawing image of their child out on the streets, lying in a gutter or living like an animal in a cage meant for criminals are declared co-dependent. How utterly dispassionate, unfair and cruel, especially knowing the very real danger of accidental overdose.

Some days I look down at my blouse, imagining that the blood that I sense leaking from my heart will soak through while I'm in denial of the devastation and busy trying to live my life. Well-meaning people advise us to detach with love. It is a nice concept, but how does it work in the real world when our adult children have failed to launch and instead have morphed into someone unrecognizable?

To all of the people who reach out to the PATH office for help, I want to assure you that we hear you and we are also frustrated with the lack of answers that we can offer you. My son's plight, although extreme, is not unique. After years of the criminal justice system wrestling with the healthcare system over the handling of people with addictive illness, and parents being bounced back and forth through this maze, willing to mortgage their homes and do anything to save their children, we are still in a very bleak place, with little support or acceptable answers as to what to do with these damaged but cherished loved ones.

We continue to be committed to finding a humane way to handle this problem and keep hope alive. Together we must find acceptable and positive ways to free trapped loved ones from the strangle-hold of addictive illness.

---

## Southern California Tribal Chairman's Association

### Substance Abuse Update

*Update from David "wolf" Diaz*

The first topic discussed at our meeting had to do with a conference call that took place on January 30th 2014 at 3 PM. The people who spoke on this conference call were Denis Turner, Chairman Anthony Pico, Eric La Chappa, Charity White, Dr.Herbert McMichael, and I. The agenda for this call was to discuss the different aspects of the planning committee for the adult residential treatment facility such as selecting a Recording Secretary, selecting planning committee members, designate meeting periods, selecting meeting date, location and agenda, and the committee's operational budget for holding these meetings.

It was decided that I will be the Secretary responsible for taking the minutes at these meetings. It was our intention to have various staff or board members from each of the four Indian health clinics. As of now the members of this planning committee will be Chairman Robert Smith who is a board member and Dr. Calac who is the chief medical officer for I HC, Dr. Herbert McMichael from SBIHC, Charity White and Gwen Parada from SIHC, and Joe Bulfer from SDAIHC. It was agreed upon that these meetings shall be quarterly. And the locations of these meetings shall take place at the four the Indian health clinics one meeting per clinic. The committee's operational budget for holding these meetings was solved by allowing each clinic to host a meeting. It was also decided that SCTCA shall host a preliminary meeting to discuss the agenda for the first meeting. This meeting has been set for April 14, 2014 time and location shall be revealed in the near future.

The the substance abuse committee also discussed the planning of two future presentations by Edward Grijalva with the topic being intergenerational and historical trauma from an American Indian standpoint. The two locations for these presentations shall be at the Rincon Indian Health Council and the Southern Indian Health Clinic. The attendees for these presentations shall be the clinic's staff and board members, the leaders and council members in relation to the surrounding reservations of these clinics. Edward Grijalva shall be presenting this information from his new position on a state level as one of four liaisons hired by the state of Arizona to establish relations and open lines of communication for American Indian reservations in regards to substance and alcohol abuse.

I will be attending a conference in Parker Arizona at the Blue Water Resort &Casino on February 20 and 21st 2014. The theme for the conference will be "Change is occurring! What is our vision for the future?" This event is the Statewide Arizona American Indian

SEE **SoCal Tribal Chairman Assoc, page 4**

---

---

# TCOYD Attracts a Full House

## Pala Casino Resort and Spa hosts major health event.

The Pala Casino Resort and Spa Event Center boasted a full house on February 8th, where more than 400 people throughout and beyond our consortium area gathered in search of health. They enjoyed a day-long wealth of activities, education, information and inspiration on the topic of diabetes, which affects 16% of Native Americans in the U.S.

The Taking Care of Your Diabetes (TCOYD) conference and health fair was co-sponsored by Indian Health Council, Inc. and Indian Health Service. It was presented by TCOYD (www.tcyod.org) specifically for the Native American population.

Entitled, "Do You Have Diabetes? Take Control: Learn, Laugh and Live Better," the multifaceted event promised, "One day can change everything!" Many participants agreed, saying they now had the motivation to change and the tools to help them do so.

A participant from Cahuilla said, "It's nice to be with so many people with a common goal to do better for ourselves and our family members with diabetes. We learned that exercise is like insulin and other facts. Most of all, we learned you can live a long and good life."

### How to Take Control of Diabetes

TCOYD founder Steve Edelman, MD kickstarted the presentations with his topic, "Well-Controlled Diabetes is the Leading Cause of Absolutely Nothing!" Dr. Edelman was diagnosed with diabetes at age 15. He said, "I was told that blindness, kidney failure and amputations were likely to occur and that my life expectancy would not exceed 20 years." The prognosis galvanized him to study medicine "to learn how to conquer this condition and help others afflicted with it."

Prior to Dr. Edelman's presentation, the day began with good-for-you break-fast burritos, a blessing, birdsinging, drumming and a welcome by several officials, including IHS' Margo Kerrigan and IHC's CMO, Daniel Calac, MD. Dr. Calac also addressed the crowd in the afternoon, advising how to "Keep Your Kidneys Kicking and Your Heart Pumping."

Positivity permeated the packed room, with information presented in a down-to-earth and upbeat manner. Native American comedian Drew Lacapa suggested ways to "Laugh Your Way to Lower Blood Sugars." A Pala participant called his routine "really funny, especially in light of the health issues he has endured, including strokes, heart attacks and surgeries. It's amazing he can find humor in it."

IHC's Physical Activity Specialist Angelina Renteria and Nutritionist Jina George explained the reasoning behind "Using Exercise and Food as Medicine." Later, Angelina led attendees in chair dancing to music so energetic many people got up off their chairs to "boogie."

Community Health Services staff organized a well-attended health fair during the event, offering blood glucose and blood pressure testing, foot screening, body fat measurements, and an opportunity for people to discuss their concerns with IHC providers, including Public Health nurses, Pharmacist Bob Schostag and Acupuncturist Anne Bailey.

Ending the event on a high note was motivational speaker Billy Mills, who wowed the world by capturing Olympic Gold in the 1964 10,000 meter race. After being diagnosed with diabetes in 2005, he immediately took control with nutrition, exercise and education. He skillfully wove the focus it took to win the gold 50 years ago with the focus it takes to lead a long and healthy life with diabetes.

From the beginning to the final presentation, people realized that yes, diabetes happens, but, like Billy Mills and Dr. Edelman, they have the power to choose how to deal with it. Dr. Calac states,

"It was rewarding to see so many people wanting to learn more about their diabetes and ready to make lifestyle changes for the health."

---

## Sober Ranch
Continued from page 1

Palomar Mountain in north-eastern San Diego County in Southern California. Sober Ranch was then a successful treatment center run strictly on the basis of the tenants of AA, which was very effective. But even more powerful is the land that this center is on. This is an ancient oak and pine grove that was once a large Cupa Indian village, with physical and spiritual evidence of their presence everywhere. It is one of the very few areas of this mountain that has never burned. The peaceful and serene atmosphere alone is healing. At 4000 feet in elevation, it is above much of the southern California pollution, and our water comes from an ancient aquifer hundreds of feet beneath us. Our electricity comes from the sun, other than the necessary pumping of the well to keep our tank full.

In the early 1900's, it was occupied by Nate Harrison, a newly freed slave who homesteaded there and became a local legend. After that it was an active horse ranch, and we use the stables and corrals and riding ring now for our equine therapy.

After working in the recovery field for years, and seeing the dismal failure of most programs, I began searching for reasons for the low rate of success, and what could be done to change it into more positive outcomes. The biggest problem was the fact that while Native Americans have the highest rates of alcoholism, drug addiction, and other dysfunctions, we have almost no culturally competent programs that address our situation specifically. AA, NA, CA, all of the A's, are great, but they lack that certain cultural aspect that makes it universally appealing and useable for Indians with this disease. It took ceremony to bring me back, after nothing else had worked. And I began to see that is the missing link in helping our people beat this disease. It is a spiritual malady, and requires a spiritual solution. And we are naturally spiritual people, if we stay away from those things that are not part of our culture and traditions. Drugs and alcohol are not part of any of our culture or traditions, regardless of what too many people may think.

I rewrote the Sober Ranch program to include and emphasize Native Culture, pan-tribal ceremony, sweat lodge, Medicine Wheel, Horsemanship, outdoor work and activities, Tipi ceremony and meetings, and other earth based healing modalities. We have Native American house managers, counselors, and therapist. And 5 nights a week all clients go down the mountain to local AA and NA meetings on the three adjacent Indian Reservations. We have specific therapy based on the concepts of childhood, cultural, and generational trauma, which has affected all Indians, whether they know it or not. It is the key to staying sober; facing our trauma, dealing with it, forgiving self and others, and moving forward from there.

This Native track is for anyone who wants to avail themselves to it, and it typically becomes the route all clients take, regardless of bloodline. Native spirituality can be a very healing experience, and everyone has there own path to recovery. But I am convinced that it is much easier for Indian people to recover using the ways we have used for thousands of years. It worked for our ancestors, and there is good reason to believe it works for us now, and will work for our descendants, 7 generations from now.

I understand there are some treatment centers in the planning stages now, and for this I am grateful. I have been speaking at Conventions and Reservations for a long time all over the country about the need for Indian treatment centers. We need thousands of them. But this one is open now, with beds available (as of right now), able to help anyone in need today. And when the new ones are up and running, I will be able to refer many clients to them. Right now the need is for a women's treatment center, I could fill that up in a week. We just don't have enough buildings to do that, and mixing the sexes only becomes a distractions to everyone's program of recovery.

Sober Ranch is for men only, 18 years and older, it is private pay, and we do not take Insurance because we have found that Insurance does not put the client first, they do not let us use our most effective programs, and want clients 'cured and sent home' much sooner than they are ready. We charge about 1/3 of the typical treatment center, and we do have some partial scholarships available under certain situations to help the client get better. I took Sober Ranch over to give back, to pay it forward, and to help those who are on the same wrong road I was once on, and show how to find the Red Road of Sobriety that I am on now. It is not about money, as our expenses usually exceed our income. But to see the life come back into a mans eyes, the color come back into his skin, and the smile to return to his face, that is the payout we are all working for. See sober-ranch.com for more information. AHo.

## Nate Harrison

Continued from page 1

as a child he had been worked so hard and fed so little) he was not attractive to buyers. They were looking for large strong men to work in the fields. During the excitement of the auction Nate saw a chance to slip away. He dropped into the river, and swam and floated for miles. At last he came to a landing where a side-wheel steamer was taking on fuel. He stole into the fuel bunker. There he stayed for days. He lost track of the number, and when he finally saw a chance to get out, he was almost starved to death. He hid out in the woods all day. When the lights in a nearby farm house went out at night, and he figured everyone would be asleep, he crept up to the house and ate food that had been set out for the dogs. He said that was the best tasting food he had eaten in all his life.

What his story was in connection with the long miles and years that stretched between the Mississippi River and California is subject for dispute. Mrs. Elsie Crooks, of Escondido, who is the granddaughter of one of California's early pioneers tells this story:

Her grandfather, John Welty, brought his family to California in a covered wagon train. At one point they met another party at a river, and the two outfits helped each other to cross. When they were across the Welty's train came right on. They wanted the others to come with them, but for some reason the other group wanted to lay over a day. They laid plans to overtake the Welty train at a place where the two outfits planned to rest for several days. When they did not arrive as planned, Grandfather Welty rode back to see what was delaying them. He found that the Indians had killed them all, burned their wagons, and made off with their stock.

As he was returning to his outfit, he came upon a women, a baby, and a Negro. They had managed to escape by hiding in some tules and willows. For fear the Indians would track them, they had put some of their clothing over their shoes, and were endeavoring to reach the others on foot.

Later, when the Welty train reached a fort, the woman and baby were left in order that they might return to the East with the first outfit going that way, but the Negro came on to California. He was Nate.

The wagon train arrived in San Bernardino in 1864. Almost all of the company settled in or near that city, but a few drifted south into San Diego County. Grandfather Welty first settled up in the mountains back of San Bernardino, where he established the first saw mill in that district. After being burned out twice by the Indians he moved his family to the Temecula Canyon, to a place called in more recent years the Keating Ranch. Mrs. Crooks says that as a child she spent a lot of time with her grandparents, and that there was never a gathering of the San Bernardino friends that Nate did not attend. Everyone always seemed exceptionally glad to see him. He would often come up to the ranch, and after spending several days would say he was going on up to San Bernardino to see the folks, meaning the other members of the wagon train. She remembers him as always laughing and as a great hand to play jokes on the children.

The first home that we hear of Nate having was in the Rincon Valley. Later he took up a homestead on the south slope of Palomar Mountain. Here he lived for years, clearing a small part of the land, planting an orchard, and raising horses. He had the one price of $150 for his horses, regardless of age, size, or kind. And he insisted he be paid in gold. He

said he wanted no truck with silver or folding money. During the summer months he acted as herdsman for a Temecula man who ran a large herd of sheep on the mountain. During the winter months he did odd jobs for his friends in the valley, and was always in demand at hog killing time.

People going to and from the mountain would always remember Nate and take him choice bits of food. These he greatly enjoyed, and amused the givers by telling them, "Just wait till I get my tooth in it." For years he only had one tooth in his head. Especially he appreciated a bottle of liquor, right up to his dying day. He always said he had been raised on corn liquor. For years he rode a white horse. He usually rode at a walk, but his friends could tell just how much he had imbibed by the way he rode. The more liquor consumed, the faster the horse was made to travel, until sometimes he would go up the mountain at a dead run.

Evidently he was not too careful a cook, for an Indian friend tells of going there one day, and, upon finding the coffee pot almost filled with coffee grounds, he decided to empty them and make fresh coffee. Down near the bottom of the pot he found a large lizard that had been boiled over and over.

Nate claimed that the meat of all wild animals was good to eat. One fall his friend Juan Disperto went up to gather acorns. Nate saw him eyeing a string of jerky that he had drying, and told him to take what he wanted of it. When ready to go home Juan took a liberal supply. In a couple of weeks he was back for more acorns. Nate asked him how he liked the jerky, and he replied it

was the best he had ever eaten. It was then that Nate told him that it was not deer meat but mountain lion. This made Disperto very angry, and he went on down the mountain without gathering any acorns.

Nate was thrifty in some ways. After he had chewed his tobacco for a long time he would put it out to dry and smoke it in his pipe. One Indian says that the pipe was so strong that all he had to do was to put a coal in it and he could have a good smoke.

Nate was a friend of the Indians and the Indians were friends of Nate's, so much so that he was adopted into their tribes to the extent that he could take part in their ceremonial dances. He was present at all the fiestas. Late in life he accepted the Catholic faith and was baptized by Max Peter's mother.

For years, when asked his age, he would reply that he would be seventy-six this coming New Year's Day. From things he said people figured he was over a hundred when Dr. Milton Bailey persuaded the old man to let him take him to the San Diego County Hospital, where he passed away.

Friends collected money and had a monument erected by the spring at the entrance to his mountain home. It is of native stone; a copper plate set in bears the following inscription:

Nathan Harrison's Spring
Brought here a slave about 1848
Died October 10th, 1920, aged 107 years
"A man's a man for a' that"

*The Journal of San Diego History*
*SAN DIEGO HISTORICAL SOCIETY QUARTERLY*
*January 1958, Volume 4, Number 1*

---

## SoCal Tribal Chairman Assoc

Continued from page 2

Behavioral Health Forum III which will have an abundance of valuable information in regards to healing and wellness for our culture. Edward Grijalva will be a presenter at this event discussing his new topic intergenerational and historical trauma from an American Indian standpoint.

At a previous substance abuse committee meeting Chairman Pico announced a beautiful suggestion that is a new approach to the 12 step principles. On March 2, 2014 Chairman Mark

Romero, Eric La Chappa, Chairman Pico and I will attend a 10:00 am meeting in San Diego that explores the mindful approach of the Buddhist way of applying recovery, wellness, wholeness, and healing on our journey. This is a way that speaks of connectedness and being in the present moment which is an eastern philosophy that parallels American Indian traditions and sacred teachings from nature itself as the example of balance and harmony. This is an important option for some indigenous people who are challenged with the Christian overtones that been associated with Alcoholics Anonymous. It is our intention that this wise and insightful approach can be incorporated as part of the curriculum at the future adult residential treatment center. We have ordered six books for the committee written by Therese Jacobs Stewart titled Mindfulness and the 12 Steps: Living Recovery in the Present Moment published by Hazelton Press.

*Substance Abuse Committee: Eric La Chappa, Mark Romero, David "Wolf" Diaz & Anthony Pico SCTCA Staff: Denis Turner, Executive Director & Recording Secretary*

Black Path Commentary: Critical Analysis on Culture, Community, & Struggle

# A Focus on Women, Health, & Movement Building: Working with our Sisters in Love & Struggle to Achieve Optimal Health

*by Min. Tukufu Kalonji*

As we move through the month of March, which we see as Black History Month II; we choose to focus on the awesomeness of our women who lived lives of ethical service, struggle, and awe-inspiring achievement so that we today can live fuller and freer lives; it's imperative that we revisit the multifaceted areas of our struggle, and thus, seek to learn lessons for us now and the future generations to come. And what better area than looking at the health of us as a people and how we as men are compelled by history, humanity, and heaven to work in the spirit of Ujima (Collective Work & Responsibility) with our sisters to heal ourselves from the mental, physical, and spiritual illness created and cultivated by the established order's mis-education, corporate culture of disease and death; and other forms of oppression that has led to and constantly refuels the plethora of health crises we face.

Undeniably, with the marking of 2014's National Women's and Girls' HIV/AIDS Awareness Day on March 10th, subsequently following National Black HIV/AIDS Awareness Day, which happened on February 7th, we without a doubt are notified and reminded of the continued calamity of the matter of HIV/AIDS in the Black community, other communities of color and indeed the world! Moreover, while a tragedy, we are also reminded of our cultural legacy of struggle and resistance to all forms of oppression that we have and will face. Thus, we are reminded to reaffirm the bonds between us as men and women, rescue, restore, and increase our capacity to define, develop, and defend our image and interest as a people, via a recommitment to self consciously engagement in mutual communal efforts to address and solve HIV/AIDS, and other serious and devastating diseases such as hypertension, obesity, diabetes, heart disease stroke et al. In the final analysis, I'm arguing here that we turn our tragedy into triumph as we work, study, and struggle to maintain our movement for liberation and constantly and continuously build within that liberation movement a clear and concise health rescue and restoration component

so that we as community; along with all of our allies will achieve a status of optimal health.

Statistics for HIV/AIDS infected peoples is overwhelmingly high for women and men, and consequently are unavoidably interrelated and inclusive of women, men, heterosexuals, gays, bisexuals and all the other ways people identify themselves via their sexual orientation and live out their daily lives. Afro Americans are nearly half of all persons living with the HIV virus, Afro American women account for 31% of all new infections; Afro American men for 69% and men having sex with men, are 75% of that number. In assessment with other ethnicities, the rate of infection of Black women is 20 times elevated than that of White women and five times higher than Latinas. It is as with obesity, high blood pressure, stroke, heart disease, as well other social ills such as failing grades, incarceration rates, rate of poverty etc, that what we need is the rebuilding and sustaining our movement for liberation.

And yes, while some argue that nothing will ever change due to the society we live in; it is without a doubt contained and written in the awesome historical legacy of our ancestors such as Mary McLeod Bethune, Ida B. Wells, Maria Stewart, Dr. Betty Shabazz, Queen Mother Moore, Sojourner Truth, Shirley Chisholm, Dr. Anna Julia Cooper, Fannie Lou Hamer and other sister heroines, too numerous to name; that with the odds against them, these sisters of struggle, all had a respectful, committed insightful, and righteous warrior man and men at their side as husband, brother, family and friends who assisted them in every endeavor of their seeking justice and bringing good into the world in the particular focus of their chose vocation. Secondly, it is important here to rightly give praise to Black women who like their ancestors cited above have prevailed as Black women have been in the vanguard of action and advocacy in the struggle for the prevention and intervention with HIV/AIDS. Both in the U.S. and abroad this is the case.

Consequently Black men must step up to the plate in supporting our

women in the fight against this debilitating disease, not only because of the unfortunate reality of the irresponsible male who is perhaps 80% of the reason women are infected with HIV/AIDS to the degree that they are but also because of the impact of those disease upon Black men and the entire Black community. Thus, it is a cultural and moral obligation for Black men to increase their advocacy and involvement in this struggle, to eradicate the diseases cited in this commentary, overturn our weaknesses and raise our community's health status to that of optimal health.

A fundamental conception of African manhood is the respect for one self as a man and simultaneously respects for ones species half, i.e. the woman/women in their life and community. Given that, males who exhibit irresponsible sexual behavior without any regard for their dignity safety and well being of their mate, partner, or themselves are in cultural, moral, and social violation of the best of what it means to be an African man. Moreover, we have asked our sisters to be more cognizant and morally compelled to work with our men who are dying at phenomenal rates of the aforementioned diseases of obesity, high blood pressure, stroke, heart disease, by being supportive in the men changing of dietary habits, supporting exercising, reduction of stress and other essential behavioral practices to improve our

health. Given that, in the final analysis, it is only righteously reciprocal that we as men do are as I have argued earlier to be compelled by history, heaven, and humanity to be the best of what it means to be an African man; and that is to do as we said in the 1995 Million Man March/ Day of Absence Mission Statement to:

*Stand up, stand together, and stand in practice; to stand up in consciousness and commitment, to stand together in harmony and unity as women and men; brothers and sisters, as partners, family and as community; to stand together in dedication, discipline, sacrifice, and achievement; by way of committing and recommitting ourselves to take personal and collective responsibility for our lives and the welfare, and future of our families and community.*
*Maulana Karenga, (1995)*

It takes a radical revolutionary movement of the masses to bring about significant and sustainable change and no doubt nothing less will suffice. Thus, being that the aforementioned diseases are a real clear and present danger to Black life, let us continue in the struggle to obtain and sustain optimal health for ourselves, our history and the generations yet to come forth by day.

*Min. Tukufu Kalonji is Founder/Kasisi of Kawaida African Ministries. For info contact @ tkalonji@hotmail.com*

## Healthy Dining Options in Restaurants

*Celebrating local healthy Asian and Pacific Islander cuisine increasing access to healthy dining options in San Diego through small food industry businesses*

San Diego, CA – In celebration of National Nutrition Month's theme of "Enjoying the Taste of Eating Right", thirteen local Asian and Pacific Islander (API) restaurants in San Diego will present their best practices and lessons learned as they shift their businesses to healthier dining options through a press conference scheduled on March 26 th , 2014, 10 am – 12 noon at the administrative office of Operation Samahan at

1428 Highland Avenue, National City, CA 91950. These thirteen restaurants, from the City of San Diego, El Cajon, National City, Spring Valley, Mira Mesa, and Chula Vista, are members of the STRIVE (Strategies to Research and Implement the Vision of Health Equity) San Diego network, a collaboration of API community-based organizations committed to addressing health disparities within and among API communities in San Diego. STRIVE San Diego focuses on risk factors, like nutrition and weight management, by connecting with local

SEE **Healthy Dining Options, page 14**

To improve the quality of life of those who recognize themselves and choose to be recognized by others as "Indigenous Peoples of Color of the Americas" and in support of The American Indian Rights and Resources Organization (AIRRO).

# Black Wall Street the Model of a Flourishing Community

Black Wall Street, the name fittingly given to one of the most affluent all-Black communities in America, was bombed from the air and burned to the ground by mobs of envious Whites. In a period spanning fewer than 12 hours, a once thriving Black business district in northern Tulsa lay smoldering – a model community destroyed and a major African-American economic movement resoundingly defused.

The night's carnage left some 3,000 African Americans dead and over 600 successful businesses lost. Among these were 21 churches, 21 restaurants, 30 grocery stores and two movie theaters, plus a hospital, a bank, a post office, libraries, schools, law offices, a half dozen private airplanes and even a bus system. As could have been expected, the impetus behind it all was the infamous Ku Klux Klan, working in consort with ranking city officials and many other sympathizers.

The best description of Black Wall Street, or Little Africa as it was also known, would be to compare it to a mini Beverly Hills. It was the golden door of the Black community during the early 1900s, and it proved that African Americans could create a successful infrastructure. That's what Black Wall Street was all about.

The dollar circulated 36 to 100 times, sometimes taking a year for currency to leave the community. Now a dollar leaves the Black community in 15 minutes. As for resources, there were Ph.D.s residing in Little Africa, Black attorneys and doctors. One doctor was Dr. Berry, who owned the bus system. His average income was $500 a day, hefty pocket change in 1910.

It was a time when the entire state of Oklahoma had only two airports, yet six Blacks owned their own planes. It was a very fascinating community. The mainstay of the community was to educate every child. Nepotism was the one word they believed in. And that's what we need to get back to. The main thoroughfare was Greenwood Avenue, and it was intersected by Archer and Pine Streets. From the first letters in each of those three names you get G.A.P. And that's where the renowned R&B music group the GAP Band got its name. They're from Tulsa.

At the end of the day, June 1, 1921, this is what remained of Black Wall Street. Lost forever were over 600 successful businesses, including 21 churches, 21 restaurants, 30 grocery stores, two movie theaters, a hospital, a bank, a post office, libraries, schools, law offices, a half dozen private airplanes and a bus system.

Black Wall Street was a prime example of the typical Black community in America that did typical Black community in America that did business, but it was in an unusual location. You see, at the time, Oklahoma was set aside to be a Black and Indian state. There were over 28 Black townships there. One third of the people who traveled in the terrifying "Trail of Tears" alongside the Indians between 1830 and 1842 were Black people. The citizens of this proposed Indian and Black state chose a Black governor, a treasurer from Kansas named McDade. But the Ku Klux Klan said that if he assumed office that they would kill him within 48 hours.

A lot of Blacks owned farmland, and many of them had gone into the oil business.

The community was so tight and wealthy because they traded dollars hand to hand and because they were dependent upon one another as a result of the Jim Crow laws. It was not unusual that if a resident's home accidentally burned down, it could be rebuilt within a few weeks by neighbors. This was the type of scenario that was going on day to day on Black Wall Street.

When Blacks intermarried into the Indian culture, some of them received their promised "40 acres and a mule" and with that came whatever oil was later found on the properties. On Black Wall Street, a lot of global business was conducted.

The community flourished from the early 1900s until June 1, 1921. That's when the largest massacre of nonmilitary Americans in the history of this country took place, and it was led by the Ku Klux Klan. Imagine walking out of your front door and seeing 1,500 homes being burned. It must have been amazing.

Survivors we interviewed think that the whole thing was planned, because during the time that all of this was going on, White families with their children stood around the borders of their community and watched the massacre – the looting and everything – much in the same manner they would watch a lynching. The riots weren't caused by anything Black or White. They were caused by jealousy.

A lot of White folks had come back from World War I and they were poor. When they looked over into the Black communities and realized that Black men who fought in the war had come home heroes, that helped trigger the destruction. It cost the Black community everything, and not a single dime of restitution – no insurance claims – has been awarded the victims to this day. Nonetheless, they rebuilt. We estimate 1,500 to 3,000 people were killed, and we know that a lot of them were buried in mass graves all around the city. Some were thrown into the river. As a matter of fact, at 21st Street and Yale Avenue, where there now stands a Sears parking lot, that corner used to be a coal mine. They threw a lot of the bodies into the shafts.

### 'The gun went off, the riot was on'

On the night of May 31,1921, mobs called for the lynching of Dick Rowland, a Black man who shined shoes, after hearing reports that on the previous day he had assaulted Sarah Page, a White woman, in the elevator she operated in a downtown building. A local newspaper had printed a fabricated story that Rowland tried to rape Page. In an editorial, the same newspaper said a hanging was planned for that night. As groups of both Blacks and Whites converged on the Tulsa Courthouse, a White man in the crowd confronted an armed Black man, a war veteran, who had joined with other Blacks to protect Rowland. Eddie Faye Gates, a member of the Tulsa Race Riot Commission, formed several years ago to determine exactly what happened, told CNN what happened next. "This White man," she said, asked the Black man, "What are you doing with this gun?" "I'm going to use it if I have to," the Black man said, according to Gates, "and (the White man) said, 'No, you're not. Give it to me,' and he tried to take it. The gun went off, the White man was dead, the riot was on." Truckloads of Whites set fires and shot Blacks on sight. When the smoke lifted the next day, more than 1,400 homes and businesses in Tulsa's Greenwood District, a prosperous area known as the "Black Wall Street," lay in ruins. Today, only a single block of the original buildings remains standing in the area. Experts now estimate that at least 3,000 died.

### 'We're in a heck of a lot of trouble'

Beulah Smith was 14 years old the night of the riot. A neighbor named Frenchie came pounding on her family's door in a Tulsa neighborhood known as "Little Africa" that also went up in flames. "Get your families out of here because they're killing Niggers uptown," she remembers Frenchie saying. "We hid in the weeds in the hog pen," Smith told CNN. People in a mob that came to

SEE **Black Wall Street**, page 10

# Native American Tribe Finds Slave Cemetery in Little Rock

*Discovery follows purchase of property on the city's east side.*

by Hubert Tate

LITTLE ROCK, AR - A group with Arkansas connections says an unmarked slave cemetery has been discovered in Pulaski County on its newly purchased property.

The cemetery has been found on a 160-acre plot of land near the Little Rock Port Authority on Thibault Rd. that was recently bought by the Quapaw Tribe to preserve its history.

"It's a very important piece of land to us. It's part of our original reservation," says business chairman John Berrey.

Berrey says the site is where the group called home before being forced to move to Oklahoma in the 1800's.

"It's a significant piece because there were a lot of Quapaws who lived in that area," Berrey says.

After buying the site, the Tribe commissioned an archaeological survey to research the property, finding more than historic, important symbols of the Quapaw culture.

"There is also an unmarked slave cemetery on this property that we haven't disclosed the location of because we want to protect it," he says.

That's why the Tribe is not saying exactly where on the property the graves are located.

The Quapaws are very passionate about preserving history. That's why they are so motivated to find someone or some organization to preserve the gravesites.

"We want to find someone in Little Rock that would like to work with us in understanding how we should treat it, whether there is a community group that is interested in slave cemeteries or someone else, we would like to find them," says Berrey.

As a result of the purchase, the Tribe also discovered several pottery pieces that have historical value to the Quapaws.

If you can help, email reporter Hubert Tate for more information at htate@kark.com.

## The Council Of American Indian Organizations Celebration

*The Monthly Meeting of the Council was held at the Sycuan Signing Hill Resort*

The torrential storm that invaded the county did not dampen the spirit of the Council of American Indian Organizations. A festive inter active meeting and luncheon captivated the attention of those in attendance. New members were recognized. Shirley Murphy guided the meeting, making sure that agenda items were addressed while gracefully dealing with the inevitable unpleasant hot button issues. Her passionate Lakota style of leadership combined with an "Think Globally act Locally "philosophy makes for a no nonsense approach to discussing serious cultural issues while affording a no holds barred dialog. Everything gets discussed from projections into the future to snagging lessons.

Members of the Sycuan Band of the Kumeyaay Nation Tribal Council sponsored the luncheon

and joined in on the meeting. Tribal Council members Jamie LaBrake and Henry Murphy graciously offered encouragement and support. Jamie LaBrake emphasized that they represent the Great Kumeyaay Nation. Tributes and prayers were offered to the veterans in the group. Self efficiency and determination was the ongoing theme. After months of hard work and organizing the Council is on the cusp of acquiring a nonprofit 501c3 status. The future is bright after a long struggle. Shirley Murphy is preparing the path for the next stage. "Once the dream is clear, the journey begins."

## 2014 National Underground Railroad Conference

*July 16-20 - Detroit Michigan*

Due to popular demand, the National Underground Railroad Conference is back! The National Park Service, National Underground Railroad Network to Freedom (NTF) Program and friends, will host its annual 2014 National Underground Railroad Conference in Detroit, Michigan, July 16-20, 2014. The theme for this year's conference is "I Resolved Never to Be Conquered": Women and the Underground Railroad. This sentiment penned by freedom seeker Harriet Jacobs, shows her determination, "though one of God's most powerless creatures," to retain control over herself and her body despite her

enslaved status.

The conference's focus on women recognizes NTF program's new organizational link with the Harriet Tubman Underground Railroad Monument (HATU), and will explore that while Tubman has been the dominant image of women and the Underground Railroad, her involvement is part of a larger story of women's participation in the movement, as freedom seekers and as operatives. During the conference, we will also take advantage of Detroit's proximity to travel on a tour to Canada, a final destination for many freedom seekers. So be sure to have your passports ready!

*Deanda Johnson, Midwest Regional Coordinator NPS, National UGRR Network to Freedom*

# The Underground Railroad Continues to Light the Path to Healing

The announcement by Deanda Johnson, Midwest Regional Coordinator

NPS, National UGRR Network to Freedom was an historically satisfying and joyous event

*by Phil Fixico*

Phil Fixico with Reverend Cecil Murray

The revival of the Underground Railroad for our community is a continuation of a the spirit of Harriet Tubman and the legions of freedom fighers of her time. This railroad has taken some detours, rest stops and fueling stations breaks along the way. Now, with the help and wisdom of National Park Service, National Underground Railroad Network to Freedom, UGR is back on the tracks and rolling down the newly minted drinking gourd path to liberation and freedom.

As I have expressed during my many media and public presentations it is time to use historic solutions for contemporary problems.

The Underground Railroad for our community once was about black people in trouble, helping other black people in trouble. This effort became all-inclusive with assistance coming from other races and countries. Today, we need to look at how well other groups have used a contemporary version of their own Underground Railroad to make progress in America. These successful entrepreneurs are to be applauded.

As the founder of the Semiroon Historical Society (a one man history club) and as a result of my activism over the years, I was confirmed as a Private Sector Partner of the National Underground Railroad/Network to Freedom 1998 Act and Program. The Law states that our society must, educate, promote and preserve, all the positive attributes of the NUGRR/NTF.

It was passed by the legislature by a vote of 415 to 2 in 1998.

It was mandated because the original Underground Railroad evolved into America's first version of a Civil Rights Movement. It is dedicated to everyone that not only used and benefitted from

it, but to those people who helped. I proudly serve as a PSP to help enrich racial harmony by achieving reconciliation of our past with our hope for the future. It is fitting that the conference will be held in Detroit, Motor City, where Motown devised its own version of a network to freedom through music.

The community is alive with sharing and caring

I was invited by Col. Franklin Henderson, President of the L.A. Buffalo Soldiers 9th & 10th Cavalry, to attended a Town Hall meeting at The Proud Bird restaurant near, LAX, in Los Angeles. to explain Public Law 105-203. All 200 attendees were interested in this important law. The guests of honor were the Tuskegee Airman. The Proud Bird houses an inside museum and outside exhibits that include many TA artifacts. The event was organized by National Association of Equal Justice in America and the Black Engineers Association. The speakers included Right Reverend Cecil Murray whose speech received a rousing standing ovation. It was an educational and healing experience.

As we look toward continuing the our journey and the revival of the Underground Railroad we have the opportunity to share, care and learn from each other.

"Let's not hate ... Let's imitate" by using legal self-help methods.

Phil "Pompey" Fixico

*"To be a good scientist you have to follow your heart because that's where the information comes first."*

*- Nassim Haramein*

# THUNDER FROM THE FOURTH ESTATE IN THE FOURTH DISTRICT

Storm clouds gave way to a sunny day in the city of San Diego March 3, 2014 when Kevin Faulconer took the stage at the standing room only gathering of the community at the Joe & Vi Jacobs Center, 404 Euclid Ave., San Diego, CA 92114.

The setting could not have been more appropriate, as the Center welcomes and supports community and culture in southeastern San Diego. The building is the place for community residents and people from around the world to meet and learn.

In a unifying speech Mayor Faulconer offered elegant words of unity for all communities to come together.

Sounding at times like his predecessor he shared a healing message for the entire city.

Following the official ceremony an upbeat reception was held on the patio. A rainbow appeared briefly as if to offer courage and strength.

# The Green Store of OB Celebrates 25 Years!

The Green Store celebrated its anniversary in grand wholistic Colleen style. Open house. The community gathered at the Methodist church to celebrate 25 years of providing peace, social justice and environmental information to the community.

Working for a Peaceful Green Planet since Earth Day 1989.

We have operated a storefront for 25 years and continue to encourage people to come to the Green Store to meet like-minded people and to utilize our amazing resource center.

Rio in the bandana-Activist and talented musician. Her dad was an activist with Cesar Chevez. Colleen, owner of the Green Store.

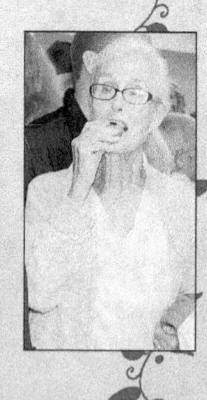

Guest eat healthy food snacks at the Feb. 17, 2014 Ocean Beach Historical Society Program celebrating the 25th Anniversary of the Green Store in Ocean Beach. This events food provided by Kathy Blavatt OBHS Board Member and Creative Director.

# Native Nation Events

The Fourth Annual Native American Human Resources Conference held January 27-28, 2014 at the Pechanga Casino Resort in Temecula, California.

# Secret Report Damning Use of Force by Border Patrol

*Border Fence By Southern Border Communities Coalition*

Southern border communities continue to call for transparency from U.S. Customs and Border Protection (CBP) after the Los Angeles Times published a story on a report critiquing the agency's use of force policy. The story indicated that reporters have reviewed a copy of the Police Executive Review Forum's (PERF) report, a document that has been withheld from the public.

The PERF Report – an independent review by the Police Executive Research Forum commissioned by the U.S. Customs and Border Protection — evidently says border agents deliberately provoked confrontations that led to avoidable violence.

us border

"Today's revealing information by the Los Angeles Times, while damning, is not shocking to southern border communities," states Christian Ramírez, Director of the Southern Border Communities Coalition (SBCC). He con-

tinues, "We have long established that a pattern of excessive force by CBP is the norm. This is a wake up call to the Department of Homeland Security: the time to clean up CBP has come and begins with making the PERF report public."

The Southern Border Communities Coalition (SBCC) and members of Congress requested the report in September when another investigation conducted by the Department of Homeland Security's Office of the Inspector General (OIG) revealed that the PERF report had indicated problems with the agency's use of force. The OIG report was heavily redacted and members of Congress still have not seen the report.

According to the LA Times, the report mentioned cases where officers resorted to use of force when it was not needed, or where they simply could have gotten out of the way. For example, the article

noted that, "in many vehicle shooting cases, the subject driver was attempting to flee from the agents who intentionally put themselves into the exit path of the vehicle, thereby exposing themselves to additional risk and creating justification for the use of deadly force."

Situations involving moving vehicles is of particular concern in light of incidents like the killing of Valeria Munique Tachiquin, a US citizen and mother of five, who was shot nine times by a plain-clothed agent. Tachiquin was shot through the windshield as she attempted to move away from the agent in a residential neighborhood near San Diego. Witnesses to the case have mentioned that they saw the agent step in front of the car and fire his weapon.

"The fact that CBP has been reluctant to release the report is deeply troubling, especially since people continue to be killed," states Christian Ramírez. "Transparency is expected of a profes-

sional federal agency. The public has a right to know how the CBP conducts its business, and clearly CBP is falling short of its responsibility," he concluded.

Earlier this week the Inter-American Commission on Human Rights (IACHR), part of the Organization of American States, expressed deep concern over the events a week earlier that led to the death of Jesus Flores Cruz, 41, a Mexican migrant. He died from gunshot wounds inflicted by a U.S. Border Patrol agent, who was pursuing him on foot in a mountainous area of San Diego, near the international border between the United States and Mexico. This is the latest in a long series of similar events.

The Southern Border Communities Coalition (SBCC) brings together more than 60 organizations from San Diego, California, to Brownsville, Texas, to ensure that border enforcement policies and practices are accountable and fair, respect human dignity and human rights, and prevent the loss of life in the region.

## Black Wall Street

Continued from page 6

Kenny Booker's house asked, "Nigger, do you have a gun?" he told CNN. Booker, then a teenager, hid with his family in their attic until the home was torched. "When we got downstairs, things were burning. My sister asked me, 'Kenny, is the world on fire?' I said, 'I don't know, but we're in a heck of a lot of trouble, baby.'" Another riot survivor, Ruth Avery, who was 7 at the time, gives an account matched by others who told of bombs dropped from small airplanes passing overhead. The explosive devices may have been dynamite or Molotov cocktails

– gasoline-filled bottles set afire and thrown as grenades. "They'd throw it down and when it'd hit, it would burst into flames," Avery said. Only a single block remains of the 1,400 homes and businesses that made up the area known as Black Wall Street.

### Unmarked graves

Many of the survivors mentioned bodies were stacked like cord wood, says Richard Warner of the Tulsa Historical Society. In its search for the facts, the commission has literally been trying to dig up the truth. Two headstones at Tulsa's Oaklawn Cemetery indicate that riot victims are buried there. In an effort

to determine how many, archeological experts used ground-piercing radar and other equipment to test the soil in a search for unmarked graves. The test picked up indications that hundreds of people have been buried in an area just outside the cemetery. Editor's note: The Tulsa Race Riot Commission, formed in 1997 to determine exactly what happened and what should be done now, delivered its final report in 2001, calling for substantial restitution. "In June 2001," according to Wikipedia, "the Oklahoma state legislature passed the '1921 Tulsa Race Riot Reconciliation Act.' While falling short of the commission's recommendations, it provided for

more than 300 college scholarships for descendants of Greenwood residents, mandated the creation of a memorial to those who died in the riot, and called for new efforts to promote economic development in Greenwood. A documentary, "Before They Die!" has been made about the survivors and their quest for justice. It chronicles efforts in Oklahoma to gain reparations for the survivors. And watch the video "One Day in May!" at www.BeforeTheyDieMovie.com.

*This story comes from the Ujamaa Network, which can be reached at mikehouse@ujamaanetwork.biz. They add these words of wisdom: "We must buy from ourselves in order to re-circulate Black dollars. If we want our dollars to return, we must spend them within our own community. 2011 will be our year if we decide it will be. Make a commitment to yourself to do as much of your spending within our community as possible."*

T-SHIRTS
JACKETS
TANK TOPS

**Full Blood** APPAREL

CAPS
STICKERS
SKATE DECKS

fullbloodskates@gmail.com
www.fullbloodskates.com
P.O. Box 3101, Valley Center, CA 92082   Ph#: (760) 445-1141   Owner: Liana Nelson

## Our Wild America Launches Wilderness Act 50th Anniversary Small Grant Program

This is year is the 50th Anniversary of the Wilderness Act, and Sierra Club's Our Wild America Campaign is supporting Chapter-based efforts to celebrate by launching a small grant program. Chapters and Groups may apply for small grants of $500 to $1500 for projects celebrating the 50th Anniversary of the Act. Projects that aim to engage a broader public beyond the core of Sierra Club activists and members will be prioritized, and those that reach youth and

diverse communities are especially encouraged. In addition, projects that are likely to bring in new Sierra Club volunteers and activists have the highest priority. The application is posted on Clubhouse at http://clubhouse.sierraclub.org/conservation/ campaigns-and-programs/Wilderness50%20Grant%20Application.pdf For more information, contact Matt Kirby matthew. kirby@sierraclub.org.

## Sacred Unions

The year of the horse runs its course
through valleys filled with snow
Distant cries fill Northern skies
and Borealis begins to glow

A hunters moon sheds its gold cocoon
and wolves begin to howl
The equinox opens up its box
for the solar winds to growl

Aurora slashes and her light storm flashes
taming a dark expanse
Her twin down south uses a fiery mouth
to encapsulate the worlds romance

Far below in the land of snow
the gathering of the pack
A timeless game that always ends the same
when the wolves begin to track

A signal here and a silence there
Hooves slow in a powdery snow
The quiet turns to din as the pack closes in
Led above by the raven and crow

Auroura Borealis entwines with the Australis
Sunlight making love in the ionosphere
A Wolf in his palace, kills without malice
Behold these Sacred Unions of the
Atmosphere

Joey Racano

## City of San Diego Unanimously Approves Bicycle Advisory Group

*Bicycle Coalition says San Diego joins numerous other bicycle advisory committees throughout the County*

SAN DIEGO, CA – This morning, San Diego City Council unanimously approved the City's first-ever Bicycle Advisory Committee. This new committee, comprising local advocates and residents, will provide guidance to the City on local bicycle projects to make a safer, more accessible and bike-able city, including the implementation of the Bicycle Master Plan Update. The San Diego County Bicycle Coalition, an organization protecting and advocating for the rights of all people who ride bicycles, celebrates that the City of San Diego joins numerous cities in the county that have formally and informally sanctioned bicycle advisory committees.

"This is a massive step for the City of San Diego, the County and the entire region," says Executive Director Andy Hanshaw. "Initiating this advisory group demonstrates the City's long-lasting commitment to all things cycling in San Diego."

With this morning's decision, San Diego joins other cities in the county that harness local bicycling input through organized bicycle advisory committees. Cities include Solana Beach, Encinitas, Coronado and Oceanside, the latter two with national designations as Bicycle-Friendly Communities for exceptional commitment to pro-bicycle infrastructure, programs and safety education.

As a countywide advocate for all things bicycling, the Bicycle Coalition congratulates the City for this extraordinary step and will continue its role uniting countywide advisory groups, transportation experts and elected officials to make San Diego County one of the most recognized bicycle-friendly destinations in the nation.

To learn more about the San Diego Bike Coalition and its advocacy efforts in San Diego County, please visit www.sdcbc.org or follow the organization on Facebook.

*SAN DIEGO COUNTY BICYCLE COALITION: (SDCBC) is a nonprofit organization that advocates for and protects the rights of all people who ride bicycles. They promote bicycling as a mainstream, safe and enjoyable form of transportation and recreation. For more information, go to www.sdcbc.org.*

## Governor Edmund G. Brown Jr. Today Announced the Following Appointments

Tiffany Conklin, 34, of Sacramento, has been appointed to the California Gambling Control Commission, where she has served since 2010. Conklin was an adjunct professor at Golden Gate University from 2008 to 2010 and chief of staff for California State Senator Tom Harman from 2001 to 2010. She is a member of the International Masters of Gaming Law. Conklin earned a Juris Doctor degree from the University of the Pacific, McGeorge School of Law. This position requires Senate confirmation and the compensation is $131,952. Conklin is a Republican.

Lauren Hammond, 58, of Sacramento, has been reappointed to the California Gambling Control Commission, where she has served since 2010. Hammond has been the principal at L. Hammond and Associates since 1994. She served as a Sacramento City Council member representing district five from 1997 to 2010 and was a consultant at the California State Senate from 1981 to 2004. This position requires Senate confirmation and the compensation is $131,952. Hammond is a Democrat.

## The 2014 Activist San Diego People's Ball
# Make Your Reservations Now for KNSJ's Next Big Event

### Saturday, March 15

The 2014 Activist People's Ball will be held on Saturday, March 15 @ 7 PM at the World Beat Center in Balboa Park. The extravaganza is a benefit for Activist San Diego and its newly-launched community radio station KNSJ (Networking for Social Justice).

For the last 12 years Activist San Diego has been hosting these gala events and this year promises to live up to the rave reviews that we have received in the past.

The featured musical group will be the world-renowned Liquid Blue, recognized by the Guinness Book of Records as the most internationally traveled band in history having performed in more countries than any other musical group (including performances for over 65,000 people at several Asian venues). Their socially conscious messages, their professionalism and their danceability are always crowd pleasers.

John Elliot, former KLSD radio personality, will be the emcee. ASD expects to make an announcement soon about a surprise keynote speaker.

Tickets for tables and individuals are available at knsj.org for advance purchase at a reduced rate thru PayPal.

Individuals $25 advance/$30 at the door

Tables for 8 – $200 advance/$240 at the door

Since there are only 250 tickets available buy early and don't miss out. Opportunity drawings, cultural performances, activist awards and other entertainment will fill the evening. Food and drink will be available for purchase from the World Beat Center's "The Prophet" Restaurant.

For more information call 619-871-9354 or info@KNSJ.org.

See more at: http://knsj.org

Featuring Liquid Blue, the World's Best Traveled Band!

## A Nessy Sighting

Many hamburger loving carnivors have been dismayed and disturbed and in the dark. What ever happened to the Nessie Burger which has been around since 1989 contained in a little roadside trailer on the west side of I-15 at Highway 76 in Fallbrook.

The popular hamburger stand has been an established fixture and stopping off point for local customers, as well as a fast-food stop for travelers between Riverside and San Diego counties. There is always a line of eager customers. We are happy to say that it has been found again, just around the corner from the old Nessy's site, on Old Highway 395, on the grounds of the Pala Mesa Market.

Nessie Burger Crew
Salvador Cuberra – Cook 22 years
Pedro Gonzales  - Cook 6 years
Ana Hernandez – Cashier 5 years
Rosalva Loera – Cashier 7 years
Edith Villa- Cashier 2 years
Charly & Sandy Rebecca Webster

*In Loving Memory ...*
## Elizabeth Cecelia Paul
Born June 23, 1941 - New Orleans, Louisiana to Nancy Walls and Boisy White.
Although she is absent from this life, her love, laughter, dedication of character will live on.

*In Our Hearts Forever ...*
## In Memory of Destiny Rose Muse
6/11/92 - 1/9/14

# TRADING POST BUSINESS DIRECTORY

### CALIFORNIA

**ADVOCACY**
Alan Lechuza Aquallo
Advocate for Native Youth and Scholarships
alan@blackphonerecords.com

**ATTORNEYS**
Marshall Law PC
Daniel E.Marshall,Attorney at Law
619-993-5778 • marslawbmw@gmail.com
sandiegoevictionattorneys.com

**BAKERY**
Historic San Luis Rey Bakery
490 N. El Camino Real Oceanside, CA 92058
760-433-7242 • www.sanluisreybakery.com

La Nueva Mexican Bakery
4676 Market St. Ste. A-3, San Diego, CA
619-262-0042

**BEEKEEPERS**
Liz • 619-504-2655

**CARE GIVER**
Private Duty– References
Terms to be discussed
619-504-2455 Ask for Liz

**CLERICAL**
Your Girl Friday International
Marketing, Operations & Promotional
Services • 619-961-0531
yourgirlfriday3512@gmail.com

**CULTURE**
Kumeyaay
www.kumeyaay.com • larry@kumeyaay.com

Worldbeat Cultural Center
619-230-1190
www.worldbeatculturalcenter.org
info@worldbeatculturalcenter.org

**DRIVER**
Driver for Hire
Clean DMV Class ABC
619-504-2455 Ask for Liz

**FINANCIAL ADVISORS**
Merrill Lynch / Elke Chenevey
Vice President & Financial Advisor
Office: 619-699-3707
Fax: 619-758-3619

Summit Funding
The Home Loan Experts
Jeff Ellenz, Branch Manager
760-568-0300 • jellenz@summitfunding.net

**FURNITURE**
Ladies Mahogany Dresser
3 Mirrors - Good condition
$2,000
619-504-2455 Ask for Liz

**HEALTH**
Rady's Children Hospital
San Diego, CA
800-869-5627 • www.rchsd.org

Regenerative Medicine Institute
www.regenerativemedicine.mx

**HEALER-SHAMAN**
Transitions / Vera A. Tucker
vtucker1212@gmail.com
619-987-0372

**HOUSEKEEPING**
Cleaning, windows, floors
4 hours $60 - 8 hours $100
619-504-2455 Ask for Liz

**INSURANCE**
State Farm / Jack Fannin
1154 E. Main St. El Cajon, CA 92021-7157
619-440-0161 Business
619-440-0495 Fax
jack.fanninjroi@statefarm.com
www.jackfannin.com

Earthquake Insurances
www.EarthquakeAuthority.com

**MARKETING**
International Marketing Systems
Eddy Michaelly
www.imsbarter.com

Jahaanah Productions
Marketing, Media, Public Relations, Graphic
Design • 832-978-0939

**NOTARY PUBLIC**
Sis. Evon X. Nana
San Diego, CA 92113 • 619-549-5792
evonx@yahoo.com

**PHOTOGRAPHY**
Peache Photo Memories
619-697-4186 office
619-549-0968 contact
www.peachephotomemories.com
peachephotos@cox.net

**PUBLISHERS**
Blackrose Communications
111 South 35th St. San Diego, CA 92113
619-234-4753
www.indianvoices.net • davis4973@aol.com

**RADIO**
91.3PM Kopa
Pala Rez Radio
www.palatribe.com • 91.3@palatribe.com

**RECOVERY**
David "Wolf"Diaz, Pres. & Founder
Walk of the Warrior, A Non-Profit Corp.
Tel: 760-646-0074 • Cell: 310-866-7057
Fax:760-689-4907
www.walkofthewarrior.com
walkofthewarrior@yahoo.com

**REGALIA**
Carla Tourville
Native Regalia Custom Design
Yokut Tule River Tribe
San Diego, CA • 619-743-9847

**REPARATIONS**
Mr. Peoples Reparations
200 N. Long Beach Blvd. Compton, CA
310-632-0577

**RESTAURANT**
Awash Ethiopian Restaurant
4979 El Cajon Blvd. San Diego,CA
619-677-3754

**RETAIL – CLOTHING**
Full Blood Apparel
P.O. Box 3101 Valley Venter, CA 92082
www.fullbloodskates.com • 760-445-1141

**SOCIAL SERVICES**
Tribal Tanf
Temporary Assistance for Needy Families
San Diego Office 866-913-3725
Escondido Office 866-428-0901
Manzanita Office 866-931-1480
Pala Office 866-806-8263

### NEVADA

**ADVOCACY**
Adams Esq.
Special Needs Children
500 N. Rainbow Blvd. Ste 300
Las Vegas, NV 89107
702-289-4143 Office • 702-924-7200 Fax

**COMMUNITY**
Native American Community Services
3909 S. Maryland Pkwy #205 Las Vegas, NV
89119-7500

**PUBLISHERS**
Blackrose Communications
111 South 35th St. San Diego, CA 92113
619-234-4753
www.indianvoices.net • davis4973@aol.com

### TEXAS

**HEALTH**
The Circle: A Healing Place
Joanna Johnson, MSW, CFAS
Longview Behavioral Hospital
22 Bermuda Lane, Longbiew, Texas 75605
www.longviewhospital.com
www.oglethorpeinc.com
850-228-0777

---

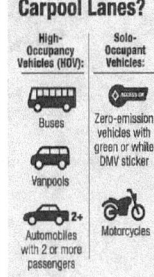

## San Francisco Institute of Architecture

"SFIA has the nation's first and most comprehensive Eco-Design programs including distance learning and continuing education. SFIA is devoted to innovation and reform in architectural education, offering open classes and a Master of Architecture program to graduate students, architectural employees, practicing professionals, and those who have yet to start their architectural education."

SFIA is the only 100% sustainably focused architecture school with the longest running and most comprehensive ecological design and green architecture programs in the world. SFIA has been offering green building and ecological design degrees for twenty years as a wholly integrated part of its architecture degree programs. SFIA also offered the first distance learning Green MBA Program. Students at SFIA have the opportunity to pursue undergraduate and graduate degrees in architecture, ecological design, green building and business administration in sustainability. People who choose to affiliate with SFIA as students, faculty members, lecturers, or advisors have three things in common:

1) They know they can help change the world.
2) They understand what's required to do so.
3) And they are busily doing it.
They work as architects, engineers,

builders, executives, administrators, writers, educators, and consultants. They work locally and globally, for private, public, and nonprofit agencies. Their numbers are growing, and we're proud to say that our current worldwide student body enrollment makes ours the largest program of its kind in the world. Phone: 1-800-634-7779 or 1-510-523-5174Fax: 1-510-523-5175 Email: info@sfia.net

Indian Voices is Proud to be affiliated with the SFIA

Architect Fred Stitt founded the San Francisco Institute of Architecture in 1990, to provide a new kind of architectural education, to encourage innovation and visionary expression, to advance education in architectural technology and management, and to make a total commitment to green building and sustainable design.

# NEVADA NEWS

For Nevada Information: 619-234-4753 • 619-534-2435

## Reid Remarks Honoring His Holiness the 14th Dalai Lama of Tibet

WASHINGTON, D.C. – Nevada Senator Harry Reid spoke on the Senate floor today to honor His Holiness, the 14th Dalai Lama of Tibet. Below are his remarks as prepared for delivery: It is my pleasure to welcome to the United States Senate, His Holiness, the 14th Dalai Lama of Tibet. I know I speak for the entire Senate family when I express our gratitude for that beautiful prayer, and for his words of encouragement and

blessing. His Holiness, the Dalai Lama, is well known throughout the world as the spiritual leader of the Tibetan people, and for spreading the gospel of peace, compassion and love for our fellow beings. But it is tradition when the United States Senate welcomes a guest chaplain to say a few words about our honored guest. His Holiness often says that he is only a simple monk, born to a farming family in northeastern Tibet. But to millions of people in Tibet and across the globe, he is much more – he is a source of hope and inspiration in a world that can sometimes seem dark.

When he was only two years old, His Holiness was recognized as the reincarnation of the 13th Dalai Lama. Four years later, when he was just a little boy, he began his monastic education. He studied logic, art, Tibetan culture, and Buddhist philosophy, among other things. At 23, he passed his exams with honors and was awarded the equivalent of a doctorate of Buddhist philosophy. And for more than half a century, the Dalai Lama has been traveling the world, raising awareness about the concerns of his 6 million fellow Tibetans and, as he would say, making new friends. In Tibetan Buddhist philosophy, the Dalai

Lamas are enlightened beings who have postponed their own nirvana – or liberation from the cycle of reincarnation – in order to serve humanity. This particular enlightened being has chosen to serve humanity by spreading a message of peace.

He motivates countless people around the world – people of every faith tradition – to practice compassion toward one another. His Holiness urges us all to, "Be kind whenever possible. It is always possible." The Dalai Lama's teachings contain lessons for people around the world and within this chamber. His Holiness also advises us that, "The best way to resolve any problem in the human world is for all sides to sit down and talk." It is advice that those of us fortunate enough to serve our country and our constituents in the United States Senate should take to heart and follow more often. And the presence of His Holiness in this chamber today inspires me – as I hope it does all of us – to renew our commitment to speak and act with a pure mind and help dispel the misery of the world.

### Academic Indian

Q: What does a mother buffalo say to a boy buffalo when she sends him off to college?

A: Bye-son

### Healthy Dining Options

Continued from page 5

small business API restaurants to offer healthier food choices and nutrition labeling. With rates of overweight, obesity, and diabetes increasing and becoming urgent public health concerns, STRIVE San Diego and its participating restaurants are finding innovative ways to increase the access to healthier dining options.

Media representatives, government officials, community leaders, other restaurant owners, and the public are encouraged to attend this press conference, which will also provide information about and experiences of participating in STRIVE San Diego as well as food samples from the partner restaurants. STRIVE San Diego, a project of Operation Samahan, Inc. was one of fifteen community-based organizations chosen nationwide by the Centers for Disease Control and Prevention (CDC) Division of Community Health to carry out a high-impact, population-wide project. Funded through Racial and Ethnic Approaches to Community Health (REACH), the national initiative aims to eliminate racial and ethnic gaps in health, including obesity, type 2 diabetes, and heart disease.

"I would like this project to have more funds to help more restaurants do more nutrition analysis... I know a lot of people want to [eat healthy] more but sometimes it's hard for them to make decisions on what to eat" said Gayle Sayyadeth, the owner of Finest Thai restaurant.

*About Operation Samahan, Inc. Operation Samahan has served San Diego County since 1973 and aims to promote better health and living conditions for all persons in the community, especially among indigent, low-income, uninsured, and underserved individuals and families. Operation Samahan provides high-quality, affordable, and culturally accessible medical and dental care, health promotion, and social services.*

## His Holiness The Dalai Lama's Opening Prayer

WASHINGTON, D.C. – His Holiness The Dalai Lama delivered the opening prayer today to convene the United States Senate. Below are his remarks as prepared for delivery:

"With our thoughts we make our world.
Our mind is central and precedes our deeds.
Speak or act with a pure mind
and happiness will follow you,
like a shadow that never leaves.

May there be joy in the world,
With bountiful harvest and spiritual wealth.
May every good fortune come to be,
And may all our wishes be fulfilled.

As long as space remains,
And as long as sentient beings remain,
Until then, may I too remain
And help dispel the misery of the world."

# Senator Harry Reid: Securing Grants to Preserve Nevada's Tribal Treasures

Indian Country and Nevada's Native American heritage will continue to be honored, strengthened and preserved with the National Park Service (NPS) grants from the Historic Preservation Fund that I helped secure. These grants assist tribes in their historic preservation efforts by locating and identifying cultural resources, comprehensive preservation planning and documenting of oral histories and traditions.

In Nevada, we have the homelands of the Washoe, Western Shoshone and Paiute peoples. The preservation efforts of the Washoe Tribe of Nevada and California include restoring Cave Rock on at Lake Tahoe and working on its designation as a traditional cultural property. On the Pyramid Lake Reservation, the tribe will use the funds to hire tribal historical preservation officers and develop a preservation plan for the east side of Pyramid Lake, a sacred area that is currently closed to due to vandalism. We need to evaluate ways to reopen this culturally-sensitive area so we can continue to share its history and heritage with the public.

The Reno-Sparks Indian Colony will be developing and organizing a two-day training for cultural resource tribal monitoring and a cultural resource forum for tribal members of all ages and employees of the tribe.

I am thankful for the work that Director Jonathan Jarvis and the National Park Service do for American Indians, Alaska Natives and Native Hawaiians tribes and for the tribal leadership in Nevada and across the nation. I will continue to work closely with my colleagues in the Senate, agencies like the NPS and tribal leaders to help protect and preserve the many oral histories, languages, and traditions of Native America.

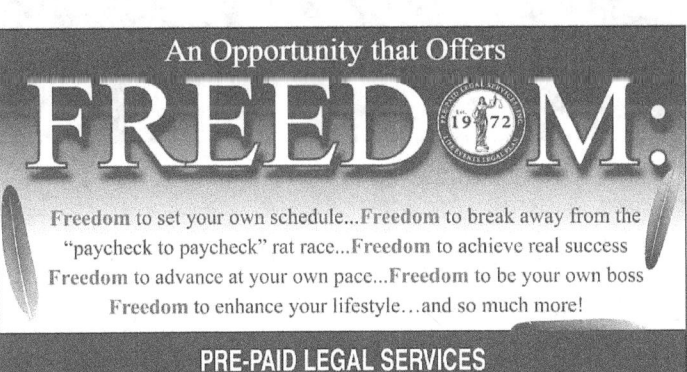

FRYBREAD                                                SAYNDAY

The PowWow Princess likes us.

How'z that?

Frybread breath!

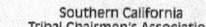

OUR 28ᵀᴴ YEAR          MULTI-CULTURAL NEWS GLOBAL NETWORK                    APRIL 2014

# Network to Freedom

*Manifest Destiny, part of the philosophy behind the taking of Indian land has been recreated at a community level through the use of corporations vs individual property owners treaties instead of governments vs tribes. The new treaties today are better known as "Bad Mortgages" that are impossible to understand and that change imperceptibly, leading to the foreclosure epidemic.*

# Doctrine of Discovery

Whether the banking industry was misregulated, deregulated or new laws fundamentally misdirected; the fact that banking risk management, or the apparatus controlling the industry are consumed by greed, is not discussed when signing on the dotted line.

What cannot be disputed is the fact that we are experiencing a foreclosure crisis that is much harder on African-Americans and Latinos, according to a many studies including the Center for Responsible Lending

People of color, African American and Latino borrowers have borne and will continue to disproportionately bear the burden of foreclosures. Nearly 8% of both African American and Latino borrowers have lost their homes to foreclosures, compared to 4.5 percent of white borrowers. Further, African-American and Latino borrowers are 76 percent and 71 percent more likely, respectively, than white borrowers to have lost their homes to foreclosure since housing prices started to tumble in January 2007.

From early 2007 to the end of 2009, the study estimates the completion of 2.5 million foreclosures and the origination of 6.9 million foreclosures across all races.

African-American and Latino borrowers were particularly vulnerable, as originators targeted traditionally underserved communities for subprime loans and steered borrowers of color to higher-cost loans. Indeed, court cases and information provided by former employees of subprime lenders describe the systematic targeting of African-American neighborhoods and other communities of color. Research shows African-American and Latino borrowers to be 30 percent more likely to get higher-rate subprime loans than white borrowers with similar risk characteristics. This may be another reason why 575,000 African Americans and Latinos have lost their homes since 2007 and 1.2 million are currently two or more loan payments behind on their mortgage.

The apparatus surrounding our country's banking system has become totally detached from reality. Were it not so painfully tragic for the innocent hard working home owner, the rampant and pervasive fraud on the part of the cabal could be entertaining theater, as corporate America and the banking industry devise ways to steal Native land again.

SEE **Network vs Doctrine, page 2**

# Airborne Honor and Courage ... At Last

*by Roy Cook*

On March 24, 2014 mostly ethnic or minority U.S. soldiers who performed bravely under fire in three of the nation's wars finally received the Medal of Honor that the government concluded should have been awarded a long time ago.

The servicemen were identified following a congressionally mandated review to ensure that eligible recipients of the country's highest recognition for valor were not bypassed due to prejudice. Only three of the 24 were alive for President Barack Obama to place the medals and ribbons around their necks. The three surviving recipients — Vietnam veterans Jose Rodela, Melvin Morris and Santiago Erevia — received a prolonged standing ovation at President Obama's side, their faces set in somber acknowledgement of the honor.

Vietnam veterans Jose Rodela, Melvin Morris and Santiago Erevia receive overdue honors.

Santiago Erevia, of San Antonio, was cited for courage while serving as a radio-telephone operator on May 21, 1969, during a search-and-clear mission near Tam Ky, South Vietnam. He was a specialist 4 when his battalion tried to take a hill fortified by Viet Cong and North Vietnam Army soldiers. The Pentagon says he single-handedly silenced four Viet Cong bunkers.

"I thought I was going to get killed when I started to advance because when you fight battles like that you don't expect to live," the 68-year-old retired postal worker told The Associated Press last month.

Jose Rodela, now of San Antonio, was a 31-year-old company commander of a

SEE **Airborne Honor, page 3**

## The Reservation System: Native American Lands Sold under the Dawes Act

By 1871, the federal government stopped signing treaties with Native Americans and replaced the treaty system with a law giving individual Indians ownership of land that had been tribal property. This "Indian Homestead Act," official known as the Dawes Act, was a way for some Indians to become U.S. citizens.

There were two reasons why the treaty system was abandoned. First, white settlers needed more and more land, and the fact that tribes were treated as separate nations with separate citizens made it more difficult to take land from them and "assimilate" them into the general population. Assimilation had become the new ideal. The goal was to absorb the tribes into the European-American culture and make native people more like mainstream Americans. Second, the House of Representatives

was angry that they did not have a voice in these policies. Under the constitution, treaties are ratified by the U.S. Senate, not the House, even though the House has to appropriate the money to pay for them. So the Congress passed a compromise bill in 1871 that, in effect, brought an end to the treaty system. The bill contained the following language buried in an appropriations law for the Yankton Indians:

"PROVIDED, That hereafter no Indian nation or tribe within the territory of the United States shall be acknowledged or recognized as an independent nation, tribe , or power with whom the United States may contract by treaty. . ."

The end of the treaties meant the end of treating tribes as sovereign nations. Attempts were made to undermine the power of the tribal leaders and the tribal justice systems. Tribal bonds were

viewed as an obstacle to federal attempts to assimilate the Indian into white society. Assimilation of the American Indians would become the basis for much of the government policy toward the Native American from the 1880s to the 1930s.

"It has become the settled policy of the Government to break up reservations, destroy tribal relations, settle Indians upon their own homesteads, incorporate them into the national life, and deal with them not as nations or tribes or bands, but as individual citizens." — Commissioner of Indian Affairs Thomas J. Morgan, 1890.

This set the stage for the passage by Congress of the General Allotment Act (the Dawes Severalty Act) of 1887.

Congressman Henry Dawes had great

faith in the civilizing power of private property. He said that to be civilized was to "wear civilized clothes ... cultivate the ground, live in houses, ride in Studebaker wagons, send children to school, drink whiskey [and] own property." This act was designed to turn Indians into farmers, in the hopes they would become more like mainstream America.

The federal government divided communal tribal lands into 160-acre parcels — known as allotments — and gave them to individual tribal members. The U.S. Government would then hold the land allotted to individual Indians in trust for a period of 25 years, so that the Indian would not sell the land and return to the reservation and/or be swindled out of it by scheming white men. The Act went on to offer Indians the benefits of U.S. citizenship — if they took an allotment, lived separate form the tribe and became "civilized."

---

## Network vs Doctrine
Continued from page 1

In response to the mounting foreclosures in recent years, the mortgage servicing industry often responds with illegal shortcuts, fees and incompetent management.

Activist Ismael Rodriguez President of Foreclosure Strategies stands with Royce Esters, National Association for Equal Justice in America.

The situation became so bad that our nation's attorneys general (AGs) joined forces with federal agencies to take action against "robo-signing" and other loan servicing abuses by the nation's largest banks. The banking industry has an insulting perception of the rest of us in this society assuming that we are incapable of understanding what they have been doing.

These shenigans are not surprising if one is aware and in tune with the Doctrine

of Discovery, the fundamental philosophical underpinning that drives the state and the corporations to follow the Papal Bulls of the 15th century. This principal, established by precedent gave Christian explorers the right to claim lands they "discovered" and lay claim to those lands for their Christian monarchs. Any land that was not inhabited by Christians was available to be "discovered", claimed, and exploited. If the "pagan" inhabitants could be converted, they might be spared. If not, they could be enslaved or killed.

The Discovery Doctrine is a concept of public international law expounded by the United States Supreme Court in a series of decisions, initially in Johnson v. M'Intosh in 1823. The doctrine was Chief Justice John Marshall's explanation of the way in which colonial powers laid claim to newly discovered lands during the Age of Discovery. Under it, title to newly discovered lands lay with the government whose subjects discovered new territory. The doctrine has been primarily used to support decisions invalidating or ignoring aboriginal possession of land in favor of colonial or post-colonial governments. The Trail of Tears is alive and well in your neighborhood and mine. People are being driven from their family homesteads.

John Marshall pointed to the doctrine as simple fact, looking at the possession-

takings which had been supported by it as things which had occurred and had to be recognized. The supposedly inferior character of native cultures was a reason for the doctrine having been used, but whether or not that was justified was not relevant for Marshall.

This Doctrine governs United States Indian Law today and has been cited as recently as 2005 in the decision City Of Sherrill V. Oneida Indian Nation of N.Y.

During slavery and Indian removals most virulent times there were always at least 3% of the dominate culture who were against both slavery and Manifest Destiny.

More benevolent influence within the

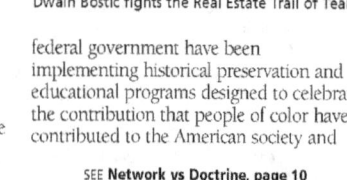

Dwain Bostic fights the Real Estate Trail of Tears.

federal government have been implementing historical preservation and educational programs designed to celebrate the contribution that people of color have contributed to the American society and

SEE Network vs Doctrine, page 10

---

# INDIAN VOICES

**Multicultural News from an American Indian Perspective**

### PUBLISHED BY BLACKROSE COMMUNICATIONS
*Member, American Indian Chamber of Commerce*

Email: rdavis4973@aol.com
Website: www.indianvoices.net
Editorial Board: Rose Davis

| | | | |
|---|---|---|---|
| Editor: | Rose Davis | Writer: | Jaclyn Bissonette |
| Managing Editor: | Yvonne-Cher Skye | Entertainment Writer/ | |
| Outside Support: | Mel Vernon | Photographer LA/SD: | Rochelle Porter |
| LV Entertainment Writer: | Z. Z. Zorn | Reporter de Espectaculos: | Omar DeSantiago |
| Associate Editor: | Sis Mary Muhammad | Reporter de Espectaculos: | Michelle Banuet |
| Writer: | Kathleen Blavatt | Proofreader: | Mary Lou Finley |
| Writer: | Roy Cook | Graphic Artist: | Elaine Hall |
| Writer: | Marc Snelling | Staff Photographer: | Abel Jacome |
| Writer: | Scott Andrews | | |

Endeavor Media Group
André Haynes
3675 S. Rainbow Blvd., Ste 107
Las Vegas, NV 89103
702-305-0973 •
www.emgnv.com

111 South 35th St.
San Diego, CA 92113
(619) 234-4753
(619) 534-2435 (cell)
Fax: (619) 512-4534

**Member of the Society of Professional Journalists**
**Member of New America Media**

# Hundreds of Tribal Representatives Join Huge Rally to Oppose Fracking

*by Dan Bacher*

Hundreds of indigenous people from California and across the country gathered with a crowd of over 4000 activists at the State Capitol in Sacramento on March 15 to send a clear message to Governor Jerry Brown: ban fracking, an environmentally destructive oil extraction practice that pollutes groundwater, rivers and the oceans.

The large Tribal contingent included members of the Miwok, Maidu, Winnemem Wintu, Yurok, Karuk, Hoopa Valley, Ohlone, Pit River, Cahto, Round Valley, Pomo and Chumash Nations and other Tribes from throughout the state, as well as members of the Dakota, Lakota Sioux, indigenous communities, native organizations and activists in the Idle No More Movement and Klamath Justice Coalitions. Many Tribal representatives emphasized the direct connection between fracking and the Shasta Dam raise and the Governor's peripheral tunnels plan, which will provide water for fracking.

"We should call the Governor

'Westlands' Brown," said Chook Chook Hillman, a member of the Karuk Tribe and the Klamath Justice Coalition, a group that has organized many direct action protests to remove the Klamath dams, halt the violation of tribal gathering rights under the Marine Life Protection Act (MLPA) Initiative to create so-called "marine protected areas," and to stop the Westlands Water District legal attempt to raid Trinity River water.

"Brown is setting aside all the environmental rules in order to ship water south," said Hillman, who held a banner proclaiming, "Stop Fracking Around – Undam the Klamath," with other members of Klamath Justice Coalition. "Fracking will take good water, put chemicals in it and then it will come out toxic forever. Fracking will affect all us - fracking is a terrible use of water, water that could be used for people and fish."

The event, organized by the Californians Against Fracking, featured diverse speakers including environmental justice advocates, farmers, student activists and other groups opposed to fracking.

Hundreds of organizations, ranging from grassroots groups to large NGOs, helped to organized the rally.

Chief Caleen Audrey Sisk, Tribal Chief and Spiritual Leader of the Winnemem Wintu, led the opening ceremony and prayer. She took aim at the Governor's peripheral tunnels plan – the "Brown Water Plan," as she calls it.

She emphasized, "Here at the Capitol a lot of Brown water planning is going on. This water is our medicine – it comes from the sacred places where the medicine comes from. We struggle to continue to take care of our waters – there is no other place we can go to practice our religion."

Warrior Woman, a Dakota Indian woman holding a sign saying, "Mother Earth Does Not Negotiate," said, "We're here to stop fracking and the rape of Mother Earth. Water is the life blood of Mother Earth. The governmental system can't continue to oppress the people and Mother Earth any longer."

Mike Duncan, Round Valley Reservation Tribe member, described

fracking as "another broken treaty."

"I'm here for tribal water waters and to stop the raising of Shasta Dam. It's the future – it's our responsibilities as tribal people to stop fracking. Fracking is another broken treaty as far as I am concerned," he said.

Penny Opal Plant, an organizer of Idle No More, pointed out that the battle against fracking and other destructive methods of oil and gas extraction is a worldwide struggle, including Lakota resistance to the XL pipeline, the resistance of Canadian First Nations to fracking and battles of indigenous people against destructive resource extraction throughout Latin America.

SEE **Fracking, page 10**

---

# Airborne Honor
Continued from page 1

Special Forces strike group on Sept. 1, 1969, in Phuoc Long Province, Vietnam, when he and his company of Cambodian soldiers whom he had helped recruit came under fire from North Vietnamese Army troops.

According to his Medal of Honor citation and supporting documents, the battle lasted 18 hours and 11 men in his company were killed and 33 others wounded.

The citation states that late in the battle, Rodela "was the only member of his company who was moving and he began to run from one position to the next, checking for casualties and moving survivors into different positions in an attempt to form a stable defense line. Throughout the battle, in spite of his wounds, Rodela repeatedly exposed himself to enemy fire to attend to the fallen and eliminate an enemy rocket position."

In an interview with the Army News Service last December, he said simply, "We trained for this and I would have done it again."

"Today we have the chance to set the record straight," President Obama said. "No nation is perfect, but here in America we confront our imperfections and face a sometimes painful past, including the truth that some of these soldiers fought and died for a country that did not always see them as equal."

U S Army Special Forces and Medal of Honor recipient Melvin Morris was born in Okmulgee, Okla., Jan. 7, 1942.

Morris entered the Oklahoma Army National Guard in 1959 and later requested to join the active Army. He became one of the first Soldiers to don the 'green beret' at the command of President John F. Kennedy, Fort Bragg, N.C., in 1961. Morris volunteered twice for deployments to Vietnam.

Melvin Morris is being recognized for his valorous actions on Sept. 17, 1969, while commanding the Third Company, Third Battalion of the IV Mobile Strike Force near Chi Lang. Then-Staff Sgt. Morris led an advance across enemy lines to retrieve a fallen comrade and single-handedly destroyed an enemy force that had pinned his battalion from a series of bunkers. Staff Sgt. Morris was shot three times as he ran back toward friendly lines with the American casualties, but did not stop until he reached safety.

The Distinguished Service Cross was awarded to then Staff Sgt. Morris in April 1970 for extraordinary heroism during this 1969 battle. After receiving the award, he returned to Vietnam the same month for his second tour. He retired at Fort Hood, Texas in May 1985. Morris

Test Platoon - First 16 qualified black paratroopers (1944) Enlisted men of the Test Platoon. Front Row from L-R: First Sgt. Walter Morris, first black enlisted man accepted for airborne duty • Sgt. Jack D. Tillis • Sgt. Leo D. Reed • Sgt Daniel Weil *S. Sgt. Hubert Bridges • Tech. Grade IV Alvin L. Moon • Sgt. Ned D. Bess • Sgt. Roger S. Walden Back Row from L-R • Cpl. McKinley Godfrey, Jr. • Sgt. Elijah Wesby • Sgt. Samuel W. Robinson • S. Sgt. Calvin R. Beal • S. Sgt Robert F. Greene • S. Sgt. Lonnie M. Duke • Sgt. Clarence H. Beavers and Sgt. James E. Kornegay. Not Shown Carstell O. Stewart, the seventeenth, who was on emergency leave and earned his wings a week later.

currently resides in Cocoa, Fla.

"I never really did worry about decorations," Morris told The Associated Press last month. But he said he fell to his knees when he received the surprise call from President Obama with news that he was to be honored.

Staff Sgt. Melvin Morris was awarded the Medal of Honor by President Barack Obama during a ceremony in the East Room of the White House in Washington, Tuesday, March 18, 2014. President Obama awarded 24 Army veterans the Medal of Honor for conspicuous gallantry in recognition of their valor during major combat operations in World War II, the Korean War and the Vietnam War.

Additionally, in Camp Mackall, North

Carolina the first all-black parachute Infantry platoon was activated on November 25,1944. They would be called the 555th Battalion, a.k.a. "The Triple Nickles." They were called the Triple Nickles because 17 of 20 soldiers selected from the Buffalo Soldiers 92nd Infantry in Arizona made it through the test platoon at Fort Benning. The unit's name came from the old English spelling and identified with three buffalo nickels joined in a triangle or pyramid.

The Triple Nickles served in more airborne units during both war and peacetime than any other parachute group in history.

In the winter of 1943-1944 twenty young African-American enlisted men were ordered to Fort Benning, Georgia to be trained as parachutists. These young men were pioneers because, never before in the segregated military system then prevalent, were 'Coloreds' considered intelligent enough or brave enough to serve in combat units of any type and certainly not capable of being paratroopers.

In early 1944 sixteen of these young men completed requisite training, overcoming numerous obstacles, and were awarded the silver wings of qualified parachutist. Shortly thereafter an additional trooper, having been delayed by a family emergency, was also awarded the much coveted parachutist badge. These men were led by former First Sergeant Walter Morris, and went on to form the cadre for the 555th Parachute Infantry Company at Camp Mackall, North Carolina.

# Tribal Flush: Pechanga People "Disenrolled" en Masse

**On the eve of what could be the largest gambling expansion in U.S. history, a tale of power, betrayal and lost Indian heritage**

*by Marc Cooper*

John Gomez Jr. parks his silver family van in the back row of one more anonymous strip mall off California's Highway 79, an hour and a half southeast of Los Angeles, on a windswept ridge overlooking the Temecula Valley.

Gomez, his dark hair barely betraying a sprinkling of gray at his temples, steps out of the van and walks away from the mall, to a barren dirt lot marked off with adobe walls. "This is where Pablo is buried," he says as we peer over the locked iron gate.

Pablo is Pablo Apis, the celebrated 19th-century "headman," or chief, of the Temecula/Pechanga Indians, who was given more than 2,000 acres of land in exchange for his work at the Mission San Luis Rey. Gomez, who is a direct descendant of Chief Apis, jiggles the lock on the gate. He has no key. "This is where a lot of our people were buried," Gomez continues, "including those killed in the famous Temecula Massacre." He's referring to the killing of several dozen Indians by Californio militias in the closing days of 1846. Apis survived and, indeed, the 1875 treaty between the Temecula tribe and the U.S. government, though never ratified, was signed at the chief's village adobe home.

Today, on a corner of Apis' original land grant, a few minutes down the road from the desolate burial ground, towers the $350 million Pechanga Resort & Casino, the glittering 14-story pleasure dome so familiar to Southern Californians from the promotional and political-advocacy commercials in near-constant rotation on local television stations. With 522 rooms, 185,000 square feet of casino floor, 2,000 slot machines, more than 150 table games and seven restaurants, along with Vegas-class showrooms, nightclubs and comedy lounges, the Pechanga Band of Luiseño Indians, as the tribe is now known, runs the largest and perhaps most profitable of California's nearly 60 Indian casinos.

And now, under terms of a deal negotiated by Governor Schwarzenegger, ratified earlier this year by the Democratic-led state legislature and set to go before voters in the February 3 primary election, the Pechanga and three other Southern California tribes may soon triple their battery of slot machines, allowing each of the four Indian groups to operate twice as many slots as any Vegas casino. If the referendums go through, the four tribes — Morongo, Agua Caliente, Sycuan and Pechanga — will be responsible for the largest expansion of gambling in recent U.S. history.

But it's Gomez's tribe no more. At least as far as the tribal leadership is concerned. Gomez and 135 adult members of his extended family (and 75 or more children) have been purged from formal Pechanga membership; they have been "disenrolled."

They were accused of no crime, no misbehavior, no wrongdoing, no disloyalty. But a series of tribal kangaroo-court hearings, bereft of even the pretense of due process, ruled that one of the family's deceased elders was not an authentic tribe member and, therefore, not withstanding their years of service to the tribe, they were all to be banned.

What it's come to goes beyond tribal pride. As a result of the disenrollment, many in the Gomez family, which accounts for some 10 percent of the total Pechanga tribe's membership, have lost their federal standing and benefits as American Indians. Some have lost their jobs at the resort. All of the adults, including Gomez, lost the generous per capita monthly payout, derived from casino profits, that was given to each adult of the tribe. When the Gomez family's expulsion was finalized in 2004, that was about $15,000 per month. Currently, for those who remain members of the tribe, the figure has risen to about $40,000 per month.

The sharp increase is due in part to a second wave of purges, finalized last year, which disenrolled another extended family, this one descended from Paulina Hunter and representing yet another 10 percent of the tribe. That second purge went ahead despite a tribe-commissioned expert probe that concluded that Hunter was, in fact, a Pechanga.

Simply put: The fewer the tribal members, the bigger the payout.

Some of the elderly disenrollees found themselves cut off from tribal clinics they helped to build. Some of the younger ones lost their education subsidies. What all the disenrollees have in common is not only the sudden loss of significant income but erasure of their collective cultural history and identity.

"Yes, we lost homes and cars. Some went into bankruptcy," Gomez says. "But mostly I was saddened for my family and for Indian country in general. It's not just your money they're taking away but also your heritage and your future."

With Indian gaming revenues now near the $30 billion mark nationally, disenrollment has rocked and divided Indian reservations from coast to coast.

"Gaming has brought in the dominant culture's disease of greed," Marty Firerider of the California American Indian Movement told the Indian Country Today newspaper.

Gomez first got into trouble with his Pechanga tribe in 2002, when, as a trusted legal adviser, he was elected to the tribal-enrollment committee, along with a cousin and a member of the Paulina Hunter family. These were sensitive positions. After the tribe won its first minor gambling concession in 1996, and after California voters approved major Indian gaming rights four years later, it was only natural that there would be an increase in those suddenly claiming membership.

"As soon as we were elected, we found that the committee was doing all kinds of strange things," Gomez says. "On the one hand they weren't adhering to an enrollment moratorium and on the other they weren't properly processing the minor children of those already enrolled."

Gomez and his new allies began an investigation.

The boom quickly dropped on them. Within weeks a letter emerged from a group called Concerned Pechanga People, a small faction closely allied with the tribal leadership and its chair, Mark Macarro, which accused Gomez and his family of not being legitimate Pechanga. By the end of the year, Gomez's extended family were notified of pending disenrollment. During an internal process that lasted more than a year and a half, Gomez put together binders of documentation proving — at least to virtually every outside observer who has reviewed them — his Pechanga ancestry.

But the tribal leadership, in closed-door sessions that adhered to no formal due process or rules of evidence, held to its position that one key elder in Gomez's lineage — Manuela Miranda — had left the traditional village after her marriage and, therefore, her descendants weren't really Pechanga. The claim, according to several experts, is prima facie absurd, as the history of American Indians is based on such dispersion and diaspora.

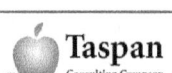

Black Path Commentary: Critical Analysis on Culture, Community, & Struggle

## Respecting the Vison & Value of Earthday: Ecological and Economic Concern, Struggle, & Possibilites of Serudj Ta

*by Min. Tukufu Kalonji*

Unquestionably, a ethical and equitable position of and on the environment has to start with us as a segment of society, reevaluating our relationship with the world, our position in it, our responsibility towards it, and all of the related rewards and/or consequences of whatever actions we engage in, change, and/or do not change. We are compelled to raise questions regarding the established orders savagery and egotism in its destroying the Earth. For what reasons does the oppressor practice ecocide? We know it is no secret, nor mystery that the oppressor ravages this planet for profit without regard even for himself! As I have argued earlier this again appears to be an episode of "the white man gone wild."

The oppressor has not only wreaked havoc upon the planets natural resources, it also in its matrix of madness has engaged in a process of creative destruction. Creative Destruction here is an economic concept rooted in capitalism whereby people are suffering via systemic and structured poverty. According to some socialist theorist, in its most fundamental sense, creative destruction is the phenomenon of capitalist economic practices that flourish as a result of some previously adhered to system and order of economic enterprise. The bottom line is the rich stay and get richer, while the masses of middle class America and its poor get poorer!

When the banks were hurting, America's elected leaders dropped everything to bail them out. The banks have rewarded politicians with more than a billion dollars, but many families are still fighting illegal foreclosures and waiting for relief from the mortgage crisis. For example, Sherry Hernandez, a member of the Home Defenders League currently is awaiting trial in Washington DC over a protest at a law firm regarding the firm's influence of Wall Street in the nation's capitol. While Ms. Hernandez and so many others are experiencing economic meltdown, Wall Street has increased their profit by over 30% since the crisis from homeowners misery, homeowners who were robbed of their homes, have had their credit rating dropped, subsequently making it difficult to begin again or pursue new business ventures or a new job."

Only through rebuilding a comprehensive liberation movement can the struggle against the savagery of major banks, multinational corporations, and their political puppets prove effective in overturning perhaps the greatest recession ever in generations past and hopefully not ever to come again. We are compelled to struggle for many corrections in the economic system as we are with our concern for the ecology of the planet. For example we can start with the battle to get a living wage. According to http://livingwage.mit.edu/counties/06073, San Diego County living wage for a family of two adults with two children should be $22.25 an hour. Well we know the minimum wage of $8.00 an hour is what many families are earning. The additional $14.25 per hour would make a significant difference. Therefore, a family would not have to stress over whether to pay their medical bills, get food, or keep the lights on etc, which is a reality often keep occurring with people working an $8.00 an hour job. Granted $8.00 an hour is better than $0.00 an hour but in a sense, it is similar to putting a Band-Aid on a gunshot wound. In short, in San Diego County and across this nation we are enslaved economically for the banks and multinational corporations are the plantation owners and the politicians they buy are like the overseers; and the masses by its lack of controlling its economic destiny are slaves to the oppression of capitalistic barbarism.

Thus, let us of cultural and social consciousness and moral grounding reflect upon and revisit Respecting the Vision & Value of Earth Day; and not only see it as time to protect and preserve the planet which is critical; but also see and use Earth Day April 22, 2014 as a marker for re-engaging the possibility and struggle for economic as well as ecologic justice. For to talk and act for the life of the planet but not the people who inhabited it is a false conception as the hard rock of reality is like the 1971 Stylistics song, People Make the World Go Round. In this classic soul jam, the matter of our environment, unionized labor, and its struggle for livable wages; and other topical issues of the time are addressed by the Stylistics. Although the song offers no solutions as it is merely a song, it does point out that the world is full of challenges and inevitably suggest in via the verse "Go underground, young man"; one can reasonably construe this verse as a call to battle for making a better world or a call to imply if you cannot correct a corrupt system, then perhaps its best to leave that system. Well if the latter was the rationale, the reality is the majority of us are going to remain right here in North America; thus subject to what systems are in place within the political economy. Furthermore, we know clearly the influential power of ones environment upon their mental,

physical, and spiritual health. Thus, it was the awesomeness of the influence of the Black Power Era 1965 to 1975, which no doubt influenced the Stylistics and so many other artists to make songs with a cultural, social and political level of consciousness in their messages.

As a final point, the American economy like its ecology is contaminated with germs and poisons rooted in the most vulgar manifestation of capitalism at its worst. And while this writer clearly does not have an all encompassing answer to the problem of ecological devastation and economic enslavement, I do contend that we can wherever we can, build allies, coalitions, and support existing movement oriented organizations working in the interest of the life of our environments ecological health, and our economical health by practicing a ancient Kemetic concept rescued and reconstructed by Dr. Maulana Karenga as an ethic and social practice of restoration; which is Serudj Ta. Serudj Ta as values and vision for Earth Day offers an African cultural concept for both areas of struggle discussed in this writing.

According to Karenga "The moral mandate of Serudj Ta is found in the ancient Egyptian sacred text, The Husia, which teaches us to see and sense the world as sacred space, as a shared heritage given by the Divine; respected and constantly renewed by the ancestors and left to us as a rich legacy to cherish, care for and continue to renew and then pass on to future generations to do likewise". Serudj Ta translates in seven fundamental ways which are:

1. To raise up that which is in ruins
2. To repair that which is damaged
3. To rejoin that which is severed
4. To replenish that which is lacking
5. To strengthen that which is weakened
6. To set right that which is wrong
7. To make flourish that which is insecure and underdeveloped

In the final analysis if we engage the struggle and practice some of these principles some of the time, a whole new change can occur on in our life and indeed the life of the world. And at the same time as we know the established order has reigned in power and enslaved us economically and wreaked havoc upon our ecology, history has shown there are rising tides; which is to say that, consequently, wealth and power acquired through ill gotten means will eventually dry up as does a weed without water. And the voice and acts of the righteous; that is, the masses will no doubt rise up in victory!

*Min. Tukufu Kalonji is Founder/Kasisi of Kawaida African Ministries. For info contact @ tkalonji@hotmail.com*

## ENDEAVOR MEDIA GROUP

*Indian Voices* is grateful to the ancestors for hooking us up with Andre Haynes and his cutting edge, forward thinking media company. Endeavor offers the perfect opportunity to push the reset button and reconnect with our friends and associates in Nevada, Las Vegas and "Sin City, who continue on the path toward healthy, social sustainability.

Established in 2011, Endeavor Media Group is a Las Vegas-based company specializing in political consulting and public relations for the arts and entertainment, politics and sports industries, with an expertise in media and events.

*Indian Voices* is more than appreciative of Andre's supportive, reverent professional assistance.
(702) 305-0973 info@emgnv.com
3675 S. Rainbow Blvd. STE. 107, Las Vegas, NV 89103

## Statement by the President on the Confirmation of Maria Contreras-Sweet to Lead the Small Business Administration

With the bipartisan confirmation of Maria Contreras-Sweet as the next Administrator of the Small Business Administration, the American people will have a fierce champion who understands what it means to start a small business, and who has a proven track record of helping other small businesses succeed.

As the founder of ProAmérica Bank, Maria helped provide loans to small businesses that needed them, especially within the Latino community. Maria also served the citizens of California as Secretary of Business, Transportation, and Housing, becoming the first Latina cabinet secretary in California history and playing a critical role in ensuring that entrepreneurs and small business owners across her state had access to the capital they needed to start and grow their businesses.

As we work to keep our economy growing, Maria will be charged with looking for more ways to support small businesses. Two years ago I elevated the role of Small Business Administrator to a cabinet-level position to make sure small businesses have the seat at the table they deserve. I'm confident that as the newest member of my cabinet, Maria will to do an outstanding job as she working with me, with America's small business owners, and with my entire Administration to increase economic growth and expand opportunity for all.

6

To improve the quality of life of those who recognize themselves and choose to be recognized by others as "Indigenous Peoples of Color of the Americas" and in support of The American Indian Rights and Resources Organization (AIRRO).

## The Lowry Band of North Carolina

*by William Loren Katz*

People of African and Native American descent have played a prominent part in North Carolina history since survivors of the Lost Colony of Roanoke in 1585 found a home among nearby Lumbee Indians and took in runaway slaves from the British colonies.

One band of these well-armed mixed bloods lived in Robeson County, North Carolina, next to South Carolina, under the name of the Lowry Band and commanded by Henry Berry Lowry, a mixture of the three races. The Lowry Band also lived under the noses of angry slaveholders.

During the Civil War the Lowry Band often had to fight off attacks by North Carolina's Confederate Home Guards. The Guards acted as police unit that seized and forced Lowry's men to build Confederate fortifications. The Lowry Band had no use for the Confederacy, forced labor and — some of their kinfolk were still enslaved by Confederates. Lowrey's men welcomed, recruited and armed fleeing Union prisoners, African American runaways and Confederate deserters.

During the Civil War the Lowry Band

and the Home Guards fought their own civil war.

Then the Union Army reached North Carolina! In late 1864 US General William T. Sherman decided he could end the war if he sliced the Confederacy in half cutting through Georgia to its capitol at Atlanta, and then on to Savannah on the Atlantic.

With 60,000 men, lacking contact with supply lines -- but aided by slave runaways – Sherman's soldiers lived off the land. From Savannah, they spun around and marched northward into South Carolina seeking to crush this fountainhead of the secession movement.

Then Sherman's army headed toward North Carolina to cut another devastating swathe through the Confederacy. His army reached Robeson County, on March 9th only to be stopped by a torrential rain, muddy roads and swollen creeks. They could not move, or even knew where to move.

Suddenly out of the downpour appeared a dark, grizzled guerilla force offering to help. Sherman called his saviors "Lumbees" because he heard were descended from Jamestown's first English colonists mixed with slave runways and Lumbee Indians.

His rescuers were "The Lowry Band" now also mortal enemies of the Confederacy and slavery. They led Sherman's army through the torrential rain and treacherous swamps. Sherman thanked the Band for "the damndest marching I ever saw."

On February 22nd Union troops including African Americans liberated Wilmington. On April 9th Lee surrendered to Grant, and two weeks later on April 26 Confederate General Joseph Johnston surrendered to Sherman in North Carolina.

Whether you call them Lumbees, the Lowry Band or Black Indians, these fighters had done their part to end the war, defeat the Confederacy and abolish slavery in the United States.

*This essay is adapted from the new, expanded [2012] edition of Black Indians :A Hidden Heritage by its author, William Loren Katz. His Black Indian website -- williamlkatz.com – has other articles on the subject and his forty other books.*

# Black Seminole Secret Identity, Revealed

### What really started the Watts Rebellion

*by refixico*

Rena Frye Price, 1916 -2013, was a Black Seminole/Seminole Freedmen of the Dosar Barkus Band of the Oklahoma Nation of Seminole Indians. Rena was born in Seminole County. This is, a public revelation of little importance to the world today. However, Ms. Frye-Price's name and the name of her son ,Marquette, received colossal news attention in August of 1965. They were scapegoated, by many, as the Mother and Son duo who , it was said, ignited the : "Watts Rebellion".

I, too, am a Black Seminole, and newly discovered family member of these unfortunate people, I prefer to say ,that the Watts Rebellion FOLLOWED their arrest. For those who never knew or can't remember, Marquette Frye and Rena's step son, Ronald Frye, were stopped by the Ca. Highway Patrol for suspicion of D.U.I. , Marquette was behind the wheel . Mothers usually love and protect their children, even those who are non-compliant adults. Unconditional love operates even when their grown children are exhibiting inappropriate behavior.

There was a history of this type of activity from Marquette and since Rena , needed her car, to survive , she had issued him a warning ( as was reported by a credible family source). Rena's warning reportedly was ,quote: "If you get in trouble, again driving my car, I'm coming after you" unquote. This is believable, and one reason, why this diminuitive Black Seminole Woman raced up to the scene. Another reason was, her other step son ,Ronald, so, the Mc Cone Report says, had been informed by the California Highway Patrol Officers, that once Marquette was taken to Jail ( since he had already, failed the Sobriety Test), that Ronald, could not drive his step mother's, 1955 Buick to the house a short distance away. Losing her car ,would certainly motivate

her to come quickly. It was, her only means of transportation, to housekeeping jobs in affluent homes where people could pay for her services.

Again, the Mc Cone Report, says that once Rena came on the scene, that she began scolding Marquette, who, according to the report, Marquette's, resisting arrest scenario began with him issuing an ultimate ( a crowd had gathered by then). "You will have to kill me before I go to jail". So far, this sounds like Saturday night all across America. When the officers went into action , so did ,Rena and Ronald and all three were subdued and transported off to jail.

The emotional climate of the community and the hot Summer Weather, populated the street with an abundance of fed-up occupants, who were tired of , no jobs, bad transportation, scarce medical services, inadequate schools, in your face Policing,  an indifferent Mayor Sam Yorty, an a agressive, no-nonsense Chief Parker of the L.A.P.D.. Rena Frye Price and her sons did not create the economic and sociological circumstances that caused the community to erupt.

The truth is, that the occupants of this area , who revolted against authority (remember, most people living in the area did not revolt) felt that they had nothing to lose, and to the contrary, they felt that they had a score to settle with society. In their hearts and minds they also vowed: "If our oppressors, make trouble for us we are coming after them".

Black Seminole, Rena Frye Price and her family did not start the ,"Watts Rebellion" ! However,the uprising followed a Police stop gone wrong, in a tinder box neighborhood, and the rest is history.

"Through Warm Tears of Gratitude"

*Phil "Pompey Bruner" Fixico, Seminole Maroon Descendant, featured in the Smithsonian Institution's: "IndiVisible": African-Native American Lives in the Americas and Private Sector Partner for the DOI/NPS/National Underground Railroad/Network to Freedom*

## San Diego Smartphone Search Case to be Heard by Supreme Court

One of the biggest Fourth Amendment cases to go before the U.S. Supreme Court in recent memory gets heard this month, and it originates from a case here in San Diego.

A man convicted of a San Diego gang-related shooting is asking for a new trial because some of the evidence was originally seized from his cellphone without a warrant when he was stopped for a traffic violation.

David Leon Riley's attorneys argue the cellphone searches violated Riley's Fourth Amendment right to unreasonable search and seizure.

Under California law, if you're arrested, police officers don't need a warrant to go through your cellphone.

In 2011, the California Supreme Court ruled these searches are legal, saying that defendants lose their privacy rights for any items they're carrying when taken into custody.

Meanwhile, law enforcement officials view cellphone searches as an invaluable tool to solve crimes.

Legal experts say this case will have a major impact on similar future cases as well as those that are pending or tied up the appeal process along with standard police procedure.

Oral arguments are set for April 29 with a decision expected by June.

## San Francisco Institute of Architecture

The San Francisco Institute of Architecture (SFIA) was founded in 1990 by Fred A. Stitt, architect, as a school devoted to innovation in design and experimental research and reform in architectural education. Its goal: to offer a new kind of architectural education, grounded in nature-based architecture and sustainable design. The school was co founded by Lou Marines, former CEO of the national American Institute of Architects. A year later Marines left SFIA to pursue independent continuing education professional development programs.

Prior to SFIA, Fred Stitt taught for three years at UC Berkeley, where he studied and documented problems and potential reforms in architectural education. He previously conducted the same kind of research on all aspects of architectural practice at various architecture firms. The results were presented over time in 18 books authored by Stitt and published by McGraw-Hill, John Wiley & Sons, and others. He also created and published over 70 architectural manuals through his own publishing company, GUIDELINES. The most recent textbook produced by Fred

Stitt, the The Ecological Design Handbook, was published by Mcgraw-Hill (recently translated into Chinese), and is used as a university textbook around the world.

Stitt and SFIA's distinguished faculty are now applying extended problem seeking and creative problem solving to every aspect of contemporary sustainable architecture. In pursuit of this work, SFIA created the first major national and international green building conferences (the Eco Wave Series) and has held recurring workshops for design professionals and educators in over 50 cities across the U.S.

Since 1997 SFIA has provided low-cost distance learning programs to architecture and engineering students and professionals in every state in the U.S. and on every continent around the world. Today, SFIA is the world's oldest and largest green building school in the world.

1-800-634-7779 or 1-510-523-5174
info@sfia.net
SFIA Information Office
Box 2590, Alameda, CA 94501

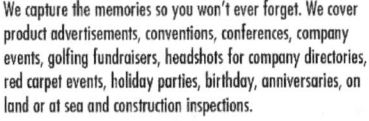

## San Diego American Indian Heritage Events Committee

Committed to providing culturally relevant events which will allow the urban American Indian community to connect with each other in order to celebrate Native history and tradition while providing a platform to raise awareness and experience of our rich heritage within the grater San Diego area.

This year we are organizing the first annual "American Indian Heritage Pow Wow"

**In Balboa Park, San Diego, CA . in May.**

This Pow Wow will occur over a Saturday and Sunday and provide a venue for our Native people to gather for dancing, food , arts and crafts and celebrating our heritage in traditional manner. This event has drawn over 2.000 in the past.

Committee Members: Honorary Chair – Randy Edmonds (Kiowa-Caddo)

Chair-Paula Brim (Choctaw Nation of Oklahoma); Secretary-Leonarda Thompson (Colorado River Indian Tribes); Cynthia Begay (Navajo/Hopi); Estelle Fisher (Colorado River Indian Tribes); Vicki Gambala (Cherokee); Connie Grey Bull (Shoshone-Bannock Tribes); John Hood (Navajo Nation); Apachee -Mims (San Carlos Apache); Richard Overdal (Ojibwe Mt Band of Chippewa); Trena Wade

Diana Williams (Cherokee/Navajo/Apache)

*Supporting Organizations: San Diego American Indian Health Center – Soaring Eagles Youth Program – Indian Education, SDUSD – Tonkawa Elders Group – American Indian Warriors Association – Kids Korps U.S.A. – American Indian Recruitment – USD Native American Alumni Council – UCSD Native American Student Alliance – Native Americana Alumni Association of SDSU-Southern California American Indian Resource*

### *In Memory*
### Edmond Andrew Harjo

Edmond Andrew Harjo, a Seminole Nation of Oklahoma tribal member and Congressional Gold Medal recipient, walked on March 31, 2014 in Ada, Oklahoma at the Mercy Hospital of Ada. He was 96 years old.

When Harjo served in the U.S. Army during World War II he was a private first class and a Seminole Nation Code Talker. During his service with the "A" Battery 195thField Artillery Battalion he received a Good Conduct Medal, a EAME Service Ribbon and a Silver Star.

In November 2013, Harjo was among those at the nations' capitol honoring code talkers from 33 tribes with Congressional Medals of Honor.

## USDA Continues Reaching Indian Country Through the Food Distribution Program on Indian Reservations (FDPIR)

Finding groceries can be difficult in many inner city neighborhoods, and in many rural areas the challenge can be even more daunting. Americans living in remote areas might easily spend half a day just making a grocery run. And for many Native Americans living on Indian reservations, simply getting to a place to purchase nutritious foods becomes a constant struggle.

Food security is a top priority for Agriculture Secretary Tom Vilsack. "Expanding access to nutritious food will not only empower American families to serve healthy meals to their children, but it will also help expand the demand for agricultural products."

One program expanding access to nutritious foods is the Food Distribution Program on Indian Reservations (FDPIR). FDPIR was first authorized under the Food Stamp Act of 1977 to provide access to nutritious foods to low-income Native American households. FDPIR is administered locally by either Indian tribal organizations (ITOs) or an agency of a state government. Currently, there are about 276 tribes receiving benefits under FDPIR, with an average of 82,600 participants each month.

Because FDPIR is administered directly on Indian reservations, it can eliminate the need for recipients to travel great distances simply to acquire nutritious foods. Eligible participants are able to choose from over 70 food options that can be used to create meals that align with the Dietary Guidelines for Americans and MyPlate. In Fiscal Year 2009, the Healthy Eating Index (HEI), which rates diets based on overall nutrition, rated the FDPIR food option package at 85.3 (an HEI score above an 80 is considered a healthy diet).

To assist in the preparation of healthy meals using FDPIR foods, FNS recently worked with tribal members to create a recipe book. "A Harvest of Recipes with USDA Foods: The Food Distribution Program on Indian Reservations (FDPIR)" provides creative, regional recipes using FDPIR food options. Each recipe features sensible levels of fat, sodium, and sugar without sacrificing taste. The recipes also list nutrition facts.

The FDPIR has made great strides in providing access to nutritious foods and reducing food insecurity on Indian reservations. For more information on FDPIR, visit http://www.fns.usda.gov/programs-and-services.

*Leslie Wheelock is the Director of Tribal Relations at the U.S. Department of Agriculture*

## APAC HOLD ELEGANT GALA AT THE TOWN AND COUNTY CONVENTION CENTER ASIAN PACIFIC AMERICAN COALITION, SAN DIEGO

APAC IS A NON-PROFIT, NON-PARTISAN LOCAL ORGANIZATION WHOSE MISSION IS TO CULTIVATE CIVIC ENGAGEMENT TO FORWARD THE VOICES OF SAN DIEGO'S ASIAN PACIFIC AMERICAN COMMUNITY.

2ND ANNUAL
APAC GALA AWARDS DINNER
MAKING HISTORY TOGETHER
MARCH 14, 2014
TOWN AND COUNTRY CONVENTION CENTER

## REGIONAL TRIBAL SUMMIT TACKLE TRANSPORTATION & ECONOMIC DEVELOPMENT

SANDAG and the Southern California Tribal Chairmen's Association (SCTCA) host the 2014 Regional Tribal Summit. Friday, April 11, 2014 at the Barona Resort Golf Events Center

The Summit engaged local tribes in important policy discussions, including the development of San Diego Forward: The Regional Plan. Scheduled for adoption in 2015, San Diego Forward is an ambitious effort to create a unified vision and implementation program for this region's future. During the one-day event, the SANDAG Board, comprising elected officials from all 18 cities and the county government, sat down with the SCTCA Board, comprising elected leaders from the 17 tribal governments in the region. Together they tackled major policy issues related to transportation, economic development, cultural resources, energy, and environmental conservation. This was the fourth summit between the two associations – the last one was held in 2010.

## Fracking

Continued from page 3

"We are not Mother Earth's failed experiment. We are her immune system. All of the our two legged relatives must stand up for Mother Earth," she stated.

She noted that the oil industry is planning ship dangerously explosive crude oil through Richmond, California – and vowed direct action to stop the trains.

"We will put our bodies on the line and we may have to sit in front of the those trains," Plant said.

"What time is it?," she shouted to the crowd. "It's time to transition!"

In a press release before the rally, Corrina Gould, Elder, Chochenyo/Karkin Ohlone, stated, "We are the ancestors of the future and it is our responsibility to be the care takers of the earth, as was given to us in our original teachings by our ancestors. We must not allow the continuous devastation and degradation of our Mother, Earth. We must be the voices for our children and our grandchildren. Fracking must stop by any means necessary."

"Fracking" is a method of oil and gas production that involves blasting millions of gallons of water, mixed with sand and toxic chemicals, under high pressure deep into the earth to extract oil and gas but it can also pollute local air, water, and endanger the lives of people and wildlife, according to Corine Fairbanks, director of American Indian Movement Southern California Chapter.

Fracking exposes people to radioactivity and numerous toxic chemicals such as lead, arsenic, methanol, and benzene.

"Fracking is also known to trigger seismic activity and earthquakes," said Fairbanks. "Anti-Fracking efforts have been led by California Native Nations throughout the state and on February 28th, 2014 the Los Angeles City Council passed a ban on fracking within its

jurisdiction. This makes Los Angeles the first oil-producing city in California to call a halt to the practice."

Fracking has been documented in 10 California counties -- Colusa, Glenn, Kern, Monterey, Sacramento, Santa Barbara, Sutter, Kings and Ventura. Oil companies have also fracked offshore wells in the ocean near California's coast, from Seal Beach to the Santa Barbara Channel. Fracking may have been used elsewhere in California, since state officials have monitored neither or tracked the practice until recently, according to Fairbanks.

Fairbanks pointed out that Indian people have been fighting against hydraulic fracking and toxic dumping for many years.

"Toxic dumping and hydraulic fracking like efforts have been happening on and around Reservations for decades, causing a multitude of problems for our people; birth defects, and twisted strands of cancer," said Fairbanks. " No one took notice or interest when Native people wanted this stopped, now all of a sudden when it is becoming more of threat in non-Native communities, there is alarm and action."

Gary Mulcahy, a member of the Winnemen Wintu Tribe, emphasized the connection between the raising of Shasta Dam, the peripheral tunnels and building of new dams that many tribal members and Delta folks made with their signs and banners at the event.

"It is interesting how fracking would bring out 4,000 to 5,000 people to a demonstration because this fracking, one way or the other, will hurt the water supply," he noted. "But when you talk about agribusiness taking water drip by drip and drop by drop by building canals, raising dams or building more dams supposed to supply more water than the system can deliver in the first place, only a few voices are heard like a candle in the darkness."

"Fracking involves your water from north to south, from east to west, water that is ultimately controlled by big corporations, including agribusiness and oil companies. If fracking is bad, then so is raising dams, building new dams and building the tunnels," he concluded.

Hopefully, this highly successful rally will be followed by even bigger rallies and demonstrations in Sacramento and throughout the state opposing fracking, the peripheral tunnels, the Shasta Dam raise and the building of new dams.

Adam Scow of Food and Water Watch, one of the co-founders of Californians Against Fracking, said anti-fracking activists will keep building the movement to put pressure on Brown to ban fracking.

"Water is a human right and fracking is a violation of that human right, as are the twin tunnels," Scow concluded.

For more information, go to: http://www.californiansagainstfracking.org

*Caleen Sisk: "We call to Olebis to look down on us and send down the good blessings. We call on sacred Mt. Shasta to help bless us with this sacred water, so it will continue to bring us and our children's, children and so on in to the future with good health and long life for all our relations. We are calling on the water and fire spirits to help bring back the balance in our world, as wild salmon, wolves, beavers and giant trees make their way back. We sing to the water that flows from the sacred spring on Buliyum Puyuk (Mt. Shasta) to the ocean and back again ... waters from Mauna Kea come back and answer the call and the lakes of fire send their blessings. We ask the fires inside of Mt Shasta and all the sacred fires inside the mountains of the world to help us bring understanding and balance to our way of life and change our lives to the good again. Bring back the original taste of water to guide the people and all relatives back to healthy thinking and acting. For nothing will be here with out fresh clean healthy WATER. No air can be produced without waters to grow the trees, the Kelp, ... this world was created in the most perfect functioning way.....but now so much destruction and toxic waste ... for mega money for a few. We pray that our words will be heard and the August Fire and Water Ceremony be good in sending our prayers up the Creator!!!"*

## Indian Peoples of California Class at SDSU

*by Norrie Robbins, SDSU*

This semester, Margaret Field and Mike Connolly (Campo) are co-teaching a class in the American Indian Studies Department at SDSU. It is called Indian Peoples of California, and is well attended. Dr. Norrie Robbins gave a talk called "Ethnobotany from the Point of View of a Paleo-Palynologist." A paleo-palynologist is a specialist in ancient pollen grains. She showed photographs of the plants and the pollen grains of the

medicinal plants that she thinks ancestors brought with them during their long journeys, such as yarrow, dull-leaf barberry, and dogbane. After the talk, Margaret and Mike laid out for the students a feast composed of shawii, dried salmon, nopales, yucca, pine nuts, elderberry jam with chia, and hot elderberry tea.

## Network vs Doctrine

Continued from page 2

the land.

The Network to Freedom recognizes that all human beings embrace the right to self-determination and freedom from oppression. The historical Underground Railroad (UGRR) seeks to address the injustices of slavery and make freedom a reality in the United States. The National Park Service, through shared leadership with local, state, and federal entities, as well as interested individuals and organizations, promote programs and partnerships to commemorate and preserve sites and other resources associated with and educate the public about the historical significance of the UGRR.

National Park Service (NPS) involvement with the Underground Railroad began in response to Public Law 101-628, enacted in November 1990, which directed the agency to study alternatives for commemorating and interpreting the Underground Railroad.

While citizens deal with this dysfunctional social scenario, stakeholders

in San Diego and nationwide are organizing to lock arms with the network of change agents suffering from greed fatigue, and are energized with a sustainable, fair and equitable vision of the future.

During this transformational age the people have drawn a line in the sand to loudly proclaim and announce to the power elite that they have struck a rock.

While impacted and threatened home owners deal with this dysfunctionally insane governmental illegal social scenario they are educating themselves and their allies within the legal and judicial system.

Stakeholders in San Diego and nationwide are organizing their indigenous intelligence and locking arms with the growing network of change agents who are suffering from "Greed Fatigue "who are energized with a sustainable, fair and equitable, earth conscious vision of the future.

The people are joining together to put the corporate banking industry on notice to show the power elite that they have stuck a rock.

## Nevada Rancher Cliven Bundy and the US Bureau of Land Management Standoff

Prior to the recent standoff with the BLM A son of embattled Bunkerville rancher Cliven Bundy spoke to the about his arrest the day before in the ongoing federal roundup of his father's so-called "trespass cattle" northeast of Las Vegas.

Bureau of Land Management officers arrested Dave Bundy, 37, Sunday along state Route 170 near Mesquite.

"They got on their loudspeaker and said that everyone needed to leave," the younger Bundy said in an impromptu press conference Monday with his father outside a 7-Eleven convenience store along North Las Vegas Boulevard. "I stood there and continued to express my First Amendment right to protest and they approached me and said that if I didn't leave, they'd arrest me."

Dave Bundy said he was taking photographs and protesting peacefully at the time.

Natalie Collins, a spokeswoman for the Nevada U.S. Attorney's office, said Bundy was released from custody and given a misdemeanor citation for "refusing to disperse and resisting issuance of a citation/arrest."

Earlier, BLM spokeswoman Kirsten Cannon said someone had been taken into custody to "protect public safety and maintain the peace," but she declined to identify the person.

"The Bureau of Land Management and National Park Service support the public's right to express opinions peacefully and lawfully. However, if an individual threatens, intimidates or assaults another individual or impedes the impoundment, they may be arrested in accordance with local, state or Federal laws," Cannon said in a written statement.

Cliven Bundy, standing next to his son, viewed Dave Bundy's arrest differently.

"What's happening is they had stole cattle from me and now they have taken their prisoner," the father said. "Davy is a political prisoner. That's what you want to call him — he's a political prisoner."

Bundy maintains his arrest was improper because he was along the side of a state highway in a state right-of-way. But BLM officials said he was in an area their agency had closed to the public.

## A New Path Celebrates 15th Anniversary Gala

Gretchen Bergman the Gala committee, board and New Path volunteers organized wonderful Anniversary celebration held at the Harbor Island Sheraton Convention center. The evening affair was an elegant celebratory networking event with many celebrities and community leaders in attendance.

A New PATH works to reduce the stigma associated with addictive illness through education and compassionate support, and to advocate for therapeutic rather than punitive drug policies. A non-profit advocacy organization of parents, concerned citizens, individuals in recovery, healthcare professionals and community leaders working together to educate the public, media and decision makers about the true nature of the disease of addiction, and to expand access to treatment services. We advocate to end discriminatory drug policies that serve as roadblocks to recovery.

A New PATH strives to assure access to quality cost-effective addiction treatment services, lessen the harms associated with addictive illness, reduce recidivism, save lives and move towards a healthier society, free from discriminatory drug policies, violent crime and wasted lives."

The organization grew out of a series of pre-Substance Abuse Summit meetings with parents, Superior Court Judges and officers of the criminal justice system in the Spring of 1999. In 2000, PATH was instrumental in passing Proposition 36 in California, mandating treatment instead of incarceration for non-violent drug offenders. Founding members are Gretchen Burns Bergman, Sylvia Liwerant and Tom O'Donnell.

Our proposals for Therapeutic Justice:
• Long-term mandatory rehabilitation in a structured therapeutic recovery environment for non-violent drug offenders
• If the nature of the crime does not allow for this alternative, sentencing should include immediate placement in a rehabilitation and recovery program within the prison system

Shirley and Hank Murphy attend the New Path Anniversary Celebration.

• Upon release from prison or recovery homes, substance abuse offenders should be mandated to a transitional program in a sober-living environment to prepare them to re-enter society

## Kay Faulconer Ambassador of Education

When Kevin Faulconer took the stage at the Jacobs Center March 3rd to be sworn in as San Diego's 36th Mayor his acceptance speech was gracious and inclusive of all of those who supported him. His tone mellowed when he reached the point in his delivery to express his gratitude and appreciation for his mother Kay. After the obligatory applause the Mayor paused and repeated his adulation and indebtedness to this woman who brought him into the world, nurtured and molded him.

His tender acknowledgment of her indicates a closeness and human bond that is shared.

It was this natural vibration that triggered a phone interview that was facilitated by Matt Aubrey, Communication Directory.

At the appointed hour the interview was underway and covered a delightful overview of this remarkable woman's achievements and vision, not only as a mother but also an academician. As a mother Kay Faulconer may point to her mayor son as a by-product of her influence. Her personal professional career is impressive in its own right.

She is self-assured yet humble as she recites her vitas, which she attributes to her love of reading and her strong Indiana Midwestern heritage. She has a BA in English and Business from Cal State Northridge. She has a double Masters in Public Communication and Business Administration from Pepperdine University and a Doctorate in Higher Educational Psychology from the University of Southern California

As one might imagine she sometimes had to call on grit and determination as she made strides while dealing with modern age challenges, which included single parenthood at one point.

Ultimately her academic success proved to be a path to a remarkable career, which continues.

Her interest in community is pervasive and includes being Dean of Ventura College.

Additionally she employs her skills to build training programs to build bridges between business and education. She is active in a multitude of community programs in Ventura County.

As Chair, of Youth Council, Workforce Investment Board of Ventura County Kay Faulconer inspires youth to achieve. She has been the recipient of many awards both statewide and national. When asked if she attributes her influence and motivation to her sons political success she modestly states with a smiling voice "you will have to ask Kevin that."

Although Kay Faulconer lives in Camarillo, CA. She views San Diego as "her home away from home" as she is here often dealing with grand parenting and family festivities and now dropping in on the Mayor of San Diego.

The interview ended with an amiable commitment to continued dialog.

### Bonnie Dumanis

Voter support for District Attorney Bonnie Dumanis far exceeds support for any of her challengers in the June primary election, but she does not have the 50 percent of votes needed to avoid a runoff, according to a poll released yesterday by the Sycuan Band of the Kumeyaay Nation.

The Sycuan Band of the Kumeyaay Nation has supported Dumanis in the past but has not yet taken a position in the 2014 elections for District Attorney, said Sycuan spokesperson Adam Day.

## Dr. Fred Simon's Prescription for America

Politics is local so the story goes. The principle that a politician's success is directly tied to his ability to understand and influence the issues of his constituents, appealing to the basic and everyday concerns of constituents is pretty simple. It is a formula that fits the style and life view of Fred Simon who is a candidate for Congress in San Diego's 52nd District.

Fred Simon defies all stereotypes of the greed motivated power-mongering tactician that we have had to suffer in contemporary times.

First of all as a local trauma surgeon and businessman Dr. Simon's worldview mirrors the humble and passive Hippocratic medicine based on "the healing power of nature."

Dr. Simon describes himself as a spiritual person.

His connection with humankind results from the intimate connection that he has with his fellows.

He worked for a year in the 80's for the Standing Rock Indian Reservation hospital.

Working in the trauma unit, the ground zero of life or death can be life altering. "The realization that everything is connected is dr.amatically evident in a hospital setting.

The entire staff is an interdependent cohesive unit, from the nurses and attendants to the janitors. We work as one symbiotically," he said.

He would like to take this simple lesson to Washington where the ruling elite have lost this vital connection and have allowed greed to conquer the heartbeat of our nation.

The long-time Coronado resident is a superior multi-tasker. He slips into a campaign mode easily. His elevator pitch is a fine science, highlighting his top priorities, including reforming the Affordable Care Act. "I have worked very hard since I was 10 years old, and have been blessed with a successful career and great family. Now I want to do my part to leave our country in better shape for our childr.en and their childr.en. We have too much debt and not enough focus on our core needs of education, healthcare, and employment opportunities."

Self funded, Dr. Simon has attended dozens of community events and meetings throughout his district over the past few months. He has been walking door-to-door and has personally talked to hundr.eds of taxpayers throughout the district. His campaign team has visited thousands more. Simon has also deployed a Mobile Campaign Office Bus so he can eat, rest, and continue to meet with voters on a daily basis

"Scott Peters and Carl DeMaio are career politicians that have raised hundr.eds of thousands of dollars from Washington D.C. leadership and special interests, so they can't be serious in their efforts to reform our broken system of partisanship and gridlock. I will continue my campaign to bring real reform and common sense solutions to the most serious problems facing our country. I meet voters everyday who tell me they are tired of politics as usual and they continue to support my campaign."

Fred Simon earned his Bachelor of Arts degree from Loma Linda University and his Medical Degree from Creighton University.

He is aware of the monumental task of taking on the power elite. Fred Simon is fortified by his vision and belief in human potential.

He and his wife, Maria, a member of the Coronado School Board, live in Coronado with their three school-aged children.

With the pride that comes with a legacy of the US Navy in his family background, Fred Simon bravely looks to revitalize and awaken the American Dream with a zeal that would please philosophers.

*"We can easily forgive a child who is afraid of the dark; the real tragedy of life is when men are afraid of the light."* – Plato

Dr. Fred Simon is not afraid and he has some strong medicine for our country.

CONTACT:
Jacqui Nguyen, Press Secretary
(858) 999-7706 •
press@fredsimonforcongress.com

# TRADING POST BUSINESS DIRECTORY

## The San Luis Rey Band of Luiseño Indians

Our Ancestors tell us that from the beginning of time our people "ataaxam" have always occupied the San Luis Rey Valley, including the coastline, the neighboring lagoons, the oak forest, the lush meadows, the vernal springs, and the creeks and rivers to the north and south of the valley. The ataaxam harvested the fertile land and sea, and their extensive knowledge of the environment was passed on through culture, songs, stories and dances from generation to generation.

The Spaniards established the Mission San Luis Rey in 1798 as part of the El Camino Real trail between Mission San Diego (1769) and Mission San Juan Capistrano (1776). During this period, the missionaries imposed the name San Luiseño on the original inhabitants of the land. Many ataaxam people suffered and died as a result of the European diseases, forced labor and loss of the way of life due to relocation and conversion to Catholicism.

The Mexican Period (1832 - 1848) inflicted further social, cultural, economic, and political limitations on the ataaxam people by forcing relocations to newly established ranchos. The ataaxam served as laborers on the Rancho Aqua Hedionda, Rancho Buena Vista, Rancho Guajome, Rancho Los Vallecitos de San Marcos, Rancho Santa Margarita y Las Flores, and Rancho Monserrate ranches.

During the American Period and treaty negotiations of 1851, the American government wanted to consolidate all the San Luiseño People in to a single representative group. It was not until the 1870's when a few reservations were established for some of the San Luiseño people near Palomar Mountain. A reservation in the San Luis Rey valley was denied the San Luis Rey Band since many homesteaders believed the coastal land was valuable for farming and ranching and wanted the land for themselves.

Many San Luiseño Indians had no land title documents and no rights under the new American government. Not until 1924 did the United States Congress bestow citizenship on Native Americans. Many of the San Luiseño Indians relocated throughout the states, wherever they could find work and a home.

There are many Luiseño people living today, some on reservations, but most of them in towns and cities. The San Luis Rey Band of Luiseño Indians has kept its identity as a people within the local communities that now exist on ancestral tribal lands. Elective leadership committees and volunteers help to oversee the affairs of the San Luis Rey Band. Today the San Luis Rey Band of Luiseño Indians is constantly being challenged to save and preserve what remains of our great cultural past, and to create and share its heritage with future generations to come. The San Luis Rey Band of Luiseño Indians is associated with the other six Luiseño and Cupeño tribes, La Jolla, Pala, Pauma, Pechanga, Rincon, Saboba and their cultural departments as a Tribal Coalition, working together to preserve our sacred ancestral cultural heritage with local governments and museums.

The San Luis Rey Band of Luiseño Indians would like to thank its members, the Elders, the Veterans, the Luiseño people, the basket weavers, the children, the dancers and singers of the Powwow, the gardeners, the students and our cultural people for sharing their time and making a presence in our community.

## Revealed: Thousands Prosecuted Under Controversial Law of Joint Enterprise

### A new investigation from the Bureau

An eight-month investigation by the Bureau of Investigative Journalism reveals, for the first time, comprehensive data showing at least 1,800 people have been prosecuted for homicide using the little-known law of joint enterprise: a law which experts have called "unclear" and "capable of producing injustice".

The revelation comes as leading members of the judiciary call for its reform. The criminal Law Commissioner, Professor David Ormerod, told the Bureau the case for reform was "overwhelming" as joint enterprise was "unclear" and posed "a risk of injustice".

Professor Jeremy Horder, former criminal Law Commissioner and now at the London School of Economics, said there needs to be major statutory reform of the law.

And Lord Phillips, former Lord Chief Justice, told the Bureau joint enterprise needs reform as it was "capable of producing injustice, undoubtedly".

Until now, there has been no information on the scale of the use of this powerful part of the criminal justice system as no official records are kept. New data collected and analysed by the Bureau shows that since 2005 at least 1,800 people and up to 4,590 have been prosecuted for homicide under joint enterprise – a legal tool that allows the prosecution of multiple defendants for the same crime. This represents at least 17.7% of all homicide prosecutions in this period.

**Indian Voices Media Project is grateful to the American Indian Veterans Association for their continued life-giving support.**

# NEVADA NEWS

For Nevada Information: 619-234-4753 • 619-534-2435

## Moapa Paiute Tribe, LADWP and First Solar Break Ground on 250MW Solar Project

*US Sen. Harry Reid Joins in Ceremony Kicking Off Landmark Power Plant on Tribal Land*

MOAPA, NV— Today, U.S. Senate Majority Leader Harry Reid (NV) joined representatives from the Moapa Band of Paiutes, executives from First Solar, Inc. (Nasdaq: FSLR) and the Los Angeles Department of Water and Power (LADWP), as well as other community, government and energy industry leaders to celebrate the start of construction of the 250 Megawatt (MW)AC Moapa Southern Paiute Solar Project. The project is located on the Moapa River

Indian Reservation just north of Las Vegas, and has a Power Purchase Agreement (PPA) with the LADWP to deliver clean, solar energy for 25 years to the City of Los Angeles.

"Today's event marks a very import milestone for Nevada, the Moapa Band of Paiutes, and tribal nations throughout the country," said Reid. "The Moapa Southern Paiute Solar project is the first utility-scale solar project on tribal land and will deliver much needed economic benefits to the Tribe and Nevada.  It will also create about 400 construction jobs, and replace dirty energy with clean solar power."

The power plant, anticipated to be fully operational by the end of 2015, is expected to generate enough clean solar energy to serve the needs of more than 93,000 homes. This amount of renewable energy will displace approximately 313,000 metric tons of carbon dioxide ($CO_2$) annually—the equivalent of taking about 60,000 cars off the road.

The project will play a key role in LADWP's efforts to build a clean energy future by expanding renewable energy to 33 percent of its total power supply and eliminating coal power. Solar energy from the Moapa plant will contribute 2.4 percent toward LADWP's renewable energy portfolio. This transformational goal also includes reducing energy use by at least 10 percent through energy efficiency measures; expanding local solar

and other forms of distributed generation; initiating a robust demand-response program; and rebuilding local power plants to better integrate renewable energy and be more flexible to meet peak demand.

"The Moapa Southern Paiute Solar Project is a significant step toward the Los Angeles Department of Water and Power's effort to achieve a major transformation of the city's power supply--one that has greater reliance on renewable energy resources and zero coal power," said Marcie L. Edwards, LADWP General Manager.

For the Moapa Band of Paiutes, the utility-scale solar project is an ideal opportunity for the Tribe to create economic opportunities while preserving the land and their cultural heritage. "This is an important step in becoming a leader in Indian Country and will help to create a model for other Tribes to follow," said Aletha Tom, Chairwoman of the Moapa Paiute Tribal Council. "If our small Tribe can accomplish this, then others can also. There are endless opportunities in renewable energy, and Tribes across the nation have the available land on which to build them."

## Sydney Smith Wakes Up Far Removed from the Familiar Surrounding of Her Birthplace. Tahlequah, OK

As a Psychotherapist for the Health Center at the Las Vegas Paiute Tribe the scenic view from her office is the asphalt foundation of the infamous Las Vegas gambling Mecca. She feels that she is following a path mapped out by destiny and guiding forces outside of her.  Her drive to become a clinician is directly related to the loss of her oldest brother to addiction. This life-altering event triggered a highly motivated academic career that has her on the path to a Doctorate in Clinical Psychology from a Depth Psychological Perspective. She has a Master's of Science in Counseling Psychology from Northeastern State University, Tahlequah, OK with emphasis in Psychometrics. Her Bachelors' Degree is also from Northeastern State University in Clinical Psychology. In addition she is a Licensed Professional Counselor (LPC), Licensed Drug and Alcohol Counselor, National Certified Gambling Counselor (NCGC) and a National Board Certified Counselor (NBCC)

As a Behavioral Health Therapist for the Las Vegas Paiute tribe she provides Individual, Family, and Group Psychotherapy focusing on both mental heath issues as well as addictive disorders.

Sydney Smiths passion relates to addiction, particularly gambling. Pathological gambling is a common

disorder that is associated with both social and family costs. The condition is classified as an impulse control disorder(addictive disorder-Pathological gambling was moved from Impulse control to addictive disorder according to new DSM-V which came out in May 2013. They now understanding this disease holds place with the other addictions) , with sufferers exhibiting many similarities to those who have substance addictions.  "This is a high risk category that has severe consequence in our community as well as devastating affects on the lives of individuals and family's living with problem gambling." Problem gambling is a powerful chronic and progressive disease. Often a lack of awareness about this addiction prevents individuals from seeking help. There are specialized treatment programs and resources available for both the gambler as well as the family. Due to the consequences of problem gambling on the family it is especially important to know they to can receive help.

The Tudinu (or Desert People), ancestors of the Las Vegas Paiute Tribe, occupied the territory encompassing part of the Colorado River, most of Southeastern Nevada and parts of both Southern California and Utah.

Outsiders who came to the Paiutes' territory often described the land as harsh, arid and barren; however, the Paiutes developed a culture suited to the diverse land and its resources. In 1826, trappers and traders began crossing Paiute

land, and these crossings became known in 1829 as the Old Spanish Trail (a trade route from New Mexico to California). In 1848, the United States government assumed control over the area.

White settlers and a booming railroad town brought an end to the Paiutes' free movement and traditional way of life, making them landless laborers in their own land.

On December 30, 1911, ranch owner

Helen J. Stewart deeded 10 acres of her land in downtown Las Vegas to the Paiutes, establishing the Las Vegas Paiute Colony. Since that time the tribe has successfully established sustainable retail businesses (Rose the Paiute also has a reservation north of town as well as the Beautiful Snow Mountain Golf Course) with many more on the drawing board.

With Sydney Smiths sensitive contributions as a Clinical Therapist for the Health Center at the Las Vegas Paiute Tribe, the community can deal with the increasing social ills with understanding and appreciation for the unique cultural needs of Native Americans.

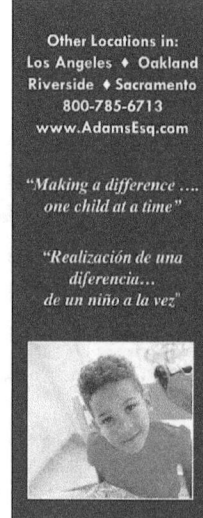

# FirstSolar's 250 Megawatt Photovoltaic Project at the Moapa Paiute Reservation

During this past March recess, I was honored to attend the groundbreaking of FirstSolar's 250 megawatt photovoltaic project at the Moapa Paiute Reservation. Anyone who has followed my career representing Nevada in Congress for long enough is sure to find that I have been a staunch advocate of conserving Nevada's wilderness, public lands, air quality, and our beautiful Lake Tahoe that we are fortunate to share with California. Clean energy is important to me. Not only does clean reliable energy keep our air breathable and limit the amount of greenhouse gasses released into the atmosphere, but the investment in domestic renewable energy also limits our dependence on foreign oil. Las Vegas, and Nevada are leading the way on deploying clean renewable energy. Recently, the world renowned Welcome to Fabulous Las Vegas sign started receiving its power from solar energy. Currently, there are projects underway all over Nevada that continue to show these industries are growing. In Moapa, the partnership between the Moapa Band of Paiutes, First Solar, the Federal Government, and Los Angeles, is a powerful example of how we can work together to achieve something big. This project in particular will deliver badly needed economic benefits to the Tribe, and to Nevada. It will create 400 construction jobs, and replace dirty energy with clean solar power. Nevada is a clean energy leader. We still have more work to do, but I'm pleased to say that we are definitely on the right track.

During that same March recess while I was in Nevada, I helped unveil a new report showing that clean energy investment in our state is nearing $5 billion. The majority of that investment has been made in solar, geothermal and wind projects in recent years, and the Moapa project will certainly add to that number. The Moapa Tribe in particular is showing the country that there is a better way to create energy, through the power of the sun. And I look forward to working with any and all Tribes, companies, or the like, that want to invest in clean, renewable energy right here in Nevada.

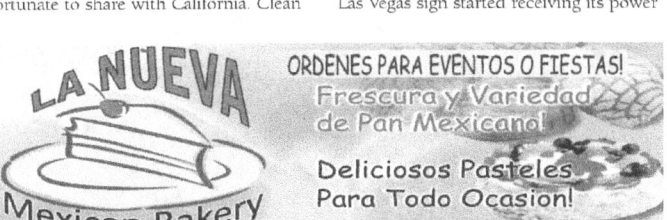

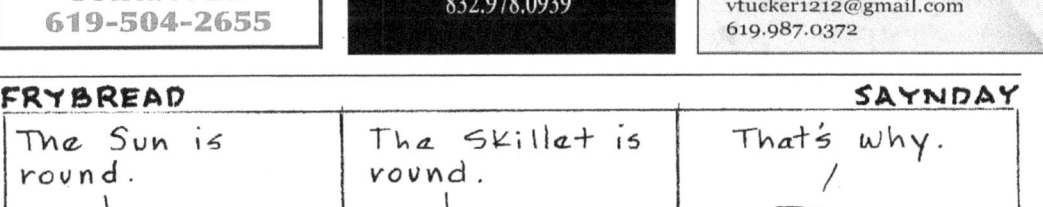

www.indianvoices.net

OUR 28TH YEAR          MULTI-CULTURAL NEWS GLOBAL NETWORK          MAY 2014

# Jane Dumas Revered Kumeyaay Elder Walks On

*Admired for her vast knowledge of plants, herbs and ancient remedies.*

The tiny chapel on the Jamul Reservation was filled with friends and family of Jane Dumas for a rosary followed by an all night wake.

St. Francis of Xavier Church, on Highway 94 is a humble and quaint structure that reflects the custom and tradition of the gentle Kumeyaay Nation who at one time lived throughout this region. The Kumeyaay people who live on and off reservations share a heritage that goes back, in their words, to the beginning of time. Jane Dumas embodied this resilient culture. She practiced and taught the gathering and preparation of acorns, making of various tools, agave harvesting and roasting. The importance of sharing and maintaining her Kumeyaay cultural heritage and passing it along to future generations was important to Jane Dumas. Those that knew and loved her were recipients of this knowledge. She

did not consider herself to be a teacher, "I'm just someone who knows the old ways and hope they will not be forgotten."

Those in attendance shared words of memory and reflection. Anthony Pico emphasized the power that this small woman had. His admiration for her was evident. "Although she was small in stature Jane Dumas was a power house. She accomplished more than any statesman or world leader could have just by her gentle but strong will." In 2006, a flag representing the Kumeyaay-Diegueño Nation was flown for the first time at Cabrillo National Monument in Point Loma. The idea for the flag came from Mrs. Dumas, who had prayed in her native language and blessed the opening ceremonies for years at the annual Cabrillo Festival. "Through her sheer will and determination this act of statesmanship represented a power that exceeded that of any world leader and strengthens our sovereignty" Pico stated.

Norrie Robbins reflected, "She taught us Ethno botany at Kumeyaay Community College. She always said that her mother was the healer; her job as a kid was to go collect the plants and bring them to her mother.

She said that her mother didn't tell her what they were for. But as the course progressed, she shared so much knowledge of the plants and how they healed us."

Ethnobotanist Richard Bugbee said, "I will miss my teacher. Her spirit has been lifted. Now I talk to her in the stars." For decades, Mrs. Dumas spoke in classrooms and at public events, sharing knowledge of Kumeyaay culture, language and medicine. She taught ethnobotany classes through Cuyamaca College and the Kumeyaay Community College on the Sycuan Indian Reservation.

In 1981, she helped found the San Diego American Indian Health Center, working there until 2000 as a traditional

SEE **Jane Dumas**, page 2

---

## Dwight Lomayesva Honored at American Indian Heritage Pow Wow

One of the most influential leaders in San Diego County is Dwight Lomayesva. A layer himself, he lives with is lawyer wife Devon on the Santa Ysabel Reservation. They puzzled over he lack of Indian students in college, and came up with a brilliant idea: the American Indian Recruitment Program (AIR). The (AIR) program started in 1993. He decided to partner with SDSU and the Dept. of American Studies to bring reservation high school students to college campuses. The program grew and grew and now it is affiliated not only with SDSU, but also UCSD, SCU-San Marcos, and Palomar and Cuyamaca Colleges.

Since its creation, more that 1000 students have been served with a majority pursuing higher education. AIR has helped many "at risk" students graduate and pursue higher education. As a result, in 2009,the program was honored with the Pacific Sociological Association's Social Conscience Award and in 2010; KPBS/Union Bank honored the program and director with the Local Heroes Award for community service. AIR students have attended Stanford, Cal State San Marcos, Northern Arizona

University, UC Davis, Humbolt State University, SDSU the University of San Diego and many more. Today many past students serve on Tribal Councils as tribal police, nurses, teachers and more. The success has come directly through the implementation of methods developed and the cooperative efforts that have been established with the native community.

The AIR program as created to address the lack of American Indian participation within higher education to promote student participation. In the beginning many statistics showed American Indian fell far behind the majority of the U.S. population. Today, although Indians have gained ground in many areas they still remain behind the rest of American society. The AIR program is working to bring greater success.

We are so happy to attend Dwight's honoring at the American Indian Heritage POW Wow where he was presented with a Pendelton blanket, and other gifts from many people who are so grateful for his actions in regards to their children. Indeed, one happy person could make a giant difference in this world.

## Jane Dumas

Continued from page 1

medicine specialist. Since 1986, she was a board member for the Indian Human Resource Center.

In 2002, she was among the first women nominated for induction into the San Diego County Women's Hall of Fame. On Oct. 1, 2004, the city of San Diego honored her by proclaiming it Jane Dumas Day. In 2005, the California State Society of Daughters of the American Revolution named her its American Indian of the Year for her social and cultural efforts on behalf of her Kumeyaay band and other American Indians.

She grew up in a dirt-floored hut on a backcountry ranch, hauling water by the bucket and eating honey and Manzanita berries for treats. A member of East County's Jamul Band of Kumeyaay Indians, she spoke Kumeyaay and Spanish before learning English in a one-room school in Potrero, where she was ostracized by classmates for being a "savage."

From her mother, a revered medicine woman and midwife, she absorbed everything there was to know about native plants and their power to heal. Mrs. Dumas made it her mission to share what she learned at her mother's side, to teach the language and culture of her people, and to advocate for the Native American community of San Diego.

"Her whole life was dedicated to helping everybody, not just the natives," said her grandson Brian Dumas. "She felt it was just as important to show the white man why we do what we do. She was a teacher right up to her last day."

"Jane was a well-respected member of our Tribe, and was known throughout San Diego County and the State of California," read a statement issued by the Jamul Indian Village Tribal Council. "Jane's knowledge and expertise of the Kumeyaay culture will be greatly missed."

Born Jane Thing on June 25, 1924, on Smith Ranch in Barrett, she was one of five children born to Ambrosia Thing and Isabelle Cuero.

Mrs. Dumas is survived by a son, Dale Dumas, of San Felipe, Baja California; a brother, Adolph Thing, of Jacumba; three grandchildren; and five great-grandchildren. She was predeceased by her daughter, Daleane Adams, in 2009, and her husband of 44 years, Cleo Dumas, in 1985.

Jane Dumas is remembered as a very special Native American with a lineal descendent of Chief Manuel Hatam She grew up in a dirt-floored home, hauling water by the bucket. She spoke Kumeyaay and Spanish before English. Jane Dumas is an enrolled member of the Jamul Band of Kumeyaay Indians in the East County. She was a well-known and widely respected elder, teacher, and leader in San Diego's American Indian community and in San Diego at-large. In 1981, Jane helped found the San Diego American Indian Health Center, and since 1986 she has been described as an "anchor, leader, peacemaker, and bridge between Indian and non-Indians in the areas of medicine and education."

As a cherished community member those who surrounded Jane Dumas shared an exceptional spiritual connection.

Rest in Peace Aunt Jane.

## US Department of Energy Office of Indian Policy Meet at Grant Hotel

Alternatives San Diego. Convened by Pilar Thomas, US Dept. of Energy Deputy Director the conference encouraged sharing and communication.

American Indian leaders from around the county came together to share information, network and socialize around environmental issues. at the Grant Hotel May 14th.

Mesa Grande Vice Chairman Virgil Oyos who is intensely involved with environmental issue at his reservation meets with Eddie Price, GRID

Virgil Oyos and Eddie Price networking.

## Partnership Created

New America Media is proud to announce the launch of our editorial partnership with The University of California. This partnership comes at a critical time for the state, amid massive demographic shifts and an increase in Californians enrolling in our colleges and universities. As California's premier public institution of higher education,

The University of California is uniquely positioned to both reflect and shape these profound changes.

As part of this partnership, over the next six months NAM will release weekly stories from the UC Newsroom for syndication to our media network. Translations for relevant stories will also be made available in Spanish, Chinese and Korean. NAM will also syndicate a monthly series profiling stories of student success.

**Multicultural News from an American Indian Perspective**

### PUBLISHED BY BLACKROSE COMMUNICATIONS
*Member, American Indian Chamber of Commerce*

Email: rdavis4973@aol.com
Website: www.indianvoices.net
Editorial Board: Rose Davis

| | | | |
|---|---|---|---|
| Editor: | Rose Davis | Writer: | Jaclyn Bissonette |
| Managing Editor: | Yvonne-Cher Skye | Entertainment Writer/ | |
| Outside Support: | Mel Vernon | Photographer LA/SD: | Rochelle Porter |
| LV Entertainment Writer: | Z. Z. Zorn | Reporter de Espectaculos: | Omar DeSantiago |
| Associate Editor: | Sis Mary Muhammad | Reporter de Espectaculos: | Michelle Banuet |
| Writer: | Kathleen Blavatt | Proofreader: | Mary Lou Finley |
| Writer: | Roy Cook | Graphic Artist: | Elaine Hall |
| Writer: | Marc Snelling | Staff Photographer: | Abel Jacome |
| Writer: | Scott Andrews | | |

Endeavor Media Group
André Haynes
3675 S. Rainbow Blvd., Ste 107
Las Vegas, NV 89103
702-305-0973 •
www.emgnv.com

111 South 35th St.
San Diego, CA 92113
(619) 234-4753
(619) 534-2435 (cell)
Fax: (619) 512-4534

**Member of the Society of Professional Journalists**
**Member of New America Media**

## San Diego Women's History Museum

**Karen Vigneault**
Iipay, Santa Ysabel

Howka, I am working on an exhibit for the San Diego women's history museum. The exhibit will be for the month of Nov.It is all about the contributions and history of Kumeyaay women I am hoping you can send this out to all the people on your mailing list/ website..here is what I am looking for ... Thanks, Karen

1. names and pictures of kumeyaay women that were in the military
2. names, pics and reservation of all kumeyaay women 90 years old or older
3. names and pics of female kumeyaay tribal leaders-dates they held office and reservation
4. names and pics of any of our women that participated in the pan am expo
5. examples of women's language word
6. artisans that would be interested in a free both at the museum for a weekend, need to know their names and what kinds of art they will be selling
7. any other ideas of how our women were a part of the history of San Diego and or represent our people.

*Karen Vigneault - MLIS, Librarian,*
*Santa Ysabel Tribal Library,*
*PO Box 130, Santa Ysabel, Ca. 92070*
*www.santaysabeltriballibrary.blogspot.com*
*Founder, KUMEYAAY HISTORICAL SOCIETY MLIS*
*Leader NATIONS OF THE 4 DIRECTIONS*
*Karen runs a virtual library for her reservation on her tribal blog at:*
*www.santaysabeltriballibrary.blogspot.com*

## Zapatista Teacher Dead, 15 Seriously Wounded in Deadly Chiapas Ambush - May 7, 2014

Jose Luis Solís López, a teacher in the Zapatista's "Little School" (La Escuelita) was targeted and murdered, and at least 15 Zapatistas seriously injured, in an ambush in which the leaderships of the paramilitary group called CIOAC-Histórica, the Green Ecological Party, the National Action Party [PAN] and the Revolutionary Institutional Party [PRI] are all implicated in directing on Friday, May 2, 2014. The same attackers damaged or destroyed both the autonomous Mayan school and the local health Zapatista Good Governance Council in La Realidad has turned this issue over to the General Command of the EZLN so that it is "investigated and justice is done."

## Relatives Say Bodies were Exhumed During Excavation for Jamul Casino

SAN DIEGO, CA - A lawsuit filed by two Native Americans in San Diego Superior Court alleges the bodies of deceased relatives were exhumed during excavation of a site for an Indian casino in Jamul, a lawyer said Tuesday.

Walter Rosales and Karen Toggery claim the bodies of Rosales' mother, brother and son were exhumed, as were Toggery's mother and son. Each had been buried along with various sacred and cultural artifacts, according to the lawsuit filed against Caltrans.

The lawsuit was brought against the state agency -- the casino is not named as a defendant -- because Caltrans allowed the bodies to be dumped on land it owns in Otay Mesa, along with other material from the excavation, according to attorney Patrick Webb, who represents Rosales and Toggery.

A Caltrans official said the agency could not comment on pending litigation.

The plaintiffs, who are seeking unspecified damages, witnessed the bodies as they were interred on land that has long been a cemetery, according to the lawsuit filed last week.

"The law still respects that people are interred and won't willy-nilly allow them to be dug up and moved," Webb said.

Glenn Revell, president of the Jamul Action Committee stated that Rosales and Toggery were deeply hurt by what has happened.

"The destruction of their home was crippling; you can only imagine how their loved ones' remains have been dug up, taken just this side of Mexico and deposited at the [Interstate] 905 and [state Route] 125 interchange as so much fill dirt, has been a crushing blow. It's an absolutely shameful situation," said Revell.

The land is being graded to make way for the $360 million Hollywood Casino at the Jamul Indian Village, about 20 miles east of downtown San Diego along state Route 94.

The three-story gaming and entertainment facility, which is slated to open next year, will encompass around 200,000 square feet, with more than 1,700 slot machines; 50 live table games, including poker; multiple restaurants, bars and lounges; and an enclosed below-grade parking structure with more than 1,900 spaces.

The development was fought by nearby residents for several years, led by county Supervisor Dianne Jacob.

The county of San Diego sued to stop construction, but a hearing is not scheduled until Aug. 22, according to county lawyer Tom Bunton.

The county lawsuit was filed in San Diego but was transferred to Sacramento and merged with litigation filed by residents of the area, he said.

## AIVA (American Indian Veterans Association) Present Colors to Open the National Indian Gaming Association Conference

### National Indian Gaming Association Meet In San Diego

It was a lively and interactive gathering at the Convention Center in San Diego. Celebrities dignitaries, movers and shakers in the gaming industry were all there.

After much preliminary celebration the event kicked off with a ribbon

cutting ceremony, and presentation of the colors by the Pala Band of Mission Indians American Indian Veterans Association Color Guard. Energized with opening remarks by Chairman Ernie Stevens and Bird Singing the crowd was ready and eager to explore the carnival like cavern of the convention hall, showcasing the latest in gaming widgets and gadgets. Hundreds of displays lured the eager conventioneer. To see each display would have required a

personal GPS.

After intrepid exploration Indian Voices finally found display 907 which housed the exhibition and showcase for Vantiv Gaming Solutions. After introductions we found a moderately safe zone for conversation.

The brief interview revealed an astonishing bit of futuristic economic and financial information

Joseph Feldkamp, Vantiv Market planning and Joseph Pappano, Managing Director are at the forefront of one of the most trusted and respected organizations in the payment processing industry, as well as the nation's largest PIN debit acquirer. Vantiv has driven many of the changes that prompted the shift from cash to electronic payments, and that innovative spirit continues to be the strength of the company. As innovators, thought leaders, boundary pushers. Vantiv is changing the face of payments. This

is particularly of interest to the gaming industry. Indian Voices eagerly looks forward to learning more about Vantiv and how the company can interact with the emerging Indian Gaming community, which seems to be on the horizon.

# California Secretary of State Candidate Forum

May 6, 2014 a forum presented by the California Voting Rights Project, Common Cause and the League of Women's Voters of California Education Fund took place at the Jacobs Center Euclid Ave in San Diego. The two-hour event made possible with the generous support of the Color of Democracy Fund featured seven candidates vying for the position of California Secretary of State. Ray Almond and Pete Peterson represented Republicans. Democratic Candidates were Derek Cressman, Jeffrey Drobman and Alex Padilla. Dan Schnur was the Independent candidate and David S. Curtis was the lone Green Party candidate.

Lori Shellenberger, ACLU Director of California Voting Rights Project welcomed the large diverse audience. Janis Hirohama former president of the League of Women Voters and Jonathan Stein, Vice Chair of the California Common Cause provided an overview. Dana Littlefield who covers San Diego

County Superior Court for the San Diego Union Tribune skillfully moderated the forum. A San Diego native, she earned her bachelors degree in mass communications from the University of Florida..

The program began with opening statements from each candidate then questions from the moderator. Each candidate was given two minutes for closing remarks and to wrap up a very informative and educational.

# St. Louis County Board Backs Bilingual Road Signs

*by John Myers*

The St. Louis County Board on Tuesday gave preliminary approval to erecting new road signs with both Anishinabe and English words identifying some lakes.

The bilingual signs will go up along county roads at two lakes within the Fond du Lac Reservation, but also in St. Louis County. Officials of the Fond du Lac Band of Lake Superior Chippewa asked for the bilingual signs, and the band will cover their cost.

"Language preservation is integral to the preservation of identity and culture," Karen Diver, chairwoman of the Fond du Lac Band, told the News Tribune on Tuesday. "Bilingual signage helps us share our culture as well as signify its importance."

The County Board's Committee of the Whole approved the concept. The full board is likely to give final approval at its May 13 meeting at the Duluth courthouse. The resolution was amended to also allow the county to work with other Ojibwe bands to offer the same agreement.

"These would be the standard white on green highway signs for lake names, but would have both English and Ojibwe (Anishinabe) language on them," said Jim Foldesi, the county's public works director.

"These lakes are adjacent to St. Louis County highways within the reservation boundaries, and we are the only entity allowed to put signing within" the road right of way, Foldesi said.

Foldesi called it "truly a cooperative agreement," in which the band will cover the cost of the new signs, and the county agrees to maintain them. The agreement is flexible, he said, and additional bilingual signs could go up within the reservation in the future.

Carlton County already has passed a similar ordinance, said Mike Tardy, Carlton County engineer. Jason Hollinday, planning director of the Fond du Lac Band, said those signs went up last year on Perch, Cedar, Rice Portage and Miller lakes in Carlton County.

Bilingual signs are common in other parts of the state, including Bemidji, where there is a large Ojibwe community and where more than 150 buildings have signs in both English and Anishinabe, including schools, public buildings and private buildings.

# Italian Hemp Seeds Held Hostage

Kentucky farmers are ready to begin planting hemp. The problem is getting their hands on the seeds. Senate Republican Leader Mitch McConnell, who wrote the Farm Bill language for legalization of industrial hemp and is seeking re-election in Kentucky, has joined the fight, asking the Drug Enforcement Administration "to release 250 pounds of Italian hemp seeds that they have held for more than a week by U.S. Customs in Louisville," Janet Patton reports for the Lexington Herald-Leader.

"The Kentucky Department of Agriculture imported the seeds for university research projects, but the DEA has blocked their release, saying the state needs a controlled-substance import permit," Patton writes. "State Agriculture Commissioner James Comer on Wednesday filed a lawsuit in federal court in Louisville to force the Justice

Department to turn them over. A hearing on the motion could come as early as Friday." DEA is part of the department; it deems illegal the seeds of cannabis sativa, which when raised for hemp contains very little of the psychoactive ingredient found in marijuana.

The Farm Bill "allows state departments of agriculture, in conjunction with colleges and universities, to grow industrial hemp for research purposes," as long as it contains less than 0.3 percent of the psychoactive ingredient, Patton notes. The DEA contends "that the language legalizes growing but does not address importation, so a controlled-substance permit is still required." They also "told Comer's office in a letter that the state and the universities cannot assign their authorities to grow hemp to private farmers."

"However, the state Agriculture Department, in its lawsuit, argues that the Farm Bill language specifically supersedes other federal laws, including the Controlled Substances Act and import/export restrictions."

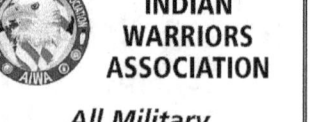

Black Path Commentary: Critical Analysis on Culture, Community, & Struggle

# Wake Up, Clean Up, Stand Up, the Liberation Ethics of Malcolm X: Reconstructing Ourselves in a Context of Optimal Health

*by Min. Tukufu Kalonji*

During this month of May, we recognize our women on Mother's Day, (May 11th), we reflect upon our global and domestic struggles and their achievements during African Liberation Day (May 25th), and without a doubt we pay homage to Minister Malcolm X, (May 19th,), the day of his birth. Thus, May is a time of marking for us to reflect upon the life and legacy of Malcolm X. Malcolm X, fire prophet, moral teacher, cultural critic, and classic living symbol of Black manhood worked, studied and struggle to build a righteous world for his people and others oppressed, may the good he gave us last forever!

Exceptionally perceptive of America' hypocrisy that he referred to as not the American dream but rather the American nightmare was and remains a timely critique. The hypocrisy Malcolm conducted his analysis on of America was and is wide ranging. Without question; this hypocrisy Malcolm teaches us on is empirically substantiated by the crisis of continued reductions in funding and services in and for education, mental and medical health care, and other critical human services. While increasingly, poverty spreads across the country like the Stutnex and Conficker viruses; considered to be the top two most dangerous virus plaguing cyberspace; the continued funding and expansion of government and private prison facilities, and the disease management system, commonly called health care system continues to keep America sick and the pharmaceutical companies and their allies with fat pockets.        Malcolm X taught us so many invaluable lessons on many issues. Of those lessons, Malcolm X gave us a straightforward and manageable prescription to follow that would and is efficient in every aspect of our life. It is summed up in his call for Black people and other oppressed peoples to Wake Up, Clean Up, and Stand Up! The liberation ethics of Malcolm X takes in consideration three essential acts of our thought and conduct: (1) bearing witness to truth_ (2) making a lived reality of our current and future history, the certainty of a recovered and reconstructed self, and, (3) engaging the struggle to correct the deficient and undignified behavior resulting from cultural psychosis in order for us to establish and reaffirm our freedom and justice in all areas of our life; which is vital in our realizing the fullness of ourselves and the inherent potential within each of us in all areas of human thought and flourishing.

Malcolm's call for us to Wake Up is a call for our deeply engaging in an educational and transformational process. Waking up is bearing truth, emphasizing the good, exposing wrong doing, and doing that which is right and good. Waking up involves in-depth study of us as a people, society, and indeed the world. Critical to waking up via our collective and personal study, we are obligated and must adhere to the critical lessons of our history. As Malcolm X teaches; "of all our studies, history is best to reward our research." the emphasis on history by Malcolm X, is not just a reading on a record of dates and deaths; rather it is for us to seek out the best practices we have achieved throughout history and emulate or reconstruct ourselves based on those best practices.

In the context of our obtaining optimal health, this study or waking up involves at a minimum two specific focal points. This focus is on first understanding and asserting ourselves in the world, which is to mean; to know our beginnings, our development, and achievements as a people in the past and present; so that we build for the future. Secondly, wake up involves us expanding this historical and awesome legacy of African peoples into every area of our life, and rationally adapting those lessons to our current social context. Therefore, in a context of our health, we should examine the means in which we lived healthier lives even in the midst of the holocaust of African enslavement. Surely if we were healthier during the height of the holocaust of our enslavement, we have no business now being the segment of society with the highest rates of health disparity. This study of necessity would be engaging practices of growing our own food, or minimally buying more produce. Also would be examining the benefits of our being physically active and its rewarding results; due to the nature of physical work and just in general. For example, although it was forced upon us, we walked much more in the past than we do now due to modernization, and for the most part we did not live a sedentary lifestyle.

Clean Up, the second pillar of Malcolm X's liberation ethics is the transformation that evolves from the waking up or education. Clean up entails our taking the lessons on living healthy from our past and bringing it to now; subsequently beginning a process of transformation. Malcolm X often used the concept of prison as a metaphor to describe the situation of Afro Americans. He implied that just as those in actual prisons are expected to "rehabilitate" themselves as a condition for their release, Black people have to transform themselves as a condition for securing our freedom from oppression. And nonetheless this is apropos for our libration from the insidious conditions of America's disease management system and its related mis-education that has resulted in our collective less oppression in the form of disproportionate rates of health disparity.

Clean up would of necessity include as a minimum, eating for nutrition, rather than fun, family, friends, or other non essential social reasons. Also a brief study of African dietary habits would illustrate the eating of more fruits, vegetables, and raw foods as opposed to eating dead animal as is the normative practices in western society. This is not to say that in ancient and modern times Africans (domestically and diasporan) didn't consume dead animals. However, naturopathic healers such as Dr. Sebi and Dr. Goss have overwhelming evidence that as a people, our most natural eating habits involved eating much healthier than what we do now, especially those of us in the wilderness of north America. Again and logically following, cleaning up would necessitate our exercising on a regular basis, getting proper rest, learning how and detoxifying our body through herbal cleansing fasting ,etc; and practicing effective stress management.

SEE **Optimal Health**, page 10

---

# Black Health Associates Examine Covered California from an Impact and Prevention Perspective

SAN DIEGO, CA – "Now That We Have health Insurance, What do We Do With It?" This is the question being asked in a community forum hosted by the San Diego Black Health Associates on Saturday, June 7, 2014 at the Jacobs Center for Neighborhood Innovation. The forum will be held from 9:00 am until 12 noon. The goal of this forum is to better examine the processes necessary to orient health insurance into the minds and behaviors of residents who have not had their own health insurance or access to health care.

"For many African Americans, access to health care has meant relying on local emergency rooms or charity care for diagnosis and treatment", explained Clovis Honore, President of the group. "With Covered California implemented, we want to make sure that community members get the annual physicals they need and begin the process of monitoring and improving their own health behaviors". Mr. Honore also felt that this is the time to begin to promote prevention and wellness into African American communities.

For more than 30 years, the Black Health Associates. have provided direct service programs, sponsored community education and information forums, conducted public policy projects, engaged in research and provided professional development to its members. The group has been particularly interested in counter-acting the e-cigarette thrust that is marketing electronic cigarettes. "We feel the marketing of e-cigarettes will stimulate addictive smoking behaviors at urban teenagers", Mr. Honore noted.

"We see that prevention and health information is not a popular subject in certain communities", explained Denise Adams-Simms, Executive Director of the SDBHA. "If we are successful in convincing our residents to lose weight, to exercise more often and to stop smoking, there will be fewer heart attacks, fewer strokes and fewer kidney dialysis visits. With the Affordable Care Act comes an opportunity for greater reliance on family-inspired prevention techniques to improve care. The message we promote is to help heal ourselves through positive health behaviors".

The forum will review 10 Essential Benefits of Covered California in the six (6) health insurance plans being offered for enrollment in San Diego. These plans include Kaiser Permanente Health Plan, Sharp Health Plan, Health Net of California, Molina Health Plan, Anthem Blue Cross of California, and Blue Shield of California. Representatives from each of these plans has been invited to attend. Access to health care is also available through the Medi-Cal plan (newly offered to single individuals). Applications for Medi-Cal will be accepted throughout the year, while access to other plans will begin during the next open enrollment period, which starts in October 2014.

Finally, the most important question to be answered will be how to promote prevention into our lives and the lives of our family members? Clovis Honore noted, "People do not become diabetic overnight. They become diabetic over time. We want our constituents to monitor their weight, their blood pressure and their blood sugar. We will note techniques that will improve outcomes at the forum". SDBHA also wants consumers to adopt healthy habits that save money and eliminate unnecessary trips to the doctor. "We will use this forum to introduce out "Fifteen Health Commandments" broadly to the residents of San Diego".

Light refreshments will be served, but seating is limited. Please contact SDBHA at (619) 906-4002 or at info@sdbha.org for reservations. The deadline is May 31, 2014.

To improve the quality of life of those who recognize themselves and choose to be recognized by others as "Indigenous Peoples of Color of the Americas" and in support of The American Indian Rights and Resources Organization (AIRRO).

# Black American Anti-Imperialist Fighters in the Philippine American War

*by Gill H. Boehringer*

*We are offered constant examples of Black sacrifice in the U.S. Armed Forces. But seldom do we hear of those Black soldiers that deserted to fight on the anti-imperialist side in the brutal U.S. war against Filipino independence, at the turn of the 20th century. As one journalist of the day put it, "the negro soldiers were in closer sympathy with the aims of the native population than they were with those of their white leaders and the policy of the United States."*

*"The Negroes deserted in scores and for the purpose of joining the insurgents, and many of them...became leaders and fought the white troops or their former comrades with zest and ability."*

The part played by black American troops in the imperialist acquisition of the Philippines has been a subject of commentary for the past century. Much of it has been praise for the loyal and positive contribution they made even in the face of the pervasive racism they experienced both in the US and in the military overseas. I want to look at a relatively little known and less remembered aspect of their participation in the "regime change" which the Americans wrought in the Philippine War. Not all the black troops (or white for that matter) remained in the US lines. A number took the decision to desert, and some of those defected to the Filipino side. It is appropriate to remember those anti-imperialist heroes from an earlier period of American expansionism and "regime change" at a time when the United States has once again, but even more dangerously to the rest of the world, shown itself to be intent on pursuing such unjustified and harmful foreign adventures.

Many commentators on the American war against the Filipino Republic have referred to the four black Regiments amongst the military forces occupying the Philippines after the defeated Spanish had sold the territory to the United States and withdrawn their troops. It is estimated that of the 125,000 troops who participated on the American side, up to 7,000 were African American. Some commentators have written about Corporal David Fagen, a black soldier who, in November, 1899, defected to the Filipino cause. Welcomed by the Army of Liberation and given the rank of Lieutenant, he fought in the Brigade of General Urbano Lacuna in central Luzon. Lacuna was thought by the Americans to be a very good military leader, one of the best after General Antonio Luna who was, unfortunately, assassinated following a serious disagreement with General Emilio Aguinaldo's policies. Aguinaldo was Commander of all Filipino forces and the President of the Republic, and was sometimes referred to as "Dictator."

*"Even after the surrender of the Lacuna Brigade the Americans could not capture nor kill David Fagen."*

As a guerrilla leader, Fagen proved highly skillful, harassing the Americans successfully for two years. His valor and guile brought military successes and led to his promotion to the rank of Captain. He gained considerable notoriety through accounts of his activities regularly published in the Manila Times, and in the USA where his exploits were covered by the New York Times and several of the San Francisco papers. Even after the surrender of the Lacuna Brigade on the 19th of May 1901, which left Fagen more vulnerable than he had been previously, the Americans could not capture nor kill him. It was the shrewd, if deceitful, Colonel (later Brigadier-General) Frederick Funston, captor of General Aguinaldo, who arranged the offer of a reward of $600 for him, "dead or alive."

There are many different versions of the end of Fagen's guerrilla days, in early December 1901. It is possible that he was killed by Anastacio Bartolome, a former insurrecto in the Lacuna Brigade, who claimed the reward. But there is some doubt about this "supposed" killing, as official American records refer to it, although they did "close" the case. It is also possible that his death was faked according to a plan conjured up by Fagen and Bartolome. After the surrender of General Lacuna, with his Brigade, resistance to the Americans had collapsed in Central and Northern Luzon. With such a price on his head and Funston's spies all over the region, it may have been Fagen's choice to retire in the mountains to live a quiet-and presumably longer-life with his Filipina wife.

Interestingly, though Fagen became the most famous of the black American guerrilla fighters, it seems there was another who joined the Filipino forces while the American black regiments were still in the USA. We do not know his name, nor how he found his way into the front lines in the early days of the war. The only reference to the presence of this "Unknown Soldier" appears to be in Funston's fascinating "Memories of Two Wars," an account not only of his very significant contribution to the crushing of the Philippine Republic but, contradictorily, of his volunteer service as a filibustero on the side of the Cubans in their struggle with the Spanish! According to Funston, on the 6th of February 1899, less than two full days after the start of the war at Manila, American troops of the Twentieth Kansas Infantry Regiment, which he commanded, completed a successful frontal assault on trenches of the Filipinos ("insurgents" as they were called then, as today in Iraq) near La Loma Church, outside Caloocan. Funston's account is worth re-visiting. He tells us in a patronizing tone, that the insurgents were given "the necessary castigation." A number, including one "plucky little Filipino," were run through with bayonets, getting "the cold steel." He notes that "These troops were fighting under a very fine silken flag with the emblem of the Katipunan embroidered on it...When we finally got the flag it had been riddled with bullets and was drenched with blood. It is now in the State House at Topeka" (The capital of his home state, Kansas.) He then, as he regularly did after each battle, gives an account of the relative losses, which in this period of the war was usually about forty to fifty Filipino casualties - mostly dead as the wounded were carried away - for every American. He then comments, "Among the dead we were surprised to find a very large and coal-black negro. As this was many months before any of our colored troops had been brought to the islands, the man could not have been a deserter from them, but was probably some vagabond seaman who had run away from a merchant-vessel in Manila Bay."

*"Fagen became the most famous of the black American guerrilla fighters."*

Like the focused military man he was, Funston moves on, literally and literarily. We learn no more about this extraordinary man. He was apparently left to be buried in anonymity and may remain one of the most interesting and mysterious of the world's "Unknown Soldiers." However, it may be possible to track down this independence fighter. The indefatigable Filipino historian George Hizon has found a picture of a black soldier in the ranks of the "boy General," Gregorio del Pilar, the hero who laid down his life at Triad Pass so that the advancing Americans could not capture General - and president - Emilio Aguinaldo.

*Gill H Boehringer is a Professor of Law and History (ret.) at Macquarie University, Sydney, Australia. He can be contacted at gil_boehringer(at)hotmail.com.*

## Foreclosure Advocates Lock Arms with "No Dirty Deeds" George Mantor - San Diego, 5-21-14

Foreclosure Strategist Ismael Rodriguez and his legion of followers came together with George Mantor, candidate for County Assessor for a loud boisterous rally at the Pacific Highway County building. They vow to expose and bring attention to the dismal and illegal activates surrounding the foreclosure crisis in San Diego and elsewhere. The group served papers to current Assessor Ernest J. Dronenbzurg Jr. indicating their intention to replace him and to start a national movement reaching the halls of congress to restore integrity, accountability and transparency to the office of Assessor.

# An Open Letter to Tribal Leaders and the American People

*FROM: Rosalie Little Thunder, Pte Oyate and Darrell Geist, Buffalo Field Campaign*

We write to you still in the aftershock of the unconscionable tribal participation in the most recent government slaughter of wild buffalo in Yellowstone National Park and Montana. We feel compelled to share our insight on how this corrosive process began.

In the early 1990s Montana cattle ranchers were in an uproar over the migration of buffalo to habitat in Montana beyond Yellowstone National Park's borders. Sounding the battle cry of brucellosis disease, cattle ranchers manipulated the Montana legislature into creating MCA 81-2-120. This new law delegates authority over the publics only wild buffalo population to livestock inspectors and the state vet.

Soon after livestock interests got control over wild buffalo, Governor Marc Racicot and the state used MCA 81-2-120 as a legal battering ram against Yellowstone National Park for "permitting" wild buffalo to naturally migrate. A court-forced legal settlement created the Interagency Bison Management Plan that has been in place since 2000. The plan is for the American people to pay the Montana Department of Livestock and Yellowstone National Park to harm and destroy our country's last wild buffalo on our National Parks and National Forests.

Irrational "permanent haze-back" deadlines and "bison-tolerant zones" have harmed the buffalo and degraded wildlife habitat. In this government-led war against the buffalo, the public will not hear about the contributions that buffalo provide to the ecosystem. The government does not bring public attention to the suffering it has caused to native plants, birds and animals when newborn buffalo calves flee Montana, driven away under the propellers of livestock agency helicopters. Harassing still pregnant buffalo and baby calves off nourishing spring grasses from our public forests and parks is an unreported crime.

Following instinctive faithfulness to calving grounds, migratory buffalo must run a lethal gauntlet of Treaty and state hunters along the Park's borders to adjoining National Forest lands. Wild buffalo must further suffer the harm of captivity in traps on public and private lands. This near-threatened and ecologically extinct native species is further subject to population control experiments with sterilizing agents. Our heritage of wild buffalo is quarantined to produce new offspring for commercial domestic profit. An arbitrary line is drawn on the map beyond which migratory buffalo can never roam again.

Sympathetic landowners who willingly share their private land with the buffalo are subject to intimidation by armed livestock inspectors and a cadre of government agents who trespass on private land to harass all buffalo out of Montana. The often-heard refrain is: "It's all part of the plan." But this heavily biased plan is man-made and can be changed.

Ignoring long standing condemnation of the government-led buffalo slaughter by American Indian Tribes and traditional leaders, the InterTribal Buffalo Council and Confederated Salish and Kootenai Tribes entered into deals with the National Park Service to take hundreds of "surplus" buffalo to slaughter this winter. The Nez Perce Tribe has also signed a slaughter deal. The Park is pursuing similar arrangements with other Tribal governments to set-up an operational quarantine - a livestock factory - to domesticate wild buffalo. Backing a trailer up to a trap in Yellowstone Park where buffalo are confined and transporting them to slaughter has nothing to do with tradition or the sacred or sovereign rights of tribes.

Our tribal councils and leaders are occupied with many challenges and do not have ready access to adequate information about the Yellowstone buffalo herd's fate. Oftentimes decision-makers are distanced from their own councils and advisors, traditional and spiritual. Unfortunately, the decisions made on wild buffalo continue to serve the interests of the Montana Department of Livestock and the National Park Service first.

With the sanction of MCA 81-2-120, Montana and Yellowstone National Park have shot or captured for slaughter 5,097 wild buffalo. This winter, with the shield of tribal involvement, several hundred buffalo were captured for shipment to slaughterhouses.

The deception that buffalo are a disease risk is not fair to the tribes or the American people. Since cattle infected buffalo in captivity on the Lamar Buffalo Ranch a century ago, there has been no case of wild buffalo transmitting brucellosis back to cattle. Our relative, the buffalo, has been found guilty while the evidence of their innocence has been buried.

## How did this state of affairs come to be?

This highly corrupt plan, and the law upon which it is based, would cease to function without the support of the U.S. Congress. Our representatives in Washington D.C. have misappropriated $40 million of the American people's money to fund a tragic and disastrous death policy for our national icon.

In spite of fourteen years of the Interagency Bison Management Plan's existence, Montana has not conceded to giving even one more acre of year-round habitat to migratory buffalo. There is no 'kill-free' zone for a native species Montana's own biologists recognize as vulnerable to "extinction or extirpation in the state."

A long overdue public process to review year-round buffalo habitat by Montana was recently blocked by cattle ranchers in collusion with the Board of Livestock. But even under the most "tolerant" alternative, wild buffalo would be confined to 0.4% of Montana's habitat.

Montana cattle ranchers now intend for the public and the tribes to swallow a poison pill: a fragment of year-round habitat in exchange for continuously slaughtering buffalo.

The boogeyman of brucellosis raised by cattle ranchers to seize management authority over the public's wild buffalo no longer exists.

Today, cattle are being managed under a U.S. Dept. of Agriculture-APHIS approved and taxpayer supported plan. Ranchers benefit $9.50 to $14 per head by vaccinating cattle. Despite the few cases of brucellosis transmission from wild elk to cattle, Montana's Designated Surveillance Area rules have protected the state's brucellosis free status. Statewide, the cost-savings for Montana cattle ranchers is $22 to $46 million dollars and multiplying. The new rules have also removed whole herd cattle slaughter and diminished the threat of state sanctions against Montana cattle that contract brucellosis.

Montana's cattle ranchers are being taken care of, but the public's one remaining population of wild buffalo is being massacred.

Montana's Constitution mandates that we take special considerations to ensure the persistence of native wildlife species for future generations. We must rally to repeal the corrupting influence of MCA 81-2-120, a misbegotten law that is destroying our natural and cultural heritage. Montanans must act together and provide a welcome home for wild buffalo.

Traditional people must guide our tribal leadership in a manner that reflects the integrity of our historical and cultural relationship with our relative, the buffalo. Montana politics has made a mockery of a keystone species. The capitalist culture has commodified the buffalo for shameless profit. The slaughter of the buffalo is not about a disease, really. It is about a commodity and profiting from that commodity. We, as a species, must take into account how our beliefs and actions are affecting the future of all species. We must make every effort to acknowledge the need for a care-taking culture that respects and honors the role of a sacred species.

Can decision-makers rise above the intense politics that swirl around this sacred species? Can we root out the entrenched, corrupt forces that threaten the future of wild buffalo? The time yet to come for buffalo now rests upon the vision, courage and leadership of our tribal leaders and the American people.

Respectfully,
Rosalie Little Thunder, Pte Oyate
Phone: (605) 939-1005
Email: rosalie.littlethunder@gmail.com

Darrell Geist, habitat coordinator,
Buffalo Field Campaign
Phone: (406) 646-0070
Email: z@wildrockies.org

## American Indian Heritage Pow Wow and Dwight Lomayesva Honoring Ceremony

Balboa Park
Park Blvd & Presidents Way
San Diego, CA.

May 10 - 11 2014

Head Staff
MC: Randy Edmonds
Northern Drum: Blue Star
Southern Drum: Hale& Co
Arena Director:
Richard Overdal

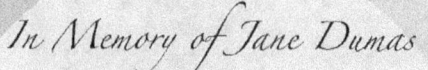

*In Memory of Jane Dumas*

GAMBLING AND THE LAW®:

# Cuba Needs Casinos

"I crapped out"
Meyer Lansky, quoted in T.J. English's
HAVANA NOCTURNE: HOW THE MOB
OWNED CUBA ... AND THEN LOST IT
TO THE REVOLUTION

Fidel Castro is gone.

He may not be dead. But on a recent trip to Cuba, I was told by both American and Cuban experts that he is beyond retired. His image may be everywhere, but he no longer has a living influence. Fidel has become to Cuba what Mao is to China.

His younger brother, Raul, is still alive, but is 83 years old. He has called for term limits, including his own. He will not run for reelection as President in 2018.

Since taking over from Fidel in 2007, Raul started introducing reforms. He had to.

Cuba is a country where nuclear physicists drive taxis, because they can make more than their $40 per month government salaries. Under Fidel, Cubans could not buy or sell cars or homes, so they arranged phony marriages. The property could then be transferred through a divorce.

Still today, everyone owns their own apartments, but literally nobody owns the apartment buildings; so, there is no one to fix leaking roofs.

Since there are no opportunities, young adults flee the country. Many are willing to risk their lives on Styrofoam rafts to try to get to America.

Change is coming to Cuba. The big questions are whether it will be slow or fast, peaceful or violent.

The old men who have led Cuba for the last 55 years – there have been 11 U.S. Presidents since Fidel took over – are survivors. They know how to hang on to power. If a charismatic leader arose who might one day challenge the Castro brothers, he was sent to work in the sugar fields. So, there is no caudillo (strong man) to lead a second revolution.

But the old men also have to keep the disappointment and anger of the general population under control. They are understandably scared by what they saw happen to dictators during the "Arab Spring."

On January 14, 2013, the government began allowing most Cubans to leave the country, without having to get approval, pay $400 for a visa or forfeiting their right to return. This may turn out to be like the fall of the Berlin Wall. Average citizens visiting countries with more than four state-controlled television channels, let alone access to the Internet, will be more frustrated upon their return, with their lack of just about everything.

The U.S. embargo, and the failures of communism, locked Cuba into 1959. Even the cars and buildings are the same. And this may provide the solution to Cuba's problems.

Classic 1950's Fords and Chevys are everywhere. Imagine the reaction of a guy making $20 a month, after trade reopens with the U.S.: "I won't give you more than $40,000 for your car."

Cuba's 1950's hotels are also still standing. More importantly, so are its casinos. Although now dark and empty, nothing else has changed; even the chandeliers are the same. You swear you hear the ghost whispering of long-gone slot machines and crap tables, when you walk around the Riviera casino.

Many of the bars and nightclubs are still open. The largest showroom of them all, the Tropicana with its multi-level, outdoor stage, sells out every night. The extravaganza features statuesque showgirls with feathered headdresses and sexy dancing, or at least what would have been considered sexy in 1959.

Fidel, through his hand-picked provisional president, Manuel Urrutia, closed the casinos immediately after seizing power, just as he canceled the national lottery. But the thousands of Cubans thrown out of work took to the streets in protest. Castro's own economic advisors told him that the country's economy would collapse unless the casinos were reopened.

They proved to be right, but too late. Castro relented, for a while. But tourists, especially Americans, stayed away in droves. The casinos were closed for good; and the economy did collapse.

Communist nations are not averse to legal gambling. Casinos in particular have been seen as a way of extracting hard currency from tourists and from the underground economy. I played in a casino in Hungary before the fall of the Eastern Bloc, with all transactions in Deutsche Marks (this was before the euro).

The Socialist Republic of Vietnam still has casinos. Surprisingly, so, too, does North Korea.

And then, of course, there is Macau. The casinos there win more than all of the privately owned casinos in Nevada, New Jersey, Mississippi and the rest of the United States – combined.

Macau, like Hong Kong, is a Special Administrative Region of the People's Republic of China. The PRC is still technically a communist country, although it would be more accurate to describe it as Marxist: widespread free enterprise capitalism flourishing under a totalitarian, one party dictatorship.

The bureaucrats who run Cuba can find a partial solution to the country's present economic catastrophe and its pending political crisis by looking east – far east. Cuba needs to pull a Macau.

Resort casinos create jobs and bring in much needed revenue. They could ease Cuba's transition out of the economic stagnation created by pure communism, as they did in China.

Of course, Cuba does not have hundreds of millions of middle-class residents with few other legal outlets for gambling. In fact, the people are so poor that it is one of the few countries where it actually is to the advantage of casino operators that locals would not be allowed to enter.

But, Cuba already attracts large numbers of tourists from Europe, Canada and Latin America; tourism is the nation's leading industry. The spectacular success of Havana's casinos in the 1950's show what legal gaming could do, especially once Americans can visit without restrictions.

The major problem is political. Havana's casinos were symbols of the prior dictator, Fulgencio Batista's, corrupt regime. When asked about the Americans who ran Cuba's gambling, Fidel said, "We are not only disposed to deport the gangsters, but to shoot them."

In the early 1960s, children could get cartoon trading cards with purchases of Felices [Spanish for happy] Frutas's canned fruit. They would glue them into their "Album de la Revolucion Cubana." One shows an angry crowd storming the Deauville Casino, with this label: "El pueblo destroza algunos casinos y casas de juegos," "The people destroy some casinos and gambling houses."

Still, this was half a century ago. Times change. Fifty years before Macau

SEE **Cuba**, page 12

## Optimal Health

Continued from page 5

i.e., mediation, yoga, prayer, or whatever one does that is healthy and relaxing to the mind, body and soul and rejuvenates that person. So stress management can not include doing those things which some folk do to escape that are damaging to the human being.

Lastly after waking up and cleaning up, comes perhaps, the most critical pillar of Malcolm's ethics in the sense of it being a constant and continuous reinforcement through practice of the first two ethics of this three pronged approach of Malcolm X's ethics. Standing Up, like Malcolm's other teaching, standing up is grounded in his personal and communitarian experiences of self critique, recovery, and reconstruction. As did Malcolm in his transformation from a being of the lumpen life to the model of Black manhood that he was in his life and remains to be as an ancestor, so it is with Black people today assuming such a position on self assessment, and rigorous challenge to overturn weakness into strength when it come to our health and well being.

Standing Up requires us through internalizing values and practicing behaviors, of eating nutritiously, exercising, getting proper rest, detoxifying and as argued earlier effective stress management to be committed to our health and well being as with other areas of our community's struggle. Thus, in the interest of our reconstructing our community to a status of optima health; I contend that we do as it states in the 5th principle of the Nguzo Saba, Nia which states; " To make our collective vocation the building and developing of our community in order to restore our people to their traditional greatness." For in the final analysis, our health is wealth, and if we don't heal ourselves, then who will, certainly not the establish order. With that said I close by saying to my readers by our personal and communitarian waking up, cleaning, up, and standing up, Wenyewe Kwa Tutajali; which is Swahili for" We Will Heal Ourselves" and what better way to restore ourselves to our traditional greatness than to bring our community to optimal health!

*Min. Tukufu Kalonji is Founder of Kawaida African Ministries,*
*For info contact @ tkalonji@hotmail.com*

# Studies Reveal that Adverse Childhood Experiences Fuel Illnesses in Adults

*by Paul B. Simms, MPH, Past President, San Diego Black Health Associates, Inc.*

San Diego, CA – For the past twenty-eight years, the San Diego Black Health Associates, Inc. (SDBHA) has been working to address the health status gap which African Americans face. For nearly every major chronic disease, Blacks suffer the highest mortality levels, the highest hospitalization rates and the most frequent visits to the emergency room of any ethnic group in the United States. Our organization has engaged in consumer education, conducted workshops, held screening sessions, provided guidance for healthier choices and promoted health through prevention. Our "Fifteen Health Commandments" reflect counsel to our communities about the importance of making the right choices.

Dr. Vincent Felitti was Medical Director of the Department of Preventive Medicine at Kaiser Permanente in San Diego for more than 16 years. During his tenure, patients who were seeking to lose weight adopted the Kaiser plan for fasting. This medically controlled denial of solid foods was directed in such a way that many persons lost significant amounts of weight. It was soon discovered that a large number of these patients dropped out of their program because the images they were protecting and the events which they had hidden were surfacing as a result of the weight loss. Come to find out, in some cases, the extra weight was protective of other events – events which happened years earlier.

Speaking at a program on Innovations in Patient Empowerment sponsored by Claremont Graduate University, Dr. Felitti described research conducted in a mail survey with 17,000 middle class patients, all of whom were Kaiser beneficiaries. African Americans represented 10% of the participants in the study. He asked the patients several questions about traumatic events which may have happened to them as children. Incredibly, over 70% of people receiving the survey responded, and these patients gave permission to connect the responses they gave to the survey to their medical records. The questions asked the consumer s inquired about whether they had been abused as a child.

This abuse could have been physical, psychological, emotional or sexual. The survey also inquired whether any adult person in their household was a problem drinker, whether they ever used drugs, whether they were mentally ill or whether a person in the household attempted suicide. Finally, the survey asked whether a member of the household had gone to prison.

Surprisingly, nearly 50% remembered at least one Adverse Childhood Experience (ACE). The research team included representatives from the Center for Disease Control and Prevention (CDC), and together, their coined the term the "Ace Score".

Several physicians at the conference sitting near the author of this story grumbled at Dr. Felitti's assertions about the abuse as a child. One felt that he would not inquire about such acts of abuse by parents or anyone so many years ago, because he would not want to "stir up" a can of worms with such an inquiry. Another physician expressed dismay that within his practice, there were only a certain number of minutes to see each patient. Asking questions about adverse childhood experiences would consume more time than he felt was available. A third physician was opposed to the inquiry by primary care physicians, many of whom had little training in psychiatry.

Dr. Jeffrey Brenner is the Founder of the Camden Coalition of Healthcare Providers and Medical Director of the Urban Institute at Cooper University Healthcare. Earlier this year, Dr. Brenner wrote a "blog" (January 29, 2014) that stated:

"For nearly 15 years, we've had the secret to delivering better care at lower cost in America. The information has sat hidden away in the medical literature, and barely mentioned among physicians. It's a remarkable story of bias. The neglect of this information by the medical community tells you a lot about our failings as a profession and the poor training we receive. It is also a powerful commentary on impacts. This is true for even for middle class patients. However, poverty magnifies the potential to have higher ACE score and possibly exacerbates any trauma that have occurred"

This past weekend, Clovis Honore, President of SDBHA and I made a presentation to the Men's Group at Bethel AME Church. Nearly 25 African American men listened while we discussed the importance of making the right health choices, why it is important to monitor one's blood pressure and why Covered California was important to African Americans for access to health care. For the first time, the ACE Score was also discussed and a pilot survey was conducted.

Information about ACE was also discussed at the retreat sponsored by the Village of Promise, a group of advocates working to provide support and resilience to children whose parents have been incarcerated.

We may be wrong but we are impressed with the findings of Dr. Felittl. He has agreed to guide our explorations into a community conversation about ACE and abuse, neglect, parenting and changing our environments for African Americans (and others). We are interested in improving the future of our children and the mindfulness of ACE may be an answer. Remember, there is no one coming to help us, but us.

# Green Store
# 25th Anniversary Celebration

The Green Store in Ocean Beach Celebrated their 25th Anniversary April 26th. Colleen Dietzel owner of the Green Store and M.C. Rio started the event with introduction of the Acoustic Blue (members of Liquid Blue) band who are a certified "Green" band that recently moved to O.B. Acoustic Blue and other local talented musicians played throughout the afternoon.

The Green Store on Voltaire Street is a resource center for many issues including global warming, promoting Mom & Pop Businesses • Advancing Social Justice • Educating people about health, farming, water and other issues • Getting residents to take part and have a voice in community issues • Working towards peace• Forming bonds with people who want a better world • Bringing people together who love O.B.!!!

Guest speakers spoke on a variety of topics including fracking, water conservation, retaining Ocean Beach's hometown appeal and activism and more.

Photos by Kathy Blavatt

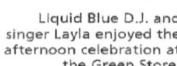

Liquid Blue D.J. and singer Layla enjoyed the afternoon celebration at the Green Store.

Justin, a local musician and song writer, put on an amazing performance singing and playing multiple instruments.

## Organic Consumers Association

On May 8, Peter Shumlin, Governor of Vermont, signed a historic bill requiring food manufacturers to label genetically engineered foods and to drop the practice of labeling these foods as "natural" or "all natural."

On May 9, the Grocery Manufacturers Association backed up Monsanto's threats and confirmed that it will sue Vermont in federal court to overturn H. 112. Vermont is prepared to fight back. The state has already established a "food fight" legal defense fund. Legal analysts say Vermont will likely win.

But Vermont isn't the only state up against the multi-billion dollar lobbying group. The GMA, whose 300-plus members include Monsanto and Dow, Coca-Cola and General Mills, is pushing a bill in Congress that would preempt all states from passing GMO labeling laws.

It's time for consumers in every state to band together to defeat the GMA's full-on assault, not only on Vermont, not only on consumers' right to know what's in our food, but on states' rights and on our basic freedoms to protect our health and our communities.

## Cuba

Continued from page 10

became the top casino market in the world, gambling in China was punishable by death.

Cuba already has tourist zones, where locals are not allowed to enter, except for work. Canadian tourists already fly directly to resorts on the southern coast of Cuba, just to go to the beach. The natural spot for the first Cuban casino-resort is, ironically, the Bay of Pigs. The scene of the disastrous failed invasion of 1961 is now a thriving resort, especially for Europeans.

But there is another spot, where a casino would be even more of a positive political statement by the Cuban government: Guantanamo Bay. It is isolated from the vast majority of the population; at more than 500 miles from Havana, it is actually closer to Miami.

There are beaches and an airport and one of the largest sea ports in the world for cruise ships, if the U.S. will allow free passage.

Cuba could set up another tourist zone, with legal gambling, on the Cuban side of Guantanamo Bay. Local residents would be barred. But visitors from every other country, including the United States, would be welcome.

Americans can travel to Macau without even having to get a visa. Wouldn't it be great if Guantanamo Bay became better known for its hotel-casino resorts than for its prison?

*© 2014, I. Nelson Rose. Prof. Rose is recognized as one of the world's leading experts on gambling law, and is a consultant and expert witness for governments, industry and players. His latest books, INTERNET GAMING LAW (1st and 2nd editions), BLACKJACK AND THE LAW, GAMING LAW: CASES AND MATERIALS and GAMING LAW IN A NUTSHELL are available through his website, www.GAMBLINGANDTHELAW.com.*

## A Three Mile 21st Birthday Hike

These two take exercise and staying in shape seriously. Unexpected circumstance found this reservation Mom and one year old toddler without a ride home on her 21st birthday. She bravely hooked up her stroller and heavy duty moccasins and made the three mile trek home on foot. She says it was a birthday to remember.

# TRADING POST BUSINESS DIRECTORY

## CALIFORNIA

**ADVOCACY**
Alan Lechuza Aquallo
Advocate for Native Youth and Scholarships
alan@blackphonerecords.com

**ATTORNEYS**
Marshall Law PC
Daniel E.Marshall,Attorney at Law
619-993-5778 • marslawbmw@gmail.com
sandiegoevictionattorneys.com

**BAKERY**
Historic San Luis Rey Bakery
490 N. El Camino Real Oceanside, CA 92058
760-433-7242 • www.sanluisreybakery.com

La Nueva Mexican Bakery
4676 Market St. Ste. A-3, San Diego, CA
619-262-0042

**CARE GIVER**
Private Duty– References
Terms to be discussed
619-504-2455 Ask for Liz

**CLERICAL**
Your Girl Friday International
Marketing, Operations & Promotional
Services • yourgirlfriday3512@gmail.com

**CULTURE**
Kumeyaay
www.kumeyaay.com • larry@kumeyaay.com

Worldbeat Cultural Center
619-230-1190
www.worldbeatculturalcenter.org
info@worldbeatculturalcenter.org

**DRIVER**
Driver for Hire
Clean DMV Class ABC
619-504-2455 Ask for Liz

**FINANCIAL ADVISORS**
Merrill Lynch / Elke Chenevey
Vice President & Financial Advisor
Office: 619-699-3707
Fax: 619-758-3619

Summit Funding
The Home Loan Experts
Jeff Ellenz, Branch Manager
760-568-0300 • jellenz@summitfunding.net

**HEALTH**
Rady's Children Hospital
San Diego, CA
800-869-5627 • www.rchsd.org

Regenerative Medicine Institute
www.regenerativemedicine.mx

San Diego American Health Center
2630 1st Avenue, San Diego, CA 92013
619-234-2158

**HEALER-SHAMAN**
Transitions / Vera A. Tucker
vtucker1212@gmail.com
619-987-0372

**HOMEMADE**
Liz • 619-504-2655

**HOUSEKEEPING**
Cleaning, windows, floors
4 hours $80 - 8 hours $120

619-504-2455 Ask for Liz

**INSURANCE**
State Farm / Jack Fannin
1154 E. Main St. El Cajon, CA 92021-7157
619-440-0161 Business
619-440-0495 Fax
jack.fanninjroi@statefarm.com
www.jackfannin.com

Earthquake Insurances
www.EarthquakeAuthority.com

**MARKETING**
International Marketing Systems
Eddy Michaelly
www.imsbarter.com

Jahaanah Productions
Marketing, Media, Public Relations, Graphic
Design • 832-978-0939

**NOTARY PUBLIC**
Sis. Evon X. Nana
San Diego, CA 92113 • 619-549-5792
evonx@yahoo.com

**PHOTOGRAPHY**
Peache Photo Memories
619-697-4186 office
619-549-0968 contact
www.peachephotomemories.com
peachephotos@cox.net

**PUBLISHERS**
Blackrose Communications
111 South 35th St. San Diego, CA 92113
619-234-4753
www.indianvoices.net • rdavis4973@aol.com

**RADIO**
91.3PM Kopa
Pala Rez Radio
www.palatribe.com • 91.3@palatribe.com

**RECOVERY**
David "Wolf" Diaz, Pres. & Founder
Walk of the Warrior, A Non-Profit Corp.
Tel: 760-646-0074 • Cell: 310-866-7057
Fax:760-689-4907
www.walkofthewarrior.com
walkofthewarrior@yahoo.com

**REGALIA**
Carla Tourville
Native Regalia Custom Design
Yokut Tule River Tribe
San Diego, CA • 619-743-9847

**REPARATIONS**
Mr. Peoples Reparations
200 N. Long Beach Blvd. Compton, CA
310-632-0577

**RESTAURANT**
Awash Ethiopian Restaurant
4979 El Cajon Blvd. San Diego,CA
619-677-3754.

**RETAIL – CLOTHING**
Full Blood Apparel
P.O. Box 3101 Valley Venter, CA 92082
760-445-1141

**SOCIAL SERVICES**
Tribal Tanf
Temporary Assistance for Needy Families
San Diego Office 866-913-3725

Escondido Office 866-428-0901
Manzanita Office 866-931-1480
Pala Office 866-806-8263

## NEVADA

**ADVOCACY**
Adams Esq.
Special Needs Children
500 N. Rainbow Blvd. Ste 300
Las Vegas, NV 89107
702-289-4143 Office • 702-924-7200 Fax

**COMMUNITY**
Native American Community Services
3909 S. Maryland Pkwy #205 Las Vegas, NV
89119-7500

**PUBLISHERS**
Blackrose Communications
111 South 35th St. San Diego, CA 92113
619-234-4753
www.indianvoices.net • rdavis4973@aol.com

## NORTH CAROLINA

**RETAIL - CLOTHING**
Passion Island
832 Washington Plaza, Washington, NC
27889; 252-402-4700

## TEXAS

**HEALTH**
The Circle: A Healing Place
Joanna Johnson, MSW, CFAS
Longview Behavioral Hospital
22 Bermuda Lane, Longview, Texas 75605
www.longviewhospital.com
www.oglethorpeinc.com
850-228-0777

# NEVADA NEWS

For Nevada Information: 619-234-4753 • 619-534-2435

## Kelly Tran Makes a Guest Appearance at the Helldorado Days Evening Parade

LAS VEGAS, NV – Although there are several pageant organizations and dozens of titleholders throughout Las Vegas in Southern Nevada, one name always resonates in the minds of industry insiders and influencers, Kelly Tran. The young and physically attractive Vietnamese pageant queen takes her community support platform to a level that until now was thought not possible as evidenced by her speaking engagements, media interviews, charitable work, and appearances.

Recently Kelly Tran, Ms. United States America International 2013 joined her mentor and friend Clark County District Court Judge Kenneth Pollock from Department J and rode with him inside a classic Mercedes Benz convertible. Tran was so popular at the parade that even a member of the parade's judge panel formally recognized her while Cox TV was filming Tran waving to a large crowd of supporters.

During a pre-event telephone interview Kelly Tran stated, "I am excited to support such a great community event for locals and families and out-of-town visitors. It is my honor to join Nevadans in celebrating 150 years of statehood and getting back to Nevada's roots by participating in the Helldorado Days Evening Parade."

Tran stays humble and modest even though she is considered to be the number one Asian pageant queen in Las Vegas, Nevada.

Kelly Tran is represented by Endeavor Media Group. To book Kelly Tran for appearances and media interviews contact Andre' Haynes by calling (702) 902-2844 or by writing to andre@emgnv.com.

**Endeavor Media Group**
**André Haynes**
**3675 S. Rainbow Blvd., Ste 107**
**Las Vegas, NV 89103**
**702-305-0973 • www.emgnv.com**

# Nevada Tribal Tourism Conference at Lake Tahoe

In April, our beautiful Silver State hosted the 6th Annual Nevada Tribal Tourism Conference at Lake Tahoe, our crown jewel and the traditional homelands of the Washoe Tribe of Nevada and California.

Nevada's Great Basin has always been the home of the Washoe, Paiute and Western Shoshone Peoples. Their stories, traditions and languages, are part of this rich cultural fabric that Nevada shares with America and the World.

Nevada plays host to millions of visitors every year and tribes play a part to help build tribal tourism and hospitality across our great state. Places like the Stewart Indian School tell the untold stories of the failed boarding school policy of the federal government that did everything it could to strip tribal people of their languages and ways of life to assimilate them into mainstream American society.

Pyramid Lake is another gem that I worked with the Pyramid Lake Paiutes to protect, and is now shared with all of Nevada for fishing and other recreation. The Nevada State Museum houses the baskets of someone I am very proud of and admire - Dat-So-La-Lee - who is recognized for her Washoe baskets around the world. Also, the Walker River Paiute Tribe hosts an Annual Pinenut Festival in Schurz each fall to celebrate the harvest of their traditional food.

Outside of Las Vegas, the Las Vegas Paiutes play host to the three-day Snow Mountain Powwow and a stunning golf resort voted one of the best places to play by Golf Digest. We need to work harder to keep building these partnerships, capacity and infrastructure so tribes can tell their stories and share their cultures.

I remain committed to ensuring that investment continues in tribal tourism which in turn helps sovereign Indian nations preserve historic and cultural resources, and build tribal economies.

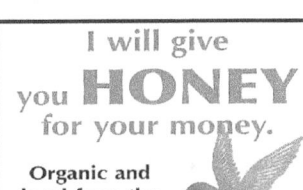

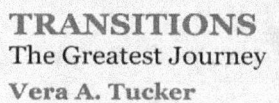

FRYBREAD                                                    SAYNDAY

What does FBI mean? | Full Blooded Inden | No. Frybread Inden!

©10-TRW

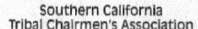

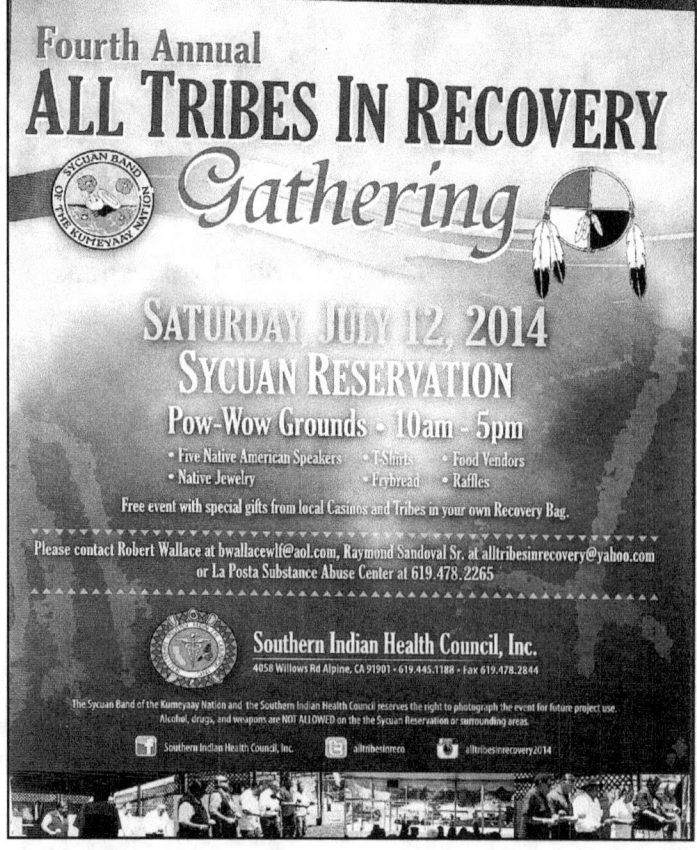

www.indianvoices.net

OUR 28TH YEAR     MULTI-CULTURAL NEWS GLOBAL NETWORK     JULY 2014

# Native Speakers and Linguists Fight to Keep Kumeyaay Language Alive

On a wildly windy day in the Kumeyaay community Juntas de Nejí, about an hour south of Tecate, Mexico, Norma Meza-Calles watches as her 6-year-old grandson, Matt, cracks open acorns. She gives him pointers in her native tongue.

Matt is Meza-Calles' hope for keeping the Kumeyaay language and culture alive.

"I'm putting all of my efforts into teaching him to speak fluent Kumeyaay," Meza-Calles said in Spanish. "I want to make up for not teaching my kids to speak Kumeyaay."

Norma Meza-Calles is teaching her six-year-old grandson, Matt, to speak Kumeyaay at home. Meza-Calles's home

language school is one small contribution to the weighty task of keeping the language from going the way of thousands of other minority languages: extinct.

"Out of 6,000 approximate languages that are spoken in the world, only about 100 of them are really safe right now," San Diego State University linguist Margaret Field said. "And those are big languages like Spanish and English, Russian and Chinese."

All but a handful of Kumeyaay speakers live south of the border. Field said the language has fared better in Mexico than in the U.S. largely because of differences in education policy.

"There's a long history of American

Indian people being forced to go to boarding school where their languages and cultures were actively repressed, and they were taught to be ashamed of their language," Field said.

"That didn't happen in Mexico. Instead what happened is people either didn't go to school or went to school for

just a little while," she said.

Meza-Calles and her three sisters only went to school for a few years as children. She said she didn't learn Spanish until she was 13.

Linguist Margaret Field works with

SEE Kumeyaay Language, page 2

# Vincent G. Logan, a Member of the Osage Nation Special Trustee for American Indians

"Vincent Logan has been a part of the fabric of Indian Country for many years as an investment professional, mentor for Native American attorneys and founding member of the Native American Bar Association of Washington, DC," Secretary of the Interior Sally Jewell said on U.S. Senate confirmation of Vincent G. Logan, "His asset management expertise, legal experience and extensive network of professional relationships in Indian Country will well serve the Office of Special Trustee as we work to build a stronger and more responsive trust asset management system for the Nation's First Americans."

The Office of Special Trustee for American Indians works to improve the accountability and management of Indian funds held in trust by the federal government. As trustee, the Interior Department has the primary fiduciary responsibility to manage about $3.7 billion in tribal trust funds and

Individual Indian Money accounts, as well as leases for developing natural resources, such as coal, oil, natural gas, timber and grazing, that generate income for those accounts.

Vincent G. Logan is the owner of The Nations Group, LLC, which works with Native American tribes on asset management, investment strategies, and financial education. He worked in the Private Banking and Investment Group at Merrill Lynch from 2006 to 2009, and was a corporate finance attorney for Schulte, Roth, & Zabel from 2001 to 2006. Prior to that, Mr. Logan worked in the Antitrust Division at the United States Department of Justice from 1996 to 1998. He was appointed to the Oklahoma State University Foundation Board of Governors in 2010. Mr. Logan is a member of the Osage Nation. He received a B.S. from Oklahoma State University and a J.D. from the University Of Oklahoma College of Law.

Vincent G. Logan

## Kumeyaay Language

Continued from page 1

three of the Meza-Calles sisters on documenting the Kumeyaay language.

Now, as adults, the sisters have a rare expertise in their endangered language and culture. Field has met with them regularly for the past five years to record and document the language.

Shirley Murphy
Lakota linguist teaches a Kumeyaay language class

Together they produced online Kumeyaay language lessons, a request from Baja California teachers. Now Field and fellow linguist Amy Miller are working on a dictionary of all five dialects of Kumeyaay spoken in Baja California.

Documenting an endangered language is a painstakingly slow process. Field met three of the Meza-Calles sisters recently at the Kumeyaay museum in Tecate. They took several hours to go over just a few sentences of a Kumeyaay creation story that the sisters had previously recorded.

"For me the most important part is getting down every morpheme on every word," Field explained. "Every little piece of a word."

The Meza-Calles family on their land in the Kumeyaay community, Juntas de Neji, Baja California, Mexico. Back in the Kumeyaay communities of Baja, the real work of keeping the language alive takes place. Meza-Calles' grandson, Matt, is shy about speaking Kumeyaay, but he seems to understand when his grandmother speaks to him in the language.

"We really started at zero," Norma said. "Our grandkids didn't even know they were Kumeyaay. Now they know and they're proud to be Kumeyaay," she said, "because we were the first inhabitants of Baja."

If Norma succeeds in making her grandson a fluent speaker of his ancestral language, it'll then be his turn to keep the language alive, and eventually to pass it on to his own children. That, at least, is his grandmother's hope.

*Read more at*
*http://www.kpbs.org/news/2014/may/27/native-speakers-and-linguists-fight-keep-kumeyaay-/*

## Looking for Your Ancestors?

Yvette Porter-Moore is a Professional Genealogist & Family Historian, and is the owner of Root Digger Genealogy Research Services. She specializes in Birth-Search & Adoption Research in California and African American Research. Yvette also specializes in research within NC, VA, WV, MA, GA, District of Columbia, and California. All research begins via online data-bases.

Yvette is currently writing "A Taste of Sugar Hill," A memoir of her mother and her ancestor's life in Sugar Hill, New York. Ms. Porter-Moore is available for speaking presentations and writing assignments.

*You can catch Yvette online at www.TheAncestorshavespoken.blogspot.com and www.yvetteportermoore.com. For more information contact 619-768-3094 or RootDigGen@gmail.com*

# Alaska Becomes the Second State to Officially Recognize Indigenous Languages

*by Casey Kelly*

Supporters of a bill to make 20 Alaska Native languages official state languages organized a 15 hour sit-in protest at the Capitol on Sunday. Their dedication paid off early this morning, when the Alaska Senate passed the measure on an 18-2 vote.

The Alaska House passed the bill last week, 38-0. It now heads to Governor Sean Parnell for his signature.

Dozens of people of all ages and races Easter finest the hall outside Sen. Lesil McGuire's office. The Anchorage Republican and chair of the Senate Rules Committee had the power to put House Bill 216 on the Senate's calendar. But with end of the legislative session looming, the bill's supporters worried it was getting caught up in last-minute, behind-the-scenes politics.

The group started their vigil just after noon, singing, dancing, and playing drums, and talking about why Alaska Native languages are so important.

*"Our language is everything. It's the air we breathe. It's the blood that flows through our veins,"* said Lance Twitchell, a professor of Native Languages at the University of Alaska Southeast.

HB 216 would add the state's indigenous languages to a statute created by a 1998 voter initiative, which made English the official language of Alaska. While the bill is largely symbolic, Twitchell said it's important to recognize all languages as equal.

"That's all we want is equal value," he said. "And there's nothing wrong with standing up and saying that. It takes a lot of courage to do that. And it takes a lot of something else to try and go against that."

Many elders who attended the sit-in recalled being punished as children for speaking their first languages. Irene Cadiente of Juneau said her teachers would hit her with a ruler when they caught her speaking Tlingit.

*"Sometimes I wonder when my hand hurts, is it on account of me speaking Tlingit?"* Cadiente asked. *"My hands were ruled. Is that why it hurts? I never forget that."*

Cadiente said she's proud that her great grandchildren are now learning to speak the language.

Heather Burge, a student in the Native Languages program at UAS, said she didn't understand how HB 216 could become controversial.

"We should be at the point where this should be a non-issue," Burge said. "But it's still scary to some people, which is a little disheartening. But hopefully we can get past this."

# INDIAN VOICES

Multicultural News from an American Indian Perspective

### PUBLISHED BY BLACKROSE COMMUNICATIONS
*Member, American Indian Chamber of Commerce*

Email: rdavis4973@aol.com
Website: www.indianvoices.net
Editorial Board: Rose Davis

| | | | |
|---|---|---|---|
| Editor: | Rose Davis | Writer: | Jaclyn Bissonette |
| Social Media Administrator: | Yvonne-Cher Skye | Entertainment Writer/ | |
| Outside Support: | Mel Vernon | Photographer LA/SD: | Rochelle Porter |
| LV Entertainment Writer: | Z. Z. Zorn | Reporter de Espectaculos: | Omar DeSantiago |
| Associate Editor: | Sis Mary Muhammad | Reporter de Espectaculos: | Michelle Banuet |
| Writer: | Kathleen Blavatt | Proofreader: | Mary Lou Finley |
| Writer: | Roy Cook | Graphic Artist: | Elaine Hall |
| Writer: | Marc Snelling | Staff Photographer: | Abel Jacome |
| Writer: | Scott Andrews | | |

Endeavor Media Group
André Haynes
3675 S. Rainbow Blvd., Ste 107
Las Vegas, NV 89103
702-305-0973 •
www.emgnv.com

111 South 35th St.
San Diego, CA 92113
(619) 234-4753
(619) 534-2435 (cell)
Fax: (619) 512-4534

**Member of the Society of Professional Journalists**
**Member of New America Media**

## Moms Fight Back Against Foreclosures

**Whereas:** Our country has not experienced a foreclosure epidemic of the magnitude that we Mothers of America are currently experiencing since the Great Depression;

**Whereas:** The numerous and widespread atrocities committed against our families and our homes by the unconscionable practices of banks and mortgage servicers is well-documented;

**Whereas:** Banks and mortgage servicers have not negotiated with the Mothers of America, the public and our families have in a good faith manner, in order to resolve the financial dilemmas that the banks created with adjustable rate interest, additional hidden fees, unreasonable increases in escrow account monies, exuberant fees, imposed legal fees, document search fees, drive by home inspection fees, forced placed insurance policies;

**Whereas:** Banks and mortgage servicers have pursued foreclosure actions against the Mothers of America, the public and our families, while simultaneously falsely making many Mothers of America believe they were on track for a loan modification, thus putting countless families on the "dual tracking system";

**Whereas:** Banks and mortgage servicers have deprived the Mothers of America, the public and our families'

opportunities to cure any delinquencies prior to the commencement of foreclosure actions;

**Whereas:** Banks and mortgage servicers have commenced forced foreclosure proceedings without proper and adequate notice thus violating the due process of American Mothers, the public and our families;

**Whereas:** Banks and mortgage servicers have not negotiated with the Mothers of America, the public, our families in a good faith manner in order to resolve the financial dilemma that the banks created with adjustable rate interest, additional fees, unreasonable increases in escrow account monies exacerbate late fees, imposed legal fees, document search fees, drive by home inspection;

**Whereas:** Attorneys for the banks and mortgage servicers have improperly commenced foreclosure actions on fraudulently created documents frequently rubber stamped by "robosigners;

**Therefore Be It Resolved:** We the Mothers of America due hereby respectfully request our President execute an Emergency Proclamation ordering financial institutions, banks and mortgage servicers to immediately cease and desist filing of any new foreclosure actions and place a moratorium on all pre-foreclosure

## Mayor Kevin Faulkner Breaks Bread with Community Press

provided.

The respect and attention given to the micro community's Fourth Estate is appreciated by this growing constituency.

True to his word about sharing his views and opinons in the open, Mayor Faulkner hosted his first Pen and Pad at City Hall June 23.

All local, weekly, community and Spanish language newspapers were encouraged to attend. The mayor shared an hour informal question and answer session with the community representatives. Lunch and coffee were

Matt Aubrey Communications Director keeping things in focus

actions, as well as pending foreclosure actions; and that this Presidential proclamation include a moratorium on all sales of foreclosed homes in process; and that this Presidential proclamation

include ordering the financial institutions, banks and mortgage servicers to provide homeowners with clean title without encumbrances or liens on their properties.

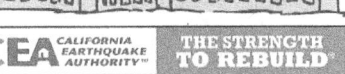

# San Pasqual Culture Day June 2014

*by Roy Cook*

In the skyline is the hazy blue silhouette of Palomar Mt. and behind lazy clouds many tribal peoples gather for this premier cultural event. Greeting each other in the bright sunlight of these first

days of summer at the June 21, 2014 they are listening to Bird songs. Many teams are looking forward to the evening and night Peon gathering. Urban visitors enjoy overlooking the valleys below. The heat of the sun this afternoon peels off the cares and layers of imposed western society. Once again, in our own Native company and our own native skin we bask in the Native tradition of this land. The Ipai tradition, the 'Yuman' language is at home in the riparian banks of the Santa Ysabel Creek, the hills and rocks of eons of generations. This is a land of significant National History and it is a chronicle of our Federal government doing right and very wrong in history. And yet, in spite of so many obstacles, we continue to survive as a native people.

The San Pasqual Culture Committee is responsible for preserving the Kumeyaay culture on the San Pasqual Reservation for future generations. It is also responsible for the maintenance of its Culture Center overlooking Lake Wohlford; its museum, resource center and archive of tribal documents and artifacts. The Committee can be reached: (760) 749-3200.

But, that aside for the moment and looking toward the future this June 21, 2014 Bird song and Peon gathering culture day at San Pasqual is evident of the quality of dedication that a community can provide, by example, for the Indian children. Tribal people from all over Southern California have come to visit with friends and relatives. They have come to enjoy the hospitality and festive traditions of thousands of years at these gatherings. There are excellent food booths to sample, beautiful gifts to select from and free T-shirts to remember this San Pasqual culture day.

As the sun dips in the west and the Singers start the Bird songs and the dancers respond as they form and reform into ever changing lines of responses to the songs and singers. These songs are a sweet sophistication of multiple related songs. The lead singer may or may not elect to bring out double step, or triple step songs, spins, turns. Facing the Singers the dancers will often assemble, mostly female, and guided by the gourd rattle and song join in the presentation. The dancing is often inspired by the moment and song selection of the lead singer. Strong songs sung by stronger singers from the River Tribes call out to the dancers, visitors and our relatives unseen that we are still here. We respected their teachings and examples. We remember them and our songs that sustain us in and thru many changes. We are still here!

Singer groups change and we realize directly of the boundary, International blockage that still keeps the flow of culture under imposed restriction and the institutionalized artificiality of colonial languages a quagmire of misunderstanding, separation of relatives and an indecent restriction on traditional burial practices. But today, these southern relations bring their songs and the same language as spoken in these Ipai hills to San Pasqual for this June 21 Bird song and Peon gathering.

Singers continue to take their turn into the dusk and night as the fires are lit for the Peon games that might last till dawn. Sometimes, after 3am and when the groups are head to head in fierce challenge, the best songs come out to encourage the teams of players.

The "Peon" competition that takes place is a highly competitive game of complex strategy, skill and calculation. The Yuman songs are thousands of years old. Not too many years ago, social opportunities to enjoy these songs were mostly at Fiestas or 'by invitation only' gatherings. Sadly, too often I have over heard comments on Bird Singing from outside observers to the Tipai-Kumeyaay culture, "They all sound alike." also "They just go back and forth, over and over." Yet, to the informed, these songs are a sweet sophistication of multiple related songs. The lead singer may or may not elect to bring out double step,

or triple step songs, spins, turns. Facing the Singers the dancers will often assemble, mostly female, and guided by the gourd rattle and song join in the presentation. The dancing is often inspired by the moment and song selection of the lead singer.

With the shadows of the evening and the lighting of the fires the youth "Peon" competition took place. This is a highly competitive game of complex strategy, skill and calculation.

It is played with eight players - four on each side, with an additional man or woman to act as umpire (Koymi). The two sides are usually made up of male or female players from different tribes or bands. The game itself is played with eight "peon sticks"- four white, and four black (usually made of sheep bone or coyote bone). They are about three inches long and half an inch in diameter. The object of the game is for one side to win all the tally sticks. The Koymi, at the end awards tally sticks corresponding to the number of correct guesses from one side to the other. The game is won when one side wins all of the tally sticks.

Much betting accompanies the game among both the men and the women. The game may be won in a short time, or it may - as frequently happens - prolonging itself through an entire night, until the early morning, with several hundred dollars or more changing hands.

Finally, with the people gathering, the songs sung and the traditional games played create a resonance with the land that is sustaining and empowering. As we do this Tribal custom and tradition we will continue to survive with and on this Indian land.

Black Path Commentary: Critical Analysis on Culture, Community, & Struggle

## Commemorating Father's Day: The Meaning of Manhood in the Context of the Black Cultural Revolution

*by Min. Tukufu Kalonji*

Appreciating this month of June is a good thing to do as it not only represents another day, week, month of our life and the possibilities that is before us; also with it comes a month of marking the recognition of fatherhood, on this Father's Day ( June 15th 2014), and by extension to a greater degree manhood. For if one is not a man, then it remains doubtful if they can fulfill the role of father. Thus, this writer brings forth this month's commentary in a context and practice of struggle in a context of the Black Cultural Revolution which is defined in Kawaida Theory as;

*The ideological and practical struggle to: 1) transform the cultural context in which people live; 2) transform the people in the process, making them self-conscious agents of their own liberation; and 3) build the institutional base to sustain and constantly expand that transformation, (Karenga, 1980).*

Furthermore this writer's point is offered as an act of self-conscious resistance to the overly stated pathological and pathogenic position on Black men and fathers that is mitiated and perpetuated by the ruling race and class's ongoing assault on the Black Man. Moreover, in the midst of the matrix of madness of the Eurocentric paradigm in this society, I argue that we of cultural, consciousness and moral vocation not be intoxicated by the structured consuming ourselves with non essential activities like that of barbecues, beaches, beer, mindless purchasing of Hallmark, Wal-Mart, or other corporate cards; and instead reflect upon a substantive position on what manhood is and fathers day should be about. And, in our demonstrating the idea and action of what it means to be Black men and fathers, we will by example provide models for those who currently are not up to par in terms of manhood, yet in struggle together; we will do as it teaches us in Kujichagulia. (Self-Determination); the second principle of the Nguzo Saba which that we will "define ourselves, name ourselves, create for ourselves and speak for ourselves" and Nia (Purpose) the fifth principle of

the Nguzo Saba which maintains that we "make our collective vocation the building and developing of our community in order to restore our people to their traditional greatness." For in the final analysis manhood and fatherhood is inextricably linked; and without question they are both self-conscious, personal and social practice, and achievements. My position is rooted in Kawaida philosophy of which I am an adherent and advocate. However for reason of propriety, it is important to note that the 7 Fold Criteria of Black Manhood, that I use here in this article, as well as live my life in consistency with; is conceptualized by Dr. Maulana Karenga, nationally and internationally known and respected cultural nationalist and Afrocentric ethical philosopher who is the architect of Kawaida philosophy; and perhaps known most for his creation of Kwanzaa, and its core value system the Nguzo Saba.

Of necessity, it is critical to define what manhood is. We know in the wilderness of North America, manhood is perpetuated by false assumptions of physicality and/or genatalia which are merely the basis of maleness. Often time sexual prowess and performances have been misconstrued as a basis of manhood. This is irrational and certainly not in line with the best of African culture and thinking. Additionally the established order has wrongly asserted that one's wealth and material gains defines manhood. Again this is merely an illusion established by a vulgar individualistic and materialistic corporate culture. Manhood thereby must be defined and made real, i.e. validated via a contextualization of social role and responsibilities in a communal context. In our position as Kawaida advocate, there are seven vital roles and obligations which are both principles and practices, thus, the 7 Fold Criteria of Black Manhood.

First there is Respect for One's Own Gender. This means being mindful and acting accordingly and creatively to the demands of being a man, and not doing anything to deform, mutilate, i.e. do damage to ones character. Secondly, there is Respect for One's Species Half. Black men and women relationships are vital to the continuance of us as a definitive ethnic /cultural group, as it with all human species. While this is a second criteria; it is equal to the first criteria as an obligation to respect members of the opposite sex i.e. girls and women. I have argued elsewhere that women are the natural, spiritual, psychological and physical binary factor which makes man complete when related as nature, the universe, and the creators intended for us to be. Likewise as it is with us men, so it is that we are for women the half that completes them in their humanity and development. In short men and women are each other's complimentary half's. If indeed we are

to heal and repair ourselves as men, it is imperative we do so in cooperation with our women and indeed this is endemic to our fulfilling our god given role of healing the world. Our cultural community enterprise in living, being devoted to one another, and struggle is as mandatory to our existence and development as sunlight, air, food, and water is indispensible to the flourishing of humanity and indeed the world.

Thirdly, is Moral Maturity, this is spiritual and moral grounding; that is to say having an ethical education and foundation upon which we think, feel, speak and act accordingly. It involves being respectful of the sacred and special, being other directed rather than self absorbed. It is in this realm of manhood where the Nguzo Saba as a value base and spiritual principles are conceptualized, internalized, and practiced in our daily living. Fourthly is Mental Maturity, which is intellectual rootedness. The third and fourth criteria of Black manhood accentuate that knowledge of self, society, and the world and being grounded in one's own cultural views and values are indispensible to our living a dignified life as African men understanding and asserting ourselves in the world. Fifthly,

is Provision, a man is compelled by culture, history and humanity to provide for his family and community, even in the midst of adverse impositions. Thus, men must be resourceful and this resourcefulness is not necessarily something to be accomplished in isolation but rather calling on the collective strength of community to meet the need I question.

Sixthly is Protection, here the emphasis is on always being security conscious and protective of one's family, community, and culture. Protection is fundamental to manhood and clearly reflects the upmost respect for one's family and community, especially its women and children. In 2004, in a lecture and discussion with political activist and professor, Angela Davis, who postulated that "men" were responsible for abusing women; I corrected her arguing that the abusive male is merely just that a male; and in fact an overgrown boy. For it is not merely chronological age that bring males into manhood; it is the practice of these seven criteria of manhood which I am outlining here that make a male transform from boy to man. And a man

SEE **Meaning of Manhood, page 7**

## Treasury Releases Tribal General Welfare Guidance to Address Unique Needs and Challenges of Indian Tribal Government

WASHINGTON, DC – On June 3rd the U.S. Department of the Treasury and Internal Revenue Service (IRS) issued final guidance specifying that a wide range of benefits and services provided by Indian tribal governments qualify for the general welfare exclusion from income. These include programs for housing, education, cultural and religious purposes, and the elderly and disabled, among others.

"Today's guidance provides important clarity for Indian tribes that certain member benefits and services are exempt from federal income tax under the general welfare exclusion. This guidance was developed as part of our ongoing government-to-government consultation with Indian Tribal governments and further demonstrates the Administration's commitment to working with the Native American community and addressing their specific needs," said Assistant Secretary for Tax Policy Mark J. Mazur.

Traditionally, payments by governments qualify for the general welfare exclusion if they are (1) made pursuant to a governmental program; (2) for the promotion of general welfare (i.e., based on need); and (3) not compensation for services.

Treasury and the IRS created this guidance to address the unique needs and challenges of Indian tribal

governments. While developing this guidance, Treasury and the IRS received over 120 written comments, convened listening sessions, and participated in other formal and informal consultations to facilitate government-to-government dialogues between the U.S. federal and Indian tribal governments and understand key tribal concerns.

The guidance specifies that certain benefits provided by Indian tribal governments to their members and certain non-members qualify for exclusion from federal income tax, including programs for housing, education, cultural and religious purposes, the elderly and disabled, and emergency and other qualifying assistance. It also provides that certain items of cultural significance or nominal cash honoraria provided to medicine men or women, shamans, or similar religious or spiritual officials to recognize their participation in cultural, religious, or social events will not be considered compensation for services.

The guidance issued today supersedes the preliminary guidance issued on December 5, 2012 (IRS Notice 2012-75), which has been effective since that date.

*For more information on Treasury's consultation with Indian tribes visit: http://www.treasury.gov/resource-center/economic-policy/tribal-policy/Pages/Tribal-Policy.aspx*

To improve the quality of life of those who recognize themselves and choose to be recognized by others as "Indigenous Peoples of Color of the Americas" and in support of The American Indian Rights and Resources Organization (AIRRO).

# Reconciliation Coming Together

Maroons (from the Latin-American Spanish word cimarrón: "feral animal, fugitive, runaway", lit. "living on mountaintops"; from Spanish cima: "top, summit") were African refugees that escaped slavery in the Americas and formed independent settlements. The term can also be applied to their descendants. The Black Seminoles who allied with Seminole Indians in Florida, were one of the largest and most successful Maroon communities in the United States. In the New World, as early as 1512, black slaves had escaped from Spanish and Portuguese captors and either joined indigenous peoples or eked out a living on their ownSir Francis Drake enlisted several cimarrónes during his raids on the Spanish.[2] As early as 1655, runaway slaves had formed their own communities in inland Jamaica, and by the 18th century, Nanny Town and other villages began to fight for independent recognition.

When runaway slaves banded together and subsisted independently they were called Maroons. On the Caribbean islands, runaway slaves formed bands and on some islands formed armed camps. Maroon communities faced great odds to survive against white attackers, obtain food for subsistence living, and to reproduce and increase their numbers. As the planters took over more land for crops, the Maroons began to vanish on the small islands. Only on some of the larger islands were organized Maroon communities able to thrive by growing crops and hunting. Here they grew in number as more slaves escaped from plantations and joined their bands. Seeking to separate themselves from whites, the Maroons gained in power and amid increasing hostilities, they raided and pillaged plantations and harassed planters until the planters began to fear a massive slave revolt.

## "I Resolved Never to Be Conquered": Women and the Underground Railroad

*July 16-20, 2014*

The theme for this year's conference is "I Resolved Never to Be Conquered": Women and the Underground Railroad. This sentiment penned by freedom seeker Harriet Jacobs, shows her determination, "though one of God's most powerless creatures," to retain control over herself and her body despite her enslaved status. The conference's focus on women recognizes NTF program's new organizational link with the Harriet Tubman Underground Railroad Monument, and will explore that while Tubman has been the dominant image of women and the Underground Railroad, her involvement is part of a larger story of women's participation in the movement, as freedom seekers and as operatives.

The five-day conference in Downtown Detroit will include renowned speakers, panel discussions, an exhibit hall, and tours of local museums and historic sites. There will also be a tour to Canada on Sunday, July 20th. So be sure to have your passports or enhanced driver's licenses ready!

Registration is available through the Association for the Study of African American Life and History (ASALH)

*For More Information, contact: Diane Miller, National Program Manager, National Underground Railroad Network to Freedom Program, 402.661.1588/diane_miller@nps.gov or Déanda Johnson, Midwest Regional Coordinator, 402.661.1590/deanda_johnson@nps.gov.*

Pencil (graphite) drawing of Harriet Jacobs, by artist Keith White, Raleigh, NC, February 1994 (PhC.122). North Carolina State Archives, Raleigh, NC.

## Seminole Maroons Caesar Bruner and "Pompey Bruner" Fixico"

Caesar Bruner was born in Indian Territory, around 1830. When the John Horse Group escaped Indian Territory and fled to Mexico in 1849, Caesar did not go with them. Those Bruner family members who did go with Wildcat and John Horse, when they returned to the U.S., in 1870, they were using the name, that they

had been called in Mexico, which was "Bruno".

The Caesar Bruner band was named after Caesar Bruner. Under his leadership, a small Freedmen community called Bruner Town was formed. Several members of the extended Bruner family settled around him.

Caesar Bruner was married to

SEE **Bruner**, page 14

## Caesar Bruner Returns

*by Phil Fixico*

When I first learned of my , true ancestry 15 years ago, I automatically, identified with, being a Seminole Maroon Descendant. Today, while reaching out to other Maroons and their Descendants, as I read the names of some of the many Maroon groups found throughout the Western Hemisphere, I looked into the eyes of a familiar face. It was found on the banner of the group known as : "Maroon Culture". The eyes on that face belonged to my Great-Grandfather "Papa" Caesar Bruner. I knew that Papa Ceasar was a, Great Leader who had fought in the U.S. Civil War, but I didn't know that he was known and revered by Maroons and their Descendants, throughout the Western Hemisphere.

*https://www.facebook.com/#!/groups/MAROONEMPIRE/*

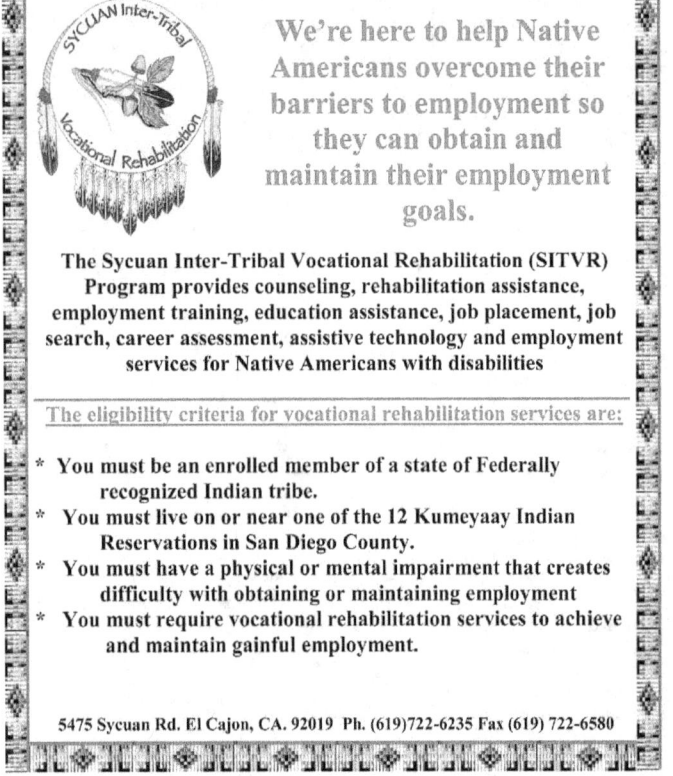

# South Bayfront Powwow

The 3rd annual South Bayfront Powwow is a traditional gathering with dance and ceremony, held on the Chula Vista Bayfront August 2nd and 3rd, 2014. Open to the public as a free educational and cultural event, we invite visitors to the bayfront for a weekend of traditional Music, Dance, Arts and Crafts and Food.

This event creates a connection to the historic past of San Diego Bay and our local diversity, highlighting our region's Native American heritage. Powwows are a traditional Native American people's way of meeting together to join in dancing, singing, visiting, renewing old friendships, and making new ones. These events serve to renew Native American culture and preserve the rich heritage of American Indians. The event activities will begin on Saturday, August 10th at 10 am. The daily schedule is from 10 am to 8 pm on

Saturday and from 10 am until 6 pm on Sunday.

This event, presented by the Soaring Eagles and South Bayfront Artists is sponsored by the Port of San Diego support from Republic Services and the City of Chula Vista's Conservation and Environmental Department. Planning and coordinating this event were members of award-winning Soaring Eagles Native American Indian cultural dance group of San Diego County, American Indian Warriors Association and Calpulli Mexican - Danza Azteca. We gratefully thank Southern California American Indian Resource Center, Inc. (SCAIR) for their support. SCAIR is a non-profit 501(c)(3) community-based tribal organization, established in 1997 under the authority of P.L. 93-638, the Indian Self Determination and Education Act of 1976.

# Native American Actor Saginaw Grant to be Honored in Oceanside

Held August 3 to 10, 2014, Oceanside International Film Festival is an annual event put out since 2009 in San Diego County's Northernmost city, Oceanside.

One of recipients of OIFF's Lifetime Achievement Awards this year is an American film and television actor Saginaw Grant. Saginaw Grant is a Native American actor, traditional dancer, and motivational speaker, respected member of the Sac-n-Fox, Iowa, and Otoe-Missouria Nations. Grant has appeared in numerous films and television shows. He played Chief Big Bear in the 2013 film

The Lone Ranger, starring Johnny Depp. The same year, he was featured in Breaking Bad. He is also known for acting and representing his nation in other TV shows: The Young Indiana Jones Chronicles (1993), Baywatch (1997), My Name is Earl (2005), Saving Grace (2007), etc. Oceanside International Film Festival also plans to have a Native American Indian element, in full regalia, on stage live at Star Theatre right before Saginaw Grant's ceremony at Closing Awards Gala taking place 2:00 pm to 5:00 pm on Sunday, August 10, 2014, at Star Theatre, 402 North Coast Hwy, Oceanside, CA 92054.

# Meaning of Manhood
Continued from page 5

is respectful and protective of this woman, children i.e. his family and community. Lastly, is Leadership; this is a man's role in his family and community and it is one characterized by right thinking and acting in taking initiative and decision making. This African leadership is not one of stifling and oppressive of women for that would be a contradiction to the best of African views and values. Evidence for this position on Black manhood and leadership is found early in our culture such as in the teachings of our heritage from ancient Kemet, found in Selections from The Husia: Sacred Wisdom of Ancient Egypt; where men are instructed

in leadership in the family. The text says;

*If you are wise and seek to make your house stable, love your wife fully and righteously. Do not order your wife around in your house when you know she keeps it in excellent order. How happy she is when you support her; and kindness and considerations will influence her better than force. Thus, every man who wishes to master his house must first master his emotions, (Karenga, 1989).*

Furthermore, we see a similar axiom taught by perhaps Afro America's best example of Black manhood, Minister Malcolm X/ El-Hajj Malik El-Shabazz. Malcolm X teaching on the Nation of Islam's educational system and the responsibilities of manhood in 1959

argues that;

*Husband means taking care of your wife, earn what you need for your family and then your family respects you. Father means taking care of your children. Be a Man, for you are accepting the responsibilities of manhood; and your family will be proud of you and say that is my father and husband. Be a Man, (Malcolm X, 1959).*

In closing, Fatherhood and Manhood are as posited earlier inextricably linked and one in order to be a father a male must first mature from boyhood to manhood. Given the historically awesome and divine role humans have bestowed upon us, men must constantly and continuously reconstruct themselves

in the most dignified ways for we humans are created in divine image as all sacred text teach; and anything less than what is prescribed in this article is doing a disservice to African culture, and the best of its ethical and historical lessons, legacy, and our collective divinity. Therefore during this Fathers Day let's reinforce those men we know who are walking upright with praise for doing the good of the creator, the ancestors, and the universe; and continue to be the model to be emulated as we Black Men in Motion Walk in the Way of Righteousness for our family, community, and culture!

*Min. Tukufu Kalonji is Founder of Kawaida African Ministries,*
*For info contact @ tkalonji@hotmail.com*

# Censored News in Solidarity with Zapatistas Will Begin Again

*by Brenda Norrell, Censored News*

In solidarity with the Zapatistas and Subcomandante Marcos, and in honor of Galeano, the murdered Zapatista teacher in La Realidad, Censored News halted publishing in its previous format on May 27, 2014, after 8 years of publishing.

Now, Censored News -- much to the dismay of our opponents -- will continue in a new format.

In the meantime, we have breaking news from Paris, where Dine' Klee Benally has challenged the auction of sacred items. Thank you to Christine Prat for the coverage.

We also have news from Lakotas Owe Aku; 'Free Peltier' photos from Western Shoshone Carl 'Bad Bear' Sampson; the latest from Mohawk Nation News;

columns by John Kane, Mohawk; the latest resolution to protect horses from roundup and slaughter on the Navajo Nation, thank you to Leland Grass; and also the voices of Dine' CARE and others protecting Navajoland from the newest poison coal development.

While we create a new name and continue to work on taking Censored News to the next level -- with increased international coverage -- the current breaking news updates are posted in a new blog Indigenous Resistance:
http://indigenousresistancejuly2014.blogspot.com/

Thanks to each of you for being part of Censored News. There are eight years of archives in Censored News, a labor of love. We continue, Brenda

**May 12, 2014 – The County Administration Center Waterfront Park converted the large 8-acre on-grade parking lots north and south of the historic Administration Center to a large community and regional open space amenity. The park include large civic greens, children's play area, intimate garden rooms and an expansive interactive fountain. The Great Kumeyaay Nation supported this massive community project.**

Photos by Bert H. Creighton III

## SAN DIEGO WATER PAR

AIVA GOLF TOURNAMENT  "ONLY T

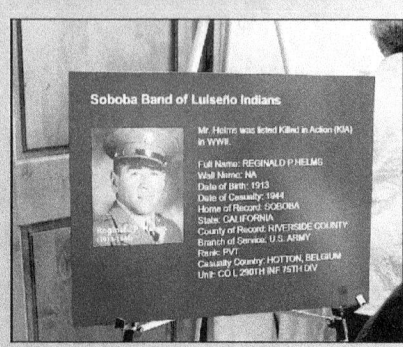

# GRAND OPENING

Michael Murphy wrote a classic book "Golf in the Kingdom" where a character, Scotsman Shivas Irons, wanders around the gorse stroking the feathery. His ghost may have been lingering in the background at the Soboba Springs Indian Veterans' Annual Golf Tournament. A trio of players, Claudio, Gus and Bob fanned out to the twelfth hole as the shotgun, best ball competition began. Most teams had four players but there wasn't a fourth available for these three golfing musketeers. Claudio hadn't really had much experience flailing the shillelaghs and he looked to be a weak link. Gus, young in

## ADOW KNOWS!"

body, could obviously crush the ball but it sometimes strayed of course. Bobolat, as he's known around sports venues, lent his non-plussed experience to the mix. Wouldn't you know, the fourth duffer turned out to be the apparition of Shivas himself. Time after time, when the chips were on the green and three shots had been blasted into duffer dumpsterville, the three gents alternated taking the fourth shot and presto, like a well oiled robot the dimpled dot guided as if by Mescalito found its way closer to the flag. The trio carded a combined 61! To top this Gus and Claudio (who though a beginner turned out to be the ringer), pocketed $156.00 each for winning shots closest to the pin. Quite a memorable feat and lots of fun to boot.

# TPP Information Town Hall Forum at World Beat Center June 29, 2014

The World Beat Center on Park Avenue in Balboa Park presented a very informative Town Hall meeting about the Trans-Pacific Partnership (TPP) Agreement, a massive trade agreement that President Obama is lobbying Congress to give him full authority to sign. Because Congress has the constitutional authority to determine the terms of trade agreement, under Article I, Section 8, Mr. Obama is asking for "Fast-Track" authority which would give him the authority instead. If they vote to give up their authority to the President, he will be allowed to ignore Congress' suggested terms and negotiate and sign the agreement on his own terms. This would create a binding trade treaty with eight other countries on the Pacific Rim. As currently negotiated - in secret - the leaked text of the TPP shows that our protections from laws governing labor, environment, health, consumer issues, Internet freedom, finance, and currency values and manipulation.

At the Town Hall, there were many speakers explaining the TPP's effects on most of these areas. Richard Barrera spoke on behalf of workers and labor unions and pointed out the threats posed by the treaty to hard-won rights and protections gained during the last century. The Sierra Club's Jean Costa presented the downgrading of environmental standards that we could expect. Matt McKinnon of the Machinists' Union spoke of his personal experiences with maquiladoras (companies established by US corporations just south of the border to replace US workers with Mexican one) and their abysmal labor conditions. There was actually a speaker from the labor coalition who told us, through a translator, of the conditions in those factories, including long hours, no benefits, no breaks, no protection from toxics, no unions, and wages that are not livable. Under the TPP, more US jobs will be sent to other countries, and more such factories will be created with the same, or similar conditions.

Although the presentations went on for about two hours, the audience of about 60 people sat spellbound and listened intently to the speakers. Each person there received a paper entitled "What We Want," and all were encouraged to reach out to their Senators and Representatives in Washington and give them the clear message that we do not want Fast-Track authority for the President. They were also encouraged to tell them that such agreements need to be negotiated AFTER the Congress, with the people's full input, has determined the standards by which all parties to the treaty must abide; that there needs to be an end to secret negotiations, and the process of finalizing the text must be completely transparent.

Many of the participants expressed their determination to make a difference by contacting their representatives and by spreading information about the effects of the TPP if it is implemented, to all their friends and contacts, through Facebook, Twitter, emails, and just talking about it whenever they get a chance. Rather than being depressed by what they heard, people said they felt energized to go and speak to their representatives, some even expressing shock that this was being secretly done by our Congress and our President.

*Christina Imhoof*

# San Diego BAYPAC Meeting ... Vibrant Animated and Informative

A decisive banging of the gavel brought the June meeting of the San Diego chapter of BAYPAC to order.

After a round table of introductions the floor was open for an orderly, energetic sharing.

It was a no show for the anticipated

Energy. It was an interactive gathering of citizens looking to join a good fight. According to overheard statements it

guest Congressman Juan Vargas, which may have been a blessing. The gathered crowd had no problem filling in.

There was a litany of information shared. Elected officials candidates, educators, social activists and anybody who had a point to make contributed to this community learning experience and forum.

The issue of prison reform was an area of concern. ACLU Policy Director, Margaret Dooley-Sammuli stuck a cord with those concerned with bringing our prison system out of the Stone Age and countering the Prison Industrial Complex. Bro Hugh Muhammad spoke of economic improvements and Green

was also fun.

For information re: BayPac membership
Contact drwillieblair@gmail.com

# San Luis Rey Mission Indian Pow Wow

Hosted by the San Luis Rey
Luiseno Mission Indians at the
Mission San Luis Rey in Oceanside,
this event draws tribal members
from all over the
United States for
contest dancing,
Native American
arts and crafts,
games and food.

# Fresno's Indigenous History

The original inhabitants of the San Joaquin Valley region were the Yokuts people, who engaged in trading with other California tribes of Native Americans including coastal peoples such as the Chumash of the Central California coast, with whom they are thought to have traded plant and animal products.

The County of Fresno was formed in 1856 after the California Gold Rush. It was named for the abundant ash trees lining the San Joaquin River. Fresno is the Spanish word for ash trees. The county was much larger than it is today as part of Tulare County, comprising its current area plus all of what became Madera County and parts of what are now San Benito, Kings, Inyo, and Mono counties.[citation needed]

Millerton, then on the banks of the free-flowing San Joaquin River and close to Fort Miller, became the county seat after becoming a focal point for settlers. Other early county settlements included Firebaugh's Ferry, Scottsburg and Elkhorn Springs.

The San Joaquin River flooded on December 24, 1867, inundating Millerton. Some residents rebuilt, others moved. Flooding also destroyed the town of Scottsburg on the nearby Kings River that winter. Rebuilt on higher ground, Scottsburg was renamed Centerville.

In 1867, Anthony "McQeen" Easterby purchased land bounded by the present Chestnut, Belmont, Clovis and California avenues, that today is called the Sunnyside district. Unable to grow wheat for lack of water, he hired sheep man Moses J. Church in 1871 to create an irrigation system.[citation needed] Building new canals and purchasing existing ditches, Church then formed the Fresno Canal and Irrigation Company, a predecessor of the Fresno Irrigation District.

In 1872, the Central Pacific Railroad established a station near Easterby's—by now a hugely productive wheat farm—for its new Southern Pacific line. Soon there was a store. Around the station and the store grew the town of Fresno Station, later called Fresno. Many Millerton residents, drawn by the convenience of the railroad and worried about flooding, moved to the new community. Fresno became an incorporated city in 1885. By 1931 the Fresno Traction Company operated 47 streetcars over 49 miles of track.

In 1877, William Helm made Fresno his home with a five-acre tract of land at the corner of Fresno and R streets. Helm was the largest individual sheep grower in Fresno County. In carrying his wool to market at Stockton, he used three wagons, each drawn by ten mules, and spent twelve days in making the round trip.

An 1897 photo of K Street High School, which was replaced by Fresno High School in 1896. The school later became Emerson Elementary School and was demolished ca. 1930.

Two years after the station was established, county residents voted to move the county seat from Millerton to Fresno. When the Friant Dam was completed in 1944, the site of Millerton became inundated by the waters of Millerton Lake. In extreme droughts, when the reservoir shrinks, ruins of the original county seat can still be observed.

In the nineteenth century, with so much wooden construction and in the absence of sophisticated firefighting resources, fires often ravaged American frontier towns. The greatest of Fresno's early-day fires, in 1882, destroyed an entire block of the city. Another devastating blaze struck in 1883.

One of the earliest buildings in Fresno, the Fresno Water Tower.

In 1909, Fresno's first and oldest synagogue, Temple Beth Israel, was founded.

The population of Fresno proper soared in the second half of the 20th century. It entered the ranks of the 100 largest United States cities in 1960 census with a population of 134,000. In the 1990 census it moved up to 47th place with 354,000, and in the census of 2000 it achieved 37th place with 428,000, a 21 percent increase during the preceding decade.

The Fresno Municipal Sanitary Landfill was the first modern landfill in the United States, and incorporated several important innovations to waste disposal, including trenching, compacting, and the daily covering of trash with dirt. It was opened in 1937 and closed in 1987. Today, it has the unusual distinction of being a National Historic Landmark as well as a Superfund site.

Before World War II, Fresno had many ethnic neighborhoods, including Little Armenia, German Town, Little Italy, and Chinatown. In 1940, the Census Bureau reported Fresno's population as 94.0% white, 3.3% black and 2.7% Asian. (Incongruously, Chinatown was primarily a Japanese neighborhood and today Japanese-American businesses still remain). During 1942, Pinedale, in what is now North Fresno, was the site of the Pinedale Assembly Center, an interim facility for the relocation of Fresno area Japanese Americans to internment camps. The Fresno Fairgrounds was also utilized as an assembly center.

Row crops and orchards gave way to urban development in the period after World War II; this transition was particularly vividly demonstrated in locations such as the Blackstone Avenue corridor.

In September 1958, Bank of America launched a new product called BankAmericard in Fresno. After a troubled gestation during which its creator resigned, BankAmericard went on to become the first successful credit card. The dance style commonly known as popping evolved in Fresno in the 1970s.

In the 1970s, the city was the subject of a song, Walking Into Fresno,' written by Hall Of Fame guitarist Bill Aken and recorded by Bob Gallion of the world-famous "WWVA Jamboree" radio and television show in Wheeling, West Virginia. Aken, adopted by Mexican movie actress Lupe Mayorga, grew up in the neighboring town of Madera and his song chronicled the hardships faced by the migrant farm workers he saw as a child. Aken also made his first TV appearance playing guitar on the old country-western show at The Fresno Barn.

Fictional residents of the town were portrayed in a 1986 comedic mini series titled "Fresno", featuring Carol Burnett, Dabney Coleman, Teri Garr and Charles Grodin, along with numerous other celebrities. The mini series was presented as a parody of the prime time soap operas popular in the 1980s.

In 1995, the Federal Bureau of Investigation's Operation Rezone sting resulted in several prominent Fresno and Clovis politicians being charged in connection with taking bribes in return for rezoning farmland for housing developments. Before the sting brought a halt to it, housing developers could buy farmland cheaply, pay off council members to have it rezoned, and make a large profit building and selling inexpensive housing. Sixteen people were eventually convicted as a result of the sting.

# TRADING POST BUSINESS DIRECTORY

## CALIFORNIA

### ADVOCACY
Alan Lechuza Aquallo
Advocate for Native Youth and Scholarships
alan@blackphonerecords.com

### ATTORNEYS
Marshall Law PC
Daniel E.Marshall,Attorney at Law
619-993-5778 • marslawbmw@gmail.com
sandiegoevictionattorneys.com

### BAKERY
Historic San Luis Rey Bakery
490 N. El Camino Real Oceanside, CA 92058
760-433-7242 • www.sanluisreybakery.com

La Nueva Mexican Bakery
4676 Market St. Ste. A-3, San Diego, CA
619-262-0042

### CARE GIVER
Private Duty– References
Terms to be discussed
619-504-2455 Ask for Liz

### CLERICAL
Your Girl Friday International
Marketing, Operations & Promotional
Services • yourgirlfriday3512@gmail.com

### CULTURE
Kumeyaay
www.kumeyaay.com • larry@kumeyaay.com

Worldbeat Cultural Center
619-230-1190
www.worldbeatculturalcenter.org
info@worldbeatculturalcenter.org

### DRIVER
Driver for Hire
Clean DMV Class ABC
619-504-2455 Ask for Liz

### FINANCIAL ADVISORS
Merrill Lynch / Elke Chenevey
Vice President & Financial Advisor
Office: 619-699-3707
Fax: 619-758-3619

Summit Funding
The Home Loan Experts
Jeff Ellenz, Branch Manager
760-568-0300 • jellenz@summitfunding.net

### HEALTH
Rady's Children Hospital
San Diego, CA
800-869-5627 • www.rchsd.org

Regenerative Medicine Institute
www.regenerativemedicine.mx

San Diego American Health Center
2630 1st Avenue, San Diego, CA 92013
619-234-2158

### HEALER-SHAMAN
Transitions / Vera A. Tucker
vtucker1212@gmail.com
619-987-0372

### HOMEMADE
Liz • 619-504-2655

### HOUSEKEEPING
Cleaning, windows, floors
4 hours $80 - 8 hours $120

619-504-2455 Ask for Liz

### INSURANCE
State Farm / Jack Fannin
1154 E. Main St. El Cajon, CA 92021-7157
619-440-0161 Business
619-440-0495 Fax
jack.fanninjroi@statefarm.com
www.jackfannin.com

Earthquake Insurances
www.EarthquakeAuthority.com

### MARKETING
International Marketing Systems
Eddy Michaelly
www.imsbarter.com

Jahaanah Productions
Marketing, Media, Public Relations, Graphic
Design • 832-978-0939

### NOTARY PUBLIC
Sis. Evon X. Nana
San Diego, CA 92113 • 619-549-5792
evonx@yahoo.com

### PHOTOGRAPHY
Peache Photo Memories
619-697-4186 office
619-549-0968 contact
www.peachephotomemories.com
peachephotos@cox.net

### PUBLISHERS
Blackrose Communications
111 South 35th St. San Diego, CA 92113
619-234-4753
www.indianvoices.net • rdavis4973@aol.com

### RADIO
91.3PM Kopa
Pala Rez Radio
www.palatribe.com • 91.3@palatribe.com

### RECOVERY
David "Wolf"Diaz, Pres. & Founder
Walk of the Warrior, A Non-Profit Corp.
Tel: 760-646-0074 • Cell: 310-866-7057
Fax:760-689-4907
www.walkofthewarrior.com
walkofthewarrior@yahoo.com

### REGALIA
Carla Tourville
Native Regalia Custom Design
Yokut Tule River Tribe
San Diego, CA • 619-743-9847

### REPARATIONS
Mr. Peoples Reparations
200 N. Long Beach Blvd. Compton, CA
310-632-0577

### RESTAURANT
Awash Ethiopian Restaurant
4979 El Cajon Blvd. San Diego,CA
619-677-3754

### RETAIL – CLOTHING
Full Blood Apparel
P.O. Box 3101 Valley Venter, CA 92082
760-445-1141

### SOCIAL SERVICES
Tribal Tanf
Temporary Assistance for Needy Families
San Diego Office 866-913-3725

Escondido Office 866-428-0901
Manzanita Office 866-931-1480
Pala Office 866-806-8263

## NEVADA

### ADVOCACY
Adams Esq.
Special Needs Children
500 N. Rainbow Blvd. Ste 300
Las Vegas, NV 89107
702-289-4143 Office • 702-924-7200 Fax

### COMMUNITY
Native American Community Services
3909 S. Maryland Pkwy #205 Las Vegas, NV
89119-7500

### PUBLISHERS
Blackrose Communications
111 South 35th St. San Diego, CA 92113
619-234-4753
www.indianvoices.net • rdavis4973@aol.com

## NORTH CAROLINA

### RETAIL - CLOTHING
Passion Island
832 Washington Plaza, Washington, NC
27889; 252-402-4700

## TEXAS

### HEALTH
The Circle: A Healing Place
Joanna Johnson, MSW, CFAS
Longview Behavioral Hospital
22 Bermuda Lane, Longbiew, Texas 75605
www.longviewhospital.com
www.oglethorpeinc.com
850-228-0777

## SAN DIEGO HAS A NEW PUBLIC RADIO STATION!
## KNSJ 89.1 FM AND KNSJ.ORG ARE CARRYING
## NATIVE VOICE ONE (NV1) MON to FRI AT 10 AM TILL NOON

Native Voice One (NV1) educates, advocates, and celebrates Native American life and culture by providing a program service from a Native point of view. This service is for everyone interested in Native American news, culture, music, events, and life. NV1 enables Native people, especially those who do not have access to the many reservation and village-based Native owned and operated stations, to stay connected.

## Carla Tourville
## Native Regalia
## Custom Design
(Yokut Tule River Tribe)

## 619-743-9847
San Diego

# Balboa Park Centennial Soaring Eagles Powwow Summer Dance Workshop in the Park

As of July 16, 2014 we are going to be moving to a new location in order to continue the powwow dance workshops. We hope that you will find it easy to get to and I hope all the SOARING EAGLES families enjoy our new location. We will continue with a Potluck Dinner before the class.

### NEW LOCATION
Pepper Grove –Balboa Park

This park is located on Park Boulevard across from the Balboa Park Activity Center, just south of the Reuben H. Fleet Science Center. Take Hwy 163 South to Park Blvd Exit. Turn left at Park Blvd and park to the south of the Science Center. There is also limited street parking available as well.

### DATES FOR JULY 2014
6:00 pm to 8:30
July 16 - Soaring Eagles Powwow Workshop

July 23 – Community Night & Soaring Eagles Powwow Workshop

Potluck Dinner bring you favorite Dish and your cold drinks & water. The main dish will be furnish by Antonio & Jennifer Garcia

Powwow Workshop Presented By San Diego American Indian Health Center, San Diego Unified School District, Indian Ed, Soaring Eagles Powwow Dance Group

*More Information: Vickie Gambala*
*619-266-2887, vickiegambala@gmail.com*

## WHAT IS FASCISM

Political ideology that imposes strict social and economical measures as a method of empowering the government and stripping citizens of rights. This authoritative system of government is usually headed by an absolute dictator who keeps citizens suppressed via acts of violence and strict laws thatgovern the people. Some of the defining characteristics of fascism are: (1) racism, (2) militarism, (3) dictatorship, and (4) destructive nationalistic policies.

# NEVADA NEWS

For Nevada Information: 619-234-4753 • 619-534-2435

## New Panel Examine Nevada Marijuana Laws

CARSON CITY — Issues raised at the first meeting of a new panel overseeing Nevada's medical marijuana program Wednesday ranged from employment protections for patients to ensuring that patients who grow their own will be allowed to continue to do so.

Another concern discussed by the Advisory Commission on the Administration of Justice's Subcommittee on the Medical Use of Marijuana was Nevada's current laws regarding driving under the influence of marijuana.

Nevada's nascent medical marijuana dispensary efforts were the subject of a wide-ranging discussion by the 20-member panel charged with overseeing and recommending improvements to the program. The first dispensary won't likely open until late this year or even into 2015, right before the next legislative session opens.

Raymond Fletcher, who moved to Las Vegas from Indiana so he could use medical marijuana to alleviate pain from a near-fatal car accident, told the panel that patients face challenges to participating in state job programs that mandate no illegal drug use. Marijuana remains illegal under federal rules despite the medical marijuana dispensary program approved by the 2013 Legislature.

"We need to make sure those legitimate patients do not get kicked out of state programs," he said.

Assemblyman Paul Aizley, D-Las Vegas, has requested a bill for the 2015 session to prohibit denial of benefits to a state or local employee who holds a medical marijuana card and uses the product.

Fletcher also asked that patients be allowed to grow their own product because of the high cost of buying it from a dispensary, a comment that was echoed by others.

"Especially for those on fixed incomes," he said. "We want to make sure there is safe access to the medicine and not make people homeless in the process."

Vicki Higgins of Wellness Education Cannabis Advocates of Nevada asked the subcommittee not to put a limit on marijuana cultivation. There are no limits yet and they could only be imposed after a public hearing process conducted by the state.

With Nevada's dispensary program allowing reciprocity with other states that authorize medical marijuana, the demand will be huge, she said.

People will come to Nevada for their vacations in part because they know they can get their medicine here without fear of legal consequences, Higgins said.

There were 5,859 medical marijuana cardholders as of the end of May, with 4,196 of those in Clark County, according to the state Division of Public and Behavioral Health.

State Sen. Tick Segerblom, D-Las Vegas, the author of the 2013 law allowing the establishment of medical marijuana dispensaries, said the panel will work on developing a bill for the 2015 session to fix any issues or concerns that arise as the program is rolled out over the next several months.

The establishment of the dispensaries and grow houses to supply the product is still in the licensing process. Regulatory approvals are required both at the state and local government levels.

The state is scheduled to accept applications from Aug. 5 to Aug. 18.

The Legislature in 2013 overwhelmingly approved Assembly Bill 374 authorizing 66 dispensaries to operate in Nevada, 40 of them in Clark County.

Segerblom said he would like to see the Legislature also tackle the driving-under-the-influence issue in a separate bill.

The panel has four state lawmakers and 16 appointees representing the legal community, law enforcement and local government, and other interests.

Las Vegas attorney and panel member John Watkins said the driving-under-the-influence issue is a top priority.

Watkins has argued that scientific evidence shows no relationship between Nevada's standard and impairment while driving. A person who smokes pot can be perfectly straight the following day but still fail the test by a wide margin.

Nevada's standard is whether a driver's blood contains 2 nanograms per milliliter of marijuana or 5 nanograms per milliliter of marijuana metabolite.

Watkins defended motorist Jessica Williams, who in a March 2000 struck and killed six teenagers collecting trash in the median of Interstate 15.

A jury determined that Williams was not impaired at the time of her crash, but convicted her of driving with prohibited substances in her blood. She is serving a prison sentence of 18 to 48 years.

*Contact Capital Bureau reporter Sean Whaley at swhaley@reviewjournal.com or 775-687-3900. Find him on Twitter: @seanw801.*

## Vincent Ochoa Family Court Judge Admitted to Violating Nevada Custody Laws!

CLARK COUNTY, NV — July 1, 2014 The Veterans In Politics has obtained information that was conducted in an interview with Michele T. LoBello and Family Court Judge Vincent Ochoa.

Judge Ochoa blatantly admitted to violating Fathers Rights.

Judge Ochoa said that he does not grant overnight visits for the first six months of the life of a child to the Father. Ochoa admitted to factoring the gender of the parent in violation of Nevada Custody Laws.

This is a clear violation of NRS

## Bruner

Continued from page 6

Prophet Abraham's granddaughter, Nancy Abraham who was the interpreter for the Seminole Chiefs, he also was a great warrior.

Sometime in 1870, Caesar Bruner found a new location for his people on Turkey Creek.

Caesar Bruner was the Band chief elected in 1879. He had served on the Union side during the Civil War. He was Band leader prior to Oklahoma statehood. He died at 93 years of age. He is buried in Mount Zion Church graveyard.

Caesar Bruner and his band promoted education for their members and making money in the cattle business. Band members were not allowed to commit crimes. If caught doing so, the band exacted harsh punishment.

Phil "Pompey Bruner" Fixico, Co-Founder of the Bureau of Black Indian Affairs, is Caesar Bruner's Great grandson, by a Full Blooded Mikasuki, Seminole (Wind Clan) woman named, Dinah Fixico, Dawes Rolls #900. Caesar Bruner is now, known throughout the Western Hemisphere thanks to the the Facebook.com group "Maroon Culture".

The early Maroon communities were usually displaced. By 1700, Maroons had disappeared from the smaller islands. Survival was always difficult as the Maroons had to fight off attackers as well as attempt to grow food. One of the most influential Maroons was François Mackandal, a houngan, or voodoo priest, who led a six-year rebellion against the white plantation owners in Haiti that preceded the Haitian Revolution.

In Cuba, there were maroon communities in the mountains, where African refugees who escaped the brutality of slavery and joined refugee Taínos. Before roads were built into the mountains of Puerto Rico, heavy brush kept many escaped maroons hidden in the southwestern hills where many also intermarried with the natives. Escaped Africans sought refuge away from the coastal plantations of Ponce. Remnants of these communities remain to this day (2006) for example in Viñales, Cuba and Adjuntas, Puerto Rico.

125.480; Best interests of child; preferences; 2.Preference must not be given to either parent for the sole reason that the parent is the mother or the father of the child.

Maybe Judge Ochoa should be a candidate for Nevada State Legislature instead of a Clark County Family Court Judge!

*Listen to link below:*
*http://www.stoffelforjudge.com/Media*
*Interview with Judge Vincent Ochoa - Michele T. LoBello, Esq. on AM720 Visit Nevada Politics at:*
*http://nevadapac.ning.com/?xg_source=msg_mes_network*

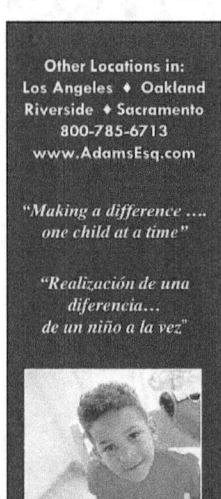

Reid All About It.

*Special to Indian Voices from Senator Harry Reid*
United States Senator for Nevada • Majority Leader • http://reid.senate.gov/

# Fighting Racism and Bigotry

Words have meaning, and sometimes these meanings can cause hurt and pain. One such word is the name of the Washington, D.C. NFL team which is a sad reminder of a long tradition of racism and bigotry.

During my time in the United States Senate, I have worked to right many of the injustices endured by Americans throughout the country. Among the most egregious in the history of our country are those injustices inflicted upon American Indians, Alaska Natives, and Native Hawaiians.

In May, I joined with 49 other Senators to call upon team owner Dan Snyder to change the name of the Washington, D.C. football team. This letter was met with hardheaded derision and defiance. The team's owner defended the racial slur of a name saying it "respects" and "honors" Native Americans.

Recently, I declined an invitation by the team to attend a home game until they change the name.

And I'm happy that in June, the United States Patent and Trademark Office issued a decision revoking six of the team's trademarks which makes one thing very clear. The writing is on the wall. It is on the wall in giant, blinking, neon lights.

Daniel Snyder may be the last person in the world to realize this, and I am sure he will appeal this decision through the federal courts, but it is just a matter of time until he is forced to do the right thing.

Even NBA Commissioner Adam Silver sent a clear message to Donald Sterling, owner of the Los Angeles Clippers, that racism will not stand in the NBA. The NFL should follow suit, and stand on the right side of history in regards to the racist, hateful name that the football team representing our nation's capital bares on its uniform.

I have been asked why I care about this issue. This is personal for me. I represent 27 tribes as the Senator from Nevada and have worked to protect their tribal interests. I will not stand idly by while a professional sports team promotes a racial slur as a team name and disparages the American people.

To learn more about this important movement, visit to www.changethemascot.org.

FRYBREAD                                    SAYNDAY

Life can be like an old frybread.    Tough    and Hard!

©10·TRW

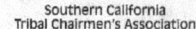

OUR 28ᵀᴴ YEAR          MULTI-CULTURAL NEWS GLOBAL NETWORK          AUGUST 2014

# California Indians Awaken The Spirit

*by Phillip Espinoza-Wellness Warrior*

Haawka ipai inyamutt, my name is Phillip Espinoza and I am a San Diego Native from the Mesa Grande Indian Reservation. I am proud to say that I am the Coordinator of the "Awakening the Spirit" Native American Outreach Program of the San Diego American Diabetes Association. The ATS Program focuses on preventing and treating Diabetes Type II in American Indian communities through the Southern California area from San Manuel to Quechan.

The work that I do to prevent and treat diabetes in the Greater San Diego American Indian Communities comes from a place of my own personal growth and transformation. For most of my youth, I was subject to poor health, poor diet and lack of regular exercise. I was obese, weighing in at around 230 lbs at

Phillip Espinoza blazing the trail for Kumeyaay cultural health.

5'0" never playing any organized sports in school or getting out much at all. I had the heart, and capability, just never the opportunity or support to participate in athletics. At the end of college, I found myself at a weight of 235lbs and decided that I wanted to make a conscious change in my life, lest I follow down a path riddled with diabetes and other health complications that disproportionately affect the lives of Native Americans. I took control of my

life as an adult and made gradual changes to my lifestyle habits that ultimately contributed to me losing a total of 75lbs down to my current healthy weight of 160lbs at 5'10". I currently am involved in endurance sports with Ironman-distance Triathlons being my main focus (2.4 mile swim, 112 mile bike ride, 26.2 mile run). I tell you my story to show you that you too can make a transformation in your life!

One of the projects we are currently working on with Awakening the Spirit is a program that would be implemented by "Wellness Warriors", which are designated tribal members who would serve as the figurehead in their tribe in the fight against Diabetes. Ideally, these Wellness Warriors would have an inspiring story of transformation, such as my own, or simply a passionate 'health and wellness' attitude that would help

SEE **Diabetes**, page 10

---

# Saginaw Grant Lifetime Achievement Award

The Star Theater in Oceanside CA was sacred ground August 10th. A gathering of tribes representing the numerous traditional Indian communities surrounding Oceanside came together to honor Saginaw Grant. It was a resonating, and powerful event. The theater was bathed in singing, dancing and traditional drumming, creating a multi-cultural spiritual happening

This historical, paradime shifting event hosted by the Oceanside Cultural Arts Foundation paid homage to a cultural icon and hero.

Saginaw Grant was born at the Indian Hospital in Pawnee, Oklahoma, the son of Austin and Sarah (née Murray) Grant. He is a member of the Sac and Fox Nation of Oklahoma His mother's ancestry was from the Iowa and Otoe-Missouria tribes of Oklahoma.

As a Native American actor, traditional dancer and motivational speaker, Saginaw Grant brought honor to the Sac-n-Fox, Iowa, and Otoe-Missouria Nations where he is a respected member.

Grant has appeared in numerous films

Alexxa Morgan presents Saginaw Grant a bouquet during the presentation of a Lifetime Achievement Award to Grant.

and television shows. He played Chief Big Bear in the 2013 film the Lone Ranger, starring Johnny Deep. The same year, he was featured in Breaking Bad. His is aso known for acting and representing

his nation in other TV shows: The Young Indiana Jones Chronicles, (1993) Baywatch, (1997). My name is Earl

SEE **Saginaw Grant**, page 11

# Rosalie Little Thunder

*September 19, 1949-August 9, 2014*

The Buffalo Field Campaign family is mourning the passing of Rosalie Little Thunder, our co-founder, leader, and a strong source of inspiration to all who had the honor of knowing her. She passed away on Saturday, August 9. Since hearing the news I've been having a hard time finding words to express who she was, the impact she made with her life, and how much she gave for the buffalo and all beings.

Seeing the Montana buffalo slaughter firsthand in 1997 inspired her to found Buffalo Nations, the organization that would become Buffalo Field Campaign. In her words:

Since I witnessed the 1996-97 slaughter, I have continued to be involved in the ongoing effort to stop the slaughter. Mike Mease and I collaborated and founded Buffalo Nations, whose mission was simply to protect the Yellowstone buffalo herd. Two strategies evolved and therefore, two projects also evolved. The immediate threats to the herd, demanding immediate action, was undertaken by Buffalo Field Campaign. The second strategy was to coordinate cultural approaches and seek tribal involvement. Buffalo Nations continued to function by its Lakota name, Tatanka Oyate.

In the winter of 1999 Rosalie led 40 Lakota men and women and 60 others from different tribes on a 507-mile walk from the Black Hills of South Dakota to Yellowstone's Roosevelt Arch, at Gardiner, MT. She carried the Sacred White Buffalo Calf Pipe Bundle of her people. The walk was, in her words, an act of spiritual activism for the buffalo. In her view, activism is an integral part of community and community is essential to survival:

Remind yourself every morning, every morning, every morning: 'I'm going to do something. I've made a commitment.' Not for yourself, but beyond yourself. You belong to the collective. Don't go wandering off or you will perish.

While we knew her as a visionary activist, artist, and organizer who dedicated a great part of her life to protecting wild buffalo, Rosalie was so much more. She was a counselor, a

SEE **Rosalie Little Thunder, page 12**

# Indian Voices is Happy to Announce that We are Branching Out to Oklahoma

Our associate Anthony Currin who we know from activist activities in San Diego has recently moved back to his hometown Oklahoma City. He has agreed to be our contact and failiator as we develop community and business relationships in the area.

Anthony has a rich historical background and is actively researching and archiving information on his family. He is the great grandson of Green I. Currin.

Indian Green I. Currin was the first African-American to serve in the Oklahoma territorial legislature. He was born October 20, 1842, in Williamson County, Tennessee. Following emancipation, he lived in Nashville until he joined the great westward movement. By 1877, he lived in Kansas, eventually establishing himself as a lawman in Topeka.

Currin staked a claim in the Land Run of 1889 in Kingfisher County, Oklahoma Territory. With the support of Republican voters, he was one of five delegates elected to the House of Representatives from Kingfisher County. On August 27, 1890, Green I. Currin took his seat in the First Session of the Legislative Assembly of Oklahoma Territory. He introduced the first civil rights legislation in the territory but it was defeated.

After one term in the legislative assembly, he served as Deputy United States Marshal and was appointed to the Colored Agricultural and Normal University (Langston) Board of Regents in 1897. Currin and his wife Caroline had five children. Green I. Currin died at his home in Dover on October 21, 1918.

We look forward to hearings some exciting things from Anthony as he develops his Oklahoma journalistic sea legs.

## Indian Message To The Moon

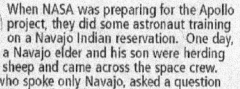

When NASA was preparing for the Apollo project, they did some astronaut training on a Navajo Indian reservation. One day, a Navajo elder and his son were herding sheep and came across the space crew. The old man, who spoke only Navajo, asked a question which his son translated. "What are these guys in the big suits doing?"

A member of the crew said they were practicing for their trip to the moon. The old man got all excited and asked if he could send a message to the moon with the astronauts. Recognizing a promotional opportunity for the spin-doctors, the NASA folks found a tape recorder.

After the old man recorded his message, they asked the son to translate it. He refused. So the NASA reps brought the tape to the reservation where the rest of the tribe listened and laughed but refused to translate the elder's message to the moon.

Finally, the NASA crew called in an official government translator. He reported that the moon message said, "Watch out for these guys; they have come to steal your land."

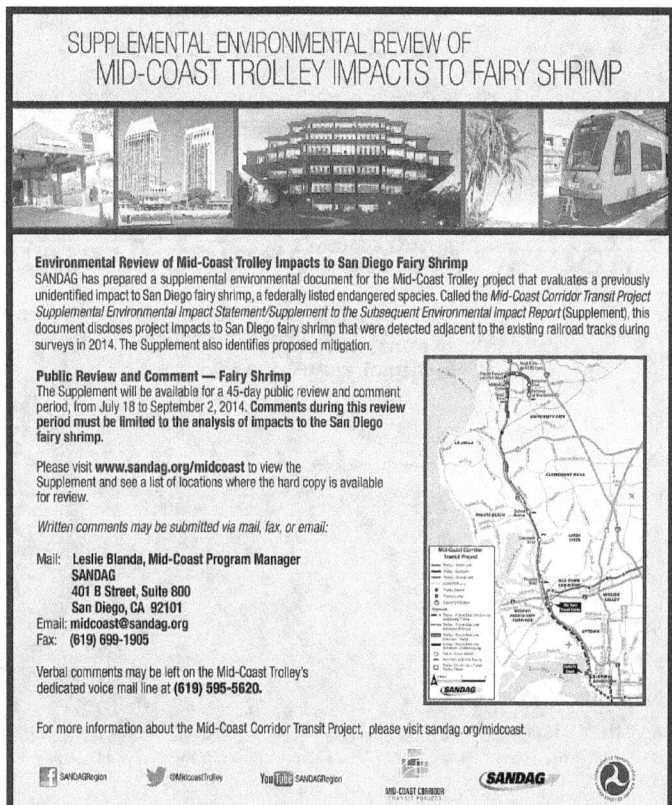

# INDIAN VOICES
**Multicultural News from an American Indian Perspective**

## PUBLISHED BY BLACKROSE COMMUNICATIONS
*Member, American Indian Chamber of Commerce*

Email: rdavis4973@aol.com
Website: www.indianvoices.net
Editorial Board: Rose Davis

| | | | |
|---|---|---|---|
| Editor: | Rose Davis | Writer: | Jaclyn Bissonette |
| Social Media Administrator: | Yvonne-Cher Skye | Entertainment Writer/ | |
| Outside Support: | Mel Vernon | Photographer LA/SD: | Rochelle Porter |
| LV Entertainment Writer: | Z. Z. Zorn | Reporter de Espectaculos: | Omar DeSantiago |
| Associate Editor: | Sis Mary Muhahmmad | Reporter de Espectaculos: | Michelle Banuet |
| Writer: | Kathleen Blavatt | Proofreader: | Mary Lou Finley |
| Writer: | Roy Cook | Graphic Artist: | Elaine Hall |
| Writer: | Marc Snelling | Staff Photographer: | Abel Jacome |
| Writer: | Scott Andrews | | |

Endeavor Media Group
André Haynes
3675 S. Rainbow Blvd., Ste 107
Las Vegas, NV 89103
702-305-0973 •
www.emgnv.com

111 South 35th St.
San Diego, CA 92113
(619) 234-4753
(619) 534-2435 (cell)
Fax: (619) 512-4534

**Member of the Society of Professional Journalists**
**Member of New America Media**

© 2001 Blackrose Communications. No part of this publication may be reproduced without written consent from the publishers. Although we try to be careful, we are not responsible for any errors. Articles are not necessarily the opinion of the publisher.

## HEAD STAFF

| | | | | |
|---|---|---|---|---|
| **2014-2015 Princess**<br>Monica Jacome | **Arena Directors**<br>Pete Buffalohead<br>John Arkeketa | **Head Man Dancer**<br>Randall Paskemin | **Head Woman Dancer**<br>Tracey Moore | **Head Gourd Dancer**<br>Cameron Saal |
| **Head Young Man Dancer**<br>Donovan Nation | **Head Young Woman Dancer**<br>Cora Milligan | **Host Southern Drum**<br>Rose Hill | **Host Northern Drum**<br>Eagle Feather | **Emcee**<br>Tom Phillips |

| FRIDAY, AUGUST 29 | SATURDAY, AUGUST 30 – SUNDAY, AUGUST 31 | SPECIAL CONTESTS |
|---|---|---|
| Gourd Dancing - 6pm<br>Grand Entry - 7pm | Gourd Dancing - 1pm and 6pm<br>Grand Entry - 7pm<br>49 Contest after Saturday evening session | Men's Fancy Dance<br>Saturday Night<br>Hand Drum Contest<br>Sunday Afternoon |

Information: Barona Tribal Office 619.443.6612 ext.120 • www.barona-nsn.gov

# A Tribute to William Loren Katz
## A Sprit Inspired Story Teller of the Peoples History

The last paragraph of William Loren Katz's book Black Indians says it all. *It is a pleasure and an honor to offer this revised edition of "Black Indians". This is story no longer hidden. I hope new readers will be as interested to meet these valiant Americans and hear their epic stories as I was to look into their lives. These men and women have earned an honored place in our history and cherished memories.*

The homegrown genealogical research resulting from The Alex Haley *Roots* phenomena in the 70s created volumes of mixed heritage family research. Much of this material floated toward Bill Katz who, due to his devoted interest in Black history was a natural magnet.

He dug further and put together a chronology of a mixed people who have been awakened. His books have been the instructional manual and guide for academics and scholars who seek factual and authentic cultural history.

Using his ability to view history from the lens of the oppressed (which often defies the colonizers version) he tells the story from a people inspired perspective. Through admirable intelligence he has managed to navigate around the down and dirty career killing academic politics that often accompanies tendentious viewpoints. He walks in two worlds with ease.

Bill Katz's career long devotion, activism and inspired research of Black Indians is the fuel that has kept the embers of the Black/Indian heritage burning while inspiring multitudes of cultural stakeholders to develop research skills. This empowering community exercise has expanded the body of knowledge and has tipped it to a critical mass.

A graduate of both Syracuse University (1950, with a BA in history) and New York University (1952, with an MA in Secondary Education), Katz taught in the New York City and State secondary education systems for 14 years. He has served as a consultant for numerous boards of education nationwide.

In 2012 he received the National Underground Railroad to Freedom Award by the National Park Service, and the Lifetime Contribution to The Literature for Children of African Descent from the Institute of African American Affairs, New York University where he has been a scholar-in-residence since 1973.

As the Congress of Black /Indians assembled for an inaugural gathering in Washington DC, multi-ethnic elders joyfully came together reconnected with their cultural memory, strengthened in spirit to clear up the clogged arteries of indigenous history and committed to handing the youth an identity crisis free life.

SEE **Katz Tribute**, page 7

## Indigenous Peoples Working Group

Our goal is to develop a strong network of Indigenous peoples throughout San Diego and (hopefully throughout the United States), to help enable indigenous people to support each other, build their capacities and work collectively in their communities.

• Implement strategy pertaining to the promotion and protection of human rights and fundamental freedoms of Indigenous Peoples.

• Collect information, produce analytical studies and reports on Indigenous Peoples of San Diego and surrounding communities.

• Plan and organize events in order to educate the local community about the Indigenous Peoples.

• Act as a focal point on Indigenous Peoples issues and promote effective collaboration.

• Liaise with tribes and various organizations and to identify needs and opportunities to promote Indigenous Peoples.

## Indigenous Peoples Working Group Youth Ambassador Program

We are currently seeking three high school students (juniors and seniors preferred) and three college students to serve as "Youth Ambassadors" for the Indigenous Peoples Working Group at the United Nations Association San Diego Chapter. You will be amongst the first to serve as youth ambassador and help bring awareness of indigenous peoples issues amongst San Diego County. We are looking for young, motivated leaders to be part of our summer program you will be an essential part of our team, as a youth ambassador you will learn about the UN system and how it all works you will conduct research and learn about issues affecting indigenous communities. Our main goal is to help educate indigenous peoples about the United Nations Declaration on the Rights of Indigenous Peoples, as a youth ambassador you will learn about the UNDRIP and help educate others.

Responsibilities and Duties include but not limited to:

• Engage other youth in UNA, San Diego activities.

• Educate the general public on indigenous people's issues.

• Public speaking.

• Media communications.

• Outreach.

• Community relations.

Youth Ambassadors will gain many new skills and be developed into future leaders for our indigenous communities, we hope to have you as our next UNA, San Diego Indigenous Youth Ambassador.

Please send your application, resume and cover letter to ipwg@unasd.org.

For more information please contact,
Ramon Montano
Co-Director Indigenous Peoples Working Group
UNA-USA San Diego | UN Foundation
(707) 845-0579 |
rmontano@unasd.org

## The Lowry Band of North Carolina

*by William Katz*

*"If you believe people have no history worth mentioning, it's easy to believe they have no humanity worth defending" --William Loren Katz.*

People of African and Native American descent have played a prominent part in North Carolina history since survivors of the Lost Colony of Roanoke in 1585 found a home among the nearby Lumbee Indians and then took in runaway slaves from later British colonies.

One band of these well-armed mixed bloods lived in Robeson County, North Carolina, next to South Carolina, under the name of the Lowry Band and commanded by Henry Berry Lowry, himself a mixture of the three races. They also lived under the noses of slaveholders who feared their presence would attract more runaways (and did). During the Civil War the Lowry Band clashed often with the state's Confederate Home Guards. This police unit tried to seize and force Lowry's men to build Confederate fortifications. The Lowry Band, in turn, had no use for the Confederacy, forced labor and that some of their kinfolk were still enslaved by Confederates. The Home Guard also claimed Lowry's men hid guns, stole meat, robbed from the rich, and wanted to overthrow slavery and the Confederacy. Lowrey's men had no intention of being made slaves again, they welcomed, recruited and armed fleeing Union prisoners, African American runaways and Confederate deserters.

During the Civil War the Lowry Band and the Home Guards fought their own civil war. Then the Union Army reached North Carolina! In late 1864 US General William T. Sherman decided he could end the war if he sliced the Confederacy in half by cutting through Georgia to its capitol at Atlanta, and then even further to Savannah on the Atlantic Ocean. With 60,000 men and no contact with supply lines -- but aided by slave runaways -- his soldiers lived off the land, as they cut a path of grim desolation. Then from Savannah, the men marched northward into South Carolina aiming to crush this fountainhead of the secession movement.

Then Sherman's army headed toward North Carolina and Virginia to cut another devastating swathe through the Confederacy. They reached Robeson County, on March 9th only to be

The Lowry Band of North Carolina

stopped by a torrential rain, muddy roads and swollen creeks. They could not move, or knew where to move. Suddenly out of the downpour appeared a dark, grizzed guerila force offering to help. Sherman called his saviors "Lumbees" because he knew were descended from Jamestown's first English colonists who had mixed with slave runways and Lumbee Indians.

But this was "The Lowry Band" under Henry Berry Lowry, and by now mortal enemies of the Confederacy and slavery. They led Sherman's army through the torrential rain and treacherous swamps. Sherman thanked the men for "the damndest marching I ever saw." Then with General Grant from the North, from the south Sherman went on to bring the Civil War to an end. On February 22nd Union troops including African Americans liberated Wilmington. On April 9th Lee surrendered to Grant, and two weeks later on April 26 Confederate General Joseph Johnston surrendered to Sherman in North Carolina.

Whether you call them Lumbees or the Lowry Band of Black Indians, these fighters had done their part to end the war, defeat the Confederacy and help abolish slavery in the United States.

*Adapted from William Loren Katz, Black Indians: A Hidden Heritage © Atheneum, 2012*

Black Path Commentary: Critical Analysis on Culture, Community, & Struggle

# The Black Freedom Movement as Cultural Context: Moving From Passion to Action in Obtaining Optimal Health

*by Min. Tukufu Kalonji*

In the context of the ongoing Black Freedom Movement; i.e. the Civil Rights and Black Power movements; emphasis on liberation permeates a multiplicity of areas of human life and it's flourishing. The status of the Black community's health is not exclusive of this focus. In examination of health disparities of Black men through a public health and community psychology lens, it is argued here the health disparities Black men specifically, Black people in general, and the need

for bringing Black folks to optimal health is clearly a project of advocacy, leadership, and social change.

As the Community Health Advocate for the Men's Health Project of San Diego Black Health Associates henceforth referred to as SDBHA, my central tasks is to educate, organize, and mobilize, Afro American men, their families in the transformation of themselves and the community in general via the rescuing and restoration of their health to a status of Optimal Health. The specific diseases and behavior focused upon by SDBHA are: (1) Obesity, High (2) Blood Pressure, (3) Diabetes, (4) Prostate Cancer, (5) HIV/AIDS, (6) Erectile dysfunction, (&) Stroke, and (7) Tobacco Cessation. In doing so I am responsible for teaching and counseling constituents on the concept and practice of *NERDS, i.e.*

*Nutrition, Exercise, Rest, Detoxification, and Stress Management.*
Utilizing the Black Freedom Movement, as a model to establishes a culturally grounded framework to define, develop, and defend our health interests. Consequently, creating a cultural context for asserting the project goals and objectives of necessity is inclusive of garnering community member's involvement; thus like the Civil Rights and Black Power Movement's; building a grassroots effort resulting in community and personal empowerment whereby community members take control of their destiny and daily lives is seeking optimal health. Moreover, application of an Afrocentric cultural framework for research, and practice of preventive and intervention strategies for Afro-Americans' has its benefits for Black people as service providers and recipients of services to foster their personal, and communitarian growth and development.

In order to accomplish this task SDBHA, as an organization must possess a value based and value driven passion to bring good health into being. However, we know that passion, which

is an intense desire or enthusiasm for something to occur, is not enough. In the final analysis, it is action that brings ideas into a definitive reality. Given that we (SDBHA) engages our constituents in an empowering process which is action oriented. The action items are (1) ongoing education via community forums and smaller educational settings, (2) sponsoring ad co-sponsoring health oriented activities involving onsite exercise programs, structured walking programs, and recreating these in various locations throughout the community, (3) working in collaboration with local churches and barbershops in increasing health literacy, and (4) constant encouraging the community to take control of its destiny and daily life with regards to its health and well-being. The work SDBHA is doing is a monumental task and no matter how big the burden it must be accomplished in the interest of life and longevity of Black peoples in San Diego.

*Min. Tukufu Kalonji is Founder of Kawaida African Ministries,*
*For info contact @ tkalonji@hotmail.com*

# Indigenous People Attend the Review of the United States by the United Nations Committee on the Elimination of Racial Discrimination

GENEVA, SWITZERLAND – Delegations representing Indigenous Nations and Peoples are in Geneva, Switzerland, to participate in the review of the United States (US) by the United Nations (UN) Committee on the Elimination on Racial Discrimination (CERD). The CERD is an 18 member UN Treaty body that monitors compliance with the International Convention on the Elimination of All Forms of Racial Discrimination (ICERD). Compliance with the ICERD is legally binding for the 177 State Parties which have ratified it. The US ratified the ICERD in 1994. Its compliance with ICERD's provisions will be reviewed on August 13 and 14 during the CERD 85th session, presided over by CERD President Francisco Cali Tzay, an Indigenous Mayan Kaqchikel from Guatemala.

The review will be based on the US government's report submitted in June 2013 as well as Alternative or Shadow reports submitted by civil society and Indigenous Peoples which provide additional information and, in many cases, directly challenge the US' own assessment of its compliance. After the review, CERD will publish Concluding Observations, including its recommendations for actions the US should take to fulfill its commitment under the ICERD to eliminate racial discrimination in its policies and practices.

Indigenous Peoples representatives are in Geneva to meet with CERD

members and present their concerns addressing a number of vital issues. The International Indian Treaty Council (IITC) submitted six Alternative Reports for this process, co-submitted by over 50 Indigenous Nations, Peoples, organizations, societies, Treaty Councils and communities. These reports addressed core areas of discrimination and human rights violations faced by Indigenous Peoples as a result of US policies and practices including desecration of sacred areas; discrimination in the criminal justice system, including for Indigenous women and youth, and denial of religious freedom for Indigenous prisoners; Treaty violations; impacts of US past and current policies of removal of Indigenous children from boarding schools and foster care; impacts of uranium mining and other forms of environmental racism; and US failure to comply with international processes for decolonization in Alaska.

The IITC also submitted two Alterative reports which focused specifically on US failure to comply with key recommendations from its last CERD review in 2008. These called upon the US to use the UN Declaration on the Rights of Indigenous Peoples "as guide to interpret the State party's obligations under the Convention relating to indigenous peoples" and to "take appropriate legislative and administrative measures to prevent acts of transnational corporations registered in the [US] which negatively impact on

the enjoyment of rights of Indigenous Peoples in territories outside the United States." The IITC's reports provided extensive documents and examples demonstrating the US lack of compliance with these recommendations.

Indigenous delegations currently in Geneva for the CERD review include the IITC, the Navajo Nation and Navajo Nation Human Rights Commission, Indigenous World Association, Chickaloon Native Village, Comanche Nation, National Indian Child Welfare Association, Laguna Acoma Coalition for a Safe Environment, Lipan Apache Women Defense and the Apache Alliance. Many organizations representing US civil society are also in attendance, including various members of the US Human Rights Network.

Lenny Foster, Dine Nation, is a member of IITC's Board of Directors representing the National Native American Prisoners Rights Coalition and is also Program Supervisor of Navajo Nation Corrections Project. He is in Geneva attending the CERD review of the US to present the issue of discrimination against Indigenous prisoners including violations of their freedom of religious practice as well as the case of Leonard Peltier. "We thank the CERD members and CERD President Francisco Cali for their consideration of these and other very important matters which will be presented by Indigenous Peoples during the review of the US this week," he stated. "We look forward to strong recommendations about how the

US can take action to correct these injustices. This is an historic occasion to present the issues that affect our lives as we continue to strive for self-determination and express our support for the human rights of our brother Leonard Peltier as we seek executive clemency".

The CERD members will hear directly from Indigenous Peoples and civil society delegations on Tuesday, August 12 and will question the US directly on August 13 and 14. Indigenous Peoples anticipate a strong response from CERD members to the issues they will present.

The CERD Concluding Observations addressing the US as well as Indigenous Peoples and other Alternative Reports are available online: http://www2.ohchr.org/english/bodies/cerd/. Visit www.treatycouncil.org for Alternative Reports co-submitted by IITC and background information about using the CERD to combat racial discrimination. For additional information regarding the events and activities in Geneva this week, contact Danika Littlechild, IITC Legal Counsel, danika@treatycouncil.org.

*The International Indian Treaty Council (IITC) is an organization of Indigenous Peoples from North, Central, South America, the Caribbean and the Pacific working for the Sovereignty and Self Determination of Indigenous Peoples and the recognition and protection of Indigenous Rights, Treaties, Traditional Cultures and Sacred Lands*

# The 1st National Congress of Black American Indians Gathering

## "Coming Together to Honor Untolded Story of the African and the Native"

To improve the quality of life of those who recognize themselves and choose to be recognized by others as "Indigenous Peoples of Color of the Americas" and in support of The American Indian Rights and Resources Organization (AIRRO).

*by Penny Gamble-Williams*
*Chappaquiddick/Wampanoag Artist, Activist and Spiritual Warrior*

On July 19, the 1st Gathering of the National Congress of Black American Indians (NCBAI) took place in the Nation's Capitol. Jay Winter Nightwolf, Founder and Director of NCBAI who is Cherokee, Shoshone, Taino, put the call out for people of mixed African and Native American ancestry to unite and tell their story. A spiritual revival was held at the Plymouth Congregational United Church of Christ and Congregation where Graylan Hagler is Pastor. Nightwolf, a radio host of the "Nightwolf Show in Washington, DC on WPFW, had a vision. This vision building on past and current efforts to tell the untold history of Afro-Native People was the catalyst for initiating a national dialogue on the shared experience and lasting contributions of people of mixed African-Native American blood.

Folks came from Massachusetts, New York, New Jersey, Pennsylvania, Maryland Virginia, North Carolina and Washington, DC. The energy in the room was high and the faces of the people told the story.

The gathering opened with a procession led by Baba Yumi Steve Hooks, Cherokee, Blackfeet and Creek. The drums and chants echoed throughout the church as the people walked making their way around the sanctuary to complete the circle. Some of the attendees shed tears as they moved to the heartbeat of the drum. Mwalim Morgan Peters of the Mashpee Wampanoag was at the piano, laid down some soulful chords and began playing a powerful rendition of Wade in the Water. It blended perfectly with the vocables. Mwalim and his group The Groovalottos rocked the church. A libation ceremony was done in the African tradition led by Nana Kwabana Brown a traditional healer in the Akan and Ewe traditions of Ghana, West Africa. Penny Gamble-Williams did a four directions prayer that was presented in the Wampanoag language, and Chief Margarito Esquino who is Nahuatl, Lencas and Mayan did a prayer and a blessing in Spanish.

Jay Winter Nightwolf shared his personal story and talked about the significance of the gathering stressing the importance of honoring the elders and the children. He reminded us that the NCBAI and "All Our Relations" includes all Indigenous Peoples of the Western Hemisphere who carry the blood of Africa and the European.

There were speakers who revisited the history the African and the Indian that is the fabric of the Americas and so

often it has been omitted from our educational institutions. We were reminded that the relationship and bond of Indigenous People of the Americas and the African existed hundreds of years before Columbus arrived. This occurred through trade and by blood. Alliances were formed during the time of enslavement when captives would escape and find shelter within some Northeast, Mid-Atlantic and Southern tribal communities. The Indigenous of the Western Hemisphere and the African suffered at the hands of the invaders. Enduring slavery, disease, murder, rape, religious conversion by force, loss of cultural ways of life and land brought the Red and the Black together. Stolen People on Stolen Land. The colonizers used the divide and conquer method that caused mistrust, misunderstanding and hatred. Much of this mindset is alive and well in the twenty-first century and as a result, many people who are African, Native and European have been stigmatized and marginalized by people who do not know or who don't want to recognize this history.

At the NCBAI gathering, the people came together to pray, talk, listen, learn, share family stories and begin the healing process. Environmental concerns, the economy and the chaos within our communities as well as around the world was included in the conversation. The discussions led to talks about utilizing the gifts that each person possesses and to put those skills to use in building NCBAI. Spoken Word Artist Sister Safiyyah Aabdullah who is Chippewa recited a powerful poem called "I Teach" that hit all aspects of how many Americans who have a distorted view of African and Native People. This was also part of the personal story shared by

Maimouna Youssef , Grammy Nominated, Singer, Songwriter, Emcee and Poet. She is African, Choctaw, Creek and Cherokee. Her words were powerful as was the chant she sang. This song was inspired by her late grandmother Mountain Eagle Woman. Maimouna spoke about learning the traditional ceremonies, dances, bead work and stories from her grandmother. She also talked about how she was mistreated by others at pow wows. She recalled at the age of six she was made to feel like she didn't belong there because she was dark. Because of those painful experiences, she told her mother and grandmother that she never wanted to dance at the pow wows again. She told her mother "Why can't I just be Black." As Maimouna got older, her mother reminded her that her African roots and the Native sweatlodge ceremonies would help her heal. Now that she is in her twenties and is a mother of a son, the traditions that she has known since childhood keeps her grounded and sustains her.

There were speakers from community organizations such as Senghor Jawara Baye of the Universal Negro Improvement Association (UNIA) in Washington, DC, and Anita Harrell who along with her husband founded the Weyanoke Association from Charles City, Virginia. W. Thunder Williams reminded everyone that we have benefited from authors such as Ivan Van Sertima who wrote "They Came Before Columbus," William Loren Katz, " Black Indians a Hidden Heritage," Jack D. Forbes, "Africans and Native Americans-The Language of Race and the Evolution of Red-Black Peoples, and Tya Miles, "Ties That Bind." There were symposiums at Dartmouth College, "Eating out of the Same Pot," National Congress of the

"Exploring the Legacy and Future of Black/Indian Relations," "The First and the Forced": Indigenous and African American Intersections, The Shifting Borders of Race and Identity Capstone Conference held at University of Kansas and Haskell Indian Nations University, Lawrence, Kansas in November 2006. In 2009 an traveling exhibit called "IndiVisible, African-Native American Lives in the Americas" opened at the National Museum of the American Indian. This was a joint project with the National Museum of African American History and Culture."

The people who attended felt joyful about coming together and they gave thanks to our Creator, The Great Spirit, honoring the Ancestors, respecting the Elders, taking care of the Children was a constant thread in the discussions. This 1st National Congress of Black American Indians brought educators, activists, healers, artists, children and elders together. This event made people feel motivated to get involved and make an impact for the seven generations to come.

National Congress of Black American Indians
ATT: Membership
P.O. Box 56274
Washington, D.C. 20040
www.ncbai.com

---

## The First National Congress of Black Native American Indians - July 19, 2014

*by William Loren Katz*

Congratulations to the hundreds of delegates and to organizer Jay Winter Night Wolf for assembling the First National Congress of Black Native American Indians.

From the sun-splashed islands of the Caribbean to Virginia's Great Dismal Swamp, the marshlands of Florida and towering mountains from Canada to Tierra del Fuego, your heroic ancestors wrote a proud history that can be found in few books. You met in celebration of the first freedom fighters of the Americas. You met to preserve their legacy and carry on their gallant traditions.

From the time of Columbus and the Spanish conquistadores your people battled slave-traders and hunters,

Europe's best soldiers and pious missionaries who sought to plant deceit and division among people of color.

You walk in the footsteps of daring and ancient revolutionary ancestors -- from Anacoana and Hatuey in the 1500s, Isobel de Olvera and Genga-Zumba in the 1600s to Lucy Gonazales Parsons in the 19th and 20th centuries.

To live in freedom your kinfolk united against armies sent by this country's sacred heroes – George Washington and Thomas Jefferson, Andrew Jackson and George Armstrong Custer – and defeated them. That is one big reason your ancestors do not appear in Hollywood movies or programs.

Your ancestors also gave birth to their own Historians – from Rosa Fay of the Black Seminole Nation, noted African

American historian Carter G. Woodson, pioneering scholar Kenneth Wiggins Porter, Dr. Jack D. Forbes, and a host of less known figures to today's William Dub Warrior of the Texas Seminoles and Phil Pompey Fixico of the Semiroon Historical Society.

Your First Gathering has carried forth the torch of justice and equality first raised by Pope' in New Mexico, Juan Andresote in Venezuela, Vicente Guerrero in Mexico, John Horse and Wildcat in Florida, Oklahoma and Mexico – and has celebrated nameless fathers and mothers who sacrificed their all for liberty, their land and the lives for their children.

May your spirit and unity at the First Gathering extend far into the future and educate people to the role of Black Indians in our common history.

# The Story of Creation Dieguños

The Mission Indian of San Diego County, California, includes the Dieguenos of Yuman heritage and fragments of Shoshonean tribes related to people of Mexican Baja California. The Dieguenos therefore have Aztec influences in their culture.

Though Mission Indians were converted long ago and "civilized" by Spanish friars, those teachings were not evident in the continuance of their early folklore passed down from generation to generation. Cinon Duro, the last of long-ago-chiefs of the Dieguenos related their traditions of very primitive people in the following legends to Constance Goddard DuBois in the late 1890's.

### Native American Legends-Margot Edmonds

When Tu-Chai-pai made the world, the earth was a woman, the sky was the man. They sky came down upon the earth. The world in the beginning a pure lake covered with tules. Tu-cahi-pai and his younger brother, Yo-ko mat-is sat together, stooping far over, bowed down by the weight of the sky, The Maker said to his brother, "What am I going to do?"

"I don't know, ' said Yo-Ko-mat-is.

"Let us go a little farther, " said the Maker.

So they went a little farther and sat down to rest. "Now what am I going to do?" said Tu-chai-pai.

"I don't know, my brother."

All of this time the Maker knew what he was about to do, but he was asking his brother's help. Then he said, "We-hicht, we-hicht, we-hicht""three times. He took tobacco in his hand, and rubbed it fine and blew upon it three times. Every time he blew, the heavens rose higher above their heads.

Younger brother did the same thing because the Maker asked him to do it. The heavens went higher and higher and so did the sky. Then they did it both together We-hicht, we-hicht, we-hicht" and both took tobacco, rubbed it, and puffed hard upon it, sending the sky so high it formed a concave arch.

Then they placed North, South, East, and West. Tu-chai-pai made a line upon the ground.

"Why did you make that line?" asked younger brother.

"I am making the line from East to West and name then so. No you make a line from North to South."

Yo-ko-mat- is thought very hard. How would he arrange it? Then he drew a cross line from top to bottom. He named the top line North, and the bottom line South. Then he asked, "Why are we doing thins"

The Maker said, "I will tell you. Three or four men are coming from the East, and from the West three or four Indian are coming."

The brother asked, "Do four men come from the North and two or three men come from the South?"

Tu-chai-pai said, "Yes. Now I am going to make hills and valleys and little hollows of water."

Then he made the forests and said. "After a while men will die of cold unless I make wood for them to burn. What are we going to do now?" "Do not know" replied younger brother.

"We are going to dig in the ground and find mud to make the first people,

the Indians." So he dug in the ground and took mud to make first me, and after that the first women. He made the men easily, but had great trouble making women. It took him a longtime.

After the Indians, he made the Mexicans and finished all his making. He called out very loudly. "People, you but can never die and you can never get tired, so you can walk all the time."

But then he made them sleep at night, to keep them from walking in the darkness. At last he told them that they must travel toward the East, where the sun's light was coming out for the first time.

The Indians then came out and searched for the light, and at last they found light and wee exceedingly glad to see the Sun. The Maker called out to his brother. "It's time to make the Moon. You call out and make the Moon to shine, as I have made the Sun. Some time the Moon will die. When it grows smaller and smaller, men will know it is going go die, and they must run races to try and keep up with the dying moon."

The villagers talked about the matter and they understood their part and the Tu-chai-pai would be watching to see that they did what he wanted them to-do. When the Maker completed all of this, he created nothing more. But he was always thinking how to make Earth and Sky better for all the Indians.

*DuBois "The Story of Creation 181-183*

---

## Katz Tribute

Continued from page 3

The ancestors have opened a window of opportunity to lock arms and drain the swamp, drive the bats from the power elites belfry and step out into a new paradeim, promoting a supportive system of information sharing grounded in Native Indigenous values and traditions while developing pioneering consensus driven efforts to build bridges with emerging grassroots coalitions who share these values.

Let us pray that we are capable of letting go of our competitive selfish egotistical old ways (learned from the colonizers) so that we can shine a light on a healthy path for our youth to follow.

We are grateful to William Katz for his spirit inspired assistance in promoting this dress rehearsal for tomorrow.

Yes indeed our story is no longer hidden.

# Lifetime Achievement Award

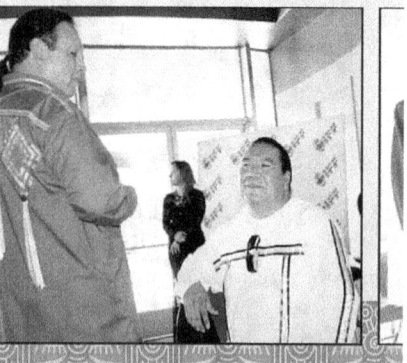

# Saginaw Grant

Photos by BlackRose Communications

# San Diego:  The Hub of Innovation

When drone makers and experts gathered at a conference in Point Loma in June, the buzz was not about drones, but that federal oversight might hamper growth of what is becoming one of the fastest growing industries in the country.

Even before the conference, San Diego was dubbed the "hub of the U.S. drone industry."

According to a National University study, more than 2,400 jobs in the county are directly related to the drone industry, which has brought at least $1.3 billion in military contracts to the region. There's even a local chapter of the Association for Unmanned Vehicle Systems International that promotes the drone industry, and more companies are waiting in the wings until the issue of federal regulation is settled.

One researcher told the Voice of San Diego: "There are some very, very smart people doing it at a garage level that are being stifled by the current policies." http://voiceofsandiego.org/category/quest-drones/

That computer-driven vehicles have taken such a hold on San Diego is a little-known fact, as is what is known about robotics.

Not too long ago, U-T science writer Dan McSwain wrote with the robotics industry "approaching liftoff" San Diego is "positioned as a major launching pad." His article in the newspaper and online recounted how robots are being made here to pick lettuce, save people from drowning, mixing drugs and carry baggage from a car to a hotel guest room, among other things. http://www.utsandiego.com/news/2013/aug/13/san-diegos-robot-cluster-poised-for-takeoff/

"In many ways, the activity resembles the early days of San Diego's biotechnology and wireless communications 'clusters,' which are famous for gathering innovators, customers and capital…" But even more, "the robot business has the potential to dwarf these giants."

Nanotechnology, bioengineering, virtual reality, sensor technology, and a host of other innovative fields, as well as one of the larger video game clusters in the U.S. – they're all here in San Diego or nearby.

However, few people here or outside the area, unless they share are related professionally, are even aware of what's taking place in what's been called "America's Finest City."

"Somebody should campaign to change the name to 'America's Most Innovative City,'" said Rosalynn Carmen, president of the Asian Heritage Society. "San Diego is THE hub of innovation."

Just up the road from san Diego, in Irvine, Oculis Rift, the virtual reality headset creator, was sold to Facebook for $2 billion http://www.theguardian.com/technology/2014/jul/22/facebook-oculus-rift-acquisition-virtual-reality while neighbor Newlight Technologies is converting greenhouses gases into a plastic material that is cheaper than what's being produced now – and lessening the carbon footprint in the process.

Seven years ago, UCSD became one of the first universities in the country to establish a Department of Nanoengineering, to research how nano components -- one billionth of a meter – are incorporated in applications as diverse as clothing and medicine.

A report released recently by the Project on emerging Nanotechnologies (PEN) said since then more than 1,200 companies. Universities and government laboratories in all 50 states are engaged in some form of nanotechnology research, with San Diego ranked seventh.

"This is the picture we want to share with the world," said Carmen, explaining the motivation behind Make It In America, a conference hosted by U.S. congressman Scott Peters, from Nov. 19-22 at the California Center for the Arts, 340 N. Escondido Blvd., Escondido. San Diego County Supervisor Dave Roberts is co-host.

Other innovations, including the growing leadership role of women in entrepreneurship and science, as well as Native American insights into corporate culture, will be among topics featured at more than three dozen panels during the four-day event, which is also attracting CEOs and business leaders from China, Taiwan, Thailand and Vietnam, who may be interested in relocating part or all of their business interests to San Diego. Ruprecht Buttlar, vice president for business, creation and development for CONNECT of San Diego, and consultant Travis Hook will be among panelists taking overseas visitors through the process of relocation.

CONNECT is a regional program that brings together innovative technology and life sciences industries and helps companies relocate to and develop in San Diego.

Other participants in the program include the San Diego Regional Development Corporation, SDG&E, U.S. Navy and City of Escondido.

For more information on the conference and to register, go to www.makeitinamerica.net

## Diabetes
Continued from page 1

motivate others to make healthy changes in their lives. As a Wellness Warrior, we would train you to deliver educational and fitness modules in diabetes prevention, diabetes awareness and general healthy lifestyle tips to your community. I am looking for tribes who see value in this opportunity and who can think of individuals in their tribe who would serve as a great Wellness Warrior. We currently have 3 Wellness Warriors: Kevin Carrizosa (Viejas), Andrej Dominguez (Santa Ysabel) and Rachel Garcia (Morongo). If you or anyone you know would make a great "Wellness Warrior", please contact me (pespinoza@diabetes.org) to find out more about this great opportunity.

I believe as Native Americans we are entirely capable of taking control of our lives again to return to the healthy and active lifestyles we once had. This is why I believe programs like "Awakening the Spirit" are vital to Native American communities, so that we all may help each other in awakening our own spirit. I am proud to be part of the American Diabetes Association and look forward to continuing the good work that needs to be done in Indian Country. 'Eyaay 'ehan (my heart is good).

## Asian Heritage Awards Honorees 2014

*Turning Points for the 21st Century*

The researcher who linked the HIV virus to AIDS, the scientist who discovered global warming 40 years ago, a child prodigy at 3 whose virtuosity on the cello has thrilled thousands all over the world, and a recipient of the French Legion of Honor.

These are among this year's Asian Heritage Awards honorees.

The four, respectively, are Dr. Flossie Wong-Staal, for public health; Dr. Veerabhadran Ramanathan, for science and technology; Tina Guo, for innovation, and Dr. Palmer Taylor, for

Tina Guo

medicine. They will be honored at a special ceremony Saturday, Nov. 22, 2014, at the California Center for the Arts, 340 N. Escondido Blvd., Escondido.

Other honorees include Dr. Anand Srivastava and Deven Petel, business enterprise; Dr. Alexander Chuang, global outreach; Dr. Charles Nguyen, opportunity in education, and Dr. Marissa Pei, entrepreneurship. In addition, California Assembly Speaker Toni Atkins will be honored as this year's Diversity Pioneer. San Diego County Supervisor Dave Roberts is serving as gala chairman.

## Asian Heritage Awards Benefit These Programs

Proceeds from the Asian Heritage Awards benefit the Asian Heritage Society's BOOSTEM program for middle school Asian and Hispanic females and Renoo's Ranch, a halfway home for female teenage victims of AIDS.

BOOSTEM, an acronym for Business, Opportunity, Outreach, Science, Technology and Entertainment for Middle School, is a program that inspires and encourages underserved females of Asian and Hispanic descent to combine the innovative skills of an entrepreneur with an appreciation of science and technology by incorporating all forms of entertainment, including music and games.

The purpose of the program is to prepare young girls for future careers in the rapidly changing technological and global landscape as innovators in science and research and as corporate leaders.

Asian and Hispanic females are the smallest ethnic groups entering the STEM college track, yet have the highest rates of completion. When Title IX took effect in 1972, only 2 percent of major CEO positions were held by females. Forty-two years later, that figure is only 3.8 percent. Less than 2 percent are held by Asian and Hispanic females.

*The purpose of the program is to prepare young girls for future careers in the rapidly changing technological and global landscape*

Worldwide, approximately 1,000 children under 15 years old are infected every day with AIDS. An estimated 270 000 children die each year from an HIV-related cause. Owing to expanded access to combinations of antiretroviral therapy, the rate of new infections in African children has decreased. However, in parts of Asia it is alarmingly on the rise. Young people between the ages of 15 and 24 account for 45 of all new HIV infections, and with globalization, according to health experts, it will grow worse, with some scientists predicting a pandemic of alarming proportions.

The AIDS epidemic already has claimed twice the lives lost during the last major global pandemic – the influenza epidemic of 1919. Complicating the problem is the ostracizing of young females by family, religion and society.

Renoo's Ranch is a place where, after treatment, teenage females can go to reclaim their lives and rebuild their hopes and dreams through programs that include followup treatment, education and job training. And where they will not be judged for their mistakes.

For more on both of these programs, go to www.boostem.org and www.asianheritagesociety.org

### Saginaw Grant
Continued from page 1

(2015), Saving Grace (2007).

The Oceanside Cultural Arts Foundation's mission is to bring quality artistic, visual and performance arts to Oceanside and the surround communities

The festival organizers stated that they were particularly honored to welcome Saginaw Grant with a special Lifetime

Achievement Award for his contribution in the film and television industry. We are thrilled to welcome Saginaw Grant in association with San Diego known for profound Native American history.

The legacy of the San Luis Rey Band of Luiseno Mission Indian is significant. The full regalia performance of the particiapnts prior to and during the on stage ceremony was good medicine for the Indigenous world.

## Ocean Beach Rides the Wave in a Perfect Storm ... San Diego City Council Approves Ocean Beach Community Plan Update

*by Kathy Blavatt, August 5, 2014*

The New York Times September 4, 2008 paper the wrote a travel piece "36 Hours in San Diego", by Brooks Barnes, that had a line the was the essence of why O.B. is still O.B., BEACH BOUND— There are dozens of beaches, but none are more authentic than Ocean Beach, a funky surfers' haven that has stayed frozen in time because of strict zoning rules from the 1970s."

Back in the 1970s the community of Ocean Beach was under threat by development interests from Point Loma and other areas. They had major redevelopment plans for this quaint beach town of one square mile.

The outside developers wanted a yacht basin and a high-rise resort; this would take out the long stretches of sandy beach and Miamidise O.B.

Little did they know they had awoken a sleeping giant who happen to have long hair, clad in tie-dye and surfed.

Along with the community folks looking at the planning process, another group of insightful visionaries were successfully putting through a 30 foot Coastal Height Limit ballot initiative to protect San Diego's coast and views.

OBceans became the first community elected planning board in the State of California. The new form of planning board, whose residents and business owners were elected by OBceans, created a new community plan. This was coupled with the Coastal Height Limit Law, which helped them shape Ocean Beach's own destiny and local character.

Fast forward to the last few years, developers had a stranglehold on San Diego. Most of the politicians are bought and paid for. Then a big storm was brewing, as developer interests got toppled into the sand struggling for the surface, when the state nixed the

redevelopment piggy bank. Another wave followed when liberal Filner won the election for mayor. Gasp, then the Barrio Logan Community Plan won approval by council. Insiders were caught outside in a riptide, struggling to get back inside.

Then those OBceans kept popping up wanting a "Community Plan Update", since it had been almost 4-decades since the last approved plan. These O.B. locals were distracting the city from the next big set of big business deals. "So what if the O.B. Community Plan Update had been worked on by residents for over a dozen years!" "So what if every major O.B. community organization supported the plan!" "So what if people are complaining about how a huge new boxy condo development blocking the view of the Ocean went up by the O.B. lifeguard station!"

Oops, maybe there was another swell building in O.B. All the Hollywood types liked having their TV shows shot there. And O.B. made the news by containing a sticky 4th of July situation by taming the marshmellow wars. And the Ocean Beach Historical Society keeps packing in the crowds that want to learn about O.B.'s history. Maybe O.B. is the iconic beach town people still love and will fight for.

Insiders, said, "Let's see if OBceans are serious about keeping their small town character".

On, July 29, 2004 a wave of OBceans rolled filling the San Diego City Hall chambers. There was a sea of blue shirts saying, "Keep the OBcean Attitude". Their presentation was on point with some O.B. humor tossed in.

City Council got the "O.B. attitude that summer day", riding the wave with a unanimous vote for the Ocean Beach Community Plan Update.

### Rosalie Little Thunder
Continued from page 2

professor, a guardian of the Lakota language and culture, and a well-respected elder who fought tirelessly for the rights of Native (and all) people. As a mother and grandmother she was devoted to her extended family and their well-being.

Rosalie was a member of the Sicangu Lakota Oyate; Burnt Thigh Band, of the Little Thunder Tiospaye and the Rosebud Sioux Tribe. She lived in the Black Hills Treaty Territory in Rapid City, South Dakota.

Rosalie remained active in the struggle to protect the buffalo until the very end of her life. In April Rosalie and BFC habitat coordinator Darrell Geist co-wrote "The Bloody Politics of Bison Slaughter: An Open Letter to Tribal Leaders and the American People," calling on tribes and tribal organizations to stop participating in the wild buffalo slaughter and calling attention to the corrupt bison management policies of Montana and the federal government:

Traditional people must guide our tribal leadership in a manner that reflects the integrity of our historical and cultural relationship with our relative, the buffalo. Montana politics has made a mockery of a keystone species.

A close friend of Rosalie's, Jacie Estes, wrote on her blog about the belief that after you pass you meet a grandmother who asks whether you have helped the people, fed the hungry, and been kind to all. "Knowing Rosalie," she wrote, "she has been having good conversations with her but we know her answer to all questions is yes."

A memorial fund has been set up in her honor. Please contribute if you can by sending a check to:
Rosalie Little Thunder Memorial Fund, PO Box 1894, Rapid City, SD 57709 or make a direct transfer to:
Rosalie Little Thunder Memorial Fund / Highmark Federal Credit Union
Routing #291479686
Acct # 341520020
*In Memory of Rosalie,*
*Daniel Brister*
*Director, Buffalo Field Campaign*

### Ocean Beach Historical Society Presents

## THE BATTLE OF SAN PASQUAL DECEMBER 1846: LOOKING THROUGH THE HAZE OF GUNSMOKE

*Featuring Richard L. Carrico, Department of American Indian Studies SDSU Thursday, September 18, 7pm at Point Loma United Methodist Church, 1984 Sunset Cliffs Blvd., O.B.*

Ever wonder what really happened at the Battle of San Pasqual on December 6-7, 1846? Who really won the battle between Andres Pico and the Californios and General Kearny and the American forces? What was Kearny's objective? How many men did he lose in the ill-fated skirmish? What was the role of the Kumeyaay at the village of San Pasqual and who was the mysterious Indian Andre who accompanied Kit Carson to seek reinforcements? How can you visit the sie of the battle and learn more?

In the context of the overall events and battles of the Mexican War the Battle of San Pasqual that occurred on December 6-7, 1846 in San Diego

County played a relatively minor role. In the history of California, however, and especially the history of southern California, the battle is of importance because of the military and political leaders involved (both Californio and American), the involvement of local Native American people (primarily Kumeyaay/Ipai and Luiseño), the fact that the sites of the engagements can still be visited, and the placement of the battle in the subtext of California's cultural history and that history's diversity.

Local historian, anthropologist, and college professor Richard L. Carrico will provide the answers to the questions posed above and many more at the OBHS Sept. 18th program. Mr. Carrico will also be available to sign copies of his newly revised edition of Strangers in a Stolen Land: The Indians of San Diego County from Prehistory to the New Deal.

# TRADING POST BUSINESS DIRECTORY

## A Eureka Moment that Saved Millions

Working at the National Cancer Institute under Dr. Rogert Gallo in the early 1980s, Dr. Flossie Wong-Staal, then only a few years out of UCLA, cloned the HIV virus, paving the way for the first genetic map of the infective agent and the development of HIV blood tests.

In 1990, the Institute for Scientific Information recognized Dr. Wong-Staal as the top woman scientist of the previous decade. That same year, she returned to UCSD to continue her AIDS research. Four years later, the university created a new Center for AIDS Research with Dr. Wong-Staal as its chairman. In 2002, she retired from UCSD and now holds the title of Professor Emerita. In addition, she is co-founder and Chief Scientific Officer of iTherX where she researches treatment for Hepatitis C.

Born in China and emigrating to Hong Kong in 1952, science was not an avocation. However, encouraged by nuns from the Catholic school she attended and her father, she decided that would be her pursuit.

Dr. Wong-Staal has said: "You need to have a passion for making discoveries because this is the most rewarding aspect of a scientific career. Eureka moments are few and far between."

## About I Love Ancestry

I Love Ancestry exists to empower people to seek knowledge of ancestral heritage, preserve historical truth, and unite like-minded people.

### Mission

I Love Ancestry exist to empower people to seek knowledge of ancestral heritage, preserve historical truth, unite like-minded people and build intergenerational relationships between communities, American Indians and Black Americans in particular

At I Love Ancestry, we envision a world where people embrace their own and each other's roots, celebrate diversity and advocate for indigenous cultures.

### Description

I Love Ancestry (ILA) is a community driven platform that bridges our past and future, engages people and reinforces cultural diversity. We share stories of unsung heroes and heroines who shaped American history and the struggle for freedom. We explore the historical alliances between American Indians and Black Americans and their contributions to history. We promote inspiring people and organizations who are making a difference in our world.

# NEVADA NEWS

For Nevada Information: 619-234-4753 • 619-534-2435

## Black Nevada

*by William Katz*

Few who seek early African American history would start with distant, remote, semiarid, largely desert area named Nevada. The earliest Spanish explorers and adventurers took one look at its winter, snow-covered mountains and called it Nevada ("snowy"). Then they pushed on. So did many others.

But for James Beckwourth, an African American with Native American ancestry, Nevada was his leap into history. A seasoned frontiersman and fur trapper, he became chief of the Crow Indian Nation and a later a US Army scout as he bounded across the United States from Florida to California. He never shied away from trouble, got into many skirmishes, and fought in wars in California and Florida. But that April in 1850 he paused on Nevada's western boundary, look into the Sierra Nevada Mountains and made a discovery that changed the country.

Just northwest of Reno, on today's Route 70 into California Beckwourth found a pass through the Sierra Nevadas that millions had only hoped for. Everyone and his brother back east was racing to California's Gold Rush, and Beckwourth Pass, as it was soon known, was a direct route to the diggings. Beckwourth personally guided the first wagon train through his Pass, and later built a hotel to accommodate eager pioneers in covered wagons – mostly men at first -- bearing picks and shovels and little else. His important pass, mountain peak and later a nearby town bear his name.

But a vital part of Beckwourth's recognition was long delayed. In 1856 when T. D. Bonner, his biographer, placed Beckwourth among the legends of the west -- Daniel Boone, Davy Crockett, and Kit Carson, he failed to mention his hero was a man of color. The book's drawings showed a white man. This erasing of truth continued into the next century. In 1951 "Tomahawk," Universal International's technicolor classic western, featured Beckwourth. However, the famed pioneer was played by Jack Oakie, a white actor. Everyone learned James Beckwourth was important, and that he was as white as Boone, Crockett and Carson. Today the people of Beckwourth Pass, Beckwourth peak and the town of Beckwourth recognize their founder was a pioneer of color.

Early African Americans settlers in Nevada then faced their set of problems based on race. In 1864 when Nevada became a state, its new government denied "Indians, Negroes and Mongolians" a public education. Speaking for the furious men and women of color who mobilized to fight this racism, Thomas Detter, their wealthy and articulate leader, called it "man's inhumanity to man" and "an "effort to keep "colored children . . . growing up in ignorance all on account of white man's prejudice." In Carson City the Black community formed the "Literary and Religious Association of Colored Citizens" to repeal the law. The Association also raised $200 to build their own school and explained, "We value our black babies a s well as other folks do theirs." Two years of determined African American community protests by women and men compelled one school to admit sixteen children of color, and another to open its doors in the evening to African American adults. By 1870 Nevada segregation had been defeated.

By then the state's Black women were playing a prominent part in building community through their churches and social events. They soon turned churches into vehicles of educational growth and agitation for equality. Virginia City's First Baptist Church was able to reach out to the Daughters of Naomi in San Francisco who then delivered their Nevada sisters "a magnificent bound pulpit Bible, and one dozen splendid bound hymn books."

By 1874 Nevada's less than 395 African American residents -- though widely scattered in the state -- were able to build secular cultural and educational societies. In Virginia City the Dumas Society enrolled 22 "ladies and gentlemen," and heard lecturer Andrew Hall told members that education will "fit us for positions where caste would be obliterated forever by the brilliancy of our intellectual attainments." For African Americans in Nevada isolation and loneliness was a leading foe. Virginia City's Black women organized a Calico Ball that extended invitations to all the men and women of color in western Nevada.

Black individuals and groups struggled to survive frontier life. 1875 Virginia City, Nevada widow Sarah Miner turned her husband's hauling business into a $6,000 enterprise, lost it in a fire and rebuilt it the next year. In 1877 Black women in Carson City initiated a literary club to educate their community. It was a sign of growth that year when Mrs. Anna Graham opened her new hairdressing establishment on Virginia City's C Street – and found she faced competition on the street from three other hair-dressing parlors run by Black women.

A clear sign of the Black community's growing prosperity and white acceptance caught public attention during the 1876 wedding of Eureka citizens Thomas Detter and Emily Brinson. The local paper reported their lavish ceremony was "attended by nearly all of the colored folk in town, besides some twenty-five or thirty white people, including some of our most prominent citizens and their wives."

Then at the dawn of the 20th century white bigotry across the country began staging a come back north and south. It reached distant Nevada when Rawhide drove out its people of color and Fallon posted signs warning them to stay away. In Reno in 1904 the police chief arrested and deported unemployed African Americans and the two daily local papers applauded his actions.

Nevada's African American communities had to mobilize again, take on old task, and face old enemies unwilling to quit or follow the Constitution.

The battle in Nevada was a part of the continuing struggle for justice and equality raging across the country. In the 1960s it drew northerners and southerners into bitter and bloody confrontations against the embedded evils of America's past so familiar to James Beckworth, Emily Brinson Detter and Thomas Detter and their friends. Finally some important victories were won in Nevada and elsewhere for people of color, for equality under law and the Constitution.

## San Diego Unified School District Presents Christopher Scott with Award

Christopher Scott owner of Calac Antiques and Collectables received an award in recognition of his community involvement and dedication to San Diego youth.

Since opening his store Christopher Scott has provided a select group of students with the opportunity to be involved with hands on experience in running a business. He offered internship and work experience under his supervision to the students. This experience is but one example of how the private sector can assist with job development and opportunities in San Diego.

Following a formal presenting by the School Board, Christopher was honored by the Indian Community at a ceremony in Balboa Park officiated by Chuck Cadott.

# Transferring Tribal Lands Back to the Tribes

For countless generations, Nevada tribes have called the Great Basin home and they remain a steadfast voice for protecting Nevada's vast, beautiful landscape. Yet throughout the history of our country, Native Americans have been removed and disenfranchised from their homelands and Nevada's Washoe Paiute and Western Shoshone people suffered great land losses through federal Indian policy. They not only lost land but lost heritage, culture and tradition. I am committed to righting historic injustices and I have introduced legislation to transfer significant amounts of land back into the hands of Nevada's tribes.

Transferring federal land back to Nevada's tribes is so important to me and Native Nevadans, who ought to be able to develop their lands and take care of their communities on their own terms. I am pleased that the US Senate Committee on Senate Affairs took the time to examine my legislation. The Moapa Band of Paiutes Land Conveyance Act and the Nevada Native Nations Land Act would together transfer more than 100,000 acres into trusts for eight Nevada tribes. The effects of this legislation are far-reaching, and will provide much-needed land for economic and energy development, housing and community development, cultural preservation, open cattle grazing and agricultural uses.

Tribes in Nevada and across Indian Country are eager for new opportunities to pursue economic development plans and my legislation will help them achieve that pursuit. During my time in the Senate, I will continue to do what I can to right some of the many wrongs by helping tribes restore their homelands and protect their sovereignty.

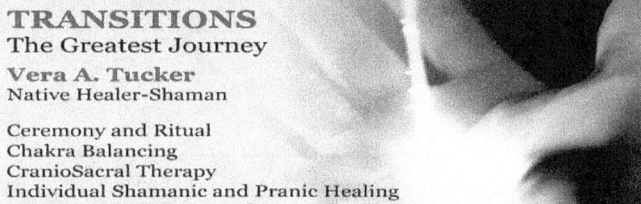

FRYBREAD                    SAYNDAY

What the...    Embarassing    Ginger bread!

©10 - TRW

# "Make It In America" Conference To Encourage Asian Investments and Entrepreneurship in the US

*First of its kind conference to take place*
**Wednesday-Saturday, Nov. 19-22, 2014**
**at the California Center for the Arts in Escondido, San Diego County, California,**
*as part of a collaborative effort by*
the Asian Heritage Society, U.S. Congressman Scott Peters and
Co-San Diego County Supervisor Dave Roberts.

### "Make It In America: Boosting Possibility Through Innovation and Entrepreneurship"

*Guests will come from China, the Philippines, Thailand and Vietnam*
*and include business leaders from the four-county region.*

The ultimate goal of the conference is to create new jobs and industry here in Southern California --
but jobs and industry with a purpose to do good.

"We can't leave progress up to corporations and government anymore," said Leonard Novarro,
secretary and board chairman of the Asian Heritage Society. "We already know what's not working.
Now it's time to find out what works, tackle the problems, change things and spread the solutions
throughout the planet to change societies. It sounds like a big order, and it is. Government and big
business had their chance. Now it's the social entrepreneurs who have seized the day."

*"Times change. We have to evolve," said Rosalynn Carmen, Asian Heritage Society President, "If anything, the last two decades
should have taught us that we can't bring back those repetitive blue collar factory jobs that eventually will be replaced by
robots and machines. We need a paradigm shift." "For 200 years America has taught the world how to build things and build
them cheaper. We can wait for the standard of living and incomes in these countries to rise so that it's less expensive to do it
here again, or we can evolve to the next stage by building a platform that combines the diligence and tenacity of Asia and the
freedom and creativity of America. That's the paradigm shift that our 'Make It In America' conference is all about. "*

### Topics Include:

- **The Future is Now:** Discoveries on the
  horizon and identifying future technologies
- **Surfing the Third Wave:** Virtual reality,
  holograms and the Internet
- **Medical Innovation:** A ground level view of
  the medical technological landscape
- **Video Games:** Good, bad and ugly -- and
  what's new
- **Video Games:** The cure that ails you; solving
  global issues and even health problems
- **Gaining and Maintaining Global Advantage:**
  National leaders share their predictions
- **What Makes San Diego No. 1:** Innovation,
  immediate access to 800 million and
  maquiladoras
- **A Hero and Heroine's Odyssey:** Asian
  American big name achievers tell how they
  did it
- **Generation Y:** Understanding the largest
  market in human history and how to reach it
- **Caring for Planet Earth:** More food, more
  water and more green energy sources that
  work and make money
- **Entrepreneurial Women:** New
  management, new leadership
- **The New Game Changers:** The Face of
  Social Entrepreneurship
- **Unleashing the Talent Within:** Innovation,
  creativity and employing right and left brain
  for corporate advantage
- **Destination San Diego:** What does it take
  to set up business in Southern California and
  prosper
- **BOOST-ing the Next Generation:** Preparing
  our youngsters for technological and global
  change
- **AND MORE**

To register, go to:
makeitinamerica.net

www.indianvoices.net

**OUR 28ᵀᴴ YEAR**　　　**MULTI-CULTURAL NEWS GLOBAL NETWORK**　　　**OCTOBER 2014**

# Descendants of Early Native Point Lomans Speak Out

*by Frank Gormlie*

Five elders of the Kumeyaay Nation spoke out in Point Loma on Tuesday, September 16th. At the invitation of La Playa Trail Association, they presented an hour-long program at the Point Loma Assembly, where roughly 60 people attending the event – with strong contingent coming from OB.

Campo chairman Paul Cuero kicked off the affair with an overview of the Kumeyaay Nation, which we learned is made up of 12 bands living in 13 reservations north of the Mexican border, and five communities spread throughout northern Baja California. Kumeyaay are responsible for the protection of a

little over three million acres in San Diego County.

Paul added that many of the place names in San Diego County, heretofore thought to be Spanish, are in fact Kumeyaay. For instance La Jolla means "close to the ocean," Jamul

means "rainwater," and Palomar means "arrow." Kumeyaay, itself, means "those who face the water from a cliff," a possible reference to Sunset Cliffs, La Jolla, and Torrey Pines.

Jaime Labrake of the Sycuan Band added that both the modern Kumeyaay and their distant ancestors have been coming to Mat Loan, -the Point Loma Peninsula -for at least the last 12,000 years. It was here that they gathered mussels, fished, and harvested a lucrative crop of abalone shells that they traded with the Arizona tribes.

Steve Benegas, of the Kumeyaay Cultural Repatriation Committee, noted

SEE **Descendants, page 2**

---

## In this issue...

THUNDER from the 4TH

**www.indianvoices.net**

## Sycuan Band Kumeyaay Nation Wins Documentary Award

*Article and photographs by Angela Wyatt*

On September 25th, San Diego Film Festival premiered Our People. Our Culture. Our History. The film was screened at the Arclight Cinema with Q & A following. Cody Martinez was inspired to put an informational piece together after he observed other tribal hotel properties had them and Sycuan did not. It was an opportunity to tell the story of Sycuan. The tribal council was supportive to the idea so he began to gather people who could speak most knowledgeably and accurately about the history of the tribe. The Kumeyaay mindset is to share. Being there for others is the Native American way. "We are not a vengeful people."- Cody Martinez "We are prideful and caring."- Jamie La Brake. It is important for people to know, Sycuan is not just a casino, but has a long historical presence. We are still here! Indigenous native people. Not something in a book, not an historical aspect. We are not victims; we survived and are going strong. Our goal is to maintain a balance, traditional ways and

modern. Jamie La Brake stated, "Sycuan has been an example of how to turn things around and contribute to society." The Bird Songs are still here, the dances and the language is being taught. There is a support system. The cultural department was possible because of the gaming. It gave an opportunity for more teachers, events appreciated element brought to the people. This environment

of building support, encouragement, community and further education. Against the odds of historical injustice, the Kumeyaay are progressing and going strong. "We fought the wars to protect our way of life."- Jamie La Brake. To view the educational award winning documentary, Our People. Our Culture. Our History. Log on to sycuan tribe.org/

**See photos page 8.**

## Neil Young, Willie Nelson and 8,000 in Nebraska Stand Up to the Keystone XL Tar Sands Pipeline

Under a warm September sun, thousands spread out across the cornfield on the Tanderup family farm in Neligh, Nebraska. We sang along with Neil Young and Willie Nelson to honor the beautiful Nebraska farms and ranches, waters and traditional lands. Willie Nelson and Neil Young both have a long track record of standing up for the family farmers. And the threat to their farms these days more and more comes from the oil industry. The proposed Keystone XL tar sands pipeline is a double-threat whammy: it hits Nebraska livelihoods with the dangers of both oil spills and climate change. This concert comes at a time when the fight against tar sands is gaining momentum and showing real results on the ground with postponement and cancellation of tar

sands projects. It also comes at a time when some in Congress are pushing for approval of Keystone XL over the head of the president even before a route has been legally identified in Nebraska. And it comes on the heels of the 400,000 strong climate march in New York City, making it clear that people are joining forces across the country to defend their land, water and climate. Keystone XL is a project that should never happen and it needs to be rejected.

When Neil Young joined Willie Nelson on stage and they sang "I went out walking, in the beautiful Sandhills... this land is made for you and me. Let's walk together and raise our voices, we're gonna stand together for the world to see." The sold-out crowd of 8,000

SEE **Keystone**, page 10

## Descendants
Continued from page 1

that the Kumeyaay's primary means of communication was via runners who effortlessly averaged 120 miles a day.

Paul Cuero interjected that on November 5, 1775, when a large confederation of local tribes burned the Mission San Diego, the Colorado River Indians were well aware of it the same day via runners.

Stanley Rodriguez of the San Isabel Band of the Ipai Nation stated that before close contact with the Europeans, many of the elders managed to live well over a century.

The night's event had began auspiciously enough with the fortuitous appearance of a gargantuan rainbow spanning the northern sky from Torrey Pines to deep in the heart of the Mexican Sierras.

To this author, this was made all the more cogent by the fact that two years ago, in November of 2012, Rainbow, a north county hamlet, was saved by the Pechanga Band of Luiseño Indians, cousins of the Kumeyaay. The Pechanga Tribe purchased 354 acres of their sacred Pu'eska Mountain, near Temecula, from a northern California mining company who had planned to exploit the property. Now, thanks to the Indians, it's forever wild.

In response to a question from the audience concerning the current re-incarnation of Cabrillo's galleon, San Salvador, currently under construction in Spanish Landing Park, Ana Gloria Rodriguez of the Sycuan Cultural Department expressed a few reservations about the Kumeyaay's supposed enthusiasm over the arrival of the Europeans.

The evening ended on an exceptionally upbeat note with a mutual desire for continued cultural interaction between the Europeans and the Indians. A video of the Kumeyaay has been made, of which they are very proud and would like to share. Additionally, Cabrillo National Monument is reported to be in the throes of making an additional video on the Kumeyaay.

Stunning displays of Indian artifacts by Kumeyaay archivist Carl Shipek, a gallery of historical photographs by Joanne Hickey, as well as a wine bar and groaning buffet table orchestrated by Dee Kettenburg lent a pleasant bit of counterpoint to the whole affair.

The annual La Playa Trail Lecture Series began in the spring of 2013 as fundraiser and means of promoting the importance of the history along the La Playa Trail, which dates from prehistoric times and boasts over 70 registered historic landmarks.

More info on the Kumeyaay can be obtained online at kumeyaay.com and the La Playa Trail Association at laplayatrail.com .

**INDIAN VOICES**
Multicultural News from an American Indian Perspective

**PUBLISHED BY BLACKROSE COMMUNICATIONS**
*Member, American Indian Chamber of Commerce*

Email: rdavis4973@aol.com
Website: www.indianvoices.net
Editorial Board: Rose Davis

| | | | |
|---|---|---|---|
| Editor: | Rose Davis | Writer: | Jaclyn Bissonette |
| Social Media Administrator: | Yvonne-Cher Skye | Entertainment Writer/ | |
| Outside Support: | Mel Vernon | Photographer LA/SD: | Rochelle Porter |
| LV Entertainment Writer: | Z. Z. Zorn | Reporter de Espectaculos: | Omar DeSantiago |
| Associate Editor: | Sis Mary Muhahmmad | Reporter de Espectaculos: | Michelle Banuet |
| Writer: | Kathleen Blavatt | Proofreader: | Mary Lou Finley |
| Writer: | Roy Cook | Graphic Artist: | Elaine Hall |
| Writer: | Marc Snelling | Staff Photographer: | Abel Jacome |
| Writer: | Scott Andrews | | |

Endeavor Media Group
André Haynes
Lakeside Business Suites
2620 Regatta Dr., Ste. 102
Las Vegas, NV 89128
(702) 902-2844 • Fax: (702) 902-2845
andre@EMGnv.com
www.EMGnv.com

111 South 35th St.
San Diego, CA 92113
(619) 234-4753
(619) 534-2435 (cell)
Fax: (619) 512-4534

**Member of the Society of Professional Journalists**
**Member of New America Media**

© 2001 Blackrose Communications. No part of this publication may be reproduced without written consent from the publishers. Although we try to be careful, we are not responsible for any errors. Articles are not necessarily the opinion of the publisher.

# Native American Tribes Adopt Bitcoin-like Currency, Prepare to Battle US Government

The programmer and Native American activist Payu Harris raised a gavel Monday night and vigorously banged the bell to open trading at The Bitcoin Center, a meeting space for virtual currency geeks that looks like an empty art gallery in the middle of New York's Financial District.

Harris was there to promote MazaCoin, a cousin of Bitcoin that is now the official currency of the seven bands that make up the Lakota nation. After an hour of questions, Harris thanked the small crowd and was promptly accosted by a tall man and a woman in red who wanted to buy some MazaCoin, which Harris was selling for 10 cents apiece. The two trailed him around the room as he hunted for a printer so he could issue the digital currency on paper. MazaCoin is a month-old cryptocurrency based on the same proof-of-work algorithm as Bitcoin, the virtual currency that approximates cash on the internet — but no one in the room was equipped to make a digital trade.

There have been a slew of copycats since the rise of Bitcoin in 2009. The first wave attempted to improve on the basic Bitcoin protocol. The second wave, which includes the meme-based Dogecoin and the Icelandic Auroracoin, are catering to specific groups.

"SINCE THE RISE OF BITCOIN, THERE HAVE BEEN A SLEW OF COPYCATS"

MazaCoin was developed by an anonymous cryptographer who had built a new implementation of the Bitcoin protocol and was looking for a good cause to associate it with, Harris says. Anyone can buy or sell the currency, but the Lakota are keeping half of it in reserve in order to prevent the wild speculation that has caused Bitcoin such price volatility. Harris has also had inquiries from other tribes that want to use the currency or start their own.

Currencies knit communities together. Having one's own currency is empowering; the Latvian 5-lat coin, nicknamed "Milda" for the woman in traditional clothing depicted on it, became a symbol of Latvian independence during the Soviet occupation. A dedicated currency also boosts economic activity within a community, the impetus behind the (questionably legal) hyperlocal currency movement that has produced alternative monies such as BerkShares, IthacaHours, and the Brooklyn Torch.

Tribes using MazaCoin automatically make it easier to spend money at the local reservation general store than changing it into dollars to spend at Walmart, for example. But perhaps more

than that, it will give the Lakota people a sense of unity and independence. "Our tribe has an idea of what sovereignty is, but not at a level like the Ukrainians," Harris says, referring to the fierce battle for democracy taking place there. "There is no sense of national identity."

"WE'RE ON SOVEREIGN SOIL SO WE HAVE THE RIGHT TO HAVE BITCOIN, LITECOIN, MAZACOIN."

That fragmentation contributes to the tribes' crippling dependency on the US government. Half the tribal members on Harris's reservation, the Oglala Lakota Pine Ridge Indian Reservation in South Dakota, live in poverty. It's a problem that afflicts tribes across the country as Native Americans have grown dependent on federal welfare after being ghettoized on reservations.

Roughly $220 million flows through the reservation every year, through the Prairie Wind casino and other venues,

Programmer and Native American activist Payu Harris explains Bitcoins.

according to Harris. But he estimates less than $45 million of that stays in the local economy. With MazaCoin, he hopes to stop that money from flowing back to Rapid City and out of the state. "We're building a new economic foundation for the reservation," he says.

The US Treasury Department has indicated that Bitcoin is legal but carries certain bookkeeping requirements related to money transmission. At the same time, some politicians are calling

SEE **Bitcoin, page 11**

# Community Foreclosure Strategists Fighting for the Rights of Foreclosure Victims

The housing foreclosure dilemma in San Diego is silent epidemic as threatening as the Ebola virus and is eroding the foundation of San Diego's minority community. A lack of news coverage has moved the foreclosure crisis off the front page leaving the general public untutored about the seriousness of the problem.

Families are being torn apart and communities fractured.

The foreclosure crisis remains an ongoing and unresolved issue in the United States. Improper

foreclosures initiated by large banks and other lenders has come to the attention of the public but few are aware of how hard hitting this matter continues to be is to San Diego minority community. The foreclosure crisis has caused significant stress and health issues to a vulnerable community. A 2014 study published in the American Journal of Public Health links the foreclosure crisis with an increase in suicide rates.

One out of every 248 households in the United States received a foreclosure notice in September 2012, according to RealtyTrac.

Many San Diegans who are coming together to

support and educate each other share this desperate situation. With backup and encouragement from sympathetic professionals within the real estate and legal professions a multicultural, non-hierarchical, populist movement is shaping up at the ground level. An alliance is growing within the community.

This people driven is coalition bubbling with enthusiasm as it becomes educated to the ways of a system that has been suppressing it.

One person who has been at the helm of this brewing issue is Ishmael Rodriguez, president of Community Foreclosure Strategists.

A non-profit community group dedicated to educating not only homeowners but also those within in the judicial system who are often misinformed. Many judges allow erroneous foreclosures and evictions, allowing banks to variously foreclose on homes, which were paid for without a mortgage, accidentally foreclosing on the wrong home, and providing fraudulent documentation in courts.

Ishmael Rodriguez has been

Ishmael Rodriguez motivates the crowd

aggressively engaged in the community on behalf of beleaguered homeowners and sees himself as a freedom fighter similar to Martin Luther King and Caesar Chavez.

Community Foreclosure Strategists is fortified with the knowledge and support of George Watts a veteran

Foreclosure Attorney as well as loyal community fighters like Francisco Crozco, Dennis Gray and Randy Thailand. They are committed to continue the struggle to pierce the veil of the legal system that is oppressing them.

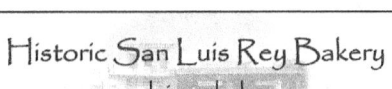

Black Path Commentary: Critical Analysis on Culture, Community, & Struggle

# The Battlefront Is Everywhere, There Are No Sheltered Rears:  Afro Americans, Police Savagery, Buck Dancing, & Engaging the Struggle

*by Min. Tukufu Kalonji*

In the wake of the murder of Michael Brown in Ferguson MO; we are reminded of the devaluing of Black life as policy and program in the wilderness of North America. Within the myriad of lame reports to justify this viciousness; and regardless of the state and city, according to a report by the Malcolm X Grassroots Movement, "1 Black Man Is Killed Every 28 Hours by Police." This is neither new, shocking, nor deserving of some self congratulatory act by the established order in trotting out its buck dancing Negroes such as Dr. Ben Carson, and Armstrong Williams in an attempt to suppress the masses who are rising up in revolt to challenge and check the police occupation in Black communities in Ferguson, and elsewhere.  Moreover, these house Negros are blaming the Black victims of these murders; which is likened to blaming a rape victim because her skirt was short and tight. That is morally bankrupt.

Armstrong and Carson speaking for their masters deny the reality of the racial climate in America and its historically evident oppression of Black people; particularly Black males, but not limited to males having any relevance with contemporary atrocities committed against Black people under the camouflage and color of law. Such as in the cases of ASU professor Dr. Ersula Ore, Sister Marlene Pinnock, or the 5 and 6 year old little Black girls handcuffed and arrested in Georgia and Florida of recent.

Reminiscent of Stephen, Samuel Jacksons's character in Django Unchained, Carson said he "is not sure if it's a police versus Black people issue." He says that "race should be factored out concerning Mr. Brown's death."  Secondly, these buck dancing Tom's keep bringing up crime in the Black community committed by Black people. That is a separate issue, and it wrong using that in an attempt to divert us from the fact of the white man gone wild via police barbarism.  The discourse that needs to be brought to the table is that police occupation and murder of Black people is a societal systemic practice

that has existed in America since the beginning of the Maangamizi, (the Holocaust of African Enslavement). Therefore, this is not just individual actions of a vicious cop in the abstract; rather it is a white supremacist socially sanctioned savagery underlined with beliefs of inferiority of Black people. This posture of the, ruling race and class as policy and practice dictates who is worthy of recognition and respect as a human being and entitled to human rights that we all desire and are deserving of.

In the final analysis there is no remedy for white supremacist policy and programming except righteous and relentless struggle. As our ancestor, the Honorable Paul Robeson argues "The Battlefront Is Everywhere, There Are No Sheltered Rears"; thus we are compelled by our history and humanity, to continue this struggle to be respected as a human being as another of our ancestor's Malcolm X, the fire prophet argued,  "By Any Means Necessary!"

*Min. Tukufu Kalonji is Founder of Kawaida African Ministries,*
*For info contact @ tkalonji@hotmail.com*

## Winona LaDuke on Returning Land to Native People

*Winona LaDuke speaks passionately about the Federal Government's refusal to return land to the Native American Indians*

*"The only compensation for land is land." ~Winona LaDuke*

Winona LaDuke is an internationally acclaimed American Indian activist, environmentalist, economist, author and orator. A graduate of Harvard & Antioch with advanced degrees in rural economic development, Winona LaDuke has devoted her life to protecting the lands & lifeways of Native communities.

*"Someone needs to explain to me why wanting clean drinking water makes you an activist, and why proposing to destroy water with chemical warfare doesn't make a corporation a terrorist." ~Winona LaDuke*

Winona LaDuke is an Anishinaabekwe (Ojibwe) enrolled member of the Mississippi Band Anishinaabeg who lives and works on the White Earth Reservations, and is the mother of three children.

She is also the Executive Director of Honor the Earth, where she works on a national level to advocate, raise public support, and create funding for frontline native environmental groups.

In 1994, Winona was nominated by Time magazine as one of America's fifty most promising leaders under forty years of age.

She has been awarded the Thomas

SEE **Winona LaDuke**, page 6

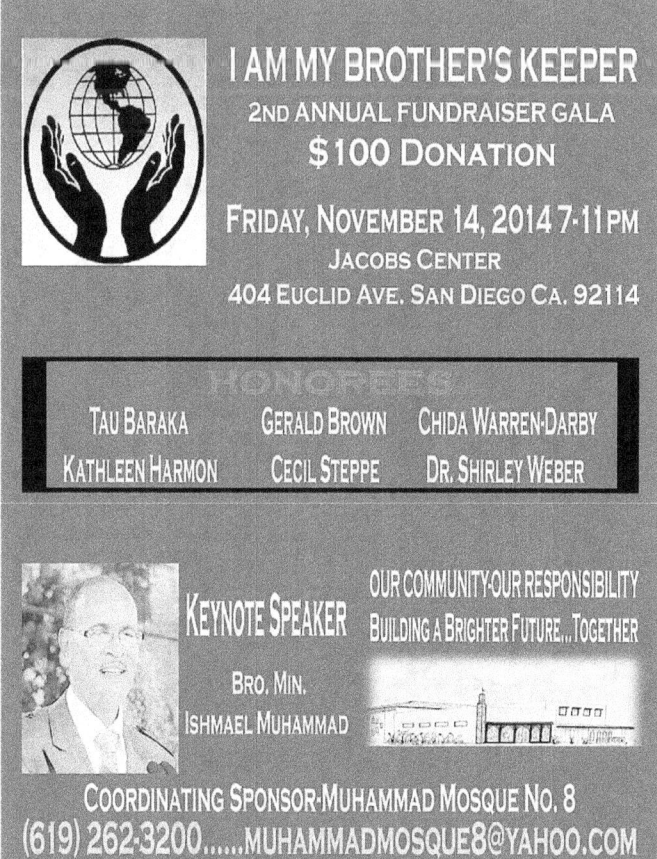

To improve the quality of life of those who recognize themselves and choose to be recognized by others as "Indigenous Peoples of Color of the Americas" and in support of The American Indian Rights and Resources Organization (AIRRO).

# Yuchi Indians of South Carolina

Yuchi Indians living in the Savannah River Basin of South Carolina and Georgia proudly honor all their ancestors: An interview with their Principal Chief, Lonzado Langley.

It is one of those many secrets of American history that have been kept out of news articles, textbooks and Wikipedia. Coretta Scott, the future wife of Dr. Martin Luther King, Jr. was more Creek Indian than anything else. Typical of many families in the Southeast, her ancestors came from three races, Native American, African and European. Perry County, Alabama, where she grew up, contains many Creek families, who were in the past forced into a "Colored" label by the South's segregation laws.

Coretta's physical features were almost entirely Muskogean. If she had worn a ribbon dress, while participating in a Stomp Dance in Okmulgee, OK, no one would have batted an eye.

Apparently, because her husband was so closely associated with the efforts to bring African-Americans political equality and economic justice, Mrs. King didn't advertise her Native

American heritage. However, she never denied that the Scott family was primarily of Creek ancestry, if directly questioned.

Among many things, the laws defining race in the South once stated that if a person was 1/64th African, they were classified legally as Colored, a

# Elders

It is not age that makes a person an Elder, it is the substance of things acquired, shared with power in a sacred way during a lifetime of learning and unlearning. That thought came to me amongst others standing before the assembly of Black Indian Elders who lived in the area of Columbia, Maryland.

Juliette Porter, a Black Nottoway/Meherrin/Cherokee grandmother, had started an Elder group in a senior citizens home there. From different nations they came with varied backgrounds, and compelling life stories for sound reasons. Older years are the time of introspection. This stage of life ask of each four questions. These four questions are the basis or the pillars of the Sweet Grass Elders Circle Juliette founded a few years ago.

"What is the responsibility of an Elder to the child, the adult and the old?"

"What is a Native Elder, and their role?"

"How do we see ourselves?"

"How does being an Elder impact life around us?"

Indians from the reservations don't have the same grasp upon what being an Indian is as a Black Indian so how, I asked myself, do I address this assembly? It is a mixed group of people who know who they are but in the context of American perception have to ask

"polite" term for Negro, and a guarantee of serf status ... even after the 13th Amendment to the Constitution freed slaves everywhere.

It was much the same for the Yuchi people along the Savannah River, who somehow survived living on the margins of Southern society for over 250 years. Those who did not move progressively westward with their allies, the Creek Indians, soon afterward either became landless serfs in their homeland or after 1832, enslaved. The blood quantum laws associated with slavery were used by county sheriffs to seize mixed-heritage Yuchi and Creek Indian farms. The families were marched in chains to the Georgia state line or sometimes allowed to be landless sharecroppers. Sheriffs and county politicians pocketed the profits.

questions a full blood does not have to ask of themselves, or others. It was an easy answer that needed time to express its enormity. From me, it was ceremony and legacy.

"How can a ceremonial approach to life be shared to a group comprised of people finally coming to terms with their identity and those raised in their particular traditions?"

Riding the subway one day in D.C. an older white man sat next to me. After greeting him I commented about a 30-something year-old couple enjoying each other. "Remember that age?" I asked. "Barely." he chuckled. The conversation led up to sharing the pleasures and wonderment about getting older.

"For me," I said, "it is the voice. Having the voice that stops and corrects young people's behavior." He eyed me astonished wanting to understand what I'd said. In answer to his question I answered that I grew up among men and

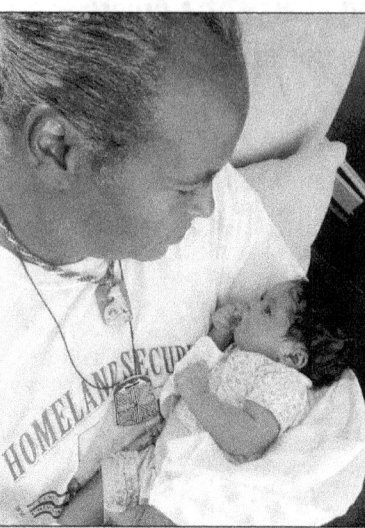

from my father I learned about power and the power of the spoken word. The voice. He was floored. I realized in that moment how powerful initiation is to the development of power and how power plays with and within stories much the same way the Earth, our Mother plays with all that grows. How as an Elder do we create change?

"Elder is a noun," Juliette Porter said recently, "It should be a verb, an action. I don't know how to do that, but it should be done." Let us think about these things in the context of our spiritual responsibility to children, adults, old people and the next seven generations hoping to live upon the Earth, our Mother.

These our my words.

Gregory E. Woods, Keeper of Stories, African/Creek/Crow

---

## Winona LaDuke

Continued from page 5

Merton Award in 1996, the BIHA Community Service Award in 1997, the Ann Bancroft Award for Women's Leadership Fellowship, and the Reebok Human Rights Award, with which she began the White Earth Land Recovery Project.

White Earth Land Recovery Project is a reservation based non-profit devoted to restoring the land-base and culture of the White Earth Anishinaabeg.

In 1998, Ms. Magazine named her Woman of the Year for her work with Honor the Earth.

In 1996 and 2000, she ran for vice president as the nominee of the Green Party of the United States, on a ticket headed by Ralph Nader.

A graduate of Harvard and Antioch Universities, Winona LaDuke has written extensively on American Indian and Environmental issues. She is a former board member of Greenpeace USA and serves, as co-chair of the Indigenous Women's Network, a North American and Pacific indigenous women's organization.

She has written extensively on American Indian and environmental issues. Author of now six books, including "The Militarization of Indian Country" (2011), "Recovering the Sacred: the Power of Naming and Claiming" (2005), the non-fiction book "All our Relations:

Native Struggles for Land and Life" (1999, South End Press), and a novel - Last Standing Woman (1997, Voyager Press).

*"We don't want a bigger piece of the pie. We want a different pie." ~Winona LaDuke*

In 2007, Winona LaDuke was inducted into the National Women's Hall of Fame.

Honor the Earth is a Native-led organization, established by Winona LaDuke and Indigo Girls Amy Ray and Emily Saliers, in 1993 to address the two primary needs of the Native environmental movement: the need to break the geographic and political isolation of Native communities and the need to increase financial resources for organizing and change.

As a unique national Native initiative, Honor the Earth works to a) raise public awareness and b) raise and direct funds to grassroots Native environmental groups. We are the only Native organization that provides both financial support and organizing support to Native environmental initiatives. This model is based on strategic analysis of what is needed to forge change in Indian country, and it is based deep in our communities, histories, and long term struggles to protect the earth.

Support her outstanding work.
Winona LaDuke Honor the Earth
HONOR THE EARTH
http://www.honorearth.org/

# Seminole Negro Indian Scouts Gather

*by Katarina Kato Wittich*

The third weekend in September is a special weekend in the tiny town of

Brackettville, Texas. Once a year, the descendants of the Seminole Negro Indian Scouts gather there to celebrate their ancestors and their unique heritage. They come from all corners of the States, from Mexico, from Europe, the Bahamas and anywhere where the Black Seminole diaspora led them. Black Seminoles are a people who were formed as escaped slaves, freedmen and maroons joined up with the Seminole Indians in the swamps of Florida and later became allies in the battle against the U.S. government

In 1870, the first unit of the Seminole Negro Indian Scouts was mustered in at Fort Duncan in Eagle Pass, The Scouts played a crucial role in the evolution of the state of Texas. They

were never given the land they were promised, and they were often the subject of extreme bigotry and violence. with in Mexico.

When the Seminole Negro Indian Scouts were disbanded in 1914, their families moved off the fort and into Brackettville, and from there spread to all parts of the US and also into Mexico. But they maintained their own unique language, a form of Gullah creole. that is now dying out with the elders. And

they kept a strong sense of themselves as "Seminol", a culturally unique black people whose ancestors had escaped slavery and lived as part of an Indian Nation for many years before splitting off and becoming their own people. They have intermarried and mingled with Mexicans and Whites and other Indian peoples like the Biloxi and the Creek

Seminole Days in Brackettville began this year on Friday September 19th.

Scout descendant Thomi Lee Perryman organized history lectures which Included presentations by the Mayor of Brackettville, Andres Rodriguez; Russell Knowell of

the Fort Clark Historical Society; John Griffin, Florida Seminole Re-enactor and historian; Daniel Romero, Chief and Richard Gonzalez Vice Chief of the Lipan Apache Band of Texas; and Doug Sivad, Historian, Actor,.

On Friday was a trip up Seminole Canyon to visit the remote site where the Scouts used to camp and water their horses. Scout descendant Cynthia Ventura Atchico arranged for any scout descendants capable of the hike to be led by the rangers into this beautiful spot.

Saturday in Brackettville began with a moving unveiling of a new plaque marking the Perryman family site that was part of the larger camp where the Scouts lived on the military reservation of Fort Clark. It was followed by the parade, which each year goes down the main streets of Brackettville and ends at the Carver School grounds where the community then gathers for a speaker program, and festivities. the parade was organized by Augusta "Gigi" Pines, the current President of the Seminole Negro Indian Scout Cemetery Association

Ms. Pines and the Association board of directors, including Vice-President Rafaela Brown and treasurer Mary Vasquez-Gamble, also organized an excellent program at the school grounds. It included speakers such as the Mayor of Brackettville and Scout Descendants including Billie Jean Frierson, Lee Young, Thomi Lee Perryman, and Elder and Honorary "Chief" William "Dub" Warrior who has been past President of the Association and keeper of the history for many years. Lipan Vice Chief Richard Gonzalez gave a moving speech encouraging the young women of the group to understand their importance as the ones who create the future, and he gave a special ceremonial necklace and blessing to the youngest teenage female descendant. After the program there was barbecue and bingo and the celebration went on until late in the evening on the school grounds with booths with displays and with all sorts of foods and souvenirs to purchase.

Saturday night there was also a semi formal banquet held on Fort Clark in the officers club, to honor "Chief" William Warrior and his wife Ethel for their many years of service to the community. Many awards were presented at the banquet, and speakers included Richard Gonzalez, John Griffin, Doug Sivad, Veronica Warrior, Mayor Rodriguez, and Retired Texas Ranger and Scout Descendant Lee Young, who is the first Black Ranger in Texas and has written a fascinating book about his

groundbreaking experiences. "Chief" Warrior spoke of his many years of gathering the history and the importance that the younger descendants take up being the guardians of the past, as it is such an important part of the future.

It was a heartwarming evening in a beautiful setting. The banquet was organized by Thomi Lee Perryman, with the help of Lovenia Raspberry, and emceed wonderfully by Billie Jean Frierson, who kept things moving so everyone could get up and dance when the program was done!

On Sunday morning the community comes together at the Seminole Negro

Indian Scouts Cemetery to honor the ancestors. The graveyard is carefully tended and flowers are placed on recent and ancient graves. Many members of the community still choose to be buried here, and there are many fresh graves as time claims the elder members of the group. Part of the ceremony is the reading of the names of those who have gone during the course of the year. This year was particularly sad because a younger and beloved member of the community, Billy Joe Pierce passed away at the beginning of the month. In addition to prayers, there was a beautiful call and response walk

into the cemetery led by the Perryman family choir, who all seem to have been blessed with exquisite voices!

As the sun rose to its full noon strength, the descendants of the Seminole Negro Indian Scouts bowed their heads in a final prayer for their ancestors, their loved ones, and a safe trip home. Hugs were exchanged and families loaded into their cars to begin the voyages toward their homes, both far away and near, knowing they will gather again next year to celebrate their connections to each other and to their rich and complex past.

San Diego Film Festival 2014

SAN DIEGO FILM FESTIVAL
Filmmaker Awards Party

Miramar Ai
Amazing

...mar Air Show Blue Angel demonstration October 4th 2014.
...nazing photo captured by Greg Nickel from a mile away.

# 44th Annual
# Barona Powwow
Friday, August 29 through Sunday, August 31, 2014
Barona Sports Park - Barona Indian Reservation - Lakeside, CA

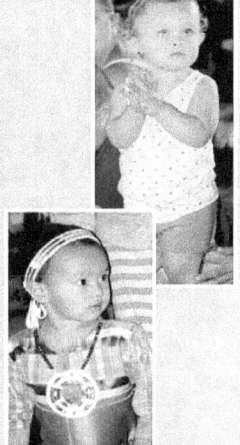

## Keystone
Continued from page 2

stretched across the field to the tepees in the far back and sang along, standing tall.

Neil Young has said: "For our grandchildren's survival we must begin to live differently. The Keystone XL pipeline is a large step in the wrong direction for the health of the earth. America must lead the world again and stop the Keystone XL." Tar sands oil is the dirtiest around. It is strip-mined or heated out from under Canada's majestic Boreal forest and from under the traditional territories of Canadian First Nations. The Keystone XL pipeline project would carry raw tar sands oil across America's heartland, through Nebraska farms and ranches and the great Ogallala Aquifer to the Gulf coast where most would be destined for export overseas. It is a risky project with all the reward going to the big multi-national oil companies and the Canadian pipeline company TransCanada.

I was honored to stand with the landowners and indigenous leaders in Nebraska fighting for their land and water in the same way we all marched in New York City for action on climate change a week earlier. Come to Nebraska and talk to the farmers and ranchers. It makes it clearer than ever that President Obama should protect our precious land, water and climate by rejecting the Keystone XL tar sands pipeline.

Our gracious hosts Art and Helen Tanderup invited us onto the farm that their family has stewarded for 100 years. Art's corn towered above my head, but he spoke about how the changing climate has already affected other crops like soybeans and he is concerned for the future of his farm. BoldNebraska, the Indigenous Environmental Network and the Cowboy and Indian Alliance - a

group of ranchers, farmers and tribal communities from along the Keystone XL tar sands pipeline route - sponsored the concert. They've been strong fighters for a long time now to protect their lands, the Sand Hills and the Ogallala Aquifer that nourishes their lives.

TransCanada, the Canadian pipeline company that has been pushing this project on landowners, responded to the project with tired arguments about the relative safety of pipelines versus rail. The bottomline is that both pipelines and rail are not safe when it comes to tar sands oil. Safe is getting energy from the wind and the sun.

We also hear lots of mistaken arguments that the development of tar sands is inevitable. The truth is that companies are finding tar sands risky and expensive while communities are saying "no" to tar sands pipelines. The Norwegian oil company Statoil just shelved one of their in situ tar sands drilling projects for at least three years due to a lack of pipeline. This means that stopping the pipelines is keeping carbon in the ground and tar sands out of our farms. In fact since Neil Young launched the Honour the Treaties concert tour in Canada to help fight tar sands expansion, three major tar sands projects have been cancelled or postponed – Total's Jocelyn mine, Shell's Pierre River mine and Statoil's Corner in situ drilling project.

Stopping the Keystone XL tar sands pipeline makes a difference for communities in Nebraska and along the pipeline pathway. Real jobs are at stake, jobs on many farms and ranches - more than a quarter of a million of them just in the five Great Plains states the tar sands pipeline would cross through. Those are the jobs that drive this region and feed the country and much of the world. And it also makes a difference for communities in Canada suffering from tar sands extraction and

communities around the world feeling the impacts of climate change to their health, homes and wallets.

The outpouring of opposition in Nebraska serves as a reminder to our nation's leaders that the Keystone XL tar sands pipeline still has no route through the state. Lawmakers in Washington DC should not try to take the decision away from the president and force Keystone XL on Nebraska's farmers, ranchers, landowners and indigenous communities. And President Obama has an opportunity to do the right thing and listen to the people in Nebraska.

Neil Young ended with his new song. He sang, "Who's gonna stand up?" and the crowd sang back, "WE ARE." Stand up for the Sand Hills, for the Ogallala Aquifer and for the climate on which we all depend. As Neil says, "Stand up and save the earth."

# San Francisco Institute of Architecture

The world's largest and longest established professional school of green building, the San Francisco Institute of Architecture (SFIA). See the SFIA Instructors, Student Testimonials, and Student/Alumni Affiliation links on our home page, for a comprehensive overview of SFIA.

We'll mentor you through the degree program on a fast track-an enjoyable, enriching, comprehensive learning experience. You can finish in as few as four months of part-time study, or take as long as you need.

All study is self paced, without deadlines. Each architecture course

earns 3 academic units. Earn Certificates of Achievement for every course completed. You can start course work at any Time.

Sign up for all 12 courses and earn a Master degree See the FALL 2014 ONLINE COURSES link at our WWW.SFIA.NET home page, for course details and enrollment form.

San Francisco Institute of Architecture Information Office Box 2590 Alameda, CA 94501 510-523-5174 1-800-634-7779 Fax 510-523-5175

Email: Director@sfia.net www.sfia.net

# Holy Goats

*Down the hill from Bayview Baptist Church*

The neighborhood around 61st Street and Imperial Ave. in San Diego has a special reverence for locals who live in the area. This piece of geography holds the memory of ancient Kumeyaay burial grounds as well as the legacy of George

Baptist Church, Gaudi Finny. Finny remembered hearing about the goats that are used as an alternative to expensive and eco-unfriendly machinery and suggested that the church use these wooly weed whackers to clear the church property of unwanted wild plants. He searched around until he found Environmental Land Management, a company that provides goat herds to clear brush on open land. The goats enjoy the dry brush, tumbleweed and greener plants equally, but alfalfa is their

Stevens, the Peoples City Council Person. It is also the home to many reverent temples of worship in the established community of the 4th District as well as the headquarters of the Black Contractor Association. It is no wonder that the sight of dozens of goats munching weeds on the hillside on the corner of 61st and Imperial Ave. suggested hallucination, illusion, or a mirage. Curiosity fueled investigative journalism instincts demanded an explanation. The resulting inquiry revealed that the inspiration for the goats came from the chief operations officer of the San Diego African American Museum of Fine Art, housed at Bayview

real treat, according to John Gonzalez, operations manager for ELM. In addition to providing an environmentally friendly alternative to weed abatement the goats help firefighters by increasing defensible space. They eat heavy scrub plants and dry vegetation that could threaten nearby commercial and residential property in the event of a fast-moving brush fire. In the case of Bayview Baptist Church the goats offered inspiration for those seeking a back to nature solution to today's high tech complexities as well as a wonderful example of mans bond with nature and God's creatures. Amen

## Bitcoin

Continued from page 3

for a ban on the currency. Harris is hoping to avoid all that with MazaCoin. Federal laws granting Native Americans special legal status provide an argument for a currency totally independent of the US dollar. Native American sovereignty is legally defined over a patchwork of treaties, laws, and precedent. "We're on sovereign soil so we have the right to have Bitcoin, Litecoin, MazaCoin," Harris says.

But Chase Iron Eyes, South Dakota legal counsel for the Lakota, believes the federal government will push back if MazaCoin succeeds. "There hasn't been a tribal nation that has declared its own currency and has mandated that that currency is used within its borders," Iron Eyes says. "But it's because of this pervasive, ever-present asserted dominion of the United States. They'll try to shut us down, try to cite us with law violations."

While the leadership of the Lakota nation has signed off on adopting MazaCoin as a national currency, there is

resistance within the ranks. Digital currencies are not always an easy sell, especially to older generations who are not accustomed to using apps constantly throughout the day. A further complication is that not all tribal members have internet access or smartphones, which means Harris has to develop a paper wallet system where members' MazaCoins are held in cold storage at a central location like a bank. In theory members can walk into the bank, get their MazaCoins in a paper wallet that can be processed by reservation businesses, then return the balance to digital storage at the bank before driving home.

There is also a fear of letting go of the US dollar, which holds the implicit threat of letting go of the federal subsidies denominated in it. Iron Eyes believes the legal battle and the public perception battle are worth fighting. "We've gone through 100 years of imposed poverty. That's the fight we're having," he says. "What we're trying to do with MazaCoin is just spark something to get us out of this cycle of victimhood."

# Manufactured News is Death Sentence for Indigenous Peoples

## Systematic Plagiarism and Deception in News Aid Corporate Genocide

*by Brenda Norrell, Censored News*

Each day the news becomes more manipulative with the truth distorted to deceive you. There is no better place to observe this than in the national Indian country news, where the news ranges from systematic plagiarism to news lite, distraction and spin.

The news coverage of the recent UN World Indigenous Conference in New York makes the point. Those who attended the World Conference on Climate Change and the Protection of Mother Earth in Cochabamba, Bolivia, in 2010, hoped this gathering would continue the work. However, they were quickly disappointed. They were not even allowed to participate, which was by invitation-only for the UN well funded.

While mining is among the top threats to Indigenous Peoples around the world -- resulting in assassinations, disappearances, rapes and torture -- mining has been kept off the agenda as a priority at UN Indigenous gatherings. Dirty coal mining, uranium mining, and metals mining, and the deaths,

homelessness and diseases that result, are among the most censored issues in Indian country news.

Further, Pacific Islanders, victims of the nuclear holocaust, withdrew their support from the UN World Conference in New York, stating that demilitarization was censored at the gathering. The voice of the peace makers who oppose war, and the spying on the peacemakers, are among the most censored issues in national Indian country news.

Photo.Brenda Norrell

Both Mexico and Canada exposed themselves at the UN World Conference in New York, Sept. 22 -- 23. First, with the presence of Mexico's President Enrique Pena Nieto, who is continuing the ongoing genocide of Indigenous Peoples, and then with Canada's rejection of the outcome document.

In Mexico, the massacre of Mayans in Chiapas in the south, and the theft of Yaqui water rights in the north, are just two of the cases in a country where Indigenous Peoples are considered both a tourist revenue for the government and expendables by both the government and its multi-national corporate crime partners.

Now, the murders and disappearances of students in Iguala, Guerrero, magnifies Mexico's role in violence, police corruption and silencing dissent as the US and Mexico continue their systematic drug and weapons industry.

Iguala has also been a stronghold of Zapatistas, where Indigenous continue to be a voice of autonomy, justice and dignity.

At the UN conference in New York, Canada asserted in a statement that it has the right to violate aboriginal rights and treaties.

The bottom line is the voice of grassroots Indigenous Peoples around the world whose voice at the United Nations has been largely replaced by well-funded non-profits and government appointees, who were never selected or appointed by grassroots Indigenous Peoples.

Grassroots Indigenous Peoples point to the amount of money spent flying around the world by the well-funded, who use their issues and suffering to obtain foundation grants. These grants often range from $100,000 to $400,000 each. Grassroots Indigenous ask what will come off all this global travel and now more talk at the United Nations.

As for the national news media in Indian country, it has collapsed after years of plagiarism and deception.

# TRADING POST BUSINESS DIRECTORY

### CALIFORNIA

**ADVOCACY**
Alan Lechuza Aquallo
Advocate for Native Youth and Scholarships
alan@blackphonerecords.com

**ATTORNEYS**
Marshall Law PC
Daniel E.Marshall, Attorney at Law
619-993-5778 • marslawbmw@gmail.com
sandiegoevictionattorneys.com

**BAKERY**
Historic San Luis Rey Bakery
490 N. El Camino Real Oceanside, CA 92058
760-433-7242 • ww.sanluisreybakery.com

La Nueva Mexican Bakery
4676 Market St. Ste. A-3, San Diego, CA
619-262-0042

**CARE GIVER**
Private Duty– References
Terms to be discussed
619-504-2455 Ask for Liz

**CLERICAL**
Your Girl Friday International
Marketing, Operations & Promotional
Services • yourgirlfriday3512@gmail.com

**CULTURE**
Kumeyaay
www.kumeyaay.com • larry@kumeyaay.com

Worldbeat Cultural Center
619-230-1190
www.worldbeatculturalcenter.org
info@worldbeatculturalcenter.org

**DRIVER**
Driver for Hire
Clean DMV Class ABC
619-504-2455 Ask for Liz

**FINANCIAL ADVISORS**
Merrill Lynch / Elke Chenevey
Vice President & Financial Advisor
Office: 619-699-3707
Fax: 619-758-3619

Summit Funding
The Home Loan Experts
Jeff Ellenz, Branch Manager
760-568-0300 • jellenz@summitfunding.net

**HEALTH**
Rady's Children Hospital
San Diego, CA
800-869-5627 • www.rchsd.org

Regenerative Medicine Institute
www.regenerativemedicine.mx

San Diego American Health Center
2630 1st Avenue, San Diego, CA 92013
619-234-2158

**HEALER-SHAMAN**
Transitions / Vera A. Tucker
vtucker1212@gmail.com
619-987-0372

**HOMEMADE**
Liz • 619-504-2655

**HOUSEKEEPING**
Cleaning, windows, floors
4 hours $80 - 8 hours $120

619-504-2455 Ask for Liz

**INSURANCE**
State Farm / Jack Fannin
1154 E. Main St. El Cajon, CA 92021-7157
619-440-0161 Business
619-440-0495 Fax
jack.fanninjroi@statefarm.com
www.jackfannin.com

Earthquake Insurances
www.EarthquakeAuthority.com

**MARKETING**
International Marketing Systems
Eddy Michaelly
www.imsbarter.com

Jahaanah Productions
Marketing, Media, Public Relations, Graphic
Design • 832-978-0939

**NOTARY PUBLIC**
Sis. Evon X. Nana
San Diego, CA 92113 • 619-549-5792
evonx@yahoo.com

**PHOTOGRAPHY**
Peache Photo Memories
619-697-4186 office
619-549-0968 contact
www.peachephotomemories.com
peachephotos@cox.net

**PUBLISHERS**
Blackrose Communications
111 South 35th St. San Diego, CA 92113
619-234-4753
www.indianvoices.net • rdavis4973@aol.com

**RADIO**
91.3FM Kopa
Pala Rez Radio
www.palatribe.com • 91.3@palatribe.com

**RECOVERY**
David "Wolf" Diaz, Pres. & Founder
Walk of the Warrior, A Non-Profit Corp.
Tel: 760-646-0074 • Cell: 310-866-7057
Fax:760-689-4907
www.walkofthewarrior.com
walkofthewarrior@yahoo.com

**REGALIA**
Carla Tourville
Native Regalia Custom Design
Yokut Tule River Tribe
San Diego, CA • 619-743-9847

**REPARATIONS**
Mr. Peoples Reparations
200 N. Long Beach Blvd. Compton, CA
310-632-0577

**RESTAURANT**
Awash Ethiopian Restaurant
4979 El Cajon Blvd. San Diego,CA
619-677-3754

**RETAIL – CLOTHING**
Full Blood Apparel
P.O. Box 3101 Valley Venter, CA 92082
760-445-1141

**SOCIAL SERVICES**
Tribal Tanf
Temporary Assistance for Needy Families
San Diego Office 866-913-3725

Escondido Office 866-428-0901
Manzanita Office 866-931-1480
Pala Office 866-806-8263

### NEVADA

**ADVOCACY**
Adams Esq.
Special Needs Children
500 N. Rainbow Blvd. Ste 300
Las Vegas, NV 89107
702-289-4143 Office • 702-924-7200 Fax

**COMMUNITY**
Native American Community Services
3909 S. Maryland Pkwy #205 Las Vegas, NV
89119-7500

**PUBLISHERS**
Blackrose Communications
111 South 35th St. San Diego, CA 92113
619-234-4753
www.indianvoices.net • rdavis4973@aol.com

### NORTH CAROLINA

**RETAIL - CLOTHING**
Passion Island
832 Washington Plaza, Washington, NC
27889; 252-402-4700

### TEXAS

**HEALTH**
The Circle: A Healing Place
Joanna Johnson, MSW, CFAS
Longview Behavioral Hospital
22 Bermuda Lane, Longview, Texas 75605
www.longviewhospital.com
www.oglethorpeinc.com
850-228-0777

---

## Slavery and the Making of American Capitalism

Edward E. Baptist's brilliant book, *The Half Has Never Been Told*, soars because of the author's decision to root his analysis in the human dimension.

Edward E. Baptist: The Half Has Never Been Told: Slavery and the Making of American Capitalism Basic Books, 498 pp , $35.00

## "Make It In America" Conference To Encourage Asian Investments and Entrepreneurship in the US

*First of its kind conference to take place*
**Wednesday-Saturday, Nov. 19-22, 2014
at the California Center for the Arts
in Escondido, San Diego County, California,**
as part of a collaborative effort by
the Asian Heritage Society, U.S. Congressman Scott Peters and
Co-San Diego County Supervisor Dave Roberts.

**"Make It In America: Boosting Possibility Through Innovation and Entrepreneurship"**
*Guests will come from China, the Philippines, Thailand and Vietnam and include business leaders from the four-county region.*

The ultimate goal of the conference is to create new jobs and industry here in Southern California -- but jobs and industry with a purpose to do good.

"We can't leave progress up to corporations and government anymore," said Leonard Novarro, secretary and board chairman of the Asian Heritage Society. "We already know what's not working. Now it's time to find out what works, tackle the problems, change things and spread the solutions throughout the planet to change societies. It sounds like a big order, and it is. Government and big business had their chance. Now it's the social entrepreneurs who have seized the day."

To register, go to: makeitinamerica.net

# NEVADA NEWS

For Nevada Information: 619-234-4753 • 619-534-2435

## EMG Rolls Out the Red Carpet Again to Honor U.S. Military Veterans on October 18th

*The 2nd Annual EMG Veterans Awards draws major support*

LAS VEGAS, NV – Cadillac of Las Vegas proudly presents the 2nd Annual EMG Veterans Awards (formerly Veterans Appreciation Awards) brought to you by Richard Scotti on Saturday - October 18, 2014 from 1300 to 1500 (1pm-3pm PT) at the EMG headquarters in the Desert Shores Community located at Lakeside Business Suites, 2620 Regatta Drive Suite 102, Las Vegas NV, 89128. Admission is FREE and ages 13+ are welcome. This year's event is hosted by actor and entertainer, Nieve Malandra. Live music will be played by DJ Liz Clark. Program supporters include Ron Q. Quilang from 360DPI, Jason Stoffel – Judicial Candidate from Dept. S, LJ Harness – Legendary Rock Drummer, Richard Knapp – 9x EMMY award winner and Judge Carolyn Ellsworth from Department 5.

EMG is honoring veterans including: Michael Smith with the 2014 EMG Veterans Awards Dedication; Veterans Talk / The Forgotten Promise with the Veteran Program of the Year Award; Veterans Reporter with the Veteran Publication of the Year Award; Judge William "Bill" Kephart with the Veteran Advocate of the Year Award; Customistic with the Veteran Owned Business of the Year Award; Tim Bedwell with the Male Veteran of the Year Award; and NV Senator Patricia Spearman with the Female Veteran of the Year Award. Award presenters include: Richard

Scotti – Judicial Candidate for Department 2, Joe Buda – Publisher of the Las Vegas Man magazine, Rosario Grajales – journalist, Vernon Fox – former NFL player, Gady Medrano – reality TV star and Judge Kenneth Pollock – Family Division in Department J.

The most prestigious award that military soldiers, veterans and advocates can receive, the EMG Veterans Awards, is presented annually by the EMG Foundation. The Annual EMG Veterans Awards presentation brings together active military, veterans, civilians and the community from Las Vegas and surrounding cities.

EMG: EMG Enterprises is a conglomerate that operates companies in the fields of non-profit, pageantry, politics and public relations. The EMG Foundation serves the community by promoting charity fundraisers, donation drives and special events to benefit non-profit organizations and programs. The Miss EMG Organization exists to promote community activism awareness and to provide a platform that women can use to enhance their academic and professional endeavors. EMG Government Affairs is non-partisan and manages statewide and local election campaigns for candidates seeking re-election and election. EMG Public Relations focuses on industries including arts and entertainment, food and beverage and sports, with an expertise in media and events. Learn more about EMG by visiting EMGnv.com.

## Parents Who Baptize Their Children May Be Charged with a Felony

*by Andre' Haynes*

Baptism is considered a sacrament and a spiritual rite of passage by several religious followers, often called believers. Some believers are baptized as infants, some as children and others as adults. Based on the religious beliefs that one embraces, the preferred method of baptism may vary from being completely submerged underneath water or pouring water on the forehead or partially kneeling inside water while it is being poured on the upper body. While believers may disagree on the preferred method of baptism, they all agree that baptism is relevant, necessary and congratulate one another for being baptized. Some church leaders feel so strongly about baptism that they have gone to the lengths of creating exclusive services for baptism only. Several believers argue that their religious rights are being trampled on and that the government is persecuting them for their religious beliefs and practices, although the American-Constitution guarantees freedom of religion in the First Amendment. If you consider yourself a believer or spiritual, if you recognize spiritual rebirth and salvation, than you may disagree with Judge Vincent Ochoa from Department S in Clark County, NV for finding a dad in CONTEMPT OF COURT after his minor children requested to be baptized and he obliged.

Kevin Beck is the father of two minor children, whom had a divorce case before Judge Ochoa. According to Dad's testimony, court minutes from Case 06D358482 and a video transcript of a September 2011 hearing, you may conclude that Judge Ochoa should be investigated for ethics violations and sued for religious discrimination. The minutes and video reveal that Ochoa found Dad's ex-wife in CONTEMPT OF COURT for violating the COURT'S ORDER by 'not giving written notice or getting consent to leave the Country' (Mexico) with the minor children. According to NV Revised Statute 125, Dad's ex-wife committed a felony and punishment may include a large fine

and incarceration in jail or prison. Ochoa found Dad in CONTEMPT OF COURT for 'not providing Notice to Mom as to the Baptism' and treated both infractions equally, thus punishing Dad for allowing his minor children the choice of baptism with the equivalency of a Felony.

Recently Judge Ochoa has been at the center of controversy for a myriad of reasons including most recently (1) having an endorsement rescinded by the Clark County School District Police Officers Association and (2) being disqualified by Judge Elizabeth Gonzalez from a custody case involving Jason Stoffel, his political opponent for a quarrel that Ochoa allegedly started.

Dad plans to discuss his legal options with an attorney and may seek the assistance of the ACLU. He is considering filing a formal complaint with the Committee On Judicial Ethics against Ochoa.

Calls to Ochoa's office went unanswered. This is a developing story.

*Andre' Haynes:*
*Andre' Haynes is a freelance writer and a talk-show host based in Las Vegas, Nevada. He regularly contributes content to online and print publications, and hosts radio and television talk-shows. Haynes primarily covers topics related to business, entertainment and sports. He is President of EMG, a conglomerate that operates companies in the fields of non-profits, politics and public relations.*
*Sources:*
*LVRJ:*
*http://www.reviewjournal.com/news/nevada/quarrel-bar-leads-family-court-judge-s-removal-custody-case*
*Las Vegas Tribune:*
*http://lasvegastribune.net/early-wrong-retract/*
*Links:*
*Website: www.emgnv.com*
*E-Mail: info@emgnv.com*

# VAWA – Milestones for Indian Country

Approximately one out of every four women suffer domestic violence in her lifetime, and 1.3 million women are victims of domestic violence each year. Domestic violence is a devastating reality for many families but this problem is much more glaring for our Native American women, who suffer rates of domestic violence disproportionately higher than any other group in our country. For this reason, we must take pause to honor those who advocated to protect our society's most vulnerable members and remind ourselves of the conditions that led to the passage of the Violence Against Women Act twenty years ago this month.

I was an original cosponsor of the initial VAWA proposal in 1990, and I supported passage of the bill when it became law in 1994. Last year, I made it one my top priorities to reauthorize this historic legislation, despite Republican attempts to block it. This law has been an invaluable tool to recognize, prevent, and combat domestic violence and it has helped millions of women affected by abuse. Since its passage in 1994, VAWA has helped reduce the rate of domestic violence by 67%.

Yet, Native American women continue to suffer higher rates of domestic violence and many of these crimes go unpunished due to gaps in our justice systems. The VAWA reauthorization tribal provisions help close those gaps and restore criminal jurisdiction to begin prosecuting non-Indians who commit crimes of domestic violence in Indian Country to Indian tribes, including the Pascua Yaqui Tribe of Arizona, the Tulalip Tribes in Washington, and the Umatilla Tribe of Oregon. The jurisdiction is limited to non-Indians who live on tribal lands, are employed within tribal boundaries, or are a spouse or intimate partner of a tribal member. These tribes must also make their criminal laws and rules available to the public, one of the new VAWA requirements.

These milestones are long overdue and important steps in strengthening Indian tribal governments and ensuring the United States meets its trust obligations to American Indians, and I support them utilizing their newfound judicial powers. As always, I remain resolute in my commitment to Indian Country, and will continue to promote policies that benefit their well-being, sovereignty and ways of life.

## Honoring Inspiring William Katz - Author & Historian

William Loren Katz is the author of Black Indians: A Hidden Heritage and 40 other books on African American history. His books have won awards and his research, writing and lectures have earned widespread praise from noted scholars such as John Hope Franklin, Henry Louis Gates, Jr., John Henrik Clarke, Howard Zinn, James M. McPherson, Alice Walker, Cornel West, Ivan Van Sertima, Betty Shabazz, and Dr. Ralph Bunche. He is an acclaimed lecturer who has spoken at more than 50 universities and dozens of museums, and libraries.

"When it comes to digging up the untold stories of black history and culture, Katz is a matchless miner." --Herb Boyd

"Bill Katz is one of the few members outside of our community who has made a significant, lasting contribution to it. Black Legacy is a good, clear layman's book on African Americans in New York." --Prof. John Henrik Clarke

"If you believe people have no history worth mentioning, it's easy to believe they have no humanity worth defending" -- William Loren Katz

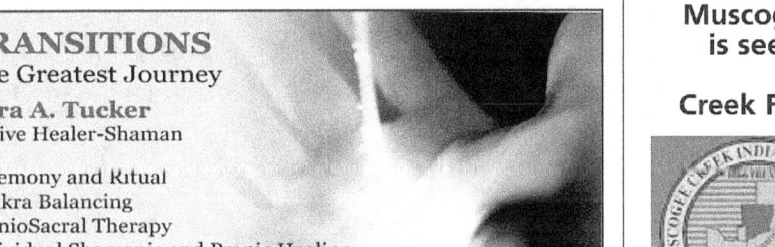

FRYBREAD                                    SAYNDAY

I wish I was Whitebread.

Why?

I sure like peanut butter.

©10- TRW

# 41st Annual Excellence in Journalism Awards!
# Winners Announced!

Tuesday, October 28 is the date of the 41st Annual
San Diego Press Club Excellence in Journalism Awards
honoring outstanding work in print, broadcast and online journalism.

The beautiful Jacobs Center at Market Creek will be the venue for this year's awards and will feature, as always, San Diego's finest restaurants, regional wines and beers, a re-imagined silent auction, and a fun evening rubbing elbows with friends.

**5:30 to 6:00 pm**
Private Reception for Honorary Committee
and their guests

**6:00 to 7:30 pm**
Gourmet Tastings from Local Restaurants
Temecula Valley Wineries, Ramona Valley Wineries
Karl Strauss Brewery, Stone Brewery, Fat Cat Brewery

**7:30 pm**
Emcee:Barbarella Fokos
Election of Board of Directors, Officers
Wild Card Category Winner
Best of Show Awards

**Special Awards:**
Harold Keen Award: Mark Sauer
Andy Mace Award: Maurice Luque
Jim Reiman Award: Joe Guerin
Drew Silvern Award: Carlsbad HS Student Filmmakers
Directors Distinguished Service Award: Phyllis Van Doren

Attire: Business Casual
RSVP: October 25, 2014

For reservations:
619-231-4340
www.sdpressclub.org

Driving and parking instructions: From 805, take Market Street exit heading East. Go approximately 1 mile, turn right (South) on Market Creek Place Driveway (there is a light there). Turn right at the end and then left to the huge parking lot. The entrance is on the South side of the building.

OUR 28TH YEAR                                   MULTI-CULTURAL NEWS GLOBAL NETWORK                                   NOVEMBER 2014

# Educator Roy Cook Selected as 2014 American Indian Heritage Month Local Hero

## American Indian Heritage Month 2014 Honoree

He is a tribal writer, self-published author, journalist, and a Native singer and American Indian artist. He's also an educator, one who carries the teachings of his elders and passes them on to the next generation. Meet Roy Cook, a 2014 American Indian Heritage Month Local Hero.

In nominating him as a Local Hero, Devon Lomayesva, board member for the American Indian Recruitment Programs, notes, "Roy has been a dynamic figure in the San Diego urban and reservation Indian community for decades, contributing to the educational, cultural, and historical presence of

Indians in San Diego County and beyond. The breadth of knowledge and information he has, and will continue to share, will have a lasting impact on Natives and non-Natives alike."

As a champion of his community, Cook's achievements are many. Yet, ask him about his life—his childhood, his dreams and from where he draws his inspiration—and he may not answer directly. Instead, he notes that the answers can be found on a website he has developed, AmericanIndianSource.com.

Cook created the site to be an educational resource on American Indian heritage and culture. It includes events Cook has participated in, such as the annual Baskets and Botany event, held every October at the Tecolote Nature

Roy Cook Writer, Cultural Warrior, Storyteller

Center.

Performing at the event were the Wildcat Singers—Cook, song leader, Juan (Jon) Meza Cuero, Ben Nance, Henry Mendibles, and Stan Rodriguez

who was joined by his son, Raymond.

On the American Indian Source site, Cook explains what it takes to sing

SEE Roy Cook, page 7

## In this issue...

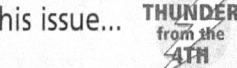

www.indianvoices.net

# NATIVE AMERICAN HISTORY MONTH: The Politics of Thanksgiving Day

*by William Loren Katz*

Thanksgiving remains the most treasured holiday in the United States, honored by Presidents since Abraham Lincoln initiated the Holiday to rouse patriotism in a war that was not going well.

Thanksgiving has often served political ends. In our own age of Middle East invasions, in 2003, President George Bush flew to Bagdad, Iraq to celebrate Thanksgiving Day with U.S. troops and rally the public behind an invasion based on lies. Bush brought a host of news photographers to snap him carrying a glazed turkey to the troops. In three hours he flew home, and TV brought his act of solidarity and generosity to US living rooms. But the turkey the President carried to Bagdad was never eaten. It was cardboard, a stage prop.

Thanksgiving 2003 had a lot in common with the first Thanksgiving Day. In 1620 149 English Pilgrims

aboard the Mayflower landed at Plymouth and survived their first New England winter when Wampanoug people brought them corn, meat and other gifts, and taught them survival skills. In 1621 Governor William Bradford of Plymouth proclaimed a day of Thanksgiving – not for his Wampanoug saviors but his brave Pilgrims. Through resourcefulness and devotion to God his Christians had defeated hunger.

We are still asked to see Thanksgiving through the eyes of Governor Bradford. But Bradford's fable is an early example of "Euro think" -- an arrogant distortion that casts the European conquest as glorious and heroic.

Bradford claims Native Americans were invited to the dinner. Really? Since Pilgrims classified their nonwhite saviors as inferiors and "infidels", if invited at all, they would be asked to provide and serve and not share the food.

After 1621 Pilgrim armies pushed

westward. In 1637 Governor Bradford, without provocation, sent his troops in a raid against their Pequot neighbors. As devout Christians locked in mortal combat with heathens, Pilgrims destroyed a village of sleeping men,

SEE Politics of Thanksgiving Day, page 2

# Native American Heritage Month

*by Kiana Maillet-Davis, MPA, Paiute-Shohone*

November is Native American Heritage Month! Every year, the President of the United States makes a declaration to dedicate this month to the indigenous people of this land. This is a great opportunity to teach your students about the many different Native American cultures throughout the United States, especially those here in San Diego County. Did you know that California has one of the largest Native American populations in the United States and that San Diego County has the most reservations? This month, dedicate part of your curriculum to this celebration in an age appropriate, culturally sensitive manner.

Teaching children about Native American culture can occur in a number of ways, some of which may be more appropriate than others. While dramatic play is an important part of child development and can teach children many things, dressing as other cultures can send the wrong the message and devalue the culture itself. Dressing children in stereotypical or even traditional costumes, making crafts such as feather headbands, and having activities such as children dancing around fake villages or fake fires should be avoided. Native American dress, crafts and artifacts created, and ceremonies cannot be generalized to all tribes and may also be considered sacred. Re-enacting these things could come off as offensive and hurtful.

Instead of trying to recreate Native culture, introduce it to children by highlighting historically accurate information and build on the important role of Native American leaders in the past and present. For example, if you want to create a Thanksgiving celebration, move away from the "Pilgrims and Indians" theme and focus on giving thanks. Perhaps also sharing information on the Fall Harvest and how this skill helped families survive. Exercise historical responsibility when sharing information with children. It's okay to enjoy a meal together and be thankful for what you have, but stay away from stereotyping a culture and continuing historical inaccuracies.

Another way to help children learn about Native American Heritage is to teach them tribe specific information keeping in mind that each tribe has its own unique culture and is its own sovereign nation. You could teach about the indigenous people specifically from this area: the Kumeyaay, the Luiseño, the Cupeño, and the Cahuilla people. If you can, take a fieldtrip to one of the museums that may be celebrating Native American Heritage or attend a local gathering or Pow Wow. Speak of indigenous people, not only in the past, but in the present as well. Today, Native Americans continue to play an important role in this country and make strides in their communities. Just recently, Diane Humetewa (Hopi) became the first Native American woman federal judge and the Schimmel sisters (Umatilla) are making headlines in women's sports.

Take the time to educate yourself before incorporating Native American Heritage Month into your own curriculum. Many colleges and universities hold special public events, lectures and performances in November. Some of these include: The Department of American Indian Studies at SDSU and Palomar College , CSU San Marcos California Indian Culture and Sovereignty Center, and the Department of Ethnic Studies at USD and UCSD. There are also many resourceful websites available such as kumeyaay.com, California Indian Education and Indian Country Media Network. Groups such as the Native Talk Storytellers are willing to come into the classroom to do presentations and they also have an extensive resource list available on their website.

Most importantly, if you have Native American families at your school, take the opportunity to learn from them, and avoid common mistakes. Ask them how they would like to see your class celebrate this month and invite them to come in and present about their specific tribe(s). The best education comes directly from the source.

## Politics of Thanksgiving Day

Continued from page 1

women and children. Bradford rejoiced: "It was a fearful sight to see them frying in the fire and the streams of blood quenching the same and horrible was the stink and stench thereof. But the victory seemed a sweet sacrifice and they [the militia] gave praise thereof to God."

Years later Pilgrim Reverend Increase Mather asked his congregation to commemorate the "victory" and thank God "that on this day we have sent six hundred heathen souls to hell."

School and scholarly texts still honor Bradford. The 1993 edition of the Columbia Encyclopedia [P. 351] states of Bradford, "He maintained friendly relations with the Native Americans." The scholarly Dictionary of American History [P. 77] said, "He was a firm, determined man and an excellent leader; kept relations with the Indians on friendly terms; tolerant toward newcomers and new religions…"

The Mayflower, renamed the Meijbloom (Dutch for Mayflower), continued to make history. It became one of the first ships to carry enslaved Africans to the Americas.

Our Thanksgiving Day celebrates not justice or equality but aggression and enslavement. It affirms the genocidal racial beliefs that destroyed millions of Native American people and their cultures.

Since Americans count themselves among the earliest to fight for freedom and independence, on Thanksgiving we could honor the first freedom fighters of the Americas – those who resisted foreign invasion.

During the century before the Pilgrims landed at Plymouth thousands of enslaved Africans and Native Americans united to fight the Europe's invaders and slavers. In the age of Columbus and the Spanish invasion they were led by Taino leaders such as woman named Anacoana and and a man named Hatuey. In 1511 Hatuey led his 400 followers from Hispaniola to Cuba to warn of the foreigners. Before the Mayflower, runaway Africans and Indians in northeast Brazil had united in the Republic of Palmaris, a maroon fortress that defeated Dutch and Portuguese efforts to storm its three walls and lasted until 1694, almost a hundred years.

Early freedom fighters kept no written records. But some of their beliefs and ideas about freedom, justice and equality were written into a sacred 1776 parchment Americans celebrate on July 4th.

*WILLIAM LOREN KATZ is the author of BLACK INDIANS; A HIDDEN HERITAGE and forty other books. His website is; williamlkatz.com*

## Union Bank and KPBS Honor San Diegans as Local Heroes During American Indian Heritage Month

SAN DIEGO, CA – In celebration of American Indian Heritage Month and as part of its ongoing commitment to cultural diversity and responsible banking, MUFG Union Bank, N.A., has partnered with KPBS to honor two inspiring individuals as local heroes. The 2014 American Indian Heritage Month honorees are: Dr. Daniel J. Calac, medical director of the Indian Health Council (IHC) and Roy Cook, tribal writer, author, journalist, native singer and artist. They will be recognized in November at a private dinner celebration

---

> "Union Bank is proud to recognize the contributions of these local heroes who have generously given their wisdom, time and resources to enrich our communities,"...

---

with their families and executives from KPBS and Union Bank.

Since 1998, KPBS and Union Bank have collaborated on the Local Heroes program and recognized more than 200 honorees. The program pays tribute to exemplary leaders who are making a difference and enriching the lives of others by improving their community, region and the world at large. The 2014 American Indian Heritage Month honorees demonstrate a shared commitment to providing their communities with the tools to thrive in today's changing world.

In addition to the American Indian Heritage Month local heroes, honorees were recognized during Black History Month (February); Women's History Month (March); Jewish American Heritage Month (May); Asian Pacific American Heritage Month (May); LGBT Pride Month (June); Hispanic Heritage Month (September 15 to October 15) and Disability Awareness Month (October).

"Union Bank is proud to recognize the contributions of these local heroes who have generously given their wisdom, time and resources to enrich our communities," said MUFG Union Bank Managing Director Pierre P. Habis, who heads the Consumer and Business Banking groups. "We are delighted to partner with KPBS as we recognize these individuals who personify our core values and reflect the vibrant and diverse communities we serve."

"KPBS is honored to continue its partnership with Union Bank to celebrate these Local Heroes during American Indian Heritage Month," said

KPBS general manager Tom Karlo. "Through their efforts in our communities, these extraordinary individuals improve the quality of life for all."

*The 2014 honorees for American Indian Heritage Month are:*

**Dr. Daniel J. Calac** is the medical director of the Indian Health Council (IHC), a consortium of nine tribes dedicated to the continual betterment of Indian health, wholeness, and well-being. A principal investigator of the California Native American Research Centers for Health (CA-NARCH), Dr. Calac was born and raised on the Pauma Indian Reservation and began his pathway in medicine as a tribal doctor. He received his bachelor's degree in biology from San Diego State University (SDSU) and his medical degree from Harvard Medical School, where he was awarded the Arthur Ashe Foundation Fellowship at Harvard AIDS Institute. Dr. Calac participated in the Four Directions Summer Program, a student-run project that brings Native American undergraduates to Harvard to perform research, shadow physicians and meet Native American medical students. He is a member of the Luiseno Band of Mission Indians, the InterTribal Youth Advisory Board and a board member of the California State University San Marcos Foundation.

**Roy Cook** is a tribal writer, author, journalist, native singer and artist born in Arizona of Ootan (Opata) and Oklahoma (Wazazee) Osage heritage. An Army veteran, Mr. Cook is the president and historian of the San Diego American Indian Warriors Association (AIWA). He also serves as the tribal historian for the Southern California American Indian Resource Center (SCAIR) in San Diego County. Mr. Cook is a member of the Golden State Gourd Dance Society and the Western Oklahoma Comanche Gourd Clan. He has served as curator of the American Indian Cultural Center Museum, San Diego Balboa Park, and the Indian Human Resource Center, Inc. He has published more than 300 stories for print and online covering many Native American topics and has taught at numerous colleges in San Diego, including Palomar College, Mesa Community College and Grossmont College, where he also served as chairman of the Multicultural Studies Department.

KPBS features a wide range of programming during American Indian Heritage Month (November). For more information or to nominate a future local hero, please visit www.kpbs.org/heroes or unionbank.com/heroes.

## Karen Hudes Battling the Corruption in the International Financial System

*by Karen Hudes*

November is Native American Heritage month. Native Americans, both in the US and Canada, have been contacting me and helping in the coalition for the rule of law. Native Americans have preserved the truth that the rest of us are now starting to see.

I am a lawyer and economist who has been battling the corruption in the international financial system together with like-minded people. Not too many people know about my story because of the censorship in the mainstream media, which is owned by a very large banking cartel that thinks it is above the law. It is not. https://s3.amazonaws.com/khudes/twitter1 0.23.14.pdf

Because I was in the right place at the right time, 188 Ministers of Finance have appointed me to safeguard the world's wealth, which Ferdinand Marcos placed in a trust fund for the benefit of humanity in 1950. This trust fund, called TVM-LSM-666, contains 1,715,000 metric tonnes of gold, precious metals, gems, and other artwork. I have filed a claim with the Inspector General of the Marines in Okinawa because some of this gold is being stolen by helicopter from an area in the Philippines controlled by the US

Military. I told the Secretary of Defense, Chuck Hagel, that he needed to court martial the Inspector General of the Department of Defense, Jon Rymer, as well as the Chair of the Joint Chiefs of Staff, Martin Dempsey, because these two traitors are working secretly for the banking cartel.

We have a limited time before all the paper currencies crash. I have been telling the UK Parliament that a small group is trying to control all of humanity. In the United States, the tentacle of this octopus is called the Federal Reserve. The Federal Reserve Notes are unconstitutional. When John F. Kennedy signed an agreement called the Green Hilton Agreement to replace the Federal Reserve Notes with currency backed by gold in TM-LSM-666, he was assassinated.

Today I called out the United Kingdom Parliament for its corruption. I started telling the UK Parliament about the corruption in 2012, and have published three statements on their website. I finally lost patience with that bunch of do-nothings when they published a report accusing everyone else of corruption but themselves. ?@KarenHudes "All the links are broken in my post calling out the UK Parliament for its craven corruption:

SEE **Karen Hudes**, page 11

# Wealth Builders Network

*People Helping People Succeed*

There is no doubt that Shawn Tillery is a change agent who has a passion to educate the community about money. More specifically his aim is to teach the untaught, historical economic truths about cash, money and wealth. This curiosity laid the groundwork for a life fulfilling economic endeavor to help others

He has had a fascination with the concept of wealth and economics since he was a child. Although born in New Orleans, LA he has been in CA since he was a toddler. His first home was in Alameda where his stepfather was stationed. He was soon transferred to San Diego, which has been home for Shawn Tillery. Shawn's fascination with wealth began as a young child. " I always wondered why the wealthy always stayed wealthy and the poor seemed to always stay poor. It was a puzzle that followed me as I developed."

Eventually this curiosity led to a personal educational pursuit that reveled the social inequities as it relates to wealth and wealth and building.

His preoccupation with analyzing the covert economic disparity that supports the worlds economic system along with his strong desire to assist those who desire to accumulate wealth has been a motivating factor for his success as an entrepreneur in the area of finance and the development of a wealth building enterprise. Along with his team of associates The Wealth Builders Network Educational Services was established in 2005.

WBNES provides members with strategies to secure a surplus of tangible wealth for financial security for families and organizations. Through passion for wanting to educate the community. WBNES has formulated the perfect plan to re-position the currencies that jeopardize the sustainability of lasting tangible wealth into more tangible asset classes like gold, silver platinum and bit coins

A Bit Coin is the new kid on the block in the financial neighborhood. It was Shawn Tillerys adamant and steadfast networking that fused the new concept with his innate futuristic instincts. Through his connections and

> **Through his connections and network he has become a true believer in this new cyber currency that is captivating the attention of futurists and creating a sea change in the financial world.**

network he has become a true believer in this new cyber currency that is captivating the attention of futurists and creating a sea change in the financial world.

Skeptics and doubters are starting to take a second look at the phenomenon. The disparity between the ultra wealthy and those on the other end of the scale has obliterated the middle class. Pope Francis condemned the world's "Cult of Money" saying that the economic crisis had left millions of people in rich and poor countries worse off.

Another persuasive aspect of Bit Coins is that The Federal Election Commission recently gave a green light to donating bit coins to political committees, one of the first rulings by a government agency on how to treat the virtual currency.

Bit Coin devotees are convinced that they represent a wave of the future. Undeterred by the tarnished early reputation of Bit Coins Shawn Tillery invisions a currency free from banks and positioned to assist Third World countries and do battle with the Billionaire Boys Club. "I see cyber currency bringing power to the people.

It is the Ninth Wonder of the World. " His enthusiasm is communicable. He has assembled dozens of clients eager to benefit from his organizational skills.

Historically, politicians have always fought for the power to create money out of thin air, so they can increase their spending without having to directly increase taxes. The staggering growth of political power throughout the twentieth century -- the century of war -- was largely made possible by replacing money limited by gold with paper currencies, which can be printed at will by government-controlled banks. Crypto currencies are the first self-limiting monetary systems in the history of mankind, and could be our greatest chance to check the growth of political power since the Magna Carta. Shawn Tillery along with his working group Gary Conner, Ryan Dennis and Richard Thompson are organizing around a crypto currency called Fuel Coins and are leading the charge to reveal the hidden political and military power of government currencies. They feel that crypto currencies could be greatest revolution in human history, and the foundation of a truly free and prosperous planet. Fuel Coins are currently in the organizational stage and preparing for a public roll our in the very near future.

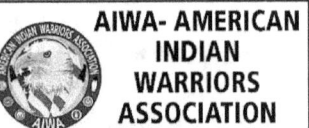

Black Path Commentary: Critical Analysis on Culture, Community, & Struggle

# Beyond The Logic & Lies of the Oppressor: A Black Power Position on Thanksgiving in America

*by Min. Tukufu Kalonji*

Holidays like history vary in their meaning and interpretation, both by those who present their perspective to the world of history and holiday as cultural phenomenon; and also by those who are recipients (either as subject or objects) of said presentations. Subsequently, the viewpoint of the ruling race and class is different from that of its oppressed members in society. As a consequence, the European celebration of lies of "discovery" of a land already inhabited by indigenous people who later we commonly call Indian is as I have argued elsewhere;

organized madness filled with gluttony in turkey dinners, self congratulatory lies of saving a reportedly savage people, whom later had havoc wreaked upon them by the European invader; and a period of time in hat contributed to laying groundwork for African enslavement in the wilderness of north America; is nothing more than a Holiday of Hypocrisy, Horror, and reaffirmation of the Holocaust of enslavement of Indian and African alike! A brief perusal of history reveals just who are the real savages.

Thanksgiving is not a day of rejoicing rather it is what an accurate depiction of history reveals it to be, and is consequently reiterated by the Wampanaog ethnic group in Massachusetts, who argue this day is a Day of Mourning for the indigenous people of this land. Clearly this not the

home of the brave and land of the free as we continue to see in the nightly news and through alternative/internet media, the continuing number of Black men, women and children, and people of color in general being criminalized in numerous form and fashion and lynched in sundry ways. Moreover, people throughout the country are still losing their homes, becoming homeless and unemployed, while the one percent of the filthy and rich maintains their status quo with government support. All the while, the ruling race and class presents itself as the overarching self declared police of the world; dropping bombs on others destroying cultures around the world in the name of "democracy."

And while havoc under the red, white and blue banner of lies is occurring both domestically and internationally, people will engage in escapism via excessive self-indulgence with fowl, swine, all the side items, and alcohol people can consume during this season of gluttony. Furthermore, for these people, they are so emotionally addicted to the notion of holiday and seek escape, they don't even see how they can celebrate and give thanks in their /our own special culturally grounded and meaningful way. Moreover

thanksgiving as an idea is a good and community building concept and practice. Yet, Min. Malcolm X teaches us that the logic of the oppressor cannot be the logic of the oppressed. Logic through cultural grounding tells us we must give thanks in a way representative of our sense of dignity and cultural heritage; not in way imposed upon us by the oppression of white supremacy. We do this specifically during Kwanzaa, however, the best of African culture, (as does the culture of first nations peoples), teaches us that we give thanks daily for the abundance of goodness we have in life, love, and liberation.

In closing let us give thanks not on November 27th, 2014, which marks White supremacist domination of native American, Africans and a land stolen by criminal's who was driven out of Europe by their own people as a day of recognition and reflection. Rather in our own special and cultural manner let us give thanks in our chosen time, space, image, interest, and according out our own needs.

*Min. Tukufu Kalonji is Founder of Kawaida African Ministries,*
*For info contact @ tkalonji@hotmail.com*

---

# I Love Ancestry

*I Love Ancestry is a national issue advocacy campaign about identity, diversity, heritage, and culture located in Miami, Florida. It was created in October 2012 and presently reaches over half a Million people online every month through proprietary social media channels and website.*

*Adrien Heckstall is the founder -director of the 'I Love Ancestry' campaign and a conscious, meticulous and thoughtful advocate for the rights of marginalized people and indigenous communities. As a creative trilingual professional with more than ten years of digital marketing and technology based experience.*

*by Adrien Heckstall*

My need to create I Love Ancestry is coming from my personal experience being born in Ibiza, an island between Spain and Morocco and raised in France within a multiracial family household. My father was American of African descent with native ancestry. My mother is French. I am proud to say that their strong union of

love made me the person I am today. However, this union was not well received by the patriarch of my mother's family. It was the usual french experience of racism where many parents claim they are not racists... Wait until their daugthers get involved in an interracial relationship and this is where the truth usually comes out. This tension between my mother's father and my father based on his race laid the foundation for a very subtle form of oppression toward me by some members of my mothers family. It started to reveal itself when my parents

seperated. I was 7 years old. In retrospective, I can see today how it was "judgement in disguise" while "being loved" at the same time.

I have been living in Miami, Florida since 1998 and while no forms of racism have been expressed towards me as I have "lightskin privilege", I have been able to witness daily the undercover racism from Anglos and Hispanics towards people of color. People you wouldn't suspect to be knowingly or unknowingly so ignorant on the sensitive subject of race. All these events happen [to name a few] at work, in public spaces, with cops, scholars, schoolteachers, and even so called "friends". I finally woke up and had to do something about it, in my own way which is where I Love Ancestry starting to emerge. This project exists today in memory of my father who didn't share with the world while living the painful stories of his past. This project also honors my own children to continue to be the beautiful and compassionate human beings they are today.

To me, I Love Ancestry is like a sanctuary where I heal myself from daily

negative energies. Through our work, I express who I am and what I am about. That is important to me. I transform negative energies into positive one by exposing the harmful behavior of undercover racism and discrimination going on within so many people. I believe this is going on towards other races, and within races controlled by the standards of a white supremacist society. I have always been moved by any injustice I have seen wherever I traveled. I always sided for the oppressed group, whoever they were. I Love Ancestry is my tool to express my truth. I strongly believe that embracing the past and historical truth of our heritage, and culture is the most valuable form of healing the scars made by racism and colorism.

Through this project, I have learned so much about myself, connecting with many like minded people who openly share their experience about identity, diversity, heritage and culture on our platform.

*For further information contact Adrien Heckstall*
*www.iloveancestry.net • iloveancestry@cox.com*

---

# Peaceful Winds

*The door to success opens widest on the hinges of hope and encouragement*

Sober Living Facility Peaceful Winds is located in the Lemon Grove, San Diego County.

A facility that predominately serves Native Americans, has a 1.25 acre panoramic mountain view with a large pool, BBQ area, garden and fruit trees. It has peaceful meditation areas and walkways contemplate life, socialize and reconnect with core values and cultural to

help break the cycle of substance abuse and violence. The Sweat Lodge is an exciting and special addition to this culturally sensitive home. A live in Manager will be available for structure and support and a resident canine mascot, gives a sense of home and unconditional love.

Peaceful Winds has zero tolerance drugs or alcohol. Residents will be tested if there is any question. Violence is never tolerated.

Residents are encouraged to work and or attend school or vocational training. Residents are required to volunteer and give back to their community and will attend three NA/AA meetings a week in

the facility, nearby Alano Club or other meetings of their choice in the community. Wellbriety will be encouraged using daily meditations and discussions. In addition, Yoga, massage, journaling, gardening, healthy cooking, self-esteem building and financial planning will all be included at this holistic facility.

Wendy Kane, RAS, M.A. (owner/administrator) has twenty five years of experience in the Substance Abuse field. Wendy has worked in many of San Diego County's most recognized programs and agencies, and with many of the most difficult populations, including parolees, incarcerated men and women, chronic

relapsers and people who were in total denial. Wendy, a Registered Addiction Specialist, who has performed many Family Interventions and counsels individuals in her private practice, is sensitive to problems that face Native Americans today.

Peaceful Winds specializes in getting in touch with Native American customs and culture and a percentage of each month's rent will be added to Peaceful Winds Scholarship Fund, helping others to get the help they need. Call Wendy Kane at 619-315-1288 or email her at Wkane@peacefulwinds.net for more information on this beautiful facility.

To improve the quality of life of those who recognize themselves and choose to be recognized by others as "Indigenous Peoples of Color of the Americas" and in support of The American Indian Rights and Resources Organization (AIRRO).

# Ill Winds Drove Columbus

*by William Loren Katz*

Columbus's Nina, Pinta and Santa Maria were driven across the Atlantic by the same ill winds that from 1095 to 1272 launched nine Crusades to capture Muslim Jerusalem. Defeated and humiliated the invaders suffered staggering human losses, left royal treasuries depleted, and convinced Christian leaders to do pay lip service to another try.

Except for Christopher Colon or Columbus. An ambitious Genoese sailor who craved adventure and was given to religious mysticism, he accepted God's personal command to free the Holy Land. He also saw God's hand in cloud formations, splashing waves, and distant stars, and had read a religious book that convinced him the world would end in 150 years. As a seaman he saw three mermaids dancing on waves, and was sure in distant lands he would meet men with tails or heads of dogs.

Above all, God had chosen him to see Christianity victorious "throughout the universe." And he would follow His further command to convert or destroy Muslims, Jews and other non-believers.

Columbus's earliest sea experiences were as a youth on Portuguese slave-trading ships along Africa's Atlantic coast. He learned captured men, women and children could be chained and sold for enormous profits. With enough slaves and gold, a Columbus could finally end the infidel grip on the Holy Land.

Weeks after first landing in the Americas Columbus thought he had found a large enough supply of gold and slaves to persuade the Christian "Sovereigns within three years [they] would undertake and prepare to go and conquer the Holy Places." Pope Urban II had launched the first Crusade. Columbus's voyage across the Atlantic to reach the riches of Asia was also a first step toward his larger goal. After five weeks in the Atlantic, lying to grumbling crewmen, claiming he was not a man

lost at sea, his food supplies running low, Columbus stumbled on a Caribbean island named Guanahani. On the morning of October 12, 1492 with a crew in heavy armor carrying swords and muskets, he left the Santa Maria for the sunny shore, and a military and nationalist operation. He planted Spain's flag in the soil, took "possession of the said island for the king and queen," and renamed it San Salvador. "With fifty men your Highness would hold them all in subjection and do with them all that you could wish," he wrote in his Diary. The Admiral was applying the new "doctrine of discovery" that granted Europe's merchant adventurers the right t claim distant lands and their inhabitants. Papal bulls of the time also divided "discovered" lands betweeen Spain and Portugal, and in 1494 the Vatican specifically drew a line dividing the Americas – and the slave trade – between these seafaring powers.

Columbus and his expedition was also a product of Spain's painful "final solution." Since 711 Spain's Muslim Arab rulers shared their cultural wealth with and practiced toleration of the country's diverse citizenry. Catholics, Jews and Muslims lived peacefully with neighbors, as Spain became a world center of books and learning.

Santiago Matamoros

Then Catholic King Ferdinand of Castille and Queen Isabella marshaled a Christian army to impose their rule. Castillian soldiers charged into battle with the cry "Santiago Matamoros" or "Kill the Moors." By January 1492 Christian soldiers stood poised for victory and an era of ethnic cleansing.

On January 2, 1492 Ferdinand's troops captured the splendid Moorish Alhambra castle, the last Arab power bastion in Grenada. An enthusiastic Columbus who stood in the cheering crowd later recorded the triumphal moment in the first sentence of his Diary. "I saw the Royal banner of your Highness placed on the towers of Alhambra ... and I saw the Moorish King come forth and kiss the royal hand of your Highness ... "

Spain's new government quickly moved to finance Columbus's voyage and against its minorities. On March 31 Spain's Jews — as integrated into commercial, governmental and cultural life as Christian and Muslim citizens – were handed an Edict of Expulsion. Families were ordered into exile, and one official suggested, "The whole accursed race of Jews, of twenty years and upwards, might be purified by fire."

The Inquisition forced many Jews to face the ultimate penalty. Even the "marranos," families who had agreed to convert to Christianity, were not exempt. Can you trust people you forced to convert? Muslims also faced persecution and exile over the next ten years. By 1609 Spain had expelled Muslims it had converted to Christianity. Exiles lost

# Lorenzo Dow Turner

Lorenzo Dow Turner (August 21, 1890 – February 10, 1972) was an African-American academic and linguist who did seminal research on the Gullah language of the Low Country of coastal South Carolina and Georgia. His studies included recordings of Gullah speakers in the 1930s. As head of the English departments at Howard University and Fisk University for a combined total of nearly 30 years, he strongly influenced their programs. He created the African Studies curriculum at Fisk, was chair of the African Studies Program at Roosevelt University, and in the early 1960s,

cofounded a training program for Peace Corps volunteers going to Africa.

Born in Elizabeth City, North Carolina on October 21, 1890, Turner was the youngest of four sons of Rooks Turner and Elizabeth Freeman. His father completed his masters degree at Howard University, although he had not begun first grade until he was twenty-one years old. His mother gained the education allowed to black women at the time (six years). Two of Turner's brothers earned degrees in medicine and law. Turner's family's strong emphasis on education inspired him and helped him achieve academic success.

# A Look at Manhood

*by Gregory E. Woods, Keeper of Stories, African/Creek*

"Looking hard upon the life I lived I remember many of the armed and dangerous challenges to my life, and that of my family and how I alone or with others made sure women and their children around us did not have to have a moment like this begging for life.

It is not from begging one's life is given respect and dignity. It is from action and an unwillingness to beg for life. As a man, I get no strength from powerlessness, and the sight of a woman holding a dead son, and hearing her grief saying to the killer, "My life matters. Black lives matter." galls me for reasons I might or might not have conveyed well enough. But, as the son of Herbert L. Woods, I could never keep a symbol like this around me unless it propelled me beyond the scope of merely existing.

When I was a little boy my father kept a picture of two Black men hanging from a noose above his office desk at home. His desk at the time was in the living room where all could see it from the kitchen or the living room. Everyday and many days I stared at it long and hard after reading or hearing something

riveting about the Civil Rights struggle, or reading a monthly publication about the number of hangings throughout the country of mostly Negro men, or listening to my father host and participate in strategy sessions about the political and social structure of the time that went squarely against the grain of his employment agreement.

When I was a man many years later, and not too many back from now, I found that old picture. Daddy told me to put it back up because it was important to remember why.

As men and sons of my father my brothers, and I feel it deep in our bones what Daddy meant. It emboldened us and made our strength stronger and our ties bound to our ancestors, and commitment to our legacies stronger, more potent, and dealt force to the enemy of who we are and stand for. The actions, and language of men tells their story and has the texture of the type of battle to come in the conflicts with those who would take freedom and power from us. Any symbol, and many things can be symbolic, that doesn't embolden the warrior does not belong amongst the warrior's arsenal. If it is not part of the strategy it is part of the tragedy!"

everything but what they could carry.

Some 150,000 refugees had trudged to southern seaports as time ran out for the Jews on the very day before Columbus left. On the day he weighed anchor at Palos, a small band of Jewish families huddled at nearby Cadiz waiting for a rescue ship.

The second sentence of Columbus's Diary shows he was well aware of the connection between their expulsion and

his departure. "After having turned all the Jews from your Kingdoms and Lordships . . . your Highness gave orders to me that with a sufficient fleet I should go." The expulsion and Columbus's departure were forever linked.

On his first night in the Bahamas, Spain's "Captain of the Ocean Sea," described in one Diary sentence how he brought the new Spain to the New

SEE Columbus, page 10

## Roy Cook

Continued from page 1

Wildcat songs. He shares a story told to him by Cuero, a Kumeyaay who lived in Mexico for a number of years.

Jon tells us this story...on how to acquire a good singing voice," he writes. "'Hattepa,' coyote, is well known for having a good, strong voice. He can sing all night long until the early morning. He can make his voice curve and move around hills in very intricate tunes. We can learn a lot by observing our four-legged friends....Jon goes on to tell us that 'Hattepa' is known to eat a lot of 'mes-hanan,' stink bug. So, it just goes to show if you want a good voice to sing Tribal songs you might follow Hattepas' example."

Cook was born in Tucson, Arizona in 1943, of Ootam (Opata) and Oklahoma (Wazazee) Osage heritage, and moved to Southern California as a child. His father worked for the railroad and found employment in National City, eventually moving to Lake Kenshaw, where Cook's earliest memories are of the people on the Santa Ysabel Reservation. It was at this time that he first met his mentor, Steve Ponchetti, who for 35 years would be the reservation's prayer leader, until his passing in 1984.

"My parents got to know Steve Ponchetti, one of the persons who really took the time to teach me the little that I do know of the local culture, the Kumeyaay," remembers Cook. "He and his wife, Florence, were exceptional human beings. They took in foster children, and I'd come and spend summers with them and got to know all the boys that lived there. I created some life-long friendships and we're still in communication with each other."

Cook, a U.S. Special Forces Army soldier, did tours with the U.S. Army Airborne, and Green Beret Special Forces during the Vietnam era. As the elected president of the San Diego American Indian Warriors Association and its official historian, as well as the historian for the Southern California American Indian Resource Center, he appreciates the opportunities he's had to teach.

"I was invited by Palomar College to teach and I took great pleasure in teaching a short summer course on the Pala Band Indian reservation," he says. "There were a lot of elders in that class and some young adolescents....I found it to be a fulfilling and a growing experience."

Cook's passion for teaching led him to a position at Grossmont College, where he ended up serving as Chairman of the Multicultural Studies Department, and had a full teaching load with classes that included Survey of American Indian Art, American Indian Lifestyles, and History and Culture of the Californian Indian.

He has also held positions at Mesa Community College, where he taught art for eight years, as well as at Southwestern and San Diego City Colleges.

But in 2005, his mother became ill, and he decided to cut back. "It required attention, so I made certain decisions," he says.

Even now, at 71, Cook continues to serve as a 36-year member of the Golden State Gourd Dance Society, and has spent the last 20 years as an associate member of the Western Oklahoma Comanche Gourd Clan. And he continues to honor those who came before him.

"Throughout my life," says Cook, "elders would just start talking to me and would find a simpatico identity and they would share their experiences. I found that to be a fount of knowledge to take with me and thereby in some way surrender that to the next generation."

## AIR Programs Annual Fundraiser Banquet

Thursday, October 30, 2014, 5:30 pm-8:30 pm
at the Sycuan Golf Resort
Serving the San Diego region for 21 years and still growing.

Norrie Robbins and Leroy Elliott

Ozzie Monge

Aaron Bruce

Gwendalle Smith and Steph Savedra

## Reparations and Chief John Willie Peoples

There is a "Grassroots Movement", to request that President Barack Obama, recognizes, the call for Reparations, by presenting, Activist John Willie Peoples, with a Lifetime Achievement Award.

This movement is supported by Juliett Porter and others.

# SAN DIEGO PRESS CLUB

# 41st Annual Excellence in Journalism Awards!

## Tuesday, October 28

The 41st Annual San Diego Press Club Excellence in Journalism Awards honoring outstanding work in print, broadcast and online journalism.

**Special Awards:**

Harold Keen Award: *Mark Sauer*
Andy Mace Award: *Maurice Luque*
Jim Reiman Award: *Joe Guerin*
Drew Silvern Award: *Carlsbad HS Student Filmmakers*
Directors Distinguished Service Award: *Phyllis Van Doren*

**Indian Voices Support Group**

Adam Rodriguez Juaneno Band of Mission Indians

San Luis Rey Captain Mel Vernon

Abel Silvas Running Grunion

# "Native Glam" Hits the Runway

Marcie Baine is the designer behind the brand, B.JASH.I Couture. Marcie creates beautiful couture gowns with a Native American influence evident in the details. In addition to creating one-of-a-kind enchanting gowns, ready to wear separates and accessories, Marcie has begun designing cozy wraps. The wrap/shawl is constructed from a weave of a wool blend yarn. Each wrap will have a basket design, beginning with her Karuk tribe basket patterns.

On the evening of October 4th, Fashion Week San Diego was wrapping up with the much anticipated finale. The event was held at a grand venue, Port Pavillion on Broadway Pier. On schedule at 7:00 pm B.JASH.I unveils her new Spring/Summer collection 2013 "Native Glam". The lights dimmed and the music began. Electric Pow Wow Drum by A Tribe Called Red echoed throughout the room. Upon hearing the traditional drum beat I instantly felt chills run down my arms. The song took a modern twist with techno sounds and a marching rythm.

The first model emerged looking stunning. Hair pulled back in a long tight braid she was adorned in a B.JASH.I Couture halter style maxi dress. A print, the colors of a winter sunset. Hues of purple, pinks, and orange shimmered on the shiny fabric as it swayed down the runway. Her earrings were a traditional statement piece, bone and bead style. One after the other the models captivated the audience displaying amazing looks.

Couture gowns, ready to wear separates and traditional accessories. From tule to silk B.JASH.I incorporated modern trend with an accent of Native American style in each piece. Marcie succeeded in offering a unique and refreshing collection. I was entranced as I watched "Native Glam" strut to the beat of the techno drum and thought to myself, what an extreme contrast. Then the voice of my Kumeyaay elder friends came to me. I remembered in conversation they stated ... "We are living in two worlds, modern and traditional." This was very evident in the seven minutes on the runway at the Port Pavillion on Broadway Pier. To view and purchase her designs visit www.Bjashi.com

*Article by Angela Wyatt*
*Photos by Chuck Fedalizo, CF photography Studios*

# San Diego Minority Community Reinvestment Coalition

The San Diego minority community organizational leaders came together with Federal Banking Regulator Meeting: November 3, 2014 to examine and

discuss Income and Racial Income Inequality. Facilitated by veteran activist and social justice soldier Hammed Abdul-Rahim. Serious issues regarding wealth disparity in San Diego were studied

San Diego Wealth Gap Facts:
• Minorities account for over 54% of the population
• Minorities account for over 71% of San Diego poverty

• Wealth Gap between whites and minorities has grown 21 to 1
• San Diego White Median Income $66,017 versus Latino Median Income of $43,601
• Minorities account for less than

14% of 2012 San Diego Conventional-FHA Home Loans
• San Diego minorities are declined for home loans more than 4 to 1 over non-minorities
• Latinos account for over 48% of California and San Diego foreclosed homes
• Less than 3% of all available private equity is invested in minority firms in any given year, despite minorities accounting approximately 54% of the San Diego population
• Less than 47% of San Diego minorities are covered by health insurance
• Over 87% of San Diego's minorities reside in low to moderate income communities

• More than 78% of San Diego minority families are headed by a single mother and are living in poverty
• San Diego Unified School District (2012): African Americans (11% of students-78% classified as socio-economically disadvantaged) Latinos (45% of students-84% classified as socio-economically disadvantaged) Asian (14.8% of students-60% classified as socio-economically disadvantaged
• San Diego Unified School District (2012) High School Drop out Rate: White (6.7%) African American (14.3%) Latino (13.2%) Asian (14.4%)
• San Diego Unified School District (2011)-4th Graders: Math Proficiency-White (66%) African American (17%)

Community Activists Judith Meeks and Curtis Robinson supporting the cause.

## Columbus

Continued from page 6

World. "I took some of the natives by force." The enslavement of American Indians was both Columbus's first act in the Americas, and a first step in his Crusade.

More Spanish troops arrived in the Americas to crush the Aztecs of Mexico, the Incas of Peru and other peoples of the Americas. Spaniards brought new weapons and a new battle cry — "Santiago Mataindios" or "Kill the Indians." They unleashed the world's largest, longest and most devastating genocide. Millions upon millions died of a harsh slavery, forced starvation and mass executions as well as European diseases. Entire villages and cities disappeared.

Along with his sailing skills and fierce ambition, Columbus carried in his heart the burning embers of his monarchy's intolerance, violence and ravenous greed. Though the Admiral found Caribbean people "tractable, peaceable" and wrote King Ferdinand, "there is not in the world a better nation" — he concluded they must be "made to work ... and adopt our ways."

Oppression built slowly. Columbus's initial voyage seized a few dozen Native men and women, some as slaves, others to present at the Royal Court. But his goal was largely exploratory. After another voyage he wrote to his King, "From here, in the name of the Blessed Trinity, we can send all the slaves that can be sold." Spain's rulers eagerly agreed

Hammed Abdul-Rahim founder and president of the Black Contractors Association of San Diego, Inc. and Bro Hugh Muhammad strategize.

Latinos (24%) Reading Proficiency-White (57%) African American (17%) Latinos (17%)

A celebration and ribbon cutting celebration was held at the San Diego Minority Construction Coalition Headquarters 345 15th Street, San Diego CA 92101 (619) 481-7624

to supply him with 17 ships, a thousand soldiers, priests who would conduct mass conversions, and orders for a brutal colonization. He began an island by island search for gold and slaves that decimated the fifty to a hundred million Native Americans.

Las Casas a Dominican Priest, denounced Spain's invaders as "ravening wild beasts, wolves, tigers and lions" whose ultimate aim . . . is to acquire gold." The only true Christians in the Americans, he stated, were Native Americans. Indians, he found, had their own name for the Spain's Christians –"Yares" or devils.

Columbus did not "discover" anything but islands filled with people who greeted him with water, food and gifts.

We should follow the advice of today's Native Americans who reject Columbus Day in favor of a Native Americans Day. All Americans need to study and celebrate the heroic battles that pitted our first Americans against Europeans who would conquer and enslave them, and their African allies.

A Native Americans Day can educate all of us about the Indians who united with Africans to fight against foreign tyranny before, during and after 1776. It will remind everyone that Native Americans still seek the lands and monies promised in ancient treaties with United States. And it will inform us anew that Americans of color whose ancestors fought and died for the principle of freedom still do not enjoy all their inalienable rights.

# Monsanto and Dept. of Defense Help Fund Pharma Company that Could Earn Billions from Ebola Treatment

There are some experimental drugs under development by pharma companies that show some promise, but nothing is commercialized yet. (9)

One fascinating development worth investigating further is that TEKMIRA Pharmaceuticals, a company working on an anti-Ebola drug, just received a $1.5 million cash infusion from none other than Monsanto. Click here to read the press release, which states "Tekmira Pharmaceuticals Corporation is a biopharmaceutical company focused on advancing novel RNAi therapeutics and providing its leading lipid nanoparticle (LNP) delivery technology to pharmaceutical partners."

The money from Monsanto is reportedly related to the company's developed of RNAi technology used in agriculture. The deal is valued at up to $86.2 million, according to the WSJ. (11)

Another press release about Tekmira reveals a $140 million contract with the U.S. military for Ebola treatment drugs:

TKM-Ebola, an anti-Ebola virus RNAi therapeutic, is being developed under a $140 million contract with the U.S. Department of Defense's Medical Countermeasure Systems BioDefense Therapeutics (MCS-BDTX) Joint Product Management Office.

Additional Tekmira partnership are listed at this Tekmira web page.

Not to invoke any charges of collusion or conspiracy here, but a whole lot of people are going to have raised eyebrows over the fact that Monsanto just happened to be giving a cash infusion to a key pharma company working on an Ebola cure right in the middle of a highly-publicized Ebola outbreak which could create huge market demand for the drugs. The fact that the U.S. Department of Defense is also involved with all this is going to have alternative news websites digging hard for additional links.

Sadly, the history of medicine reveals that drug companies, the CDC and the WHO have repeatedly played up the severity of disease outbreaks in order to promote sales of treatment drugs. I'm not saying this outbreak isn't very real and very alarming, of course. It is real. But we always have to be suspicious when windfalls profits just happen to line up for certain corporations following global outbreaks of infectious disease. Vaccine manufacturers, remember, made billions off the false swine flu scare, and tens of millions of dollars in stockpiled swine flu vaccines later had to be destroyed by the governments that panicked and purchased them.

## Karen Hudes
Continued from page 3

http://www.theguardian.com/business/2014/oct/21/government-borrowing-10-percent-higher-budget-deficit#comment-42581114
    then this:
http://www.publications.parliament.uk/pa/cm201213/cmselect/cmpubadm/writev/publicpolicy/m03.htm
    then this (ignoring bogus warnings of virus contamination on the UK Parliament website)
http://www.parliament.uk/documents/commons-committees/public-administration/Complaints-1-consolidated-13-sept.pdf

then this: https://s3.amazonaws.com/khudes/international+gold+reserves.pdf
    then this: https://s3.amazonaws.com/khudes/Twitter10.31.14.1.pdf

The chances that we all work together to clean up this corruption are excellent. A very accurate power transition model has been predicting that we will win ever since Elaine Colville, another World Bank whistleblower from Scotland, and I started getting our statements published by the UK Parliament. Native Americans will have an important role to play in helping us to reclaim our worth as individuals.

Last week, Pope Francis condemned the world's "Cult of Money" saying that the economic crisis had left millions of people in rich and poor countries worse off.

## Jake Dakota Jacome with AC Green Ex-Lakers Player

Jake Dakota Jacome is a whirlwind of social-cultural networking. Keeping up with his appearances is an adventure.

Jake is leaving a cheerful trail from mountain reservations to Hollywood.

Jake's positive influence in the community is as inspiring as the Jacome family who work tirelessly for the collective good. The supportive energy is strong medicine for all of us.

Thank you for illuminating a positive path.

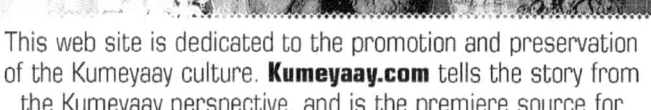

# Professor Charles Ogletree Enlivens San Diego's Diverse Commnity

It was a power packed two days for the politically engaged community and change agents in San Diego, particularly in the 4th District. Powered by the supreme authority and control of the Black Church the call went out. On October 15-16th a gathering of concerned citizens assembled to pay honor and respect to an esteemed community and national leader, Charles James Ogletree, Jr.

The Guest of Honor, Charles Ogletree is Professor at Harvard Law School, the founder of the school's Charles Hamilton Houston Institute for Race and Justice,

and past national president of the Black Law Students Association. These accomplishments are but a back story when added to the fact that Ogletree taught both Barack and Michelle Obama at Harvard and has remained close to Barack Obama throughout his political career.

The community confab, which was masterfully coordinated by Frank Jordan, had a glimmer of a small town political convention.

The Christian Fellowship on Kelton Ave was the setting for the first evening. There were awards and presentations from a cross section of civic and community groups.

The reception and conduct of the San Diego's diverse community was at its prideful best. For a moment the 4th District became a village. SDUSD Board Trustee, Marne Foster opened up the

session at St. Stevens Church with an impassioned delivery about the importance of education. She pointed out the responsibility that all factions of the community have a part to play in the healthy, sustainability of the collective whole. Councilwoman Myrtle Cole elegantly represented her district.

Photos: Rochelle Porter

There was much sharing and deliberating. Photo-ops were a high priority. There was a noticeable abundance of hugging. Community leaders and other strange bedfellows mixed and blended with the impassioned proltariat and the loyal opposition.

The Chief of Police Sally Zimmerman emphasized the Officer Friendly mission of her department. District Attorney Bonnie Dumanis stressed her exhaustive efforts to bond and relate with the electorate from the throne of the ruling class. St Stevens Church offered a respectful, jubilant space to blend

futuristic civic ideas void of progessive or conservative labels.

The spirit of the community reigned supreme. Professor Charles Ogletree ended the forum with the humble advice to care for each other and step forward with love.

San Diego is grateful to Rev. George McKinney and all of the ecclesitical community for their spiritual inspiration and hospitality.

# TRADING POST BUSINESS DIRECTORY

## "I Didn't Get No Wake-Up Call"

A Drama Play, Written and Directed by Paul Wm. Taylor, Sr.

This honest depiction of contemporary life, offers an in-depth look at a family in the late 1970's. This universal story concerns the characters struggle as they deal with the effects of alcohol. With the help of Alcoholics Anonymous and their beliefs in a higher power, they are able to overcome their obstacles and live full and rewarding lives. Don't miss "This Wake-Up Call".

Running November 14, 15, 16, 21, 22, & 23, 2014

Friday & Saturday at 8:00pm.

Sunday Matinée at 3:00pm. $14.00 for Seniors, Students, Military & Disabled. $16.00 General
Reservations/Tickets.
http://www.communityactorstheatre.com
ARTS Tix, Goldstar, or 619.264.3391

# NEVADA NEWS

For Nevada Information: 619-234-4753 • 619-534-2435

## Latinos in USA tells their Idol, Harry Reid, "If You Mess with Us You Are Messing with the Best"

*by Rolando Larraz*

Latinos in the USA send a message like Tony Montana to their favorite idol, Senator Majority Leader Harry Reid, saying that "If you f*** with us you are f***ing with the best,"

Well, the election is over and now we may be able to enjoy a few days of tranquility, peace, and calm before everyone starts complaining again; and most likely, the complaints will come from those who did not vote in this election, or did not do their homework regarding who to vote for.

One thing we can be sure about is that the Latino community took some words from Tony Montana's Scarface to send a message to their favorite idol, Senator Majority Leader Harry Reid, saying that "If you f*** with us you are f***ing with the best," and replaced him as Majority Leader for lying and playing political games with them on the immigration issues.

Reid, who up to now has been the Latino's second God, has been lying to them by promising them immigration reform, amnesty and many other promises that would lead them (Latinos) to believe they were going to be allowed to stay in the country and get citizenship; he has been playing political games with the Latinos in every election and now he gets the payoff for playing those games.

Every time I told the Latinos that Reid and Obama were playing games, they got really upset with me and thought that I said that just because I didn't like Reid or I didn't like Obama or because I was probably a hardcore Republican, but none of that is true.

I don't like Harry Reid because for a very long time, in my humble opinion, he has been a hypocrite; I am not going to call him a liar because as a senator and as Majority Leader, he deserves respect, so I am going to say– because it sounds better and more polite — that he didn't tell the truth all the time.

I cannot say that I dislike Obama; after all, the Las Vegas Tribune was the first newspaper in Clark County to endorse Obama for President, before the Culinary Union and many other organizations, but when we were presented with a picture of the Obama headquarters office in Houston, Texas showing a picture of the Cuban Flag and a picture of Argentinean mercenary Ernesto "Che" Guevara on the wall, we immediately withdrew that endorsement.

We tried to talk to the national headquarters to get some sense of why the picture of a socialist mercenary and the flag of a communist country were displayed in the headquarters of a man running for the presidency of the United States of America, and no one ever answered our question, so we withdrew that endorsement.

I am not a Republican; neither am I a Democrat. I believe that I am a journalist with a mission to clean out our government of corruption and eliminate police abuse and end the police state system that we now have; I believe that I am a journalist with a dream to have a judicial system equal to none with judges that follow the law and do not think that they above everyone and every law.

I am the kind of person that on many occasions gives the wrong impression, and I know that; but I believe that we are all entitled to have the best government there is and one we can be proud of.

I was not born in this country but I have been in Clark County more than half of my natural life and I love Clark County, Las Vegas and the United States and I want to turn the time around and make this city the way it was in the old days.

Sure, it was a time of favors; there were friendships and there may have been some "help" to someone in need; but there were no lies, no extortions, no slandering of one's "non-friends" as there are in the present day.

I remember one time a man I used to know — who I am not going to name because he is already dead — made a terrible mistake that no one was allowed to make in the gaming world; he had a very high profile job in one of the best — if not the best — casinos of the time, and ended up driving a taxi. I went to see the sheriff, Ralph Lamb, and asked him for leniency to allow him to go back to work in what he knew.

Ralph Lamb told me, "Ask me anything but that, please." The Sheriff did not BS me; he did not tell me that he was going to think about it; he did not tell me that he would let me know in a few days; he was straightforward, honest, kind and polite — and humble enough to see me when I was a nobody, because that is the way the people in power, the important people in this community, used to be.

I remember when Senator Floyd Lamb used to go to my office at the La

Verdad newspaper; remember that Floyd Lamb was at that time one of the most powerful persons in Nevada and some of the Spanish people that happened to be there on unrelated business could not believe that the humble gray-haired man that walked into my office was the most powerful senator of the time.

Sheriff John McCarthy used to visit me in my office or at my home very frequently and people could not believe that that single man, driving his own car, was the number one law man in our county.

On my wedding night, John Moran and his wife Goldie were at my home, and as always, they did not come with empty hands; they brought us a wonderful wedding present that up to today I still have and cherish as a sweet memory.

Please understand this: I am not bragging about the people I used to know; I am just comparing how the people act nowadays even when in reality they are not that important. Notice that I am not using some of the present personalities as an example, because that is what I would call bragging.

If Reid and Obama would have kept their promises to the Latino community — in particular, the Mexican community, which for a long time and up to now have idolized the senator and today feel betrayed by both Senator Reid and President Obama — there might have been a different outcome.

I have always been a firm believer that many Latinos, when they become American citizens, register as Democrat because they may confuse Democracy with being a Democrat; but that is a big mistake.

Tuesday night was a good example of what happens when someone politically betrays or double-crosses a Latino — plain and simple, they lose control of the U.S. Senate.

Hopefully the new Republicans at the Senate and the House will not make the same mistake of double-crossing anyone and do a good job for the country; and hopefully the new majority leader will not let his new position go to his head as happened with his predecessor.

My name is Rolando Larraz, and as always, I approved this column.

*Rolando Larraz is Editor in Chief of the Las Vegas Tribune. His column appears weekly in this newspaper. To contact Rolando Larraz, email him at: Rlarraz@lasvegastribune.com or at (702) 868-NEWS (6397)*

## Warren was Honored Sunday by the ACLU in Beverly Hills along with Participants Jim Berk, Cyndi Lauper and Cameron Strang

Massachusetts Sen. Elizabeth Warren, regarded by many progressive Democrats as their party's alternative to Hillary Clinton, told attendees at an ACLU gala in Beverly Hills on Sunday that "economic opportunity is slipping further and further out of reach" for average Americans.

She said bluntly: "We have to face it: The game is rigged in Congress."

# Funding for Tribal Economic Development

Before any settlers came to the Silver State, Nevada has been the home to the Washoe, Western Shoshone, and the Paiute people. The United States has trust obligations to our country's tribal nations based on treaties, laws and Supreme Court decisions. Because of our state's strong connection to American Indians, I take the United States' obligations to the twenty-seven tribes in Nevada very seriously. Sometimes on Indian reservations in rural and remote areas faced with seemingly limited opportunities, tribes in Nevada and across Indian Country are eager to pursue economic and community development plans. I was pleased that the Department of Housing and Urban Development (HUD) announced in October that more than $3.5 million dollars in grants will be directed to seven different tribes to kickoff important small business, healthcare, infrastructure and housing projects.

The grant funding comes from the Indian Community Development Block Grant (ICDBG) Program which assists Indian tribes in accomplishing their self-determined community development goals. Nevada tribes stand to benefit tremendously from these crucial, job-creating grants. For example, the Duckwater Shoshone Tribe will use its grant funding to expand a health and medical facility. The Elko Band of the Te-Moak Tribe of Western Shoshone's grant will provide funds for new manufactured homes for tribal members who are living in overcrowded situations. Additionally, the Fallon Paiute Shoshone Tribe will use its grant to renovate a Head Start building.

I am proud to announce this funding, which promotes tribes the flexibility to decide for themselves how best to meet their own community development needs. I will continue to work so Nevada tribes and others have the tools they need to pursue development efforts in their communities and continue to build their economies.

# Don't Let Congress 'Fast-Track' Dangerous Trade Deals

Corporations like Monsanto are pressing the President and Congress to fast-track international trade deals—deals that would allow corporations to sue entire countries in order to get what they want.

If these deals are rammed through Congress, without scrutiny or debate, countries could lose their right to, among other things, regulate factory farms and genetically modified organisms (GMOs).

Tell Congress: Don't 'fast-track' undemocratic international trade deals! Then, follow-up with a phone call and tell your lawmakers that you oppose fast-track. Capitol Switchboard: 202-224-3121.

FRYBREAD                                    SAYN DAY
You look nice...    Self rising?    No Commod!
©10· TRW

**www.indianvoices.net**

**OUR 28TH YEAR**　　　　**MULTI-CULTURAL NEWS GLOBAL NETWORK**　　　　**DECEMBER 2014**

# Indian Heritage Month
# Honoring Tim RedBird Kiowa

## A Profound Gathering

*by Chamese Dempsey & Rose Davis*

The Honoring of Tim RedBird could not have been better timed. On November 29, 2014 at the Centro Cultural de la Raza, 2004 Park Blvd., San Diego, CA, the stars lined up to publically recognize and celebrate a community icon and spiritual leader, while providing an opportunity for cultural change agents to fulfill their mission.

Community Members, Emerson Joe (Dine') owner of Native Grill and Native Inc., Chamese Dempsey (Paiute), San Diego American Indian Health Center's Community Engagement Coordinator and Mia

Alvarado-Ruffner (Purepecha & Mexica), the Art Advisory Chair of the Centro Cultural de la Raza had gathered together to coordinate a celebration for Native American Indian Heritage Month. Nothing could have been more appropriate than honoring Tim RedBird

Tim, also known as Whitefox, is a 64yr old Native American Indian, full blood Kiowa. Known as a traditionalist artist of sight and sound. He's a singer/composer. His drum group is the Red Warrior singers for Pow Wows and Cultural events. He is a member of these Kiowa warrior societies: Gourd Clan, Oh Ho Mah, Black Leggings & Native American Church, Kiowa chapter. He's self taught in the arts

of painting and music. Raised in the house of Whitefox (Grandfather), Ernest and Ruth Redbird (parents), all famous Kiowa singers. He is proud to be a Native Son of the Kiowas.

Emerson Joe has long envisioned ways to bring the Indian Community together to carry on our tradition of gathering as a tribal group. Young and the old singing, dancing feasting and socializing while coming together as one is much needed in our urban community. We consider it to be a blessing that Tim RedBird offered us this opportunity to rediscover our medicine.

Tim RedBird shared with us his

SEE **Tim RedBird**, page 10

---

**www.indianvoices.net**

---

# Balboa Park Holiday Nights 2014

*by Roy Cook*

Balboa Park Holiday Nights, December 5 & 6, 2014, is the opening activity for the events recognizing the San Diego 1915-2015 Panama Exposition. All this was originally done 100 years ago for the commemoration of the opening of the Panama Canal. A major Native American change this Centennial time is this San Diego regions Bands and village clan participations. A native focus theme for the year long Centennial is; Native American Century of Prosperity.

This Holiday Nights Balboa Park Centennial has local representation of many Tribal Bands all are invited all to attend the Centennial event. Many of the events took place in the east room of the Museum of Man.

The opening singing group on Saturday was the Aukas: Jon Meza Cuero-Lead singer, Roy Cook, Henry Mendibles, Ben Nance and Stan Rodriguez, sing traditional Tipai Wildcat songs from Southern California.

Auka is a Tipai term for greeting. It is also analogous to the break of day and thus enlightenment. Jon has often said, "One of my goals with these songs is to plant these songs like seeds and bring the brightness of the culture to the children."

He was taught these FAMILY Wildcat songs by Alfonso Meza Jon's father and his uncle Bennito Carranza and they also taught him songs by a historical and

Barona Reservation Tribal Leader Larry Banegas, Kumeyaay educator, guides the proceedings.

well-known Tribal singer of songs: Amaay Ta Qwas or Pinta el Cielo Amarillo or Yellow Sky, in English. Yellow Sky composed many songs. Then, as he traveled from village to village-he composed more songs describing those

SEE **Holiday Nights**, page 2

## Holiday Nights
Continued from page 1

locations. Many of his inspirations were from sights seen, stories and emotions experienced. The Aukas will sing some songs composed by Yellow sky describing the very area of this San Diego Matayum. Songs of the Ipai, Tipai, Kwaimi and Kumeyaay.

As a teacher and song composer, Jon strongly emphasizes the need to learn the tune first. He has often said, "First the song, then the words, and then what the words mean." We feel he offers his instruction in a traditional manner and often speaks to us from the heart in a traditional way.

Speaking of the local history and spirituality was Paul 'Junior' Cuero, Campo, and his group of Bird singers. Larry Banegas, Barona, presented a rich content account of the local Kumeyyay in a concise talk. Stan Rodriguez, Santa Ysabel, also spoke on the local Art and traditional materials and in addition he sang a set of Tipai "tin can' songs.

There was a very gracious introduction by Mr. Anthony Pico, Viejas and announced the names of the members of the organizing committee. He gave special credit to our committee point man, Mr. Michael Connelly, Campo.

The Maataam Nakashin Intertribal Centennial Committee consists of representatives of the two language groups and many of the 21 recognized Bands in Southern California.

Events held in the Museum of Man East room: Traditional storytelling gatherings, Bird singing, Wildcat singing, and maybe a little dancing.

Finally, I would be remiss to not mention Charlene and her family, Sycuan, in glorious Kumeyyay array.

This Museum of Man East room is in sight of the traditional Hattam Kumeyaay Village. Kumeyaay Chief Manuel Hatam, 1834-1875 was the popular leader of the Tribal people living on this Balboa Park location. Our recently passed Respected Elder Jane Dumas is a lineal descendent of Chief, Manuel Hatam. For thousands and thousands of years the Kumeyaay people lived all over this coastal area as Florida canyon, Indian point, and Chollas Creek. We might ask ourselves, where are they today? The answer is, right here in the greater and San Diego City proper! That is correct! There are hundreds of tribal people still living near to their original locations. Many more are scattered by many events: historical, political or military.

For more information and changes see the website: WWW.nakashin.org

LETTER TO THE EDITOR

*Dear Friend,*

Yesterday, the US Senate Intelligence committee released its long-awaited report of the CIA torture practices.

As some of you may remember, six years ago I brought some of the same information about illegal torture in Article XVIII of the Impeachment President Bush.

One surprising response in the Senate report is that the torture, called 'enhanced interrogation techniques,' was "ineffective," as if torture would have been OK if the torturers at the CIA had gained 'useful' information!

The CIA's post-911 history of the use of torture, documented in the Senate report should cause every American to demand release of the full, unredacted report. There should be no hiding place nor refuge for anyone who was involved in the program. Torturers and those who authorized them ought to be brought to justice.

Sign the petition here demanding full release of the Senate's Report on CIA Torture. Please contribute to our on-going efforts to keep the American people aware of the truth and of a path to action to reclaim our nation.

Once again we see the need for a US Commission on Truth and Reconciliation, where the American people can finally come face to face with the lies which our nation has been living since 911, address those lies and chart a new course of truth, at home and in the world.

It is imperative that the American people know what was done in our name and what continues to be done by our government and its agencies to promote division and war around the world.

Last week's Kucinich Action post, " No War with Russia, Hot or Cold", received a powerful national response, igniting a petition response and beginning a new debate over the direction of US–Russia relations, which are sadly bristling with violence. Thank you to everyone for their personal messages, which I am endeavoring to answer.

Today, December 10, 2014, is the 50th Anniversary of Dr. Martin Luther King Jr.'s Nobel Peace Prize Acceptance Speech. I have been asked by Dr. Bernice King, the youngest daughter of Dr. Martin Luther King, Jr., to make a special presentation, sponsored by the King Center, at the National Center for Civil and Human Rights, in Atlanta, as part of the 50th Anniversary commemoration, celebrating her father's life work for peace. I will send you the details of my presentation.

I am always grateful for your support and I humbly ask that you contribute to enable our continued communication efforts.

*Thanks so much, Dennis*
*www.facebook.com/Dennis.kucinich*
*www.Kucinich.com*

## INDIAN VOICES
### Multicultural News from an American Indian Perspective

## PUBLISHED BY BLACKROSE COMMUNICATIONS
*Member, American Indian Chamber of Commerce*

Email: rdavis4973@aol.com
Website: www.indianvoices.net
Editorial Board: Rose Davis

| | | | |
|---|---|---|---|
| Editor: | Rose Davis | Writer: | Jaclyn Bissonette |
| Social Media Administrator: | Yvonne-Cher Skye | Entertainment Writer/ | |
| Outside Support: | Mel Vernon | Photographer LA/SD: | Rochelle Porter |
| LV Entertainment Writer: | Z. Z. Zorn | Reporter de Espectaculos: | Omar DeSantiago |
| Associate Editor: | Sis Mary Muhahmmad | Reporter de Espectaculos: | Michelle Banuet |
| Writer: | Kathleen Blavatt | Proofreader: | Mary Lou Finley |
| Writer: | Roy Cook | Graphic Artist: | Elaine Hall |
| Writer: | Marc Snelling | Staff Photographer: | Abel Jacome |
| Writer: | Scott Andrews | | |

Endeavor Media Group
André Haynes
Lakeside Business Suites
2620 Regatta Dr., Ste. 102
Las Vegas, NV 89128
(702) 902-2844 • Fax: (702) 902-2845
andre@EMGnv.com
www.EMGnv.com

111 South 35th St.
San Diego, CA 92113
(619) 234-4753
(619) 534-2435 (cell)
Fax: (619) 512-4534

**Member of the Society of Professional Journalists**
**Member of New America Media**

© 2001 Blackrose Communications. No part of this publication may be reproduced without written consent from the publishers. Although we try to be careful, we are not responsible for any errors. Articles are not necessarily the opinion of the publisher.

# Working for Sovereign Nations as the Creator Intended

As the year draws to an end grassroots journalists, as well as our brothers and sisters working diligently for a positive, equitable, healthy and sustainable social future are confidant, cheerful and full of hope. It has been a bumpy, drama filled and turbulent year filled with a kaleidoscope of emotional drama from tragedy to ecstasy.

Dueling with an archaic unyielding militarized government has galvanized our creativity and perfected our networking skills. Unlikely bedfellows are redefining our social/political apparatus.

We have managed to lock arms and march through difficult times. Our collective spirituality has tapped into our indigenous intelligence making us more informed, wiser and stronger.

As we move forward, Indian Voices is pleased to have the opportunity to affiliate with Cash Community Development a 501c3 with dba division Native American TIO (Trade Information Office) whose stated mission is the responsibility to our American Indian community and Vets/Military. Their

services are intended to help all tribal groups to aspire to self-sufficiency through self-determination and sovereignty.

The founder of this program is John T. Moss who is a proud member of the Caddo Nation of Oklahoma. John has served as consultant to a leading international investment and merchant bank based in the US, active in Asia, Mexico, and Middle East. He has been involved in advising on cross border merger and acquisition involving billions in commercial banking from the emerging markets. John is also one of the most respected sales and service trainers with his applicable methods for any industry in the United States and internationally, and author of the ethically recognized book "The Millionaire Loan Officer" (www.johntmoss.com). Since 1981 John's successful business experience has served to support Indian County and Military. He founded the the non-profit "Caddo Assets Services Help Community Development" with the "Native American Trade Information Office". This Indian

managed non-profits goal, is to provide options of funding, and tribal ownership in economic development projects John knows that economic strength and jobs, enhances our Indian Nation's ability to better ensure generational preservation of our cultures, music, dance, language, & arts. The Per-Capatia program provides opportunities for John and his associates to provide common sense financial and business solutions utilizing "Financial Literacy and Business Development" for the community good.

His team is honored to be working on over $11.5 billion dollars in projects to Indian Country including projects around the world with Indigenous Nations.

John T. Moss co- founded Indigenous Development Collaborative (IDC http://bluestone-idc.com/pdfs/IntroductiontoIDC-RDL.pdf) who assists Tribes/Businesses in the structuring and implementation of successful economic development opportunities on and off reservation land; this has included Casinos, to Hotels, to Housing. The Principals of IDC are

seasoned development and finance professionals who work cooperatively with Tribal Governments and NATIO around the world.

John has been able to bring his years of credibility in the financial business world to Indian Country, focused on the support to human resource departments with financial literacy programs. John through CASH-CD/NATIO is acting as liaisons with the Indian Nations, Military Collaborative, & the Obama Administration in coordinating all aspects of his business development, and Call Center development programs with those Tribes who qualify. John's non-profit board has vast experience within Indian County supporting Military/Warrior needs with such honored members like Randy Edmonds founder of SCARE, Bernard Kahrahrah, , Roy Sampsel and RIP David Lester. These networks are ethically working hard to enhance Indian Country and Warriors while working towards self-sustainability as sovereign nations as the Creator intended.

*John Moss is Grandson of Indian Actor/Artist Chief Silvermoon. The Indian Voices Media Project is excited about kicking off the New Year while networking with John T. Moss.*

# Interior Disburses $13.4 Billion in FY14 Energy Revenues to Benefit Federal, State, Local and Tribal Governments

*Disbursements to States increase; American Indian Revenues top $1 Billion for first time*

WASHINGTON – Secretary of the Interior Sally Jewell today announced that the Department of the Interior disbursed more than $13.4 billion in revenue generated by energy production on Federal and American Indian lands and offshore areas in Fiscal Year 2014, with increases in state and Indian Country revenues over the prior year.

The disbursements include more than $1 billion to American Indian Tribes and individual Indian mineral owners, marking the first time disbursements from energy production on American Indian lands topped the billion-dollar

mark.

The Interior Department distributes energy revenues to state, local, and federal accounts to support critical reclamation, conservation, recreation, and historic preservation projects. Local governments apply the revenues to meet a variety of needs, ranging from school funding to infrastructure improvements and water conservation projects.

"Revenue generated from developing public energy resources that belong to all Americans helps fund critical investments in communities across the United States and creates American jobs, fosters land and water conservation efforts, improves critical infrastructure, and supports education," said Jewell. "This year's disbursements continue to reflect significant energy production from public

and tribal lands in the United States."

The $1.1 billion disbursed to 34 American Indian Tribes and more than 34,000 individual Indian mineral owners for resources held for them in trust or restricted status represents an increase of more than $200 million over FY 2013 disbursements that totaled $937.9 million. This increase to Indian Country is attributed primarily to increasing oil production from the Ft. Berthold Reservation in North Dakota.

The Interior Department disburses 100 percent of the revenues received for energy and mineral production activities on Indian lands directly to the Tribes and individual Indian mineral owners through Interior's Bureau of Indian Affairs and the Office of Special Trustee for American Indians. Tribes then use the

revenues to develop infrastructure, provide healthcare and education, and support other critical community development programs, such as senior centers, public safety projects, and youth initiatives.

Secretary Jewell in June announced a package of regulatory initiatives intended to help tribal leaders to spur investment opportunities and economic development in Indian Country, including efforts to remove regulatory barriers to infrastructure and energy development in Indian Country; increase tribal community access to expanded, high-speed Internet resources via broadband; eliminate leasing impediments to land development; and support the growth of new markets for Native American and Alaska Native businesses.

"While some tribes continue to experience recent economic progress from energy development, these tribes

SEE **Energy Revenue**, page 7

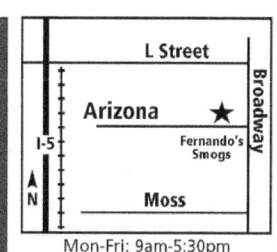

## How Dogs Can Help Veterans Overcome PTSD

*New research finds that "man's best friend" could be lifesavers for veterans of the wars in Iraq and Afghanistan*

by Chris Colin

"I would constantly be scanning for who was going to come stab me from behind," says Robert Soliz, a 31-year-old former Army Specialist from San Joaquin, California. He was discharged in 2005 after serving in a heavy artillery quick-reaction force in South Baghdad. But fear, anxiety, depression and substance abuse swept into his life, and Soliz became one of 300,000 U.S. veterans of the wars in Iraq and Afghanistan with a diagnosis of post-traumatic stress disorder.

Isolated, his family deteriorating—"I couldn't show affection, couldn't hug my kids"—Soliz turned to the Palo Alto V.A. Medical Center. One recent morning, he talked about his progress. Hanging from his belt was a container of doggie treats, a link to the treatment he credits with saving his life. Soliz participates in Paws for Purple Hearts, one of four experimental programs nationwide that pair veterans afflicted

by PTSD with Labrador and golden retrievers. Launched in 2008 by a social worker?named Rick Yount, the program arranges for a veteran to spend six weeks with a dog, training it to be a mobility-assistance animal for a physically disabled veteran.

It's no surprise that a doe-eyed creature like the one at Soliz's feet can soothe, but other benefits are less predictable. The animals draw out even the most isolated personality, and having to praise the animals helps traumatized veterans overcome emotional numbness. Teaching the dogs service commands develops a patient's ability to communicate, to be assertive but not aggressive, a distinction some struggle with. The dogs can also assuage the hypervigilance common in vets with PTSD. Some participants report they finally got some sleep knowing that a naturally alert soul was standing watch.

Researchers are accumulating evidence that bonding with dogs has biological effects, such as elevated levels of the hormone?oxytocin. "Oxytocin improves trust, the ability to interpret facial expressions, the overcoming of paranoia and other pro-social effects— the opposite of PTSD symptoms," says Meg Daley Olmert of Baltimore, who works for a program called Warrior Canine Connection.

About 300 vets have participated in these programs, and some graduates who Yount worried "wouldn't make it" report impressive strides. Congress has commissioned a study, underway in Florida, to assess the effectiveness of canine-caretaking on PTSD.

Soliz says his life is slowly coming back to him. He now can go to the movies without panicking—and hug and kiss his two kids.

## Remembering the Wades, the Bradens and the Struggle for Racial Integration in Louisville

by Rick Howlett

*On a October morning, Ebbs is standing next to a historical marker erected near the Wade home site a few years ago. "I've made sure that my children understand the significance of the fact that there's a monument here and it is our blood relatives that went through what they did to receive something like this. So I make sure that I definitely give it the respect that it's due."*

Andrew, Charlotte and Rosemary Wade stand on the front porch of their new home in Shively the day after someone hurled a rock through the front window. , Credit Al Blunk / The Courier-Journal,

Andrew, Charlotte and Rosemary Wade stand on the front porch of their new home in Shively the day after someone hurled a rock through the front window.
Credit:  Al Blunk / The Courier-Journal

This year, many in Louisville have been marking the anniversary of a touchstone event of the Civil Rights era.

It started 60 years ago when white activists, led by Carl and Anne Braden purchased a home on behalf of a young black family.

That act touched off weeks of racial violence and led to serious criminal charges against the activists.

Today, the neighborhood in Shively seems a most unlikely place for cross-burnings, gunfire and a dynamite attack, but that's exactly what happened along the street over the course of several weeks in 1954.

The hostility began when an African-American family—Andrew Wade, his pregnant wife, Charlotte and their 2-year-old daughter Rosemary—moved into their new home at 4010 Rone Court.

Andrew Wade was an electrician who wanted to move his family to the suburbs but was turned down by a

succession of white real estate agents, who refused to cross the illegal but still highly observed line of segregation.

In an interview from the 1980s featured in the documentary "Anne Braden: Southern Patriot," Wade recalls a piece of advice he received from agent.

"He said 'Wade, let's be realistic—if you see a house, you like the house, regardless of where it is, get a white person if necessary if it's in a white neighborhood to buy the house for you and transfer it to you. It's that simple.'"

So, that's what he did. Wade enlisted the help of acquaintances Carl and Anne Braden, left-wing activists who had been vocal in their opposition to Louisville's housing segregation laws.

The transaction was completed but trouble began as soon as the Wades moved in.

"That night, they heard gunshots, and somebody was firing at the house, and

SEE **The Wades**, page 11

## Veterans Charities Don't All Make Grade

Lehmkuhler said she has little time or money to spend on fundraising the way many national charities do. Her last tax filing showed $329,000 in spending and $1.3 million in net assets for the year. "I don't want to disparage anyone else but yes, it's sad to me that they would choose to worry about raising more money rather than getting out there helping the guys and gals," Lehmkuhler said. "It's hard, but I'm not going to waste money on (promotional) blankets and postage. I'm going to keep pure to our mission." University of San Diego law professor Robert Muth runs a veterans legal clinic that, like Disabled American Veterans, helps survivors secure federal benefits.

Local veterans-services organizations

are well aware of the fund raising prowess of many national charities with eight- and ninefigure budgets, Muth said. "It's not necessarily that the large organizations are doing anything illegal, they just have a different focus: to raise money," he said. "Smaller nonprofits focused on veterans services here in San Diego simply can't compete."

National veterans' charities often turn up at local news conferences to tap the generosity of a community that cares about veterans, Muth said. Then they leave.

"It's frustrating," he said. 'They're not necessarily here providing direct services to San Diego veterans."

Black Path Commentary: Critical Analysis on Culture, Community, & Struggle

# Standing Steadfast on the Battlefield: A Black Power Position on the Ferguson Revolt & Continuing Struggle

*by Min. Tukufu Kalonji*

Of the varied scantly credible reports and continued media justifying of the bloodthirsty savagery in blue; that is the police oppression and murder in Ferguson of Michael Brown; or the murders of Oscar Grant, Tamir Rice, Eric Garner, and Trayvon Martin by a wanna be cop; and all the Black men, women, and children maimed and killed by the so called authorities; is reflective of the inhumane devaluing of Black life in America. Furthermore, the consistent and immoral act of the criminal system of injustice for failing to indict,

prosecute, and bring the perpetrator police to justice is not new, shocking, nor out of the norm for the ruling race and class and its occupying forces in American cities.

History provides a blatant picture of the clear and present danger Black folk face in America since the beginning of the Holocaust of Enslavement of Africans in the wilderness of North America. If America is honest and disassociates itself from the hypocrisy of its arrogant, immoral, and self aggrandizement illusions of being a land of the brave an home of the free; and truly does a critical self examination, then perhaps the ruling race and class might come to a solution to its sociopathic behavior of devaluing the life of Black peoples and other oppressed in the USA. Should this happen perhaps America would realize

the critical need for a serious process of deconstruction and reconstruction on all levels in and throughout society and its institutions. However, it is clear the dominant society does not have the moral consciousness or capacity do such an act of rightness, thus the need for revolution and revolt.

Moreover, the people's righteous indignation and revolt, in all its forms is reflective of our right and responsibility to fight for justice as we have demonstrated since the 1960's. It is of necessity to make note that the masses are reported "rioting" in the nightly news, but that is misleading for the people of Ferguson MO and across the country are engaged in Revolt! A riot is an unstructured outburst without any self-conscious political goals. In contrast a revolt is a collective act of a people to achieve three fundamental objectives which are; Self-Determination; Self-Respect; and Self-Defense. Liberation and the acquisition of social justice require revolution and revolution requires revolt(s). Whether it's in the policy making halls of congress, senate, city council et al; or varied board rooms, or where it typically takes place initially,

in the streets, with the masses igniting the flames of radical reconstruction in the forward thrust of resisting occupation and seeking justice; revolt and revolution is implemented and sustained via out in the open actions as well as through clandestine maneuvers which are necessary and sufficient for any battle being engaged.

My posture is to encourage our readers to the stand, as I do, with our ancestor Paul Robeson, artist, athlete, and revolutionary leader who argued; "I stand here struggling for the rights of my people to be full citizens in this country and they are not. You want to shut up every Negro who has the courage to stand up and fight for the rights of his people. That is why I am here today; for the battle front is everywhere there is no shelters." (Robeson, 1985; the Whole World In His Hand).

Let us stand steadfast on the battlefield for liberation and a higher level of human life as we say in Swahili Mapambano Inaendelea (the struggle continues)!

*Min. Tukufu Kalonji is Founder of Kawaida African Ministries,*
*For info contact @ tkalonji@hotmail.com*

---

# Sustainability and Exclusion

*by Nic Paget-Clarke*

Can sustainability exclude? Apparently so. Sustainability may be one of the most overused words in language. Though the marketing spin on sustainability implies good health and care for the environment there is no reason that it should -- and truth be told, it doesn't. Sustainability is a noun, a thing, yet it does not exist. It is a human-inspired concept as applicable to anything as any word. According to their website, Monsanto practices both responsibility and sustainability. Used judiciously, it can easily mean nothing. You choose: sustainable agriculture, sustainable democracy, sustainable military occupation, sustainable development, sustainable capitalism. How about sustainable exclusion?

In October of this year, I visited the Southern Cone of South America, specifically Argentina, Uruguay, and Chile. I went as part of an ongoing search to understand just what sustainability is. How can humans survive on Earth? Is life sustainable?

Within minutes of landing at the Buenos Aires airport, I was heading into this thirteen-million-person metropolis and chatting with the taxi driver. I asked him about the "villas". His assessment was there are four large villas (or barrios) around Buenos Aires with a population of about two million. I learned as the days slipped by that the people in these villas are "excluidos" – excluded from society.

The next day, I walked downtown by the Presidential Palace – The Pink House and the Plaza de Mayo. I stared at skyscrapers and gazed at huge government buildings, at remnants of the Spanish colonizers, the English invaders – even the statue of Columbus which President Cristina Fernández de Kirchner has had disassembled in preparation for relocation. I stopped and listened to a reggae jazz band. I walked down the tourist-targeted Florida alley. I stumbled onto lines of ambling riot police.

To my left, down one of Buenos Aires' main avenues, came a march, a family outing of excluidos. From one side of the street to the other, with a Givenchy perfume billboard as a backdrop, came bright blue banners, barrio identification, images of Che!, rhyming drums – came excluidos. I'm told that a large percentage of the villistas are migrants from the Argentine countryside, from Paraguay, from Bolivia, even Chile. They are peasants. They are Indigenous people. They are people in general. They come because their land is no longer theirs; they have no income; they can't survive. They are drawn to this huge metropolis in search of survival. Just like people come to the United States.

I joined the march, took photos, had short chats. I had a people-guided tour of downtown Buenos Aires.

A couple of hours later, I was in the offices of CTEP in the Constitución neighborhood. CTEP is the Confederación de Trabajadores de la Economía Popular -- the Confederation of Workers of the People's Economy. When you have been excluded from society, you have to create your own society, with your own culture and

economy. CTEP, organized without hierarchy and based on horizontal relationships, makes it decisions in networks of community assemblies in the villas of Buenos Aires and throughout Argentina. They create cooperatives and small enterprises to create and share products and income. They work with the movement of recuperated factories in Argentina which are owned and run by their workers. They grow vegetables and raise animals without landlords. They collect used materials and recycle them. As artists they make clothing, pots, all sorts of things, and sell them on blankets in the streets, at fairs and markets. They wash windscreens at traffic lights. They deliver messages and items on motorbikes.

But what does it mean to be excluded? Excluded by who and from what? CTEP has realized that the world economy, the world culture is no longer simply about exploiting people -- whether they be wage workers, farmers or peasants -- and concentrating that wealth, that land, those mines, that capital in the hands of fewer and fewer investors and corporate owners. According to their analysis, those who are privatizing the Earth have such wealth, such power, and such access to

Working in a recycling cooperative in Buenos Aires, Argentina.
Photo by Nic Paget-Clarke

technology that they simply don't need all of us people to sustain their system of depredation. They have written off millions. There is no rational economic reason to continue to include them. And this view of sustainability demands exclusion.

I've never quoted a Pope before, but the new Pope Francis who is from Buenos Aires puts it this way: "Just as the commandment 'Thou shalt not kill' sets a clear limit in order to safeguard the value of human life, today we also have to say "thou shalt not" to an economy of exclusion and inequality. Such an economy kills. How can it be that it is not a news item when an elderly homeless person dies of exposure, but it is news when the stock market loses two

SEE **Sustainability**, page 14

To improve the quality of life of those who recognize themselves and choose to be recognized by others as "Indigenous Peoples of Color of the Americas" and in support of The American Indian Rights and Resources Organization (AIRRO).

## Are Indian Casinos the New Smallpox?

*by YoNasDa LoneWolf Hill*

Greetings Relatives,

Many moons ago the United States government needed to find strategies to exterminate the Native people of this land called the Americas. They attempted to use them as slaves even transporting them to England as slaves. In North and South America Native Americans knew the land, so many ran away from the slavemasters. So after that the government began to build on America but realized they couldn't control their "Indian epidemic" so they began to figure out ways to move them away from their growing communities and a strategy where they wouldn't have to see the Native Americans again. So in many states offering "peace gifts" while they were en route to unknown territories that other tribes may have occupied or places they never been. The US government gave native men, women and children blankets infected with smallpox. This was the first of many germ warfare tactics the government used. Millions of indigenous people of this land died.

So fast forward today there is 566 federal recognized tribes (federal recognized means being recognized by the federal government for assistance in food, shelter , health and education. Many tribes were forced on land that wasn't useful to grow crops, hunt, etc. so they worked out deals to still keep their sovereignty on land but to receive assistance. So starting in the 80's some of the tribes began to build casinos to use an income source to help the needs of the tribal members and began their 100% soveirgnty.

Like smallpox in the blankets it's disguised to be used to comfort the tribe but in many ways it's killing the tribe. It has opened up the gates of hell of Caucasians that never cared for Native people now all of a sudden they have Cherokee in their family, just enough to enroll with tribes that have casinos so they too can benefit from the millions that are coming into the tribe. They are coming into tribes as "advisors" and outsourcing PR firms, managers, lawyers, etc creating jobs to non native people so they can use these tactics to exterminate indigenous people.

Currently as my people are preparing themselves for war for the XL keystone pipeline the government is trying to build through America including several Native lands. So just like history repeats itself it may not be small pox blankets to kill Native people that are in the way of a still growing America, the government have came up with a better way to kill off the "Indians" and that's through alcohol, drugs, diabetes and suicide all coming from welcoming casinos in. There are other ways to get income for a tribe.

I have opened up cultural tours called "Rez Tours" to organizations, community leaders, artists and youth groups. It gives people an opportunity to physically learn about Native people by Native people. Dec 11-14 is the Houma Nation: Rez Tour leaving Atlanta, GA if you want to come please email me at thereztours@gmail.com

Mitakoye Oyasin
Wacipi Ola Win - Star Song Woman
Yonasda LoneWolf Hill
@queenyonasda
www.facebook.com/queenyonasda

*Greetings to All from Phil Fixico,*

My Indian Heritage presentation this year at AC Bilbrew Library in Los Angeles was entitled: "Seminole Maroons in the Civil War". Most of my installed exhibit, consisted of the documented evidence about my direct Ancestors. Three of them, one of my g-grandparents, and 2 of my g-g-grandparents were combatants in the First Indian Home Guard, including other family members in the "Loyal Indians", 1st Kansas Colored Infantry and the  79th Reg. USCT. They were the first "Troops of Color" to fight Confederate Forces as "Loyal Indians" in the  Indian Territory in November and December of 1861. During the Civil War their units participated in 30 engagements. They suffered many causalties, among the troops  and their family members who in December of 1861 fled to Kansas on the "Trail of Blood on Ice". When the Seminole Maroons returned to Indian Territory, in tribute to achieving a new level of "Marronage" they, named their two Black Bands, the: "John Brown" and Jim Lane Bands, they would later become the Dosar Barkus and  Caesar Bruner Band. I need to thank so many , who have participated over the years, this makes my 6th presentation at the beautiful and spacious AC Bilbrew Black Resource Center. I must thank Mr. Pare Bowlegs, who , was the Historical Preservation Officer for Oklahoma Seminole Nation, Some years ago, it was he who ,so generously  gave me links, websites and information about my g-grandmother Dinah Fixico's Band history, Octiarche/Mikasuki/Meccosukke. Of course Dr. Kevin Mulroy, currently the Dean of Claremont College's, Library Sciences facilities. Dr. Mulroy is recognized as the "World's Leading Authority " on Seminole Maroons, my friends at the National Archives and Records  Administration, Oral and Family Tree Historians, C. Edwards, Charles Gibson, Charlesetta  Bruner and Virgie Fixico. Of course the Smithsonian Institution's Dr. Gabrielle Tayac Editor/Curater for the "indiVisible": African-Native American Lives in the Americas, The Journal of  Ethnohistory, for feauturing my family's hisitory in their Winter 2011 edition , Diane Miller Nation Program Director  for National Underground/Network to Freedom, the Los Angeles Chapter of the 9th & 10th (horse) Cavalry and Mr. Wm. L. Katz author of "Black Indians" and the "Father of Black Indian Studies of  in the United States. There are so many more who should be mentioned here, however , time does  not permit. Thank you, one and all for your many years of crucial support.

*"Through Warm Tears of Gratitude"*
*Phil "Pompey Bruner" Fixico,*
*Seminole Maroon Descendant*

P.S. Special Thanks, must go to Rose Mitchell Head Librarian, at the AC Bilbrew for fighting to keep the presentations going. Also , Rose Davis of www.indianvoices.net, over the years has donated a barrel of ink and space in her newspaper. Our friends at the Seminole Producer Newspaper in Seminole County, Oklahoma have been wonderful, in their coverage. Let us, not forget Mr. Kevin Brinker, who solved the family's longest running mystery, about my grand aunt, Lucinda Fixico and another great Humanitarian Mr. Ralph Wagner. Two other longtime and notable contributors are Steve Riley of mixedracestudies.net and Dr. Angela Molette.

# John Brown: A White Role Model

*by William Loren Katz*

John Brown was born in 1800, and he was executed by the state of Virginia on December 2, 1859. This year (2006) a PBS documentary film continued an effort that began even before his execution to sully his reputation. Why? He was a white man who gave his life fighting slavery but he did so before Lincoln issued the Emancipation Proclamation. He was a premature "emancipationist." However, two years after John Brown's death Union soldiers marched into the South singing of the man—"his truth goes marching on." In the year 2000 PBS film finds no truths about Brown worth repeating. The documentary begins with a long, slow scene showing Brown being led to the gallows and ends with a long slow scene showing him being led to the gallows. This could seem like a warning to similarly inclined white people, and the public deserves better.

Brown was a devout Christian who saw slavery as violence and whose favorite Biblical quote was "Remember them that are in bonds, as bound with them." He swore his entire family to the anti-slavery struggle; led armed bands that rescued enslaved people, and was an active agent of the underground railroad. In 1856 Brown fought slaveholders' fire with rifle fire in the Kansas Civil War. He was not a man to be trifled with. When President James Buchanan offered a $250 reward for Brown's capture, he offered $2.50 for Buchanan's.

In 1858, he met in Canada with dozens of African Americans, including the father of Black nationalism, Martin R. Delany, to develop his liberation plan. The next year Brown led five African Americans, and 17 whites including three of his sons, to seize the government arsenal at Harper's Ferry. Their goal was to arm enslaved people, help them reach the Allegheny mountains, help them wage a war against bondage.

## John Brown, The Blackest White Man (1800 – 1859)

John Brown was an American abolitionist and a True Hero who used violent actions to fight slavery. During 1856 in Kansas, Brown commanded forces at the Battle of Black Jack and the Battle of Osawatomie. Brown's followers also killed five pro-slavery supporters at Pottawatomie. In 1859, abolitionist John Brown led a small group on a raid against a federal armory in Harpers Ferry in an attempt to start an armed slave revolt and destroy the institution of slavery. Brown was arrested, tried, and hung.

John Brown, The Blackest White Man in American History (1800 – 1859)

## Sarah Harnendez Continues Working for the People

"December brings many blessings. One in particular for me is starting a new position as the Career Counselor for SCAIR (Southern California American Resource Center, Inc.). This will be for their new Native NetWorks Program. Employment and Training for American Indians. I am blessed and my heart is anywhere helping the people. My starting date is December 22nd. It is just an honor to be in staff with the amazing people at SCAIR! A veteran to this position, I held a similar position at the age of 19 when IHRC was down on 30th. I love assisting our people and watching them succeed!"

### Energy Revenue
Continued from page 3

and many other tribal communities continue to face formidable economic hardship," said Jewell. "In our efforts to foster tribal self-determination and improve our federal regulations to meet the needs of the 21st century, we will continue to look for opportunities to provide greater deference to tribes to help remove barriers to economic development on tribal lands. Working hand in hand with tribal communities and with my colleagues across the Administration, we hope to help lay a solid foundation for economic development and improve the quality of life for American Indians and Alaska Natives in their homelands."

More than $2.2 billion of the FY 2014 energy revenues were disbursed to 36 states as their cumulative share of revenues collected from oil, gas and mineral production on federal lands within their borders and from U.S. offshore oil and gas tracts adjacent to their shores. In FY 2013 disbursements to the states totaled about $2 billion. Among the top states receiving FY 2014 revenue are Wyoming ($1 billion); New Mexico ($579 million); Utah ($171 million); Colorado ($169 million); California ($100 million); North Dakota ($68 million); Montana ($38 million); Louisiana ($24 million); Alaska ($20 million); and Texas ($12 million).

Included in the state disbursements is $4.1 million sent directly to 37 individual counties in eight states from geothermal energy production. State disbursements also include $4.3 million to four coastal states and 42 eligible political subdivisions (counties and parishes) under provisions of the Gulf of

Mexico Energy Security Act of 2006. A complete list of states receiving revenues through Fiscal Year 2014 is available on Interior's Office of Natural Resources Revenue's website at: http://www.onrr.gov/

A total of $7.2 billion was disbursed to the U.S. Treasury to fund programs for the entire nation, making the Department's mineral revenue disbursements one of the nation's largest sources of non-tax revenue. The disbursements also fund several special use accounts in the U.S. Treasury, including FY 2014 transfers to the Land & Water Conservation Fund, the Reclamation Fund, and the Historic Preservation Fund.

The Land and Water Conservation Fund, established by Congress in 1964, receives revenue from energy development to provide grants to state, federal and local governments to acquire land, water and easements for recreation use and to protect natural treasures. Receipts deposited in the Reclamation Fund are made available by Congress through annual appropriation acts for authorized water management and efficiency programs that directly benefit 17 Western States. The Historic Preservation Fund provides matching grants to help state and tribal historic preservation offices preserve cultural and other historic resources.

All federal energy revenues are collected and disbursed by Interior's Office of Natural Resources Revenue (ONRR), which is under the Assistant Secretary for Policy, Management and Budget. ONRR makes disbursements on a monthly basis from the royalties, rents and bonuses it collects from energy and mineral companies.

## John T. Moss

CEO/Founder of 501 c3 CASH Community Development, Native American TIO, & Wise Debt Relief

The Caddo Assets-Services Help (C.A.S.H.) Community Development Organization and div. Native American Trade Information Office (T.I.O.) is a non-profit based in Huntington Beach, California. Our organization is geared to enable various tribes around the country obtain federal and private grants that will develop sustainable, long-term community projects.

Our 100% Indian-managed non-profit provides services in facilitating funding, economic project development, education in business and personal finance, economic strategies, employment opportunities, and instruction on implementation. Our goal is to bring self-reliance to our great Indian Nations and our work with all of the USA Military branches past and present.

John T. Moss developed a non-profit organization to respond to contract needs of the USAID program of the U.S. Dept of Commerce as well economic development via our networks like "IDC" Indigenous Development Collaborative. This organization provides expertise in sustainable economic development through a network of qualified and experienced practitioners of sustainable design and implementation techniques. This organization works in concert with the Consortium for International Development world wide with our main focus being Native American Federally Recognized Tribes/Nations and Indigenous Nations.

---

**The San Diego American Indian Community Salutes Eleanor Miller**

Eleanor has been a willing worker at the heart of our world. Her friendship, loyalty and smile has bonded us together. Our love and deep appreciation goes with her as she sets up camp in Arizona.

---

*"When we walk upon Mother Earth, we always plant our feet carefully because we know the faces of our future generations are looking up at us from beneath the ground. We never forget them."*
*– Oren Lyons - Onondaga Nation*

---

# Harvest Dinner 2014

**San Diego American Indian Health Center Annual Winter Celebration**

Food, games for kids.
Indian Entertainment
Saturday, December 6, 2014
Barrio Station
2175 Newton Ave., San Diego, CA

# MAYAN GOLD

**Kenneth Barlis**

On November 7th, 2014, under the full moon, guest gathered at the historic La Fayette Hotel Ballroom in San Diego. It was designer Kenneth Barlis second fashion show. The debut of men and women's 2015 Spring/Summer collection. Known for his whimsical, romantic patterns, this collection had a twist. The collection was inspired from the Mayan culture. Couture gowns in unexpected tons of gold, copper and bronze. Each piece had intricate detail, resembling ancient Mayan shapes and symbols. The fabrics are created by the Barlis team. Detailed by hand, each Swarvoski crystal and bead is sewn on one at a time. The quality is unsurpassed. Each gown was seriously stunning. They were constructed of intricate hand sewn details, precise shapes and cut-outs. Swirling patterns reflecting Mayan art and the Mayan calendar. The fabrics used were fine. Gold lame, silk taffeta and soft tulle in unexpected colors of copper and bronze. The couture collection had an interesting mix of textures. Ultra soft draping with constructed pieces around the body. There were also black dresses with silver accents in the dark, sexy, mysterious, and sophisticated collection. The designer, Kenneth Barlis was born in Pagadion City, Philippines. He had always had an eye for luxury and pursued his dream after moving to America. Kenneth received top honors at Fashion week San Diego 2012 and was in an exclusive for LA Fashion Magazine as "San Diego's Leading Fashion Designer."

*Article by: Angela Wyatt*
*Photography by: Chuck Fedalizo, CF photography Studios*

---

# A SUCCESS STORY

2014 marks 15 years of service for the Dress for Success Organization San Diego. Throughout the years, the organization has served nearly 9000 local women by assisting in providing a network of supportive services including career development.

Leonard Simpson, founder of Fashion Forward, produces an annual Gala in November. This year it was Leonard Simpsons 10 Best Dressed Awards Benefitting Dress for Success San Diego. It is a theatrical production, over the top fun Broadway style that includes a beautiful fashion show with over 10 designers, a live auction, a fabulous dinner and an award ceremony.

Among the award recipients Sylvia Evans-McKinney, Founder and Executive Director of Dress for Success was honored. In the Special Awards category she received Founder Award for Charitable Contribution. In an interview she states "I have walked their path before, I know what it takes." The organization partners with 65 agencies that teach hard

skills. DFSSD teaches the soft skills piece, the social aspect. It offers many support groups and programs to help women that are disadvantaged. Sylvia states the most rewarding part of her position is when her clients return and say they are employed.

Maryanne Parker approached the podium at the gala wearing a beautiful Adriana Papell designer gown. She was the elected spokesperson for Dress for Success San Diego that evening. Here is her testimony. "I am a former Dress for Success client. I came to the U.S. 9 years ago. I didn't have a family, friends, money or a car. But I had a responsibility to my two children to create a dignifying life. I was

directed to the organization. After efficient training, I got employed, retained my job and purchased my first home only 5 years after my arrival. Through Dress for Success I received a scholarship and studied with International School of Protocol and Diplomacy. I started my own company, Manor of Mannors. A company for business, social and youth etiquette. Today I am a home owner, a business owner and a private counsel to Middle Eastern Dignitaries.

I was impressed that this single mother of two arrived in a foreign country with nothing and was able to succeed beyond expectations with the guidance and tools from

Dress for Success San Diego. This organization is a jewel of San Diego to disadvantaged women. Their clients are diamonds in the rough and Maryanne Parker is a prime example of a polished professional shaped by a network aimed to promote women to thrive in work and in life.

To contact San Diego Dress for Success log on to www.dressforsuccess.org/sandiego
To contact Manor of Manners Intl., log on to www.manorofmanners.com

*Article and photographs by Angela Wyatt*

# Tribes Can Legalize Pot, Justice Department Decides

*Marijuana may displace casinos as reservation cash cows.*

by Steven Nelson

Four western U.S. states have decided to allow recreational marijuana sales, but legal pot may soon be within driving distance of many more Americans following a new Department of Justice decision.

In a memo released Thursday, the department outlined new policies allowing American Indian tribes to grow and sell marijuana on reservation lands.

Possession of marijuana is a federal crime, but the department announced in August 2013 it would allow states to regulate recreational marijuana sales. The nation's first recreational pot stores opened in Colorado and Washington this year.

Residents of Alaska, Oregon and the District of Columbia voted in November to also legalize marijuana, though Congress appears likely to block sales in the nation's capital.

The new federal policy will allow tribes interested in growing and selling marijuana to do so, if they maintain "robust and effective regulatory systems," John Walsh, the U.S. attorney for Colorado, told the Los Angeles Times.

Tribes will need to avoid eight enforcement triggers that currently apply to state marijuana sales, including a prohibition on sales to minors and the diversion of marijuana to states where it remains illegal under local law.

It's unclear how many tribes will take advantage of the policy directive. Some tribes are well-known for using their special legal status to host casinos or sell untaxed cigarettes, but addiction and substance abuse are major concerns for some communities.

Federally recognized tribal reservations are scattered around the country. Click here to see a more detailed map of reservation locations.

Federally recognized tribal reservations are scattered around the country. Click here to see a more detailed map of reservation locations.

There are 326 federally recognized American Indian reservations, according to the Bureau of Indian Affairs. Many reservations are in states that don't allow marijuana for medical or recreational use, such as Oklahoma, Utah and the Dakotas. Others are located near major East Coast cities and far from legal pot stores in the West.

"The tribes have the sovereign right to set the code on their reservations," U.S. attorney for North Dakota Timothy Purdon, chairman of the Attorney General's Subcommittee on Native American Issues, told the Times.

In a statement, the Department of Justice said U.S. attorneys will review tribal marijuana policies on a case-by-case basis and that prosecutors retain the right to enforce federal law.

"Each U.S. attorney will assess the threats and circumstances in his or her district, and consult closely with tribal partners and the Justice Department when significant issues or enforcement decisions arise in this area," the statement says.

Kevin Sabet, a former presidential drug adviser and co-founder of the anti-legalization group Smart Approaches to Marijuana, says he's concerned the new policy opens the door to pockets of legalization across the country.

"A situation is quickly forming where people living in states who do not want legalization will in fact be living 10 minutes away from a marijuana store," Sabet says.

Mason Tvert, a spokesman for the pro-legalization Marijuana Policy Project, says tribal leaders "will have a tremendous opportunity to improve public health and safety, as well as benefit economically" by legalizing marijuana.

"Regulating and taxing marijuana like alcohol would ensure the product is controlled, and it would bring significant revenue and new jobs to these communities," Tvert says. "Studies have consistently found above-average rates of alcohol abuse and related problems among Native American communities, so it would be incredibly beneficial to provide adults with a safer recreational alternative."

## Tim RedBird

Continued from page 1

World Beat Center Makada (r) and entourage attended.

many delightful talents such as his exceptional art display of Native American art that mounted on the walls of the Centro; he also shared with us his remarkable poetry he composed, sang many Southern Kiowa songs with his drum group Red Warriors while the Soaring Eagles danced to the heart beat of the drum. Tim ended the evening off with singing a variety of songs, some he composed himself, while playing his guitar.

The event committee gifted Tim with a beautiful Pendleton blanket while thanking him for being a positive role model to our people as well as sharing his talents for all of us to see and experience. Emerson set up his food booth, Native Grill and cooked Bison burgers on fry bread and Indian Tacos. The event turnout was a success with approximately 300 people. The event had an Indian market with several Native Arts & Crafts Booths and a raffle at the end that consisted of items from each of the vendors, sacks of blue bird flour donated from Native Grill, Christmas packages and gifts donated by Connie Grey Bull on behalf of Title VII Indian Education and hand-made beaded Christmas ornaments donated by Estelle Fisher and other items donated by the committee.

The event committee would like to thank the Centro Cultural de la Raza for opening their doors to help make this event happen. The event Committee and other community members also plan to continue to host more Native Events at the Centro in the near future to continue to bring our community together to celebrate our cultural. Nothing is more important than carrying on our cultural tradition while shielding it from influences that my exploit and otherwise neutralize us as a people. We must become self-sufficient and avoid the temptations of the colonizer and the modern day seduction of social technology.

Tim RedBird and our change agents and cultural warriors are shining a path for us to follow.

Richard Overdall and Tim RedBird team up.

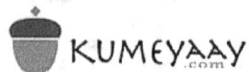

## Juaneno Band of Mission Indians

*by Abel Silvas Running Grunion*

The Juaneno Band of Mission Indians have always been a one nation tribe since Father Serra came to their homeland in 1776. Even to this day they continue to be a strong tribe protecting their history and homeland without a reservation. Thanks to the great leadership of Chairman David Belardes for keeping the Band together for the last 25 years and hopefully for many more years to come.

David continues to pursue the United States for Federal recognition and for a reservation.

## The Kumeyaay Redefine Wealth

The Kumeyaay family come together in a human coalition of indigenous ancestral preservation.

## The Wades

Continued from page 4

Andrew says he told his wife to get down, but it didn't hit anybody. And they looked out and there was a cross burning in the field next to them," Anne Braden recalled in the documentary.

There would more trouble in the days to come; a stone bearing a racial epithet hurled into a window, the local dairy refused to deliver milk; the Wades' newspaper subscription canceled because the carrier wouldn't deliver it.

Police were stationed nearby for protection, but the Wades and their white allies didn't trust them, so they formed a committee whose members would take turns staying in the house.

One of the guards was Lewis Lubka.

"I was in the back kitchen with a gun. And when we were shot at we shot back. I was working days and helping guard the house at nights," said Lubka, the last surviving activist who's now 88 and lives in Fargo, North Dakota.

Several weeks went by and tensions seemed to ease a bit. But just after midnight on June 27 1954;

"We was coming in and a bomb went off under the house," Lubka said.

The home was blown up with dynamite. The explosives were placed under Rosemary's room. No one was in the house at the time.

Cate Fosl is a biographer of Anne Braden and heads the Anne Braden Institute for Social Justice Research at the University of Louisville. She said it was no secret who was responsible for this and other attacks, but:

"No indictments were returned against any of the neighbors, even though they had admitted to burning a cross and being hostile to the idea. But all of the indictments were against the whites who supported the Wades in this quest for a house," Fosl said.

Anne and Carl Braden and the five other whites were charged with sedition, accused of hatching a Communist plot to buy the home, blow it up, touch off a race war and overthrow the Commonwealth of Kentucky.

Today, it sounds outrageous. But in an interview from the collections of the Kentucky Historical Society, Anne Braden provided some context: this happened at the confluence of McCarthyism and the Supreme Court's 1954 Brown v. Board of Education ruling that outlawed school segregation.

"And I always felt that the Wades and us became lightning rods. They couldn't get at the Supreme Court but that could get to us," Anne Braden said.

Carl Braden was convicted of sedition and spent eight months in prison.

The following year a ruling came down from the U.S. Supreme Court in a

Anne and Carl Braden during Carl's sedition trial in Louisville. He was convicted on December 13, 1954. Credit: Charley Darneal / The Courier-Journal

Pennsylvania case that said, in essence, sedition is a federal crime, not a state offense.

Carl Braden's state conviction was later reversed and the charges against the other defendants were dropped.

Branded as Communist troublemakers, all the defendants had trouble finding work in the following years. Carl Braden died in 1975. Anne Braden continued her work opposing housing and school segregation.

The Wade family attempted to repair their home, but amid continuing hostility, sold the house at a loss and moved back into west Louisville, where Charlotte Wade still lives. She no longer speaks publicly about the case. Andrew Wade died in 2005.

Anne Braden, who died in 2006 at the age of 81, told the Kentucky Historical Society she had no regrets about helping the Wades buy their dream home.

"It would have been unthinkable for us to say no, because this is something we believed in. You live by what you believe in or you don't, that's all."

Fosl said the Bradens and the Wades would be proud of how the once-troubled Shively neighborhood has changed.

"It is one of the most integrated, multi-racial, multi-cultural neighborhoods in Louisville today," Fosl said.

It's also the home of 31-year-old postal worker Steve Ebbs, his wife, and two young daughters.

On a October morning, Ebbs is standing next to a historical marker erected near the Wade home site a few years ago.

He's the great-nephew of Andrew and Charlotte Wade, and lives down the street from 4010 Rone Court, now called Clyde Drive.

Ebbs has been the family's spokesman during the anniversary commemorations.

"It's something that I really take pride in," Ebbs said.

"I've made sure that my children understand the significance of the fact that there's a monument here and it is our blood relatives that went through what they did to receive something like this. So I make sure that I definitely give it the respect that it's due."

# A Killer Among Us that No One Wants to Talk About

*by Wendy Kane*

Drug Abuse has reached epidemic numbers in our society. The money spent for police involvement, lost and stolen property, hospitalizations, the loss of jobs and homes, children removed from their parents and deaths have reached an all time high. Drug and alcohol addiction has touched families, friends and our community. Many of our friends, neighbors, co-workers and family members are dealing with this problem. People, in their addiction, are often told by friends and family to "just stop," as if it's a loss of will power, morals or weakness. They are often told, "if you love me, your children or your family, you would stop drinking / using drugs."

Years ago the only hope for alcoholics or drug addicts was sanitariums or locked psych. hospitals. Many people felt that there was no hope for these poor souls. Today the AMA (American Medical Association) recognizes addiction as a disease and substance abuse is included in the DSM (Diagnostic and Statistical manual of Mental Disorders).

Statistics (www.AddictionsandRecovery.org) show that drug /alcohol addiction is 3x more common than diabetes. It crosses all socio-economic boundaries. At least two times more people die from alcohol related deaths than die from car accidents.(AMA Journal 3/10/04). Alcohol intoxication is associated with 40 – 50% of traffic fatalities, 25 – 35% of non - fatal vehicle injuries, and 64 % of fires. Alcohol is present in nearly 50% of all homicides (either victim or perpetrator), in 31% of fatal injuries and 23 % of suicides.

Parents, spouses, co – workers and friends ask again and again what it will take to stop those they care about from this addiction? Pawning a great grandmother's ring, sleeping on the streets, acquiring Hepatitis C or HIV, going to jail or prison, or losing their children should be the bottom for those affected, but often it is not. When it is not, their loved ones continue to watch the downward spiral of destruction hopelessly standing by and praying that they will quit. With each phone call comes a fear that our loved one has overdosed.

Help is available. There are residential rehabs, outpatient day programs, AA, NA, individual and group therapy, and intervention. Few alcoholics and addicts stop using the first time they try recovery, but each time they hopefully will learn more about living life on life's terms.

The following screening and questionnaire concerning substance abuse is based on criteria from the American Psychiatric Associations DSM and the World Health Organization.

1. Do you use more and more drugs/alcohol over time?

2. When you stop using have you experienced physical, emotional withdrawal, irritability, anxiety, shakes, sweats, vomiting or nausea?

3. Do you drink/ use more than you planned ? Once you start, can you stop?

4. Despite negative consequences to your self esteem, job family and finances do you still continue to drink or use?

5. Have you spent a significant amount of time4 obtaining, using, planning, or recovering from using? Have you ever concealed or minimized your use? Have you ever made up stories or lied to avoid getting caught?

6. Have you ever thought about cutting down or controlling your use? Have you ever made unsuccessful attempts to cut down or control your use?

7. The substance use is continued despite knowledge of having a persistent or recurrent physical or psychological problem that is likely to be caused or exacerbated by the substance?

Addictions can be caused by many factors including negative childhood experiences, environmental factors, emotional disorders, genetics, and addictive personality and several other factors. If you are having a problem in this area, get help. If it's a loved one, listen to them and encourage them to get help. I believe, by working with hundreds and hundreds of people, that there is hope for anyone who has a desire to want to get better and live a healthier happier life.

Wendy Kane, a Registered Addiction Specialist with 25+ years in the Recovery field, has recently opened Peaceful Winds Sober Living for Native Americans in Lemon Grove. Wendy also sees individuals in her private practice and specializes with people who chronically relapse, family interventions, and people who need help putting the pieces of their lives back together. Contact Kane for more information (619) 315-1288.

---

# Once Again, John McCain is the Darling of the Coyotes and Snakes

*by Brenda Norrell, Censored News*

Sen. John McCain's new mode of genocide is no where more obvious than in the slick theft of Apache sacred lands for the benefit of a foreign corporation for copper mining. Of course, McCain's theft of sacred lands in Arizona is nothing new, nor is the complicity by the corrupt media who are in the saddle with fellow politicians and corporate bedfellows.

With deception and spin, McCain and his team of thieves hid away the theft of Oak Flat, sacred lands of Apache, in the National Defense Authorization Act passed by the Senate on Friday, after being passed by the House. McCain and his fellow thieves in Congress have duped the public once again. And they all came out smiling.

The snakes used similar spin and deception for the so-called Navajo Hopi land dispute, which was actually to clear Navajos off their land at Black Mesa for Peabody Coal. The coal fuels one of the world's dirtiest coal-fired power plants, Navajo Generating Station, on the Navajo Nation in Arizona.

The stench of this government and media deception is also found in the secret files of the United States internment camps where Aleuts were forced to live, and many died of starvation and disease, during World War II. Even in the mid-Twentieth Century, the US government carried out a secret program of sterilizing American Indian women in Indian Health Service hospitals.

---

# Winter Solstice 12/10/14 Soaring Eagle Dance Workshop

The December Soaring Eagle Dance workshop was a joyful busy event. The program, which encourages the education and advancement of tribal traditional cultures is a program of the San Diego Unified School District They meet regularly at the Ballard Parent Center 2375 Congress St. San Diego, CA 92110.

Randy Edmonds spread Xmas joy and distributed gifts.

Chuck Cadott Dancing instructor and all around organizer took care of program details and gave out certificates of appreciation for contributions made daring the Pow Wow season. New students lined up for their first lesson. Carla Tourville made sure the dance regalia were is in good order.

To stay up to date regarding

Chuck Cadotte presents Kiana Davis with an achievement award.

SOARING EAGLES  contact:
 Vickie Gambala 619-266-2887
vickiegambala@gmail.com
 Jennifer Garcia 619-540-4688
mariposa2172@yahoo.com
 Carla Tourville 619-743-9847
carlatourville@yahoo.com

---

# TRADING POST BUSINESS DIRECTORY

## CALIFORNIA

**ADVOCACY**
Alan Lechuza Aquallo
Advocate for Native Youth and Scholarships
alan@blackphonerecords.com

**ATTORNEYS**
Marshall Law PC
Daniel E.Marshall,Attorney at Law
619-993-5778 • marslawbmw@gmail.com
sandiegoevictionattorneys.com

**BAKERY**
Historic San Luis Rey Bakery
490 N. El Camino Real Oceanside, CA 92058
760-433-7242 • ww.sanluisreybakery.com

La Nueva Mexican Bakery
4676 Market St. Ste. A-3, San Diego, CA
619-262-0042

**CARE GIVER**
Private Duty– References
Terms to be discussed
619-504-2455 Ask for Liz

**CLERICAL**
Your Girl Friday International
Marketing, Operations & Promotional
Services • yourgirlfriday3512@gmail.com

**CULTURE**
Kumeyaay
www.kumeyaay.com • larry@kumeyaay.com

Worldbeat Cultural Center
619-230-1190
www.worldbeatculturalcenter.org
info@worldbeatculturalcenter.org

**DRIVER**
Driver for Hire
Clean DMV Class ABC
619-504-2455 Ask for Liz

**FINANCIAL ADVISORS**
Merrill Lynch / Elke Chenevey
Vice President & Financial Advisor
Office: 619-699-3707
Fax: 619-758-3619

**FINANCIAL SERVICES**
The Caddo Assets-Services
(C.A.S.H.) Community Development
Organization and div. Native American
Trade Information Office (T.I.O.) is a
non-profit based in Huntington Beach,
California 949-287-4687

**HEALTH**
Rady's Children Hospital
San Diego, CA
800-869-5627 • www.rchsd.org

Regenerative Medicine Institute
www.regenerativemedicine.mx

San Diego American Health Center
2630 1st Avenue, San Diego, CA 92013
619-234-2158

**HEALER-SHAMAN**
Transitions / Vera A. Tucker
vtucker1212@gmail.com
619-987-0372

**HOUSEKEEPING**
Cleaning, windows, floors
4 hours $80 - 8 hours $120

619-504-2455 Ask for Liz

**INSURANCE**
State Farm / Jack Fannin
1154 E. Main St. El Cajon, CA 92021-7157
619-440-0161 Business
619-440-0495 Fax
jack.fanninjroi@statefarm.com
www.jackfannin.com

Earthquake Insurances
www.EarthquakeAuthority.com

**MARKETING**
Jahaanah Productions
Marketing, Media, Public Relations, Graphic
Design • 832-978-0939

**NOTARY PUBLIC**
Sis. Evon X. Nana
San Diego, CA 92113 • 619-549-5792
evonx@yahoo.com

**PHOTOGRAPHY**
Peache Photo Memories
619-697-4186 office
619-549-0968 contact
www.peachephotomemories.com
peachephotos@cox.net

**PUBLISHERS**
Blackrose Communications
111 South 35th St. San Diego, CA 92113
619-234-4753
www.Indianvoices.net • rdavis4973@aol.com

**RADIO**
91.3PM Kopa
Pala Rez Radio

www.palatribe.com • 91.3@palatribe.com

**RECOVERY**
David "Wolf" Diaz, Pres. & Founder
Walk of the Warrior, A Non-Profit Corp.
Tel: 760-646-0074 • Cell: 310-866-7057
Fax:760-689-4907
www.walkofthewarrior.com
walkofthewarrior@yahoo.com

Peaceful Winds Sober Living
619-315-1288

**REGALIA**
Carla Tourville
Native Regalia Custom Design
Yokut Tule River Tribe
San Diego, CA • 619-743-9847

**REPARATIONS**
Mr. Peoples Reparations
200 N. Long Beach Blvd. Compton, CA
310-632-0577

**RESTAURANT**
Awash Ethiopian Restaurant
4979 El Cajon Blvd. San Diego,CA
619-677-3754

**RETAIL – CLOTHING**
Full Blood Apparel
P.O. Box 3101 Valley Venter, CA 92082
760-445-1141

**SOCIAL SERVICES**
Tribal Tanf
Temporary Assistance for Needy Families
San Diego Office 866-913-3725
Escondido Office 866-428-0901

Manzanita Office 866-931-1480
Pala Office 866-806-8263

## NEVADA

**ADVOCACY**
Adams Esq.
Special Needs Children
500 N. Rainbow Blvd. Ste 300
Las Vegas, NV 89107
702-289-4143 Office • 702-924-7200 Fax

**COMMUNITY**
Native American Community Services
3909 S. Maryland Pkwy #205 Las Vegas, NV
89119-7500

**PUBLISHERS**
Blackrose Communications
111 South 35th St. San Diego, CA 92113
619-234-4753
www.indianvoices.net • rdavis4973@aol.com

## NORTH CAROLINA

**RETAIL - CLOTHING**
Passion Island
832 Washington Plaza, Washington, NC
27889; 252-402-4700

## TEXAS

**HEALTH**
The Circle: A Healing Place
Joanna Johnson, MSW, CFAS
Longview Behavioral Hospital
22 Bermuda Lane, Longbiew, Texas 75605
www.longviewhospital.com
www.oglethorpeinc.com
850-228-0777

---

# "OB Time": the Old OB Hippie – Proud of OB Coming Together

*OB Parade*

Yup, kids, the Old OB Hippie is full of pride these days about OB (... but not so much from other stuff) and how the community came together around the annual OB Holiday Parade.

The OB Parades are always a gas, but this year was special, as the OB Town Council, who hosts the parade, named the OB Community Plan as the "Grand Marshal" of the parade! Wow! This is tremendous – and I've never in all my decades seen the local town council join up in solidarity with the local planning board like this. Plus I don't think there's ever been a Grand Marshall that hasn't been an actual person. I could be wrong, and I'd love to know if I was on this. But this is / was very significant in this community's history.

The OB Parade always has surprises and fun floats and entries. This year, the "OB Pause" was crazy great. They had a airplane outline in lights and then they all came to a halt. The Innocence Project was there as was the Amnesty International folks, plus the anti-war themes of some of the others. Hey, did you notice the guerrilla float advocating for marijuana legalization with the smoking VW bus and large joint – or was that a rocket? (But hey guys, that one decal sticker mocking the homeless

was not cool.)

I'm also full of pride about how OB donates money, food and toys for those more needy than the rest of us. The Town Council raised at least $7000 at its recent annual Christmas Auction last week. The big item: the old OB entry way sign still with the termites that forced it to come down and be replaced. And don't forget, the old sign still has the guerrilla "O" in the "OB" painted red – the new one doesn't. Did you notice that? Plus OBceans dished out more donations at the end of the Parade. And lots of people emerge from the proverbial woodwork this time of year and volunteer for the various events – this is great.

# NEVADA NEWS

For Nevada Information: 619-234-4753 • 619-534-2435

## The Nevada Commission on Tourism Authorize $414,854 in Grants

CARSON CITY, Nev. — A project to support air lift to Elko and another to create webisodes about Ely's historical railway are among the 70 proposals approved for funding from the state's Rural Grants Program, Lt. Gov. Brian Krolicki announced today. The Nevada Commission on Tourism has authorized $414,854 in grants for programs and activities designed to deliver more tourists to rural Nevada.

"I am delighted to announce these investments into our rural tourism communities," Krolicki, NCOT chairman, said. "Competition for these grants is intense because the opportunities to leverage this funding into new revenue opportunities and new tourism-related assets are substantial. Working with rural Nevada to increase visitation to some of Nevada's hidden treasures is one of the commission's main objectives and a real passion of mine."

The Rural Grants Program funds are disbursed twice a year. This recent distribution is the second in fiscal year 2015; a total of $1.4 million was awarded in fiscal year 2015.

Among the funded projects:

• A $10,000 grant was awarded to the Elko Regional Airport to advertise SkyWest air service to Elko from Salt Lake City in the Utah market. SkyWest is one of two airlines flying into Elko, home of the National Cowboy Poetry Gathering as well as several mining operations. Through this project, grant applicants hope to increase area visitation by 5,000 people.

• A $10,000 award was given to the White Pine Historic Railroad Foundation in Ely to create 20 webisodes about the Nevada Northern Railway that will be posted to the railway's YouTube channel. The project, Railroad Fun Facts and Trivia, is designed to draw up to 36,000 visitors to the Ely area.

• An $8,000 grant was approved for the Lake Tahoe Visitors Authority to promote the Amgen professional women's cycling race in May 2015. About 84 athletes are expected to compete in two races that will raise awareness of the destination through coverage on AEG Sports, the race producer. Grant applicants estimate the value of the media coverage of this event to be in excess of $200,000.

• An $8,000 award was granted to the Dam Short Film Society in Boulder City to promote the Dam Short Film Festival, which takes place in February 2015. Promotional materials, including video for social media and B-roll footage for broadcast news, would be funded in part from the grant. Festival organizers estimate that the event's total promotional effort will reach more than 1 million people.

• A $6,500 grant was approved to Indian Territory, a nonprofit organization promoting tribal tourism, to hire a photographer to complete a comprehensive photo library of the state's American Indian tourism destinations. The photos will be used by Indian Territory as well as individual tribes to create marketing materials for their destinations.

• A 3,800 award was granted to Nevada Silver Trails, a nonprofit group promoting tourism to the state's central and southern rural areas, to create a brochure about attractions off the U.S. 95 corridor between Reno and Las Vegas. The brochure would augment three destination signs already in the Tonopah area; the goal is to encourage longer stays in central Nevada by visitors driving between Reno and Las Vegas.

"We are pleased that destinations throughout the state are embarking on programs that will build the state's tourism infrastructure and drive domestic and international visitation today and into the future," Nevada Department of Tourism and Cultural Affairs Director Claudia Vecchio said. "Most importantly, these programs extend the state brand through enhanced use of technology and marketing programming."

Grants are given to nonprofit entities for tourism marketing projects that will result in overnight stays, ultimately increasing room tax revenue for the state. Grant recipients must provide a 50-50 match in funds or volunteer hours. NCOT distributes the grants in the form of reimbursement to the recipients after the projects are completed and labor and funding details are documented.

NCOT advises the Nevada Division of Tourism, which receives three-eighths of 1 percent of room tax revenue as its operating budget. A portion of those funds are expended on the Rural Grants Program, which helps nonprofit groups and government agencies in rural Nevada enhance visitation and boost revenue from overnight stays. Funding for the Rural Grants Program does not come from the state's general fund.

The Nevada Commission on Tourism (NCOT) is a 15-member commission that advises the Nevada Division of Tourism, which is part of the Nevada Department of Tourism and Cultural Affairs. NCOT is responsible for promoting and marketing Nevada as a travel destination to domestic and international travelers. For more, visit www.TravelNevada.biz.

## Paiutes Fight Against Water Rights to Pyramid Lake

PYRAMID LAKE, Nevada -- Pyramid Lake Paiutes continued to fight for their water rights to Pyramid Lake, one of many Indian Nations battling corruption and new legislation in the US Congress to steal Native water rights.

"A little over 150 natives show up at the meeting. Thanks to all concerned people and the one's who commented," said Ray Bones Lowery about the meeting on Dec. 6, 2014.

## Sustainability
Continued from page 5

points? This is a case of exclusion. Can we continue to stand by when food is thrown away while people are starving? This is a case of inequality. Today everything comes under the laws of competition and the survival of the fittest, where the powerful feed upon the powerless. As a consequence, masses of people find themselves excluded and marginalized: without work, without possibilities, without any means of escape.

"Human beings are themselves considered consumer goods to be used and then discarded. We have created a 'throw away' culture which is now spreading. It is no longer simply about exploitation and oppression, but something new. Exclusion ultimately has to do with what it means to be a part of the society in which we live; those excluded are no longer society's underside or its fringes or its disenfranchised – they are no longer even a part of it. The excluded are not the 'exploited' but the outcast, the 'leftovers'."

We have exclusion and it can certainly be sustained. Additionally, there are those who need exclusion for their own sustainability. So, yes, sustainability can exclude. At the same time, though, if we want to, we can listen to and learn from those who seek balance and inclusion -- and sustain that.

*Nic Paget-Clarke is publisher of In Motion Magazine (inmotionmagazine.com) and author of "... and the echo follows" (facebook.com/AndTheEchoFollows).*

## Assisting Tribes in Pursuing Their Self-Determined Goals

As we prepare to celebrate the holidays with our families and reign in the New Year, we can reflect on the events that have occurred in the past and that will influence the future.

I am so pleased that the President signed into law legislation that affirms a water settlement agreement between the Pyramid Lake Paiute Tribe and a private water company. This legislation is important to moving Nevada forward.

Indian Country, especially Chairman Arlan Melendez, Reno-Sparks Indian Colony, worked very hard in getting legislation to the President's desk that will put Indian tribes on equal footing with states by excluding Indian general welfare benefits from gross income in calculating income tax.

I was honored to testify before the US Senate Committee on Indian Affairs to advocate for the passage of the Moapa Band of Paiutes Land Conveyance Act and the Nevada Native Nations Land Act, which would transfer tens of thousands of acres back into federal trust for the benefit of various Nevada tribes. This legislation would convey much-needed land for housing, cultural preservation, and economic and energy development.

Restoring land to Nevada's tribes is so important to me. And I believe the tribes ought to be able to use their lands and develop their communities on their own terms. To assist tribes in pursuing their self-determined goals, the Department of Housing and Urban Development (HUD) announced more than $3.5 million dollars in grants for seven Nevada tribes this year. These competitive Indian Community Development Block Grants (ICDBG) will help these tribes kick start crucial small business, tourism, and housing projects.

Earlier this year I was fortunate to attend the groundbreaking of FirstSolar's 250 megawatt photovoltaic project at the Moapa Paiute Reservation. This project will deliver much needed economic benefits to the Tribe, and to Nevada. It will create 400 construction jobs, and replace dirty energy with clean solar power.

I remain committed to doing everything I can so Nevada Tribes, and all tribes, have new opportunities to flourish. I wish you all a joyous holiday season, and a happy new year.

*Editorial note: see page 145. Pyramid Lake Piautes continue to fight for their water rights*

*The Rainbow Warriors*
*This new Tribe shall be made up of all colors and creeds ...*

Late one night a burglar broke into a house and while he was sneaking around he heard a voice say, "Jesús is watching you." He looked around and saw nothing. He kept on creeping and again heard, "Jesús is watching you." In a dark corner, he saw a cage with a parrot inside. The burglar asked the parrot, "Was it you who said Jesús is watching me" The parrot replied, "Yes." Relieved, the burglar asked, "What is your name?" The parrot said, "Clarence." The burglar said, "That's a stupid name for a parrot. What idiot named you Clarence?" The parrot answered, "The same idiot that named the rottweiler Jesús."

FRYBREAD                                    SAYNDAY

What is soft, round and brown?

Me?

No. That Ndan babe!

©W. TRW

Rose Davis of African and Seminole heritage has been indefatigably and independently producing the Native American media product INDIAN VOICES for over twenty-five years. She has diligently developed her singular brand of grassroots journalism that has inspired trust and loyalty of dedicated volunteers and readers.

Born in Wilmington, North Carolina a half century after the infamous *coup d'etat* and race riots of 1898 that were generated and cheer led by a biased media whose purpose was to suppress a minority population, Rose has always had a keen sense of journalistic justice. Related by family ties to the groundbreaking Chicago Defender Rose cut her teeth on observing the effect media neglect has on marginalized communities and the impotence of giving a voice to isolated minorities.

www.indianvoices.net

**MISSION**
*To promote a supportive system of information sharing grounded in Native Indigenous values while building relationships with grassroots coalitions of labor and community groups.*

### GENERAL INFORMATION
A monthly publication targeted to a diverse readership as a multi-cultural networking tool. Distribution to educational institutions, native reservations, health clinics, urban Indian centers, fairs, public events, employment fairs, libraries, hotels, tourist centers and information centers nationwide.

**Publication Dates: First day of month**
**Material / Ad Deadline: 20th of month**
**Dimensions: Tabloid Frame Size**
**(10.25" X 13")**

### ADVANTAGES OF ADVERTISING IN "INDIAN VOICES"
*Indian Voices* offers advertisers the opportunity to reach out to unique clientele from a variety of cultures and heritages.

### NETWORKING AND COMMUNITY BUILDING OPPORTUNITIES
*Indian Voices* is a portal to access many talented and skilled journalists, artists and business owners. Because of its reputation with our readers, it is a viable resource for consumers to discover your products and services.

### INCREASE AWARENESS OF YOUR PRODUCTS AND SERVICES WITH OUR DIVERSE AND UNIQUE DEMOGRAPHIC
By utilizing *Indian Voices* as a marketing tool, an untapped demographic is exposed to your existing products and services. For 27 years, *Indian Voices* has delivered award-winning coverage of the American Southwest from San Diego to Las Vegas cultural and business communities. Our print and online formats are one of the indigenous community's most valuable business tools.

### MARKET TRENDS
Our marketing department can identify trends in local market forces, detect emerging competition and uncover new opportunities.

### CONTENT AND GOALS OF "INDIAN VOICES"
• From weekly schedules to targeting specific issues or seasons, *Indian Voices* provides a variety of sizes and rates that are extremely cost-effective. Also, an insert can be placed within the publication to promote your products and services.

• *Indian Voices Media Project* supports the development of an entrepreneurial journalistic endeavor dedicated to bringing the voices of indigenous members of our society into the national discourse. To influence policy makers, provide educational materials, and public outreach regarding the important role of indigenous people whose enduring presence in the development of our history and society assures its future.

• A vendor's circle for Powwow vendors to promote their products and services.

• Calendars
1. An entertainment venue calendar to provide a social calendar for the public who is seeking indigenous cultural and entertainment events.
2. Student events and sports events with a focus on Native American students and athletes.

• Tourist Education is a partnership with local tour guides who provide cultural and educational tours with a focus on accurate representation of indigenous people.

www.indianvoices.net

## PRINT ADVERTISING RATES

Outside Back Cover       $2000*
(10.25" x 12.125") full color available

Inside  Back Cover       $1500*
(10.25" x 12.125")

Inside Center Fold       $1800*
(10.25" x 12.125") full color available

Full Page                $1000*
(10.25" x 12.125")

Half Page Horizontal     $600*
(10.25" x 5.875")

Half Page Vertical       $600*
(5" x 12.125")

Quarter Page Vertical    $325*
(5" x 5.875")

Quarter Page Horizontal  $325*
(10.25" x 2.875")

Eighth Page Vertical     $175*
(2.5" x 5.875")

Eighth Page Horizontal   $175*
(5" x 2.875")

Business Card            $125*
(3.75" x 2")

\* Rates are per issue

**Contract Discount** ~ contact us for special
discount rates:
• Three (3) issues: 5%
• Six (6) issues: 10%
• Twelve (12) issues: 15%

## ONLINE ADVERTISING RATES

Digital media have been one of the few beneficiaries of the
recession, with internet advertising outperforming television
for the first time. Advertising with *Indian Voices* provides
cutting edge exposure.

• Top Banner $95/month (728 X 90 pixels)
  Rotated on EVERY page

• Left/Right Column $25/month  (350 x 250 pixels)
  Rotated on EVERY page

## PRINT GRAPHIC SPECS

Camera-ready art for the print edition must be mailed before
the 20th of the month or may be e-mailed in JPEG, TIFF or
PDF format.

All artwork must be 300dpi @ 100% size.

Graphics and photos from the internet are low resolution and
will not print clearly.

To inquire about web advertising or to submit an ad for the
*Indian Voices* website, please contact us.